Anxieties of Experience

OXFORD STUDIES IN AMERICAN LITERARY HISTORY

Gordon Hutner, Series Editor

Anxieties of Experience

THE LITERATURES OF THE AMERICAS FROM WHITMAN TO BOLAÑO

Jeffrey Lawrence

OXFORD

UNIVERSITY PRESS

OXFORD

UNIVERSITY PRESS

Oxford University Press is a department of the University of Oxford.
It furthers the University's objective of excellence in research, scholarship,
and education by publishing worldwide. Oxford is a registered trade mark of
Oxford University Press in the UK and certain other countries

Published in the United States of America by Oxford University Press
198 Madison Avenue, New York, NY 10016, United States of America

Library of Congress Cataloging-in-Publication Data
Names: Lawrence, Jeffrey, 1983– author.
Title: Anxieties of experience : the literatures of the Americas from
Whitman to Bolaño / Jeffrey Lawrence.
Description: New York, NY : Oxford University Press, [2018] |
Series: Oxford Studies in American Literary History |
Includes bibliographical references and index.
Identifiers: LCCN 2017014043| ISBN 9780190690205 (hardback) |
ISBN 9780190690229 (epub)
Subjects: LCSH: America—Literatures—History and criticism. |
National characteristics, American, in literature. |
National characteristics, Latin American, in literature. |
Literature and history—United States. | Literature and history—Latin America.
Classification: LCC PN846 .L39 2018 | DDC 809/.897—dc23 LC
record available at https://lccn.loc.gov/2017014043

For my mom, Karen, my best reader

He was an American; he wanted to submerge himself in the flow of experience to distill the art of fiction.

Era un norteamericano; buscaba hundirse en el fluir de la experiencia para destilar el arte de la ficción.

—RICARDO PIGLIA, *Prisión Perpetua* (1988)

{ CONTENTS }

{ ACKNOWLEDGMENTS }

This book was written, read, and edited in various places throughout the United States and Latin America, and I'm indebted to friends and colleagues both near and far. At Rutgers, I have benefited from discussing the book with many of my colleagues in the English Department. I'm particularly grateful to David Kurnick, Rebecca Walkowitz, Carter Mathes, and Nick Gaskill for reading portions of the manuscript. During my graduate studies at Princeton, I was fortunate to work with faculty members in several different departments: Comparative Literature, English, Spanish and Portuguese, and Classics. My first thanks go to Gabriela Nouzeilles, who believed in this project from the time it was just an idea for a dissertation prospectus. Michael Wood, Susana Draper, and William Gleason gave me valuable feedback during the dissertation process, and Daniel Rodgers, Eileen Reeves, Arcadio Díaz Quiñones, and Rubén Gallo commented on early versions of several chapters included here. My fellow graduate students at Princeton provided so much of the intellectual (and anti-intellectual) force behind this book. I especially want to thank Luis Othoniel Rosa, Carlos Fonseca, Dora Zhang, Carl Fischer, Luis Moreno-Caballud, Ron Wilson, Charles Samuelson, Carolina Alvarado, Ana Sabau, Gavin Arnall, Leah Klement, Andy Lemons, Sergio Delgado, Alejandra Josiowicz, Ivan Ortiz, Jill Jarvis, Javier Patiño, Cate Reilly, Rachel Galvin, Kameron Collins, Sarah Wasserman, Ritwik Bhattacharya, and Joel Suarez. I also owe a great deal to Jay Garcia, who helped me find my disciplinary footing during the dissertation's first stages. Going back even further, *Anxieties of Experience* has its roots in an undergraduate thesis I wrote on Roberto Bolaño with Ilan Stavans at Amherst College.

Parts of this book have been published in *American Literary History*, *Twentieth-Century Literature*, and *Pensamiento de los confines*. During the course of writing it, I consulted archival materials in the Centro de Documentación e Investigación de la Cultura de Izquierdas en Argentina (CeDInCI) in Buenos Aires, the Department of Rare Books and Special Collections at Princeton's Firestone Library, the Waldo Frank papers at the University of Pennsylvania, and the Katherine

Anne Porter papers at the University of Maryland, where the archivist and scholar Ruth Alvarez was of invaluable assistance.

Gordon Hutner has seen this book through the entire publishing process, and I thank him for his editorial advice as well as his mentorship over the past few years. At Oxford University Press, Sarah Pirovitz, Gwen Colvin, Robert Milks, and Abigail Johnson have done an excellent job shepherding the manuscript toward publication. Jordan Brower, my college roommate and now colleague in the profession, has read more versions of these chapters than I can count. Paul Franz also provided a sharp editorial eye in the final stages of revising the manuscript. Additionally, I wish to acknowledge the generous support of the Rutgers University Research Council toward the publication of this book.

My family has tolerated my obsessions for seven years. Thanks to my dad, Peter, and my brother, Andy, for challenging me to make my thinking and writing intelligible to those outside of the discipline. My mom, Karen, deserves the entire dedication page I've devoted to her and more.

Anxieties of Experience no existiría sin los aportes de varias personas e instituciones latinoamericanas a lo largo de los años. Debo mis primeras impresiones de Bolaño a la materia "Roberto Bolaño y la tradición latinoamericana" que cursé con Hugo Achugar en 2006 en la Facultad de Humanidades de la Universidad de la República Uruguay. Desde entonces, mantengo una conversación constante sobre Bolaño con otro ex-alumno de la facultad, Franco Laviano, uno de los mejores lectores que conozco. En Princeton, los seminarios del historiador Rafael Rojas y del escritor Alan Pauls influyeron de modo profundo sobre este proyecto. Finalmente, no puedo dejar de mencionar a dos personas claves para mi formación intelectual, Ana Amado y Ricardo Piglia, que fallecieron en la última etapa de la escritura del libro. De Ana recordaré no sólo sus agudas lecturas de la historia cultural argentina sino también su generosidad como anfitriona en mis viajes a Buenos Aires. De Ricardo, no sólo su literatura, que ya pertenece a la tradición, sino también su genialidad como interlocutor. Espero que haya tanto homenaje como traición en este libro.

Anxieties of Experience

{ INTRODUCTION }

In the summer of 2011, while drinking with friends in a Mexico City *pulquería*, I met a writer from Los Angeles who had just finished reading the English translation of Chilean novelist Roberto Bolaño's *Los detectives salvajes* [*The Savage Detectives*, 1998]. The novel, which follows the founders of a 1970s Mexican avant-garde literary movement across four continents and a span of twenty years, had appeared in the United States with much fanfare a few years earlier. Since the *pulquería* was on Avenida Insurgentes, close to many of the haunts of the novel's characters, we began enthusiastically to evoke the rough-and-tumble world of Mexican poetry that Bolaño describes through the diary of young García Madero and the other ex-members of the "visceral realist" group. But when our conversation turned to those parts of *The Savage Detectives* set in Southern California, the writer asked me a question that took me by surprise: "So how long did Bolaño live in Los Angeles?"

At first I thought he was confusing Los Angeles, California, with Los Ángeles, Chile, the capital of the little-known province where Bolaño was born and raised. Almost immediately, though, I realized he was referring to an effect produced by the novel itself. "Bolaño just has this way of describing Southern Cal like he knows it from the inside," the writer explained. "It's amazingly true to life." I nodded my head in agreement, even as I responded that, so far as I could establish, *Bolaño never once set foot in the United States*. The writer's astonished reaction made the irony of our situation almost palpable. Here we were in Mexico City, in part trying (let's be honest) to live or relive or revive the "Mexican experience" so vertiginously narrated in the pages of *The Savage Detectives*. And suddenly we were forced to accept that Bolaño had captured the "American experience" without ever having visited the country. That conversation stayed with me throughout my time in Mexico City, and eventually gave rise to the question that animates this book. How can we explain Bolaño's desire to represent the United States, a place he had never been—and, just as importantly, how can we explain the (North) American desire for Bolaño, that is, the explosion of interest in Bolaño's work and life among US readers?

Latin American Readers and US Experiencers

In an influential article, Sarah Pollack has argued that Bolaño's popularity in the United States derives from a market logic of substitution, whereby his "visceral realism" has replaced Gabriel García Márquez's "magical realism" as the new stereotyped image of Latin America.[1] Yet if Bolaño may have gained currency in the United States in part through his portrayal of a late-twentieth century Latin America replete with sex, violence, and drugs, his texts also appeal to the US reading public by confronting it with its own reflection. Bolaño populated his works with American writers, from the profanity-spewing *poeta maldita* Barbara Patterson of *The Savage Detectives* and the journalist Oscar Fate of *2666* to the eponymous Vietnam War veteran of the short story "Jim," who leaves the United States for Mexico in the 1970s. How was Bolaño able to create so vivid a Wildean looking glass for the North, despite never having crossed the Rio Grande? It would be tempting to explain this capacity as evidence of Bolaño's powers of invention, but the fact is he drew almost all these characters and scenes from a lifetime of reading US fiction. Indeed, his posthumous book of essays, *Entre paréntesis* [*Between Parentheses*, 2004], is filled with references to American writers, from Mark Twain, William Burroughs, and Patricia Highsmith to contemporaries such as Cormac McCarthy and Walter Mosley. Though Bolaño never went to the United States, he obsessively read its authors.

In this sense, we must approach Bolaño's literary relationship to the United States as part of a broader defense of reading by contemporary Spanish-language writers, including the Argentine Ricardo Piglia, the Spaniards Enrique Vila-Matas and Javier Cercas, and the Mexicans Sergio Pitol, Cristina Rivera Garza, and Juan Villoro. For these "addicted" readers, as Piglia calls them in *El último lector* [The Last Reader, 2005], "reading [*la lectura*] is not only a practice; it's a way of life."[2] Bolaño underscored this existential appetite in various articulations of his literary creed. In his "Preliminary Autobiography,"

he asserts, "I'm much happier reading than writing," and in a later
essay describing his first encounter with Albert Camus, he tells us:
"I went from being a cautious reader to a voracious reader [un lector
voraz]....I wanted to read everything."[3] In Cercas's novel *Soldados de
Salamina* [*Soldiers of Salamis*, 2001], where Bolaño appears as a fictional character, the first words he speaks come straight from that
quintessential novel about obsessive reading, *Don Quijote*: "I read
even the papers I find on the street."[4] Bolaño shocks Cercas the narrator, a down-and-out writer, by claiming to have read every novel
Cercas has written. He walks up to Cercas, books in hand, a sideways smirk on his face signaling his triumph. I've read you. Have
you read me?

Without a doubt, this exaggerated emphasis on the activity of reading stems from global anxieties about the disappearance of the book
and a worldwide decline in print readership in the digital age. Piglia
renders such anxieties explicit in his very title—*The Last Reader*. And
Bolaño shares this preoccupation with the extinction of the reader,
to the extent that his fiction often seems like a refuge for an endan-
gered species. Compulsive reading becomes almost a natural function within Bolaño's narrative universe: his characters bring books
into bathrooms, bars, showers, and beds. Yet these contemporary portraits of the artist as reader also establish a more specific link to a
long Iberian and Latin American tradition of obsessive readers hark-
ing back to Cervantes, Miguel de Unamuno, José Vasconcelos, and
Jorge Luis Borges. There is little doubt that the intertext of Bolaño's
statement about his predilection for reading over writing is Borges's
famous line from the 1935 preface to his *Historia universal de la infa-
mia* [*A Universal History of Infamy*]: "good readers are swans even
more shadowy and singular than good writers."[5]

The image of the quixotic writer who reads even the papers he or
she finds on the streets has spread throughout the Spanish-speaking
world like the rumors that circulate through the small towns of
García Márquez's novels. However, this image comes not from the
repertoire of the magically real but from what the Uruguayan critic
Ángel Rama long ago dubbed the Latin American "lettered city." In
modern Latin American countries characterized by what Rama
calls an "idealized vision of intellectual functions," the figure of the
letrado—a word in Spanish that has a wide semantic range from "man
of letters" to lawyer—continues to attract tremendous social prestige
all the way from the bastions of political power to the enclaves of

rebellion.[6] And indeed, the scholarship of Sylvia Molloy and Roberto González Echevarría has highlighted the predominance of the activity of reading and the importance of the literary and historical "archive" in the construction of the Latin American subject in various contexts from the colonial period to the 1970s. It is true, as more recent scholarship has argued, that some of the most significant Latin American texts of the past half century have challenged the authority of the lettered city.[7] Yet the resurgence of the writer-as-reader in twenty-first-century Latin American fiction should cause us to pause before consigning the category to the historical dustbin. Contemporary works by writers such as Rivera Garza and Pola Oloixarac have reconstructed a line of Latin American *letradas*, exemplifying the process by which the figure of the writer-as-reader has expanded beyond its traditionally masculinist role.

The family resemblance among this generation of Latin American writers resides not only in their similar habits of reading (and of depicting readers). It also extends to their view of North American literature. In their fiction and essays, contemporary Latin American reader-writers consistently describe the US literary field as one organized around the principle of "writing from experience." Bolaño makes this point in a late essay on the Beat writer William Burroughs: "literature, from which [Burroughs] made a living for thirty years, interested him, but not too much. In this sense he is similar to other North American classics who concentrated their efforts on the observation of life and experience."[8] For these Latin American authors, it is the experiential impulse, and its concomitant turn away from the activity of reading, that constitutes the guiding thread of US literature. Thus, in typically citational fashion, Villoro borrows from Ernest Hemingway in proclaiming that the US literary tradition begins with the "invitation to a voyage [el viaje]...to go out into the world in search of experience."[9] While North American culture has often been identified as an external force that Latin American authors either welcome or resist, these comments suggest that the Latin American writer-as-reader has developed dialectically in relation to an entire tradition of US experiential literature. Here too Bolaño proves instructive. His essays, reviews, manifestos, and diary reveal an unwavering fascination with US experiential literature dating back to his teenage years in the 1970s. As he explained in an interview in 1998, "The voyage [el viaje], in my generation's imaginary, was the voyage of the Beatniks."[10] Bolaño was not merely interested in the formal characteristics of the Beat road novel. He was compelled by how these US writers had lived—and, more specifically, by how they had made the pursuit of variegated experiences the very condition of possibility of their literature.

"Jim," one of the last texts Bolaño published in his lifetime, presents a composite picture of the US writer as experiencer. First published as a nonfiction piece and later included in the short-story collection *El gaucho insufrible* [*The Insufferable Gaucho*, 2003], it briefly narrates the life of the "saddest North American" that Bolaño/the narrator has ever seen. Asked by a group of young children about the source of poetry, Jim responds first by vomiting, then by speaking of the "search for truth," and finally by proclaiming that he "seek[s] the extraordinary to say it in everyday language."[11] Having journeyed through Central and South America, Jim ends his quest in Mexico City, where the narrator encounters him inching toward a fire-breathing street performer. His slow movement toward the intense heat of the flame, which simultaneously illuminates and threatens to annhilate him, disquiets the narrator, who eventually shoves Jim out of the way. The American poet's willingness to test his human limits becomes representative of an attitude toward experience that at once attracts and terrifies the young Latin American narrator.

At first glance, it might seem that Bolaño's work offers only a superficial portrait of US writers. Yet I will demonstrate that the identification and representation of a North American "literature of experience" by this current generation of Latin American writers-as-readers in fact reveals the deep structures of both the US and Latin American literary fields. Of course, we are all familiar with Ernest Hemingway's aphorisms on the link between writing and authorial experience, the belief, as Hemingway put it in a 1935 *Esquire* article, that good writing "will be true in proportion to the amount of knowledge of life that [the writer] has" and that "[t]he more [the writer] learns from experience the more truly he can imagine."[12] Much of the scholarship of the past forty years has tended to see Hemingway's words less as a serious literary creed than as a sententious, satirical, or even self-aware evasion of how fiction actually gets written. Yet important scholarly studies over the past ten years have called attention to the power and durability of the concept of experience in twentieth-century US culture, underscoring both its relevance to the American pragmatist tradition and its pervasiveness in modernist and postmodern literary discourse.[13] And in fact, appeals to the authority of experience surface in the novels, essays, prologues, and magazine articles of a surprisingly diverse group of US writers. Bolaño's fiction therefore reflects a more profound insight into North American literature than we might initially suppose.

The central claim of this book is that two dominant subject positions structure canonical twentieth-century literature in the Americas: in the United States, the subject position of the writer as *experiencer*, and in Latin America, the subject position of the writer as *reader* [*lector*]. I maintain that these subject positions have been embedded, in turn, within two cultural formations I refer to throughout this book as the "US literature of experience" and the "Latin American literature of the reader." Borrowing the concept of "cultural forma-tion" from Raymond Williams, who defines it as a complex of inter-related "tendencies and movements" best identified in retrospect, I contend that from our current vantage point, the US literature of experience and the Latin American literature of the reader must be seen as the *dominant* cultural formations in the Americas during the twentieth century.[14] Critics have long recognized the authority of experience in US literary production and the centrality of the writer-as-reader in the Latin American literary field, but rarely have they examined the interaction of these positions across the hemi-sphere. Over the course of this book, I show that the US literature of experience and the Latin American literature of the reader were mutually constitutive. Far from arising in the isolation of national or regional contexts, these literary formations were forged out of the long history of US and Latin American political and cultural rela-tions. I argue here that Bolaño's work functions as both symptom and diagnosis of this history. By rendering visible the vexed dynamic between the US literature of experience and the Latin American lit-erature of the reader, Bolaño has compelled contemporary writers throughout the hemisphere to revise their literary practice. In the post-Bolaño era of the past decade, the effort to synthesize these for-mations, to bridge the gap between reading and experience, has emerged as one of the primary features of both the US and Latin American literary fields.

As a comparatist whose early training was in the literatures of the Spanish-speaking world, I began this study as an effort to think US culture from the outside—that is, to reconstruct representations of American literature and society by Latin American writers. That proj-ect would have had many important precursors, and indeed studies that attempt to "read North by South" have become a veritable academic subgenre over the past thirty years. Yet even as I was inspired by this scholarship, I quickly intuited that my own project was more concerned with analyzing the different languages—and language games—used to talk about literature in the United States and Latin America than with studying the Latin American reception of US literature as such. This intuition was strengthened by the difficulties I was encountering as a translator of Latin American literature when rendering commonplace Spanish words, phrases, and tropes into an American English in which they sounded utterly strange. As my opening anecdote suggests, I gradually trained my attention on the term *experience*—or, more specifically, on the ways in which "experience" emerged as a fundamental yet contested keyword in literary debates in the hemisphere. I was captivated by the extent to which this polarizing, almost talismanic word continues to fuel literary debates throughout the Americas even as it is frequently written off as naïve and passé.

The book I ended up writing examines how the term "experience" has served as a flashpoint in a series of literary "misencounters" across the North-South divide.[15] *Anxieties of Experience* studies the complicated forms of attraction and disavowal that writers across the Americas have displayed toward firsthand experience as the ultimate authority for literary work. It also analyzes how the activity of reading has variously been seen as inimical to and coterminous with the process of experiencing. My title, which echoes Harold Bloom's iconic study of poetic tradition, *The Anxiety of Influence* (1973), refers to the extraordinary amount of energy that writers both North and South have devoted to exploring the relationship among what one writes, reads, and lives. But whereas Bloom's Oedipal model of literary influence emphasizes the psychological battles that (typically male) writers wage against their precursors, the "anxieties" I explore are geopolitical as much as they are personal, social as much as spiritual, historical as much as poetic. They are also shared, albeit differently inflected, across genders. These are anxieties that so deeply pervade a cultural ecology that it takes a sustained effort simply to render them visible. Yet they remain, lodged in the cultural imaginary and the texts it generates. If anxieties of experience plague writers in all cultures to a certain extent, I make the case that US and Latin American writers have employed substantially different strategies for coping with them.

Figuring (Out) Experience

A major contention of this book is that the word *experience* under-went a seismic semantic shift in the United States in the twentieth century, a shift that transformed basic assumptions about the activity of writing in the US literary field. Martin Jay has observed that "ex-perience" is one of the most universally invoked terms in modern thought and one of the most difficult to define, such that no totaliz-ing "account of what 'experience' really is or what it might be" is pos-sible.[16] In the spirit of Jay's insight, I wish to dispel any notion that this book will capture an ultimate truth about that protean concept. I will argue, however, that the *term* "experience" has accrued specific meanings in twentieth-century US cultural debates, and that recon-structing those meanings teaches us something important about US literature itself.[17]

The *Merriam-Webster* dictionary defines experience as "direct ob-servation of or participation in events as a basis of knowledge," and the word's most common usage among US writers likewise empha-sizes unmediated contact and close proximity. In their fiction and in their statements about the creative process, twentieth-century US writers consistently privileged firsthand knowledge over knowledge acquired through books, abstract systems, and highly codified bodies of information. That said, it was in the pragmatism of John Dewey and William James that US writers found a more capacious defini-tion of the concept, one that altered its meaning in both philosophi-cal and literary contexts. In critiquing the standard empiricist episte-mology grounded in cognitive reflection on prior events, Dewey proposed that our mental pictures of the world are not only means "for reporting and registering past experiences," but also "bases for orga-nizing future observations and experiences."[18] In *Art as Experience* (1934), Dewey turned this future-oriented conception of experience to the study of aesthetics. Taking issue with the Kantian legacy that prioritized "contemplation" and "pleasure," Dewey insisted that the creative process began with the artist's initial "impulsion" into the world. "Every experience, including the most generous and idealistic," Dewey remarks, "begins with an element of seeking, of pressing for-ward."[19] As Jay correctly asserts, Dewey harbored the "belief that the fruits of experience were in the future rather than the present" (295), and his works consistently emphasized the more active valences of the term. My book explores how US writers transformed this future orientation of experience into a literary practice, both by invoking the vocabulary of "experience" and by doing things with the word.[20]

While the US literature of the twenties and thirties has often been read under the sign of Anglo-American modernism and Ezra Pound's celebrated injunction to "Make it New," much of the debate in the interwar period centered on the correlation between "life experience" and literary creation. In his well-known cultural critique *Our America* (1919), the novelist and essayist Waldo Frank maintained that "Experience…is the sole true norm of culture, the sole measure of growth."[21] In a lecture before the American Women's Club in Paris in 1934, Katherine Anne Porter asserted that "[t]he value of a writer can be measured best, probably, by his capacity to express what he feels, knows, is, has been, has seen, and experienced."[22] Although these formulations, along with those of Hemingway, accented the individual texture of lived experience, others highlighted the degree to which experiential insights accrued to entire groups and even the nation as a whole. In the immediate aftermath of World War I, W. E. B. Du Bois put a slight spin on his famous concept of double consciousness by speaking of the wartime trajectory of young African American soldiers and expatriates in terms of a "double-experience" of "devilish persecution from their own countrymen" and a taste of "real democracy" in the Old World.[23] And in an influential 1941 essay "The Cult of Experience in American Writing," Philip Rahv consecrated "the writing of experience" as a foundational American paradigm, insisting that "the American creative mind…has found the terms and objects of its activity in the urge toward and immersion in experience. It is this search for experience, conducted on diverse and often conflicting levels of consciousness, which has been the dominant, quintessential theme of the characteristic American literary productions—from *Leaves of Grass* to *Winesburg, Ohio* and beyond."[24] Rahv's language of "urge," "activity," and "immersion" indicates how deeply the rhetoric of Deweyan aesthetics permeated the cultural common sense in the United States during the interwar period.

Rahv's "The Cult of Experience" is one of the most thorough inquiries into the literary and cultural dimensions of the US literature of experience. Yet the essay, which relies heavily on a mid-twentieth-century interpretive matrix that framed American culture in teleological terms, tends to naturalize what was in fact a historical process. Rahv's argument hinges on casting the thirst for experience as a necessary development in a country emerging from the strictures of

Puritan morality onto the international scene, and he goes on to suggest that this phenomenon distinguishes American literature from the French, German, and Russian national traditions. Understandably, the strong essentialist undertones in Rahv's essay have made scholars reluctant to take its claims seriously. My own approach will refer to the US literature of experience as a historical formation, produced by a particular constellation of cultural, literary, and geopolitical factors. Although I will call into question the exceptionalist claims of Rahv's essay and its reduction of the experiential paradigm to a restricted group of primarily white male authors, it provides a particularly acute lens through which to bring into focus the formation of twentieth-century US literary culture.

To understand "experience" as a contested keyword is not only to attend to the longstanding debate about the relationship between writing and experience in the US literary field. It also requires examining how the US literature of experience emerged in tandem with the geographical expansion of American culture itself. An influential critical argument in American literary studies holds that the primary strand of experiential discourse in the United States arose domestically in early twentieth-century debates about cultural pluralism before becoming institutionalized in postwar identity politics. According to this argument, formulated by Walter Benn Michaels in *Our America: Nativism, Modernism, and Pluralism* (1995) and *The Shape of the Signifier: 1967 to the End of History* (2004), and given a more positive articulation by Mark McGurl in *The Program Era: Postwar Fiction and the Rise of Creative Writing* (2009), the US literary field has increasingly become committed to the belief that literary authority arises from (re)affirming one's personal identity: justifying "who you are" (Michaels) and "writing what you know" (McGurl). Despite their disagreements over the consequences of this shift, Michaels and McGurl construct a similar map of postwar US literature as a territory divided into a series of overlapping but discrete "domains of experience" representing different identity-based groups. As powerful as this narrative of national US literary culture may be (and I will return to it at various points in my study), it fails to account for how the discourse of experience appealed to postwar US writers as diverse as Toni Morrison, William Burroughs, and Sandra Cisneros precisely because it allowed them to escape from the logic of bounded sectional, class, and race identity. Even as the idea of literary multiculturalism gained traction in the US public sphere in the 1970s and

1980s, American writers continued to invoke the pragmatist vocabulary of impulsion and immersion alongside (and against) the multiculturalist language of identity and roots.[25] These writers suggested that an expansive and global trajectory authorized them to absorb a variety of different cultures rather than to reify a single group "experience." Indeed, it could be argued that the US literature of experience persisted after the social upheaval of the 1960s and the Vietnam War because of its unique capacity to incorporate both dominant and oppositional visions of the country's role in the world, alternately (or even simultaneously) positioning its writers as the most far-seeing observers of the global "American century" and as privileged witnesses uniquely situated to critique US hegemony.

Recent Americanist studies and older internationalist analyses of expatriate American literature have equally neglected the special role that Latin America played as a field of experience for US writers. Critical accounts of American modernist literature that take the transatlantic line connecting the United States and Europe as their main axis elide the formative Latin American journeys of many US writers, including Hemingway, Katherine Anne Porter, Waldo Frank, Hart Crane, Langston Hughes, John Dos Passos, Wallace Stevens, Eugene O'Neill, and Zora Neale Hurston, to name only the most famous. To retrace these hemispheric itineraries is to see how Latin America began to function as the privileged space for experiential writers during a time of increased US economic and political imperialism in the region. Porter, a key figure in this book who lived and wrote in Mexico for much of the 1920s and 1930s, followed Hemingway in identifying experience as the fundamental source material for the writer. Yet she was far more acutely aware than Hemingway of the degree to which the restless desire to "have an experience" often functioned as a sublimation of more muscular and expansionist US cultural discourses. The irritable gringo Kennerly of her 1934 story "Hacienda," who bulldozes through Mexico while guzzling beers and bragging about the book he is going to write, seems to be constantly "slamming himself into a fight in which there are no rules and no referee and the antagonist is everywhere."[26] Porter's mistrust of this type of propulsive force, which she associated with the bullfighting culture so precious to the young Hemingway, would lead her to theorize the difference between "mere adventure," which is "something you seek for pleasure, or even for profit, like a gold rush or invading a country," and "real experience," "what really

happens to you in the long run; the truth that finally overtakes you"
(*CS* 808). While Porter initially situates herself at the "truth-seeking"
end of the spectrum, she ultimately recognizes the complexities and
complicities of her own secret fascination with bullfighting, which
becomes a symbol of the incessant feedback loop of impulsion and
experience: "no matter how we...attempted to deceive ourselves,
our acts had all the earmarks of adventure, violence of motive, events
taking place at top speed, at sustained intensity, under powerful
stimulus and a willful seeking of pleasure" (*CS* 819).

Latin American writers of the twentieth century were highly attuned to the accent on expansive experience in US literary works
about Latin America and what we might call the definitional battle
between "experience" and "adventure" that Porter describes. Studying
the US literature of experience in relation to writers who traveled to
Latin America helps to explain why a long line of Latin American
writers felt the need to challenge, undermine, and appropriate the
discourse of experience as it emerged in US literature and pragmatist
aesthetics. Already in the 1920s, we begin to detect friction across
the hemispheric divide between US and Latin American writers who
otherwise shared many common features. This was certainly the
case for the Jewish-American writer Waldo Frank and his Jewish-
Argentinian counterpart Samuel Glusberg, whose epistolary correspondence of the late 1920s reveals their starkly different attitudes
about the relationship between culture and experience. In proposing
the launch of an inter-American literary journal, Frank insisted that
he would first need broad firsthand knowledge of the hemisphere:
"I am more deeply than ever convinced that the problem today is that
of *The* American Culture.... South America is part of it. I feel this.
I shall not understand my feeling, however, until I have experienced
South America."[27] Glusberg, however, frequently pushed back against
this experiential inter-American vision, calling attention to the
cultural constraints that restricted his own geographic mobility.
Referring at one point to the ever-changing postmarks on the letters
of Frank, who was making plans to visit Argentina for the first time,
Glusberg stressed the limits of their shared Jewish heritage in defining their vision of US–Latin American cultural relations: "Lucky you
who can travel. I'm still here [in Buenos Aires] without being able to
move and the worst thing is that I don't know how long it will
last.... Being a Jew is not enough to be a wanderer."[28] In rendering
visible Frank's experiential transformation of the diasporic figure of

the Wandering Jew, Glusberg identifies how the appeal to the authority of experience among US writers could subsume and transform discourses of ethnic and cultural affiliation.

In his *crónica* "Conversations with Langston Hughes," the Afro-Cuban poet Nicolás Guillén gives an account of a 1929 meeting in Havana that bears striking parallels to Glusberg's response to Frank. Guillén reproduces lengthy excerpts of a "conversation" with Hughes in which the US author's commitment to becoming *the* representative black poet in the world intertwines with his desire for intimate knowledge of the entirety of the African diaspora. "After studying for a year at Columbia," Guillén's Hughes reports, "I dedicated myself to exploring the globe, free of all obstacles, outside of all conventions.... I have visited Dakar, Nigeria, Luanda.... In those lands the feeling of love for the Negro was strengthened in my soul, a feeling that has never since abandoned me. In contact with those sweet people.... I understood that it was necessary to be their friend, their voice, their crutch: to be their poet."[29] Guillén frames Hughes's visit to Havana as part of an aesthetic project aimed at solidifying the American writer's position as the "*poeta de los negros*" by relentlessly expanding his "contact" with the black Atlantic. Guillén perceives in Hughes a variant of what Glusberg recognizes in Frank: the overriding conviction that the sympathetic literary imagination must be cultivated through extensive firsthand contact. Guillén also drew attention to those aspects of Afro-Cuban culture that US writers often overlooked in their search for the black experience, referring in his poem "Pequeña oda a un boxeador cubano negro" to a black Cuban boxer who "isn't worried about Waldo Frank or Langston Hughes."[30] Despite inhabiting opposite poles of the Spanish-speaking Americas, Guillén and Glusberg expressed a similar frustration with US writers using the language of experience to validate their Latin American literary projects.

In the second half of the twentieth century, there was an explosion in the range and number of US writers who composed in situ in Latin America. Burroughs, Elizabeth Bishop, Jack Kerouac, Amiri Baraka, Jane Bowles, Allen Ginsberg, Sandra Cisneros, Hunter Thompson, Joan Didion, Paul Theroux, Robert Stone, Lucia Berlin, and Francisco Goldman all wrote significant works in and about the region. During this same period, the US experiencer emerged as an archetypal figure within Latin American literature. In an interview, the Argentine novelist Ricardo Piglia described Steve Ratliff, the protagonist of his 1988

novella "En otro país" [In Another Country] in the precise terms of
the US literature of experience: "he was a very cultivated and refined
man who was seduced by the myth, so typically North American, of
lived experience [la experiencia vivida]; he embarked on a journey
to see the world and spent close to a year wandering around and had
a tragic history with a woman in Buenos Aires and never again left
Argentina."[31] Though Ratliff is a fictional character, Piglia's portrait
of the US writer as experiencer is clearly meant to evoke and invoke
the *actual* US writers who wrote about Latin America. His novella
sets up a number of elaborate parallels between Ratliff and Hemingway,
and much of its action occurs in a bar called Ambos Mundos, which
takes its name from Hemingway's real-life hangout in Havana. When
we set "En otro país" alongside a series of other Latin American
texts, we see that it is far more than a metafictional "who's who in
American literature" game for a Spanish-speaking audience. Together
with Edmundo Desnoes's *Memorias del subdesarrollo* [*Memories of
Underdevelopment*, 1965] and Leonardo Padura's *Adiós, Hemingway*
(2001), two important Cuban novels treating Hemingway's expatriate
life on the island, Piglia's text participates in a sustained literary dialogue about the US writer's relationship to Latin America. Significantly,
all three works take seriously the Hemingwayesque equation between the quantity of a writer's life experience and the quality of his
or her fiction. As Padura's narrator puts it, "[Hemingway] knew that
his imagination had always been weak and deceiving, and that the mere
telling of the things he had seen and learned in life had allowed him
to write books that were capable of exuding that veracity that he demanded of his literature. . . . He knew the truth: he needed to live the
life he did to produce his literature."[32] Rejecting the logic of those "critics" who suggest that Hemingway's experiential method was simply a
construction of his persona, Padura's narrator details Hemingway's
methods for expanding his "actual observation" of events from the
Italian front and the bullrings of Spain to the Gulf Stream off Padura's
home country of Cuba.

Piglia and Padura are among the many Latin American writers
who have drawn from and reshaped the cultural legacy of the US
literature of experience. My use of the word "experiencer," what lin-
guists call an "agent noun," highlights the complex mechanisms by
which the activity of "experiencing" accrued such value and authority in the US literary field that it came to rival the act of writing as
the primary marker of literary production. At the same time, it calls

attention to the way Latin American writers began to attach the idea of a "literature of experience" to a series of real and imagined twentieth-century US writers, blurring the line between historical and fictional registers in their texts.

Literary Fields of the Americas

Anxieties of Experience draws primarily (though not exclusively) from US writing about Latin America and Latin American writing about the United States. My objects of study are diverse: works of fiction, travel narratives, autobiographies, poems, letters, cultural criticism, newspapers, and literary textbooks. Although I reflect on the differences among various genres and registers across the Americas, this book is ultimately concerned with distinct literary practices and identity formations of writers in the US and Latin American literary fields. Similarly, while I address a number of topics that have received significant attention in hemispheric studies, such as translation, circulation, empire, border crossing, and the politics of movement, I treat such material conditions mainly as a way to understand literary formations in the hemisphere, not the other way around.

This account of US and Latin American literature and literary relations must reckon with two major methodological objections. Perhaps the most formidable obstacle to this study resides in the very conceptual opposition I pose between reading and experience. According to Jay, the rise of a widespread poststructuralist inclination in the American academy during the late twentieth century "challenge[d] 'experience' (or even more so 'lived experience') as a simplistic ground of immediacy that fail[ed] to register the always already mediated nature of cultural relations and the instability of the subject who is supposedly the bearer of experiences" (3). Whether in its deconstructive or Foucauldian iteration (the former more concerned with the philosophic contradictions of the discourse of experience, the latter more attuned to its ideological grounds), the poststructuralist challenge to the claims of experience shadows every interpretive move taken in this book. The various references to "strategies of representation," "scenes of not reading," and similar critical terms should alert the reader to my recognition that both the "US experiencer" and "Latin American reader" are cultural constructions. Even the most experience-bound writer must read, just as the most bookish writer must have nonliterary experiences.

Nevertheless, I am ultimately unsatisfied with the reduction of literary or philosophical appeals to experience as so many instances of textuality. My own experience with various interpretive communities in the United States and Latin America persuades me that different structures of feeling surrounding the concepts of experience and reading do, after all, exist.[33] Indeed, I will make the case that Latin American writers have been highly attuned to how "major" US authors have attempted to monopolize both the discourse and the practices of experiential writing. Moreover, many key scholarly works in postcolonial studies and world-systems analysis have convincingly shown that cultural influences often replicate or recode broader imbalances across political and geographical lines.[34] Thus, while literary influence in the twentieth and twenty-first centuries has increasingly moved north as well as south, cross-cultural readings between the United States and Latin America continue to be asymmetrical. The scholarship of Irene Rostagno and Helen Delpar, among others, has provided empirical evidence for what must quickly become obvious to those working with hemispheric archives of the twentieth century: Latin Americans have tended to translate and read many more works by Americans than vice versa.[35]

The other major objection would presumably arise from the discipline of inter-American, hemispheric, or Americas studies itself. A focus on disparate literary identity formations in the United States and Latin America seems to strike at the very foundations of a field that has typically stressed commonalities over contrasts. Indeed, since the rise of the discipline in the late 1980s and the subsequent publication of Gustavo Pérez Firmat's edited volume *Do the Americas Have a Common Literature?* (1990), many have followed Pérez Firmat in searching for the "common ground" of the two regions as a means of analyzing patterns of mutual influence and shared aspirations across the hemisphere.[36] In this vein, in their introduction to a 2009 special issue of *Comparative Literature* on the Americas, Lois Parkinson Zamora and Silvia Spitta urge Americanists and Latin Americanists alike to "overcom[e] the North-South divide."[37] Even scholars such as José David Saldívar, whose *The Dialectics of Our America: Genealogy, Cultural Critique, and Literary History* (1991) seizes on the unequal relations of power, influence, and cultural capital within the Americas, have operated with a notion of underground solidarity and "resistance" across national and regional borders. These methodologies have compellingly demonstrated the limitations of national or regional frameworks for studying literary production in the hemisphere, providing an important genealogy for eschewing an exclusively Americanist or Latin Americanist approach.

Yet the "common grounds" approach to literature in the Americas also conceals significant differences. Recently, several scholars have argued that comparative work on US and Latin American literature must be aware of the "pitfalls of trans-American comparisons."[38] Drawing from a growing critical literature in transnational studies, this scholarship has questioned the dominant assumption of equivalence and correspondence across geographical boundaries in the hemisphere. In fleshing out numerous instances of "misencounters" between US and Latin American writers, my book contributes to this recent trend. However, by identifying the US literature of experience and the Latin American literature of the reader as the tectonic forces that increasingly impelled such misencounters over the course of the twentieth century, I offer a new model for studying the literatures of the Americas in addition to a critique of existing frameworks.

My methodology in this book rests on the conviction that scholars should treat the literatures of the Americas as a set of overlapping literary fields that are at once regional, national, and hemispheric. In Pierre Bourdieu's usage, a literary field defines the "social universe" in which literary works are written and valued, a semiautonomous system in which external factors such as economics and politics are "always retranslated according to the specific logic of the field."[39] Building on Bourdieu's insights, my approach will highlight how the cultural, geopolitical, and linguistic relationship between the United States and Latin America was mobilized in the construction of the identity formations of the US experiencer and the Latin American reader.[40] As we will see, the US authors I discuss prove their experiential bona fides in Latin America through a series of writerly practices that include prolonged immersion in the region, emphasis on extensive and intensive geographical coverage, and a vernacular model for appropriating the Spanish language. The Latin American authors I examine cultivate their relationship to the United States through an opposing set of writerly practices: prolonged immersion in the US archive (i.e., the repository of *mediated* representations of US culture), emphasis on the constrictions on geographical mobility for Latin Americans in the United States, and a citational model for appropriating the English language. Though it goes without saying that not all writers in these respective literary fields conform to these modes of writing, I will insist that these are the dominant cultural formations that developed in the hemisphere over the twentieth century. I realize that such a statement risks implying that the authors who appear in this book are mere players in a hemispheric drama over which they have no control, delivering lines—indeed, whole books—according to a predetermined script. On the contrary, I hope to communicate the sheer creativity that each of these literary actors brought to the task of inventing, improvising, and revising the drama as it was being performed. If this is in many ways an account of how cultural and geopolitical systems impinge on the work of writers, it is no less a study of how writers transform cultural and geopolitical systems.

My comparative approach to literary fields in the hemisphere also seeks to move inter-American studies into recent debates about the category of "world literature." Although Bourdieu's project was mainly confined to French cultural production, Pascale Casanova has persuasively illuminated the dynamic relationship among national and regional literary fields, positing a World Republic of Letters structured by antagonistic *literary* rather than political forces. The weakness of Casanova's theoretical paradigm, however, is that it locates this global literary space almost entirely in the domain of what writers have said and done, rather than in the literary texts they have written. My burden will be to show how an analysis of the logic of literary fields can inform our understanding of textual forms, proving that a field-based approach can account for what Franco Moretti has referred to as the "complex literary features" of a global (and hemispheric) literary terrain.[41] I will also remain attentive to the fact that, as Ignacio Sánchez Prado has signaled, both Casanova and Moretti privilege Latin American writers and critics who have been canonized in Europe and the United States over those whose primary influence is internal to the region.[42] An important aspect of my study will be to evaluate the work of major Latin American authors who are less visible in US literary and academic debates, such as Ricardo Piglia and Cristina Rivera Garza, alongside hypercanonical writers like Borges, García Márquez, Rigoberta Menchú, and Bolaño.

In adopting a field-based approach, I am aware of the very real political, linguistic, and cultural variations within and among the countries that compose Latin America, and of the national paradigms that still influence much of literary culture in the region. If

I nevertheless take a supranational view, it is because the literary field that has developed in the region since the second quarter of the twentieth century—its institutions, cultural routes, publishing houses, and market relations—has largely been determined along the lines of language. My focus is therefore principally on Spanish-speaking Latin America, or what Josefina Ludmer has called the "territory of the language," with its main publishing centers in Barcelona, Mexico City, Buenos Aires, Madrid, and Havana, and with its primary actors living throughout Latin America and Spain.[43] Despite cross-cultural exchange among the Spanish-, French-, and Portuguese-speaking regions of the Western Hemisphere, I do not address Brazil and the French Caribbean, whose fields of literary production have different loci and are organized by a different logic. It would perhaps make more sense to speak of "Spanish America" or "Hispanic America" than "Latin America," but since these designations are much less common in English usage than they are in Spanish, I settle on "Latin America" as the primary name for the region. When I occasionally wish to make visible the gap between this signifier and the geographical region it purports to represent, I will refer more specifically to writers of the "Spanish-speaking Americas."

Although this project may initially appear to naturalize the geopolitical boundaries of the United States and the Spanish-speaking Americas, I will show that transnational networks traverse the literary identity formations of both the US experiencer and the Latin American reader. First, as I suggest in my opening chapter, these identity formations incorporated long-standing historical traditions that extend across centuries and an even wider geographical terrain than I map in this book.[44] Second, and more central to my argument, the US and Latin American literary fields were accessible to writers from outside them who could develop what we might refer to, paraphrasing Bourdieu, as a *feel* for the hemispheric game. Several of the most important contributors to the formation of the US literature of experience were neither born in the United States nor held American citizenship at the time of their most influential writings. Participating in the US literature of experience often depended as much on one's ability to incorporate the codes of the US literary field as it did on one's country of origin.

The work of the poet and novelist Claude McKay, who was born in the British West Indies in 1889 and arrived in the United States in 1912, illustrates how non-US writers adapted to and manipulated the subject position of the US experiencer. McKay's transnational trajectory from Jamaican dialect poet to Harlem chronicler to radical diasporic intellectual in Europe has been much discussed, but the careful reworking of his complicated personal history to both incorporate and challenge US literary codes merits further attention.[45] McKay's *Home to Harlem* (1928), the best-selling novel of the Afro-modernist movement that would come to be known as the Harlem Renaissance, dramatizes the pull of the literature of experience within the US literary field through the divergent trajectories of its two main characters, Jake and Ray. Jake is an attractive African American twenty-something who returns from the Great War to a rollicking lifestyle in New York. A born adventurer who seems to glide effortlessly from railroad cars to nightclubs and cabarets, he relates to life primarily through experience. Ray, on the other hand, is a pensive Haitian expatriate who spends most of his time immersed in books. In many ways Ray more closely resembles McKay himself: a black intellectual steeped in the history of the Americas, a multilingual expatriate who reads Wordsworth, Toussaint, and *The Negro World* alike, a radical internationalist who lambasts races and nations as "things like skunks, whose smells poisoned the air of life."[46] Yet Jake is unquestionably the protagonist of the novel. As Wayne Cooper has documented, McKay's choice to make Jake the main character was not an easy one, and in "Color Scheme," the unpublished novel that preceded *Home to Harlem*, Ray was the leading man.[47] At some point in the composition of *Home to Harlem*, however, McKay decided, as he put it to his literary agent, that Ray functioned far better in a "secondary role" than "as the principal character."[48] Ray's diminished status in *Home to Harlem* thus represented a deliberate displacement of the activity of reading and the subject position of the reader from the novel's center of gravity.

Home to Harlem provides a paradigmatic example of the narrative strategies by which the writer-as-reader was marginalized within the US literature of experience. In the novel's final version, McKay devalues Ray's broad knowledge of hemispheric history and his literary formation in non-English languages and literatures. When Ray disappears at the end of the second part, he laments that "[t]he more I learn the less I understand and love life" (274). Jake, on the other hand, winds up reuniting with his long-lost sweetheart, the aptly and significantly named Felice. Though contemporary opinions in the United States were split on McKay's depiction of Harlem's black working class and its boisterous nightlife, ranging from Langston Hughes's exuberant claim that *Home to Harlem* was "the finest thing 'we've' done yet" to Du Bois's famous quip that the novel left him "wanting to take a bath," reviewers almost uniformly took Jake rather than Ray as the embodiment of the novel's aesthetic.[49] McKay's repositioning of Ray as *Home to Harlem*'s foil enabled Jake's experiential characteristics to emerge more fully from the narrative. The novel itself consecrates the US experiencer, relegating Ray's more radical and literarily transnational formation to the interstices of the text.

The US literature of experience was therefore permeable to certain non-American writers, but it had its limits and logic of exclusion. McKay's "success" in participating in the US literature of experience depended on his familiarity with American literary institutions, his use of the English language, and his ability to lay claim to firsthand knowledge of the United States. This linguistic, cultural, and experiential threshold excluded a large number of writers who did not or could not publish English-language texts in the country, conditions that continued to be imposed, *mutatis mutandis*, on Latina/o, Asian-American, and African writers in the second half of the twentieth century. More specifically, it created different conditions of reception for English- and Spanish-language writers of the hemisphere, regardless of where they produced. My focus on the Latin American reading of the US literature of experience acknowledges this cultural, linguistic, and material barrier as a constitutive factor in the disparate identity formations across the Americas. That we may be in the midst of a significant reorganization of these formations in the first decades of the twenty-first century only makes it more necessary to understand their history.

Anxieties of Experience tracks the evolving relationship of the US literature of experience and the Latin American literature of the reader from the nineteenth century to the present. The book consists of two parts and an epilogue. Part I, "Hemispheric Literary Divides," enacts a sustained critique of the "common grounds" approach to the literatures of the Americas. Tracing a series of misencounters between US "experiencers" and Latin American "readers" across the terrains of literary history, hemispheric cultural initiatives, and canonical texts, I explain the distinct yet mutually constitutive logics of literary production in the hemisphere. Part II, "Literary Fields of the Americas," turns from a hemispheric framework to an examination of how the subject positions of the writer as experiencer and the writer-as-reader structured the twentieth-century US and Latin American literary fields respectively. If part I uses the discourses of experience and reading as a means of intervening in major hemispheric debates of the past twenty years, part II suggests how an analysis of these discourses alters our understanding of US and Latin American literary studies. The epilogue, "After Bolaño: Toward a Literature of the Americas," argues that the US literature of experience and the Latin American literature of the reader are already converging in the twenty-first century, as the transnational processes of globalization have reconfigured both the circulation and cultural imaginary of contemporary US and Latin American literature. The recent work of several US Latina/o writers suggests that we are currently at an important juncture in literary history, in which writers in the United States not only increasingly read Latin American fiction but also fashion themselves as voracious readers of it. Or to put it slightly differently, if writers and scholars have recently begun to speak of a *literature* of the Americas in the singular, we should attribute this terminological shift more to a complex transformation of contemporary literary practice than to the triumph of a hemispheric cultural outlook that was always already there.

Chapter 1, "Cultural Divergence: The US Literature of Experience and the Latin American Literature of the Reader," periodizes the literatures of the Americas from the nineteenth century to the postwar period. After acknowledging the emergence of a brief "transamerican literary imagination" forged in the wake of the Latin American independence movements of the 1810s and 1820s, I chart the gradual breakdown of this shared literary imagination in the second half of the nineteenth century. The chapter links this process to the rise of the US literature of experience and the Latin American literature of the reader, two distinct modes of literary production inflected by (without merely reflecting) US and Latin American political and cultural processes in the late nineteenth century and the twentieth century. Outlining the historical transformations of the US and Latin American cultural terrains, I assert that a hemispheric divide can be located in the texts and contexts of the literatures of the Americas, encompassing narrative strategies as well as dominant national and regional discourses.

In chapter 2, "An Inter-American Episode: Jorge Luis Borges, Waldo Frank, and the Battle for Whitman's America," I focus on a paradigmatic misencounter between an American experiencer and a Latin

American reader, following the trail of Waldo Frank's and Jorge Luis Borges's implicit dispute about the source material of Walt Whitman's poetry and his vision of the Americas. I show how Frank, one of the main literary ambassadors between the United States and Latin America in the twentieth century, positioned Whitman as the representative US writer whose antibookish experiential aesthetics could serve as a model for "American" writers both North and South. Drawing from Frank's speeches, letters, and essays during his visit to Argentina in 1929, I argue that Frank's framework provided a foil for Borges's idiosyncratic view that Whitman's poetry about America derived entirely from his readings of European and US writers. Although much of the best scholarship on the reception of Whitman in Latin America has concentrated on poets like José Martí and Pablo Neruda who adapted Whitman's naturalism, I contend that Borges's iconoclastic portrait of Whitman as a reader profoundly influenced a range of antiexperiential literary practices in Latin America.

Chapter 3, "Uncommon Grounds: The Representation of History in *Absalom, Absalom!, One Hundred Years of Solitude,* and *Song of Solomon,*" turns from a historical account of the development of the US literature of experience and the Latin American literature of reading to a textual analysis of US and Latin American historical novels. Hemispheric and inter-American scholars often treat the novels I study here—William Faulkner's *Absalom, Absalom!* (1936), Gabriel García Márquez's *One Hundred Years of Solitude* (1967), and Toni Morrison's *Song of Solomon* (1977)—as exemplary instances of literary borrowing and shared thematic concerns across the North-South divide. Yet I demonstrate that as each of these canonical texts transforms the text that came before it, it simultaneously realigns its predecessor's historical imaginary to conform to the dominant logic of the US and Latin American literary fields. While the American works present us with experiential models of reconstructing the past and conveying knowledge from generation to generation, García Márquez's Latin American novel contains the recurring motif of reading as the fundamental mode of comprehending and transmitting history. I claim that even where hemispheric literary exchanges genuinely occur, they remain thoroughly traversed by the disparate representational strategies of the US literature of experience and the Latin American literature of reading. I suggest that tracking the migration of formal structures and the treatment of history *across* literary fields helps delineate the structures of these fields in ways that a

purely immanent reading of US literature or Latin American literature cannot.

The second part of the book moves on to explore the internal
logics of the US literature of experience and the Latin American
literature of the reader, respectively. Chapter 4, "Full Immersion:
Modernist Aesthetics and the US Literature of Experience," argues
that the modernist fiction of Katherine Anne Porter and Ernest
Hemingway articulated a link between good writing and expansive personal experience that appears most clearly in their works set
in Latin America. I begin by reconstructing how Hemingway and
Porter each developed the literature of experience in the 1920s as an
internationalist mode of expanding their knowledge of the world. I
then track the turn in both authors' writings of the 1930s toward a
more political argument about experiential literature. In the context
of the rise of the literary left and Popular Front aesthetics, Hemingway
and Porter both highlighted the danger of producing literature derived from ideological positioning as opposed to firsthand witnessing. This section focuses on two key texts about the long experience
of Latin American revolutions: Hemingway's *To Have and Have Not*
(1937), a novel whose plot incorporates a series of episodes from the
1933 Cuban Revolution; and Porter's "Hacienda" (1937), a story chronicling the retrenchment of radical aesthetics and politics in Mexico
in the aftermath of the Mexican Revolution of 1910-1920. The chapter closes by demonstrating the surprising degree to which debates
about the relationship between authorial experience and literary
production animated the New Critical movement, as critics such as
Robert Penn Warren and Cleanth Brooks re-envisioned the writerly
emphasis on firsthand experience of place as a question of formal
style. I conclude that the "disciplining" of the US literature of experience in books like Warren and Brooks's *Understanding Fiction* (1943)
set the critical tone for debates about authorial experience in the early
post-1945 period.

Chapter 5, "Voracious Readers: The Latin American Lettered City
and the US Literature of Experience," considers how Latin American
writer-readers of the late twentieth century and early twenty-first
century have defined their work in relation to the US literature of
experience. Through analysis of the works of Ricardo Piglia, Roberto
Bolaño, and Cristina Rivera Garza, I contend that contemporary Latin
American writers have made visible the implicit cultural and geopolitical codes of the US literature of experience while simultaneously

constructing an alternative paradigm for literary production based on what Bolaño refers to as "voracious reading." This chapter examines both the dissemination of US literature in the Spanish-speaking world and the way it was received and rewritten by Latin American writers. First, I show how Piglia developed a politically engaged model for the reader in the 1970s and 1980s. Then, I demonstrate how Bolaño's work of the 1990s and 2000s merged the positions of the reader and experiencer through a decades-long engagement with the US literature of experience. The chapter ends with an examination of how the contemporary Mexican novelist Cristina Rivera Garza has challenged the masculine codes of the Latin American voracious reader.

My epilogue, "After Bolaño: Toward a Contemporary Literature of the Americas," addresses the US and Latin American literary fields in the "post-Bolaño" era. Since the posthumous publication of Bolaño's *2666* in Spanish in 2004, and the translations of *Distant Star* (2004), *The Savage Detectives* (2007), and *2666* (2008) into English, Bolaño has become one of the most important contemporary literary models for writers in both the English- and Spanish-speaking worlds. Even when not explicitly acknowledged as such, Bolaño's merging of the reader and experiencer has forced US and Latin American writers to confront the cultural expectations of their literary practices. I show how the figure of the reader-experiencer has become an emergent formation in the post-Bolaño literatures of the Americas. Now that US authors are reading Latin American literature more than ever, Latin American authors are more frequently writing about their "experience" of the United States. I attempt to explain and substantiate this claim through an analysis of contemporary works by Latina/o writers composing in English in the United States, including Francisco Goldman, Ana Menéndez, and Junot Díaz; by non-Latina/o US writers such as Ben Lerner and Kenneth Goldsmith; and by Spanish-language writers such as the Mexican novelist Valeria Luiselli and the Puerto Rican poet Mara Pastor. The book therefore ends on a speculative note, as I consider how recent works in the literatures of the Americas might point the way to new literary possibilities in the future.

PART I

Hemispheric Literary Divides

Cultural Divergence

THE US LITERATURE OF EXPERIENCE AND THE LATIN AMERICAN LITERATURE OF THE READER

We are different, we are other: North Americans (by which I mean the citizens of the United States) and Latin Americans.

—CARLOS FUENTES, *Latin America: At War with the Past*

In *The Idea of Latin America* (2005), Walter Mignolo announces that the turn of the new millennium is the perfect time to reverse the "excess of confidence" that has "spead all over the world regarding the ontology of continental divides," and more specifically, of the "ideology of a continental divide between 'Latin' and 'Anglo' Americas."[1] This imperative to reject a binary vision of the hemisphere might be considered all the more urgent in light of Mignolo's convincing argument that the historical emergence of the "ideas" of Latin and Anglo America in the mid-nineteenth century were intextricably entwined with Eurocentric discourses of modernity and colonial power.[2] Given Mignolo's analysis, why would we continue to reinforce the binary between the United States and Latin America in the twenty-first century? Shouldn't inter-American scholars embark on a collective project to bridge the hemispheric divide, healing what Mignolo calls the "colonial wounds" of a violent and fractured geography?

The answers to these questions, however, are far from obvious. On the one hand, there is no disputing Mignolo's claim that a broad variety of social actors and grassroots initiatives over the past twenty years have effectively challenged the hemispheric cultural logic that tended to pit "Anglos" against "Latinos." Mignolo is right to point to the limitations of the ideas of Latin and Anglo America as totalizing frameworks for approaching the cultures and history of the hemisphere. To carry this point over to the literary sphere, Mignolo's cautionary words remind us that a range of oral traditions and writing practices have existed for centuries outside the dominant public spheres and European languages in the hemisphere. On the other hand, Mignolo's epistemic reduction of an entire complex of marginalized discourses to a "decolonial paradigm of knowledge and understanding" (xii) stretching back to the sixteenth century risks undermining the very historical argument he makes. The same reasons that cause him to be wary of reifying categories such as "Anglo" and "Latino" should also caution us against essentializing and dehistoricizing alternative epistemelogies and forms of resistance. While the divide between the United States and Latin America may be a construction of the nineteenth century, it is neverthless a construction within which writers, readers, and other cultural actors have lived and produced. If we understand the "hemispheric divide" not as a fatal geographic separation but as a set of historically determined yet variable cultural systems, we can begin to trace both the dominant categories in the hemisphere and the specific strategies by which they have been contested. The question I address here is therefore not *whether* a hemispheric divide "really" exists at the ontological level, but rather *how* its discursive construction shaped the various literary fields of the Americas. My aim is to show that such a divide, as both a political and a cultural phenomenon, has at once limited and enabled the conditions of literary production within each respective region.

This chapter excavates the formation of the US literature of experience and the Latin American literature of the reader as the major *literary* fault line that developed in the hemisphere in the twentieth century. It periodizes the literatures of the Americas from the nineteenth century to the post–World War II period, mapping the broad contours of the US literature of experience and the Latin American literature of the reader in order to set the historical foundations for the chapters that follow. I examine this process with a view to what are commonly held to be the key periods in US and Latin American literary history: in the United States, the "American Renaissance" of the mid-nineteenth century, the "age of realism" of the last quarter of the nineteenth century, the "modernist" period between the two world wars, and the "postmodern" era of the late twentieth century; in Latin America, the *modernismo* of the late nineteenth and early twentieth century, the *vanguardia* movement of the 1920s and early 1930s, and the boom decades of the 1960s and 1970s. In recent years, scholars have persuasively demonstrated that a "transameri-can literary imaginary" coexisted with and rivaled national and regional cultural paradigms in the decades following the consolidation of the continental Latin American independence movements of the 1810s and 1820s.[3] In this chapter I track how this common framework for conceptualizing literary production in the Americas broke down at the turn of the twentieth century. I argue that major "hemispheric" events such as the Spanish-Cuban-American War of 1898 fueled the creation of distinct but mutually constitutive US and Latin American literary fields. What will primarily be at issue here is the fundamental asymmetry of that relationship. While US writers increasingly used Latin America as a "field of experience," Latin American writers used the US literature of experience to define their own cultural aims: first, through the "arielist" distinction between North American materialism and Latin American spirituality, and then through the invention of the figure of the Latin American reader of the US literary archive. Thus, although I address numerous contact zones in the hemisphere, I suggest that such contact zones have been thoroughly permeated by the disparate expectations of the US literature of experience and the Latin American literature of the reader.

The US Literature of Experience

The rhetoric of experience was not, of course, invented in the United States. As Martin Jay has demonstrated, explicit appeals to the authority of experience among European philosophers and writers surface as early as the sixteenth and seventeenth centuries.[4] And in the North American context, scholars have found evidence of the vocabulary of experience in the writings of British-American colonial settlers.[5] Though one can certainly find aspects of these various discourses in contemporary American usages of the term "experience," I contend that the experiential strain of US literature that became dominant in the twentieth century arose amid the intense cultural national debates of the mid-nineteenth century. To trace the emergence and development of the US literature of experience means revisiting a narrative about American literary history that will already be familiar to many scholars. Yet by situating this narrative within the matrix of hemispheric geopolitics, new angles and accents appear. They bring into view both the peculiar resiliency of the discourse of experience in the US literary field and the ways it was reshaped and reimagined in each successive literary-historical period.

EXPERIENCE AND EXPANSION (1848–1918)

For decades after the United States achieved political independence, scores of American writers, editors, and publishers wondered how and when the country could produce an "independent" national literature. This is the question that animates Ralph Waldo Emerson's address "The American Scholar" (1837), which ultimately arrives at the conclusion that "we have listened too long to the courtly muses of Europe."[6] In Emerson's eyes, the best way for the American writer to defy Old World traditions was to look to experience instead of books. Mandating a "strictly subordinated" role for reading and lambasting "bibliomaniacs of all degrees" (58, 57), Emerson insists: "Only so much do I know, as I have lived. Instantly, we know whose words are loaded with life, and whose not" (60). The bulk of Emerson scholarship over the past twenty years has sought to recover the intertexuality of his thought and writings, and critics are right to point out that later essays such as "Experience" and "Books" often reverse his earlier judgments about the possibility of unmediated access to nature and the noxious effects of reading.[7] Nevertheless, the New World troping of the quintessentially Romantic image of the poet closing the book to go out in search of experience—a gesture whose *locus classicus* is Wordsworth's 1798 "The Tables Turned"—emerged as a key rhetorical move of the post-Emersonian literary field.

In the mid-nineteenth century, the influence of Emerson's anti-bookish, experiential discourse of national self-reliance only grew deeper, in spite of the evident irony that he himself was a bibliomaniac. Emerson's discourse had the powerful effect of inspiring a younger generation of writers, including Walt Whitman and Henry David Thoreau, to radicalize his positions even further. Whitman's preface to the 1855 *Leaves of Grass* proclaims that "[w]hat I experience or portray shall go from my composition without a shred of my composition," and in one of the three anonymous self-reviews of the first edition that he published, Whitman described himself as a kind of illiterate savant: "Self-reliant, with haughty eyes, assuming to himself all the attributes of his country, steps Walt Whitman into literature, talking like a man unaware that there was ever hitherto such a production as a book, or such a being as a writer."[8] This anticipatory figuration of the national poet soaking up the country through a series of experiential journeys would be ratified in such poems as "Song of the Open Road," where the poet, "done" with libraries, studies, and "indoor complaints," invites his audience to leave the "book on the shelf unopen'd" and join him on the open road.[9] The explicit targets of Whitman's antibookish rhetoric were mainly European literature and writers, a testament to the postcolonial cultural imbalances between Britain and the United States in the antebellum period.[10] But the rest of the Americas often appeared in Whitman's work as a future path for discovery and exploration. It should not be forgotten that all these open roads eventually led to the territories that had recently been acquired in the Mexican-American War (1846–1848), the military effort that Whitman vociferously supported while editor of the *Brooklyn Daily Eagle*. As many scholars have recognized, the language of "generosity" and "affection" in Whitman's call to American poets to "incarnate" US geography from the "long" Atlantic Coast to the even "longer" Pacific (7) marks a deliberate recoding of the mid-nineteenth-century rhetoric of Manifest Destiny.[11]

To be sure, *Leaves of Grass* never explicitly promotes the expansionist views of Whitman's *Daily Eagle* pieces. Yet a passage in "Song of Myself" recounting the "massacre" of Goliad during the Texas War of Independence exemplifies how Whitman's hemispheric interventionism was nonetheless refracted through his most famous poem. In section 34, the speaker recounts the "tale" of the "murder in cold blood" of Texan soldiers by the Mexican army in 1835 (226), a conflict that served as a prelude to the greater violence of the Mexican-American War. The Goliad section follows many of the conventions of patriotic poetry, particularly in its selective emphasis on the "enemy['s]" violation of the codes of *jus in bello*. Yet Whitman's most decisive compositional strategy in representing the Goliad conflict was to revise the passage in later editions of "Song of Myself" to give the speaker the aura of testimony: "Now I tell what I knew in Texas in my early youth" (226). Though in truth Whitman, like most other civilians in the Northeast, had only read newspaper accounts about the conflicts of the 1830s and 1840s, his first-person narration allowed him to claim experiential authority for the nation- and empire-building process he had earlier championed as a journalist. From his vantage point on the border between Mexico and the soon-to-be-annexed Texan territory, the speaker authoritatively reports on the "glory of the race of rangers" and the perfidy of the Mexican "assassins" (227), justifying the extension of US national borders through a supposedly eyewitness account. For Whitman, this rendering of history as experience became an important precedent for *Drum-Taps* (1865), where he used the more "authentically" situated knowledge he gleaned from his three-year stint as hospital nurse in Washington, D.C. as source material for his poetry about the US Civil War. Although we are accustomed to thinking of Whitman's poetic "I" as either an integrating force for national unification or, in poems such as "Passage to India," as a kind of disembodied cosmopolitan spirit, the Goliad passage demonstrates how Whitman mobilized the discourse of personal experience to render specific hemispheric geopolitical concerns into poetic form.

Few could believe that the Whitman persona of *Leaves of Grass*, with its ever more elaborate descriptions of embodied experiences, was the actual life history of a single empirical author (especially in those moments when the speaker claims insight into the origins of night and day). Yet for subsequent generations of US writers, the poem's diversity of voices, perspectives, and topographies functioned as a model for incorporating new people and places into the national literary project. The relentlessly proleptic and pluralizing tone of Whitman's verse made better sense as a promise of what the US literary field could be than as a statement of what it actually was. It is important to recall that the experiential rhetoric of Whitman's verse was only one of many discursive modes available to US authors in the antebellum period. As Gretchen Murphy observes, a number of US-authored literary works about Mexico in the decades surrounding 1848 were historical romances that centered on the nation's Aztec past and presented themselves as found manuscripts, a framing technique much more in line with Hawthorne's *Scarlet Letter* than with Whitman's *Leaves of Grass*.[12] And although David Reynolds has suggested that the elder Whitman significantly overstated the degree to which his poetry initially went unsold and unrecognized in the United States,[13] what is certain is that Whitman's share of the literary marketplace—or Emerson's for that matter—did not come close to rivaling those of the sentimental novels of Harriet Beecher Stowe and Susan Warner, the two best-selling American authors of the 1850s. To borrow Raymond Williams's influential terms, the US literature of experience might best be described as an emergent rather than a dominant discourse in the mid-nineteenth century.

From the roots of the Whitmanesque and Emersonian naturalist argument for the primacy of lived experience, scholars have traced the first flowering of pragmatist philosophy and the literary realist and regionalist movements that flourished in the United States in the last decades of the nineteenth century.[14] And a full account of the US literature of experience in the second half of the nineteenth century would also include analysis of the growing skepticism toward the acquisition of Old World "culture" in American travel narratives such as Mark Twain's *Innocents Abroad* (1869) and Henry James's *Daisy Miller* (1877). The eponymous protagonist of *Daisy Miller* is only the most famous example of the late-nineteenth-century expatriate American who "care[s] little for feudal antiquities" and the "dusky traditions" of Europe, deliberately eschewing the well-charted itineraries of the Grand Tour in favor of a more vital experience of the Continent.[15] But in the midst of a sharp increase in US interventionism in the Americas at the turn of the twentieth century, Latin America began to replace Europe as the preferred destination for US writers of experience. Here, Stephen Crane and Richard Harding Davis, two leading authors of the 1890s and foundational figures of modern literary journalism, provide the guiding line. Unlike Whitman, both Crane and Davis did in fact observe a major hemispheric conflict, having traveled to the Caribbean as war correspondents during the Spanish-Cuban-American War of 1898. The long buildup to the War of 1898, which culminated in the United States' intervention in the independence struggle of the Cuban *insurrectos* against the Spanish Crown, provided material for many important works of the period. As political unrest in the Caribbean began to attract the attention of the American public (and eventually the US military), Crane and Davis used their Latin American "experience" to produce some of their best-known fiction. Davis's *Soldiers of Fortune* (1897), a swashbuckling romance about an American engineer-cum-revolutionary in the fictional Caribbean republic of Olancho, suggests that an appetite for experience as well as political intrigue fueled such Latin American adventurism. At the end of the novel, the two main characters, Robert Clay and Hope Langham, return from their successful expedition in satisfied exhaustion, while the character who refuses to take part in the action, Hope's sister Alice, sits smoldering in readerly anxiety, "look[ing] after them somewhat wistfully and bit[ing] the edges of her book."[16] Although Clay had initially courted Alice in cosmopolitan New York by referring to their shared appreciation for European civilization, once the scene moves to Latin America, his desire flows toward her sister, a fellow adventurer rather than a companion in culture.

Whereas Davis used his journalistic coverage of Central America and the Caribbean coast of South America in the 1890s primarily as background material for *Soldiers of Fortune*, Stephen Crane produced a series of short stories about the Spanish-Cuban-American War in which journalists themselves figured as avatars of the US writer of experience. After traveling to Cuba by way of Florida in 1896 as a journalist for William Randolph Hearst's *New York Journal*, Crane spent the next three years in and around the island, dispatching battle reports, impressionistic first-person accounts, and opinion pieces to Hearst and Joseph Pulitzer before composing several short stories later included in the volume *Wounds in the Rain: War Stories* (1900). Amy Kaplan has shown how Crane's journalistic account "Vivid Story of San Juan Hill" helped to construct an official US-centric narrative of the most famous battle of the Spanish-American War that depicted the invading US Marines as heroic and the Cuban insurgents as lazy, incompetent, and incapable of self-rule.[17] But Crane's fictional stories about wartime journalism consistently explode such tightly orchestrated political plot lines, focusing on the angles that the Hearst and Pulitzer articles either omit or leave unexplored. In stories such as "God Rest Ye Merry Gentleman," the choppy passage between Cuba and Florida doubles as a physical and psychological barrier the journalist must pass through in order to capture the full experience of the conflict. Crane's fictional journalists are always in the act of such exploration, seeking to unveil the verities of the US occupation mile by mile, village by village, and person by person. Although US writers of the early twentieth century acknowledged that Crane's most canonical work, *The Red Badge of Courage* (1895), had been published before he had witnessed a single moment of combat, they tended to see his writings in Cuba as the culmination of a literary trajectory marked by a zeal for both first-person witnessing and geographical coverage. In an essay commemorating Crane's death in 1900, Willa Cather remarked that he had "established himself as the first writer of his time in the picturing of episodic, fragmentary life.... He went from country to country, from man to man, absorbing all that was in them for him."[18] Crane's self-fashioning as an experiential journalist made him an important precursor not only of the war-correspondent-turned-fiction-writer of the modernist period but also of later Latin American–based writer-reporters such as Hunter Thompson (*The Rum Diary*, 1960, published 1998), Joan Didion (*Salvador*, 1983), and Francisco Goldman (*The Long Night of the White Chickens*, 1992).[19]

It is therefore worth underscoring that the foundational document of American pragmatism, the philosophical movement that martialed the concept of "practical experience" to combat what John Dewey would later describe as the "spectator theory of knowledge," appeared in the immediate aftermath of the war in Cuba, when the entire country was debating the potential scope and limitations of US expansionism. William James's address to the Philosophical Union at the University of California–Berkeley in August 1898, entitled "Philosophical Conceptions and Practical Results," introduced the word "pragmatism" to the public through an elaborate metaphor of philosophy as a form of "trailblazing," wherein the pragmatist philosopher wields "the axe of the human intellect on the trees of the otherwise trackless forest of human experience."[20] His talk begins by playfully converting the Turneresque rhetoric of the frontier into a figure for American intellectual progress: "I ought to give you something worthy of your hospitality, and not altogether unworthy of your great destiny, to help cement our rugged East and your wondrous West together in a spiritual bond" (1078). And it proceeds mock-seriously to adduce Britain's support of the United States against Spain as a reason for replacing German transcendentalism with English empiricism as the primary course material for students in the United States. Though James at one point avows that "national jingoism…has no place in philosophy" (1096), at another he champions the American pragmatism of Charles Sanders Peirce as the only philosophy that can rectify the "failure" of English philosophers "to track the practical results completely enough to see how far they extend" (1095). "Experience," "extension," and "path-finding" are James's key terms in describing how the "principle of practicalism" will emerge triumphant in the United States, coming into its own on "this wonderful Pacific Coast, of which our race is taking possession" (1097). In moments like these, as Deborah Whitehead has observed, James unmistakably—and seemingly unapologetically—"places pragmatism and US imperialism in uncomfortable relation."[21] It is crucial to insist that James's Berkeley address is a far more mediated and complex response to the war in Cuba than Teddy Roosevelt's notorious 1899 speech in praise of the "strenuous life," and Alexander Livingston has recently documented James's turn toward an anti-imperial stance in the lead-up to the Philippine-American War of 1899–1902.[22] My point is that the emphasis on "practical experience" in the pragmatist discourse of the turn of the twentieth century cannot be divorced from the realities of US geopolitics or the cultural imaginaries they engendered. Both "classical" pragmatism and its rhetoric of experience were marked by a complicated blend of appropriation and critique of dominant views about the country's expanding role in the hemisphere.

As debates in the United States about interventionism in the Americas shaded, post-1898, into debates about the comparative advantages of engagement or isolationism in the First World War, the discourse of experience largely jettisoned the metaphorics of conquest discernible in the language of James. Dewey's writings in particular help to trace the shift in the US discourse of experience from the post-1898 period to the interwar years, when the United States fully emerged as a political and economic power on the world stage. Dewey's use of "experience" in political contexts was largely aligned with the language of Wilsonian internationalism, advocating not only the exportation of American-style democracy but also, in equally exceptionalist terms, of the "American experience." Indeed, in his defense of Woodrow Wilson's endorsement of the early blueprints for what would eventually become the League of Nations, Dewey explictly promoted the concept of federalism based on the idea that it had sprung "*directly out of our own experience*, which we have worked out and tested on a smaller scale in our own political life"[23] (emphasis mine). This would be the guiding line of the US literature of experience as it evolved in the 1920s and 1930s: less overt in flexing its muscles, more disposed to "testing" its methods and hypotheses around the globe.

MODERNIZING THE AMERICAN EXPERIENCE (1918–1945)

It would be difficult to overstate the degree to which the ideas of "experience" and "American" became intertwined in US literary discourses of the interwar period, permeating the very notion of "American literature" itself. Americanist scholarship of the past thirty years has compellingly argued that the canon of the nineteenth-century "American Renaissance" was largely the invention of twentieth-century cultural and literary criticism.[24] For the purposes of this study, I wish simply to highlight how completely the conceptual framework of the literature of experience undergirded this canonizing process, beginning with the resurgence of interest in Whitman in the late 1910s and the so-called Melville Revival of the 1920s. Carl Van Doren's discussion of *Moby Dick* in *The American*

Novel (1921) is typical of an early critical tradition that presented the novel as a transmutation of its author's vast firsthand knowledge of the globe: Melville "brought...an imagination which worked with lurid power over the facts of his own experience, swinging resistlessly [*sic*] over the seven seas and the seventy regions of the earth."[25] In *Studies in Classic American Literature* (1923), which laid the groundwork for later studies of what came to be known as the period of the American Renaissance, D. H. Lawrence asserts that Whitman's "essential message" was "to go down the open road, as the road opens into the unknown...accomplishing nothing save the journey, and the works incident to the journey."[26] Lawrence goes on to argue that this message is "the inspiration of thousands of Americans today...a message that only in America can be fully understood, finally accepted" (157). Although Lawrence's rhetoric owes much to the tropes of New World primitivism that crisscrossed the Atlantic in the early twentieth century, the influence of his critical paradigm depended in large part upon his translation of these tropes into a cultural program that lent legitimacy to the emerging experiential rhetoric in the US literary field. Indeed, in his proposed introduction to the British version of *Studies in Classic American Literature*, Lawrence made the controversial assertion that the United States had surpassed England in its "quality of life-experience, of emotion and passion and desire" (168). His critical work was instrumental in persuading English-speaking audiences on both sides of the Atlantic to accept that this greater intensity of lived experience, what he refers to at one point as a "change in experience, a change in being" (168), was the warp and woof of the greatest American literary works.

This belief in the correlation between life experience and artistic quality similarly pervades the major US narrative texts of the interwar period. The Whitmanesque trope of closing the book as a means of opening oneself up to experience is ubiquitous in what we now consider canonical US modernist novels. If Deweyan pragmatism would lament the gap between the cloistered spaces of art (the library, the museum, the studio) and the "realities of the actual world," US modernist works often address this gap by describing characters whose thirst for experience is signaled by symbolic acts of inattention or indifference to books and other artifacts that epitomize these privileged sites of culture. Scenes of reading in these novels are often scenes of not reading, scenes of getting tired while reading, scenes alluding to the dangers of reading. We find a full repertoire of these gestures in Hemingway's *The Sun Also Rises* (1926), where the novel repeatedly contrasts the writer-narrator Jake Barnes (who knows, as he says after a few minutes of reading Turgenev, when "it [is] not necessary to read any more") to Robert Cohn, the petulant young writer who constantly looks for answers in books.[27] It isn't exactly that Jake doesn't read, so much as that his reading always occurs in the interstices of the text, in the lulls before sleep that also function as narrative interludes. Jake is, in this sense, perhaps the most convincing fictional instantiation of the Emersonian principle that books are only for the writer's "idle times." When Jake criticizes Cohn for hating Paris and wanting to move to Latin America, it is not Cohn's thirst for adventure that draws Jake's ire but rather the fact that his desire to travel derives from his reading of a novel about the South American pampas: "He got the first idea out of a book, and I suppose the second came out of a book too" (20). The implication of Jake's critique is that the writerly impetus to "go beyond" stale literary conventions should be motivated by an equal commitment to going beyond those places that have been described *ad tedium* by other writers.

While Hemingway's antiliterariness has often been seen as a peculiarity of his thirst for masculine adventure and penchant for authenticity, variations on this attitude are constitutive of what we've come to understand as US modernism, crossing lines of region, race, and gender. Nowhere are such scenes of not reading more prevalent than in the novels, poems, and autobiographies of the "New Negro" movement that came to be known as the Harlem Renaissance.[28] A recurrent plot device in New Negro texts is the movement of an African American protagonist from the sheltered precincts of cultural production—usually, but not always, elite educational institutions—to a modern world that directly contradicted the intellectual expectations of what Du Bois notoriously dubbed the "talented tenth." The "Kabnis" section of *Cane* (1923) opens paradigmatically with the eponymous character deciding that there is "no use to read," before throwing down his book and stepping out into the "serene loveliness of Georgian autumn moonlight."[29] Similarly, Nella Larsen's *Quicksand* (1928) begins with a scene of the protagonist Helga Crane "discard[ing] her book" and "wish[ing] it were vacation, so that she might get away for a time."[30] Larsen's novel propels Helga on a journey of discovery from her teaching position at Naxos to Harlem to Copenhagen, a movement that only slows at the end of the novel when she settles into married life in the South with a traditional black preacher—the existential "quicksand" to which the novel's title refers.

Although many canonical US authors of the period continued to imagine such experiential journeys within the limits of national or regional borders, the modernist appropriation of the Whitmanesque trope frequently took on more global dimensions. Langston Hughes's autobiographical work *The Big Sea* (1936) opens with a famous scene in which the young poet dumps his books into the ocean: "I leaned over the rail of the S.S. *Malone* and threw the books as far as I could out into the sea—all the books I had had at Columbia, and all the books I had lately bought to read."[31] This scene, which anticipates the logic of Sal Paradise's flight from the "stultified" campus life in Jack Kerouac's *On the Road* (1957), culminates in the narrator's arrival on the African coast of Dakar. It is almost impossible to separate the pan-Africanist discourses in Hughes's writing from the aesthetics of experience that motivates the narrator to reverse the causal relationship between life and literature. While "books had been happening to [Hughes]" in the United States (4), the transatlantic journey finally allows him to merge his affective relationship to Africa with an experiential absorption of the place itself: "My Africa, Motherland of the Negro peoples! And me a Negro! Africa! The real thing, to be touched and seen, not merely read about in a book" (10). Hughes quickly reveals his ambivalent sense of belonging in Africa, and later portrays his decision to abandon his studies as itself influenced by reading. However, casting off his books in the opening pages clearly marks Hughes's initiation as a writer and his awakening to his diasporic identity. For Hughes, as for other interwar writers, moving beyond mediation ("I was glad [the books] were gone") often meant moving beyond the United States ("New York was gone, too," 4).

The narratives of Toomer, Larsen, and Hughes thus inaugurated a significant shift in the discourses surrounding reading and experience in the African American cultural tradition. As Henry Louis Gates and others have argued, displays of literary competence—through scenes of reading and metaphors of the "talking book"—were a central feature of African American literature through the antebellum period up to the early part of the twentieth century. A major turning point in the *Narrative of the Life of Frederick Douglass* (1845) occurs when Douglass realizes that the prohibition on reading among slaves in the South is one of the primary tools of oppression: having been told by his master that literacy would make him "forever unfit to be a slave," he vows "at whatever cost of trouble, to learn how to read."[32] As late as 1912, the narrator of James Weldon Johnson's *The Autobiography of an Ex-Coloured Man* could claim that his reading of *Uncle Tom's Cabin* "opened my eyes as to who and what I was and what my country considered me; in fact it gave me my bearing."[33] The narrator's sense of empowerment through his reading of Stowe's sentimental abolitionist novel, which he champions in opposition to critics who "brush it aside" as a "direct misrepresentation" of the slaveholding South (41), suggests the degree to which oppositional reading—that is, reading against the grain of dominant cultural stereotypes—had become an important narrative strategy in African American literary works. Yet the mounting interest in vernacular speech, folk culture, and musical tradition among the authors of the New Negro movement also manifested itself in a growing mistrust of the activity of reading itself.[34] The major works of the Harlem Renaissance thus not only responded to earlier texts in the African American tradition; they also helped initiate a broad US modernist reconfiguration of the literature of experience.

Both the expansive and the antibookish strains of the US literature of experience find their most elaborate theoretical framework in Dewey's aesthetic treatise *Art as Experience* (1934). Employing a conceptual language congruent with that of Hughes and Hemingway, Dewey insists that the artist is a born "experimenter," "a lover of unalloyed experience, [who] shuns objects that are already saturated, and [who] is therefore always on the growing edge of things. By the nature of the case, he is as unsatisfied with what is established as is a geographic explorer or a scientific inquirer."[35] If Dewey drew parallels between artists and explorers by way of analogy, US writers of the interwar period often took the connection quite literally. While we might tend to conceive of "writing from experience" as a creative transmutation of remembered experiences into a linguistic medium in the moment of composition, for US modernist writers this aesthetic also implied the need to go out in search of fresh material, or in Dewey's words, to "have an experience."

The discourse and practice of experience that had become constitutive of the US literary field by the early 1920s was particularly strong among those American writers who composed in situ in Latin America. Although US writers had long been writing in and about Latin America, as we have seen in the cases of Stephen Crane and Richard Harding Davis, the 1920s and 1930s witnessed an explosion of interest in the region, fundamentally altering US literary production. Katherine Anne Porter's writings on Mexico, which I examine in more depth in chapter 4, suggest how the antibookishness represented *within* interwar US fiction about Latin America often coincided with a failure to engage with the region's *actual* literary tradition. Recent scholarship in hemispheric studies has tended to see Porter as an exemplary model for what Rachel Adams describes as the "sustained cross-cultural pollination" between the United States and Mexico in the 1920s, a claim based on Porter's interests in the Mexican muralist movement, pre-Columbian art, and the revolutionary *corridos*.[36] And indeed, in addition to composing the catalogue for a major state-sponsored exhibit of Mexican art in Los Angeles in 1922, Porter wrote that she found in the Mexican "renascence" of the 1920s "a feeling for art consanguine with my own."[37] What this scholarship has largely missed, however, is the degree to which Porter privileged Mexico's visual culture and folk art over its written expression, essentially refusing to read its contemporary literature. In a notebook entry of 1931, she was categorical in this respect: "There is no Mexican literature. The subject is embarrassing to think about."[38] Incredibly, from 1920, when she arrived in Mexico during the last months of the Mexican Revolution, to 1942, when she was commissioned by Ángel Flores to introduce a collection of Latin American short stories, *Porter never mentioned a single twentieth-century Mexican poet, short story writer, or novelist* in her published writings.[39]

To a certain extent, Porter's elision of twentieth-century Mexican literature reflects the broad cultural imbalances of the period. As Helen Delpar remarks about the rising Mexican "vogue" in the United States in the 1920s and early 1930s, "Although American periodicals were dotted with verse reflecting the Mexican experiences of Americans, only a few examples of Mexican poetry were translated and published in the United States."[40] Even as interest in Mexico and its popular arts grew in the United States, and as the Good Neighbor Policy placed a renewed emphasis on restoring inter-American cultural relations, publishing ventures seeking to bring translated Latin American literature before a US audience continued to founder.

At a deeper level, however, Porter's failure to engage with the Mexican literature of the period demonstrates how the identity formation of the US writer as experiencer *contributed* to, as well as reflected, the hemispheric imbalance in literary exchange. An overview of Porter's reviews of literature about Mexico over the following ten years testifies less to her role as a cultural maven introducing Mexican literature to the United States than to her strategy of positioning herself as gatekeeper of the Mexican experience, an authority she never ceased to attribute to her prolonged in situ immersion in the country. In a review of Stuart Chase's *Mexico: A Study of Two Americas*, for example, Porter writes, "there is not one shred of evidence that Mr. Chase ever set foot in this country, except for some sketchy glances at the scenery. Everything else, he could, and did, I believe, read from books, and most of them very silly books recently published on Mexico."[41] Such critical comments exist on a continuum with Porter's short stories, which frequently contain object lessons that serve to warn other writers about taking source material from books rather than experience. "That Tree" (1934), based on the life of her erstwhile friend Carleton Beals, sketches the portrait of a bohemian American poet in postrevolutionary Mexico who belatedly comes to realize he "had notions about artists that [he] must have got out of books" (82). Ironically, Porter's Mexican writings outline an argument for why US writers shouldn't read books about Mexico. From this perspective, Porter should be seen less as a forerunner of later efforts to bolster hemispheric literary relations than as one of the many cultural actors who inhibited the translation and incorporation of contemporary Latin American literature into the US literary field. It is perhaps for this reason that the Chilean novelist José Donoso once quipped that Porter was "under the impression that she invented Latin America."[42]

There were, of course, interwar US modernist writers who challenged the evolving codes of the literature of experience. As I have suggested elsewhere, T. S. Eliot increasingly pitched his "classicist" argument for European cultural assimilation to a British reading public, providing an important example of how an antiexperiential literary program could lead writers to depart from the US literary field both literally and aesthetically.[43] Several authors writing "internally" for a US audience also formulated critiques of the literature of experience, taking aim at its antibookish model of absorption as well as its deployment in Latin America. One of the more radical alternatives to the aesthetics of experience was announced by William Carlos Williams in *In the American Grain* (1925). A revisionary account of US history that replaces the twice-told tale of English discovery and settlement with an international saga of the New World as a vast territory of contest and competition, *In the American Grain* ventriloquizes the voices of a range of Spanish, French, and English historical figures. Midway through his rewriting of these historical sources, Williams pauses to reflect in the first person on the hazards of the prevailing attitude toward literary production in the United States:

> It is an extraordinary phenomenon that Americans have lost the sense, being made up as we are, that what we are has its origin in what *the nation* in the past has been; that there is a source in America for everything we think or do.... That unless everything that is, proclaim a ground on which it stand, it has no worth; and that what has been morally, aesthetically worth while in America has rested upon peculiar and discoverable ground. But [Americans] think they get it out of the air or the rivers, or from the Grand Banks or wherever it may be, instead of by word of mouth or from records contained for us in books—and that, aesthetically, morally we are deformed unless we read.[44]

Williams's description of the general climate of US interwar writing is important for two reasons. First, it complicates the seemingly inevitable choice for American writers between a kind of weary Old World assimilation and a naïve New World naturalism by advocating for the "intelligent investigation" of the historical and literary traditions of the Americas. Second, and even more important for our purposes, it implies that an experiential approach to writing American literature—extracting poetry from the land as if it were a natural resource—had become the dominant tendency in the US literary field in the 1920s.

Vera Kutzinski has persuasively argued that *In the American Grain* performs an overcoming of the mythological view of the United States as a "virgin land" through its "hybridized" and "cross-pollinated" weave of English, French, Spanish, and indigenous traditions.[45] She also notes that Williams linked his mistrust of the essentializing tendencies of most "Americans" to his own "mixed ancestry" as the son of an English father and a Puerto Rican mother. In a 1939 letter to Horace Gregory explaining how he came to write *In the American Grain*, Williams recounted that "I decided as far as possible to go to whatever source material I could get at and start my own valuations there: to establish myself from my own reading, in my own way, in the locality which by birthright had become my own."[46] Williams's self-proclaimed "localism" coexisted in the early 1920s with this attempt to find a usable past through a program of intertextual New World writing. Moving back and forth between colonial and post-Independence Spanish- and English-language archives, Williams initiated a powerful project for capturing the *longue durée* of hemispheric history.

Nevertheless, Williams's failure to find a public for his rewriting of the historical archives of the Americas only further impressed upon him the difficulty of displacing the dominant assumptions of the US literature of experience. Years later, Williams admitted that the book's lack of critical and commercial success affected him deeply: "As a book, it fell flat. I made trip after trip to the publisher's offices until they got so sick of seeing me that all of them would give me a nod and walk by, talking together, and close themselves in before me, leaving me sitting there: a beautiful brushoff. . . . I had to see my high hopes of success go skittering out the window."[47] The failure almost literally sent him back to the drawing board. Not only did Williams scrap plans to compose a sequel to *In the American Grain*, he increasingly turned to a different mode of writing in the American grain, shifting from stylistic vamping of figures of the past to what Rick Moody calls the "warm plain speech" of his later poetry (x). It was only in the early 1960s, which saw the publication of the collected edition of Williams's similarly intertextual *Paterson*, that writers and critics would recuperate *In the American Grain*'s readerly aesthetic. That Williams's experiment was released the same year (1925) as Hemingway's *In Our Time*, and by the same publisher—Boni and Liveright, the modernist press par excellence—highlights the strikingly disparate fates of two works whose titles indicate analogous desires to be *in* our time and work *in* the grain. *Time* magazine, the very arbiter of the now, capped its glowing review of *In Our Time* by declaring that "Ernest Hemingway is somebody; a new, honest, un-'literary' transcriber of life."[48] In contrast, Williams was faced with the crushing realization that his ambitious demonstration of the cultural necessity of reading had attracted almost no readers.

Although Williams's more capacious historical mode of translation would find echoes in Archibald MacLeish's Pulitzer Prize–winning poem *Conquistador* (1933), as well as in Hart Crane's aborted attempt to write an epic poem about the Spanish conquest on the model of "The Bridge," these experiments in historical intertextuality were largely superseded in the US literary field by the linguistic practices of the literature of experience. Experiential writers such as Hemingway and Porter tended to eschew formal citations of foreign literary texts in favor of the incorporation of colloquial expressions, region-specific terminology, and popular and folk songs. From Jake

Barnes's "C'est entendu" in *The Sun Also Rises* to Thomas Hudson's "Todo el mundo me conoce" in *Islands in the Stream*, Hemingway deployed a communicative model that held out to its English-speaking audience the promise—one is tempted to say the illusion—that a basic grasp of a foreign vernacular was all one needed to successfully navigate the international scene. Although Michael Soto is right to suggest that Hemingway's "translingual didacticism" as "a form of instruction...testifies to Hemingway's success as a translator," this translational model was decidedly limited in scope.[49] Hemingway's protagonists might more accurately be characterized as interpreters rather than translators, since their language transactions and code switching always occur in the moment and in the flesh, never in the solitary encounter of a reader with a text.

This mode of US modernist translingualism, largely at odds with the citationalism of Eliot and Ezra Pound, became particularly entrenched in the case of the Spanish language. Looking across the spectrum of US literary production in the thirty years after Hemingway's *The Sun Also Rises*, one is astonished by how dominant this form of incorporating the everyday idioms of Spanish became. When Joe Williams travels to Buenos Aires with the US Merchant Marine in Dos Passos's *1919* (1932), the narrative voice mimics the most (stereo) typical of Argentine phrases: "Che...pobrecito...Che."[50] In Raymond Chandler's *The Long Goodbye* (1954), the hard-boiled detective Philip Marlowe peppers his comments to Spanish-speaking characters in Hollywood with *amigo, señora, señor*.[51] Though Langston Hughes translated the works of Nicolás Guillén and Gabriela Mistral and co-edited the groundbreaking hemispheric poetry anthology *The Poetry of the Negro, 1746–1949* in the late 1940s, his own literary works favored the use of idiomatic language over intertextuality. His first poem composed in situ in Cuba, "Havana Dreams," ends with the colloquial code switching typical of his Latin American–themed texts: "¿Quién sabe? Who really knows."[52] The US literature of experience thus entailed a vernacular model for appropriating foreign languages alongside its antibookish mode of identity formation.[53]

STILL EXPERIENCED (1945–1995)

From a certain perspective, the fifty-year period following the end of World War II witnessed the closest rapprochement of the US and Latin American literary fields since the surge of hemispheric solidarity in the early post-Independence period. At the most basic level, this proximity could be seen in the unparalleled opening of the US literary field to translations of Latin American fiction, a significant corrective to the cultural imbalances of the interwar period. During the twenty years following the seminal 1962 publication of *Labyrinths*, a collection of Borges's stories translated by Donald Yates and James Irby, the works of canonical Latin American authors such as Gabriel García Márquez, Mario Vargas Llosa, Carlos Fuentes, Julio Cortázar, Octavio Paz, and Isabel Allende were translated, reviewed, and (often) celebrated by important US writers and critics. Additionally, as much recent scholarship has shown, the state-sponsored funding and promotion of hemispheric journals, events, and translation initiatives played an important role in encouraging literary reciprocity during the period, albeit under the guise of Cold War cultural diplomacy. Finally, the rise of a reader-centered "postmodernism" in the literature of John Barth, Thomas Pynchon, Ishmael Reed, William Gass, and Kathy Acker–a phenomenon accompanied by the turn toward poststructuralism in the American academy–seemed to augur the end of antibookish experientialism as the dominant literary aesthetic in the United States. Nevertheless, the US literature of experience remained influential in a variety of ways.

In the first place, the degree to which most post-1945 US writers actually turned against the experiential aesthetics of the modernist generation has often been exaggerated in scholarship on the period, perhaps partly because of the confirmation bias of a generation of academic scholars determined to apply poststructural critiques of experience to the texts they were studying. Mark McGurl's *The Program Era* deftly tracks the way that the MFA slogan "write what you know" motivated a surprising number of literary movements in the postwar period, from the Native American Renaissance and the Black Arts Movement to the lower-middle-class neorealism of Raymond Carver. Furthermore, critics have often downplayed the continuities between the Beat writers of the 1950s and 1960s, whose redeployment of the discourse of experience I explore in chapter 5, and the canonical postmodern writers who came of age in their wake. Pynchon's only autobiographical writing to date, the 1985 preface to *Slow Learner*, registers the continued relevance of the aesthetics of experience in the United States to a writer often adduced as exemplifying its demise:

Somewhere I had come up with the notion that one's personal life had nothing to do with fiction, when the truth, as everyone knows, is nearly the direct opposite....I wasn't the only one writing then who felt some need to stretch, to step out. It may have gone back to the sense of academic enclosure we felt which had lent such appeal to the American picaresque life the Beat writers seemed to us to be leading....I had published a novel and thought I knew a thing or two, but for the first time I believe I was also beginning to shut up and listen to the American voices around me, even to shift my eyes away from printed sources and take a look at American nonverbal reality. I was out on the road at last getting to know the places Kerouac had written about.[54]

Such anxieties about the debilitating effects of "academic enclosure," and appeals to the commonsense solution of hitting the open road, surface even among the most hardened "postmodern" writers. Even during the postwar period when, as McGurl has demonstrated, many writers migrated into the universities, the ability to stake a claim to substantial extracurricular experience remained a significant technique of legitimation. The bumbling Jack Gladney of Don DeLillo's *White Noise* (1985), a leading scholar of Hitler studies who does not know a single word of German, was a stark reminder of the corrosive effect of allowing one's academic credentials to trump one's absorption of "nonverbal reality."

Second, Latin America itself remained a privileged site for writers from the United States to get their fill (or "fix," as the case might be) of nonliterary reality, even as Latin American literary works increasingly found a sympathetic audience in the United States. As Latin America became a key battleground of Cold War geopolitics, from the US-backed coup against Jacobo Árbenz in Guatemala in 1953 to the intensified campaign against Cuba in the post-Soviet "special period" of the 1990s, a number of important American literary works appeared that explored the contradictory "experience" of moving back and forth between the "First World" and the "Third World" conditions of Latin America. Many of these works were written by US Latina/o authors, whose emergence "into the mainstream" in the 1980s (as the editors of the *Norton Anthology of Latino Literature* put it) coincided with the publication of several highly regarded English-language works that centered on the lived experience of transnational travel and migration.[55] The works of Sandra Cisneros and Cristina García, two of the most canonical figures in post-1945

Mexican-American and Cuban-American fiction respectively, offer insights into the mechanisms through which Latina/o writers reformulated the US literature of experience to adapt to the hemispheric political and social climate of the late twentieth century.

Sandra Cisneros's The *House on Mango Street*, a foundational work of Chicana/o fiction, has often been read in the tradition of postwar US multiethnic literature. The novel's main plot line follows a young Mexican-American girl, Esperanza, who struggles to find her place in a Chicago neighborhood fraught with race, gender, and class tensions. Yet to track Cisneros's literary trajectory over the 1980s and 1990s is to see how her preoccupation with racial and national identity was gradually subsumed into a broader inquiry into the "experience" of moving between the United States and Latin America. Though the action of *A House on Mango Street* rarely strays from the urban American environment where Esperanza comes of age, a scene in the vignette "Laughter" highlights the significance of the protagonist's status as a Chicana with firsthand experience south of the border:

> One day we were passing a house that looked, in my mind, like houses I had seen in Mexico. I don't know why. There was nothing about the house that looked exactly like the houses I remembered. I'm not even sure why I thought it, but it seemed to feel right.
>
> Look at that house, I said, it looks like Mexico.
>
> Rachel and Lucy look at me like I'm crazy, but before they can let out a laugh, Nenny says: Yes, that's Mexico all right. That's what I was thinking exactly.[56]

In a social milieu in which Esperanza constantly plays the role of the outsider, this scene temporarily infuses her with an insider's authority: she has the advantage of a comparative perspective of both North and South. Faced with the potential embarrassment of explaining her intuitive juxtaposition of Chicago and Mexico to two girls from the United States, Esperanza finds legitimation in her sister's affirmation that such transnational observations—and therefore such transnational observers—are inherently "right." In her own authorial statements, Cisneros draws a similar conclusion about the different Chicana/o communities in the United States. She contrasts the Chicanas/os of Texas, who identify primarily as "Texan" and rarely "[venture] south of the border," with midwestern Chicanas/os like herself, who participate in a yearly summer "migration" and "cannot be taught through

Texas text books," because they "know better what Mexico is."[57] Here she implies that her Mexican-American identity is as much an acquired as an inherited characteristic, a process to be wrought from continuous exposure to both Mexico and the United States.

In Cisneros's next fictional work, the short-story collection *Woman Hollering Creek and Other Stories* (1991), this transnational perspective becomes even more pronounced, as nearly all the characters crisscross the border in a perpetual movement toward "*el otro lado.*" In the short story "Mericans," for example, a young Mexican-American girl visits the Basilica of Our Lady of Guadalupe on the outskirts of Mexico City. Standing at the entrance to the famous church, she finds herself midway between the "awful" Mexican grandmother who prays inside and the gringo sightseers outside who speak to her in broken Spanish because they don't realize that she too is from the United States.[58] The "Mericans" of the title alludes not only to the narrator's cultural and linguistic hybridity–Mexican and American, English and Spanish speaking, though neither fully one nor the other–but also the bifocal perspective she gains at the threshold of the local "interior" and the touristy "exterior." Like Esperanza, the characters in *Woman Hollering Creek* encounter misunderstanding and discrimination in their interactions with the gringo and Mexican worlds; nevertheless, this liminality and marginalization often gets recoded in the narrative as an improvement in artistic depth. Absorption of the cultural, linguistic, and ethnic violence of the US-Mexico border becomes the painful yet necessary compositional key of the entire sequence.

Whereas Cisneros's writings of the 1980s and 1990s repeatedly return to the crossing of the US-Mexico border as a vital experiential act, Cristina García's *Dreaming in Cuban* (1991) focuses on an even more treacherous transnational passage: the journey between the United States and Cuba. In the wake of the 1959 Cuban Revolution and the US government's prohibition on travel to the island after severing ties with the Castro regime in 1961, Cuba proved to be one of the most difficult—and therefore enticing—countries for US writers to visit in the last decades of the twentieth century. Although the ideological effort to demonize the Cuban regime could be (and was) taken up by US state apparatuses and the vehemently anti-Castro political right, the specifically *literary* task of conceptualizing Cuba was often pursued by those who could rely on their "personal experience" of the transformation of Cuban society. Although Cristina García moved from Cuba to the United States at the age of four, her family's status permitted her to visit the island several times in the 1980s, thus making her one of the few writers with US citizenship to spend significant time in Cuba after the rupturing of diplomatic ties. Her firsthand experience of the island is crucial both to her construction of the novel and to our reading of it.

Dreaming in Cuban, a National Book Award finalist in 1992, follows the members of a Cuban household that splits up in the aftermath of the Revolution, with half the family staying on the island and half moving to the United States—some to Miami, some to New York. The novel describes Cuba primarily through its sights and sounds: the island's visual, sensory, and musical ecologies take precedence over its literary traditions. The scenes in the novel that take place in Cuba are often presented as an unfiltered view of events in the country from the beginning of the Revolution to the mass exodus of the 1980 Mariel boatlift. The novel contains many of the signature gestures of US postmodernism: pop-culture references to the songs of Cuban musicians such as Celia Cruz and Beny Moré, high-literary allusions to Wallace Stevens, Molière, Gustave Flaubert, and Hemingway, as well as textual citations (in Spanish) of lines from the Andalusian poet Féderico García Lorca, the favorite poet of Abuela Cecilia. At the same time, the novel *does not refer to a single Cuban (or even Latin American) literary author*. The text elides a range of Cuban literary works that shaped the public sphere in Cuba in the twentieth century, from the "official" poetry of José Martí and Nicolás Guillén to the experimental novels of Alejo Carpentier and José Lezama Lima.

Much of the criticism on *Dreaming in Cuban* has focused on how its American- and Cuban-based characters negotiate the rupture of family ties and the vagaries of exilic life in the aftermath of the Revolution. And indeed, as the novel progresses, the New York—raised protagonist Pilar becomes a symbol of the desire to reconnect with her Cuban ancestry. A passage from an interview with García from the 1990s, however, suggests the degree to which she staked her own literary authority on her firsthand knowledge of Cuba at a time when few foreigners were allowed into the country, as well as how she recast her experiential journey as a privileged means of access to the "other side" of the gulf.

As a child I used to listen to accounts of family history from my mother. But then, when I first went back to Cuba, in 1984, I developed a strong relationship with my grandmother and realized how distorted those accounts from my mother were, how nostalgia and anger had clouded her version of events. My mother's family is still in Cuba and lives in Guanabo and in Havana. Before 1984 I did not have any contact with my family in Cuba.[59]

The description of García's "first contact" with Cuba—which allows her a corrective to the "distorted" views of her upbringing in the United States—is coded into the deep structure of the novel itself. The narrative tracks Pilar's escape from her rabidly anti-Castro mother, Lourdes, in New York to her extended family in Florida, where she embarks on a clandestine trip to Cuba to reconnect with Abuela Cecilia and her cousin Ivanito. Pilar's eyewitness testimony of the opposing actualities of the United States and post-Revolution Cuba forms the structural core of the novel, a kind of experiential equivalent to the "balanced viewpoint" that mediates between Cecilia's paranoid fears of another US invasion and Lourdes's hyperbolically anti-Communist rhetoric. The waters of the gulf figure in *Dreaming in Cuban* as the physical manifestation of the ideological split between the US and the Castro regime during the Cold War; Pilar's decision to cross the gulf offers a cultural solution to a political problem. By visiting Cuba and seeing the "other side," she takes the first step toward integrating the seemingly irreconcilable aspirations of her transnational family. Pilar may begin by dreaming of Cuba, but her most important act in the novel is to travel to the island to experience it.

The late twentieth-century writings of Cisneros and García demonstrate perhaps the most fundamental aspect of the US literature of experience: its sheer elasticity and longevity as a cultural discourse. Despite the fact that Cisneros and García incorporated vastly different political, social, and cultural themes about hemispheric migration in the Americas in the 1980s and 1990s—their Mexican-American and Cuban-American "experiences" are by no means the same—they share a common conviction that firsthand authorial experience must provide the source material and foundation for their literary work. Of course, there were other models for conceptualizing Latina/o literary production in the United States in the late twentieth century, and in the epilogue I discuss how writers of the US-Mexico borderlands such as Rolando Hinojosa and Gloria Anzaldúa offered a competing model of Latina/o literature as a hybrid cultural weave that destabilized dominant discourses in both the United States and Latin

America. But while Hinojosa's and Anzaldúa's texts circulated largely among academic, activist, and regional publishers in the 1980s and 1990s, the texts of Cisneros and García distinguished themselves by their broader visibility (and legibility) in the US literary field.

The Latin American Literature of the Reader

In an important sense, the Latin American literature of the reader can be seen as no less durable and resilient than the US literature of experience. In the wake of Ángel Rama's influential study of the "lettered city," scholars have frequently commented on the outsized role of the practices of reading and writing in the formation of Latin American culture from the colonial period forward.[60] I will suggest here, however, that it was during the *vanguardia* period of the 1920s and 1930s that the figure of the writer-as-reader rose to dominance in the Latin American literary field. I argue that key works by José Vasconcelos and Jorge Luis Borges rearticulated the turn-of-the-century *arielista* antinomy between Latin American spirituality and American materialism as an opposition between the Latin American literature of the reader and the US literature of experience. Tracing this trajectory requires us to revisit a series of cultural discourses about the United States and its literature that developed in the Spanish-speaking Americas in the nineteenth and twentieth centuries. The emergence of the Latin American literature of the reader cannot be divorced from the modes by which writers and thinkers in the Spanish-speaking Americas have conceptualized hemispheric literary, cultural, political, and even psychological difference.

FROM LATINITY TO *ARIELISMO* (1848–1918)

The US invasion of Mexico in 1847 and the subsequent Treaty of Guadalupe Hidalgo (1848), which formalized Mexico's cession of nearly half its territory to the United States, was the first major jolt to the hemispheric cultural aspirations harbored by many in the Spanish-speaking Americas during the early post-Independence period. As numerous studies have shown, the idea of an "América Latina" was generated by a group of French and Spanish American writers and politicians in mid-nineteenth-century Paris who championed the shared "Latin" roots of Mediterranean Europe and the

Romance language-speaking countries of the Americas as a means of opposing what they perceived as the growing threat of US hegemony in the "New World." [61] The Colombian author and diplomat José María Torres Caicedo's 1856 poem "Las dos Américas" [The Two Americas], which advocated an "alliance" among the Spanish American countries based on their common "language," "religion," and "traditions," imagined a deeply rooted cultural and historical split between "Anglo" and "Latin" America that political independence had accentuated rather than erased. Over the next thirty years, the term "Latin America" increasingly gained currency throughout the Spanish-speaking Americas. Yet the call for a millenarian hemispheric battle between North and South found its greatest adherents among conservative elements, and the most direct political manifestation of this ideal pan-Latinist alliance was the French intervention in Mexico from 1863 to 1867, when the Hapsburg prince Maximilian was installed by Napoleon III's French imperial army alongside internal forces of the Mexican Conservative Party. Within the liberal republican currents that increasingly dominated public discourse in Latin America during the second half of the nineteenth century, from the Argentine Generation of 1837 to the *liberales* of Mexico's La Reforma, the United States continued to be viewed as a force of progress.

As Doris Sommer has shown, in the process of imagining their own national romances, nineteenth-century Latin American novelists frequently turned to the US novel to evaluate existing "formula[s] for writing about America."[62] Hence the midcentury rise of what Sommer dubs "Coopermania," in which prominent writers such as Domingo Sarmiento speculated as to whether James Fenimore Cooper's *The Last of the Mohicans* (1827) could provide them with an adequate "model for New World writing" (55). For a great number of nineteenth-century Latin American writers, this cross-cultural conversation implied shared political as well as aesthetic ideals. The protagonist of José Mármol's *Amalia* (1854), the most famous of Argentina's foundational fictions, lauds the United States as the "freest and most democratic nation of the nineteenth century" before placing his friend under the protection of the US Embassy during a particularly violent period of the Argentine civil war.[63] When Mexican president Benito Juárez invited William Cullen Bryant to a commemorative event in Mexico City in 1872, five years after the defeat of Maximilian (and the Mexican Conservative Party itself) by Liberal forces allied with the US military, it was only the most tangible sign of a renewed political and cultural alignment with the United States during the period. As James Sanders has argued, *liberales* of the 1860s and 1870s such as Juárez frequently positioned Spanish America at the vanguard of hemispheric democratic republicanism, a partner more than a follower of the United States in the aim of defending New World liberties against Old World tyranny.[64]

As the nineteenth century came to a close, these two visions of the relationship between the United States and Spanish-speaking America—the hemispheric liberal republican emphasis on shared cultural values and the pan-Latinist insistence on deep-seated and irreconcilable cultural traditions—alternated as the dominant modes for representing the Americas, at times even within different works by the same writer. This is certainly the case with José Martí, perhaps the most important late nineteenth-century Latin American chronicler of the United States. Born in Havana in 1853 and exiled by the Spanish authorities at the age of sixteen for his proindependence writings, Martí arrived in New York in 1880 and remained in the city until his return to Cuba in 1895, where he died in the very first battle of the Cuban War of Independence. Scholars of transamerican studies, citing his iconic essay "Nuesta América" ["Our America," 1891], have often seen Martí as a precursor of the ideological tensions between the United States and Latin America in the twentieth century. Several recent studies, however, have indicated the degree to which Martí's work is indebted to earlier republican and liberal discourses that looked far more favorably on the United States.[65]

Martí's initial attraction to the political ideals of the United States helps explain his admiration for the nineteenth-century US literature of experience. His influential essays on Whitman and Emerson appropriate the antiliterary and naturalist tropes of their poetry and prose: he describes Whitman as a "natural man" who has written a "natural book" and claims that for Emerson "a child on the ranch is closer to universal truth than an antiquarian."[66] And his well-known *Versos sencillos* (1891) open with an evocation of the literature of experience's central aspiration toward full geographic coverage: "I come from all places, / and toward all places I go" [yo vengo de todas partes, / y hacia todas partes voy]. Even as Martí's view of the US role in Latin American affairs darkened after the first Pan-American Conference in New York in 1888, where he reported on the strongarm tactics of US secretary of state James Blaine, his writing continued to reflect the impact of North American cultural discourse. Though "Our

America" warns of the growing danger posed by the "colossus of the North," the essay mobilizes the very language Martí earlier attributed to Whitman, asserting that "the imported book has been defeated in América by the natural man. Natural men have defeated the artificially lettered men [letrados artificiales]."[67] As this passage makes clear, Martí continued to borrow the rhetoric of the US literature of experience even as his view of the United States itself grew increasingly pessimistic.

The Spanish-Cuban-American War from 1895 to 1898 altered Latin American culture at the most fundamental level. In material terms, the war caused a wave of displacement among writers of the Hispanic Caribbean, exacerbating the condition of exile that had been a staple of Latin American life since the early nineteenth century. Martí's death on the battlefield in 1895 is only the most obvious reminder that during this period in Latin American history, military violence, forced emigrations, and shifting political borders were the norm. It is true that the rise of journalism as a profession offered a new space for Latin American writers in the late nineteenth and early twentieth centuries, just as it did for authors in the United States. Yet the political and economic precariousness of these Latin American *modernistas* differentiated the conditions of their literary production from the expansionist enterprise of Crane and Davis writing in the Caribbean.[68] As Arcadio Díaz Quiñones observes, the writers and critics who were most influential in constructing the pan-Hispano-American literary canon of the early twentieth century conceived of a literary *patria grande* through a series of geographic displacements.[69] Such precariousness of place and livelihood was an inherent condition of literary production in the late nineteenth-century Latin American cultural field.

The material difficulties of many *modernista* and post-*modernista* writers and intellectuals only serve to highlight the broader shift in the Latin American literary imaginary after 1898. Indeed, scholarship on *modernismo* typically divides the movement into two basic phases: a cosmopolitan period governed by the attempt to enrich Hispanophone literature through the incorporation of diverse foreign poetic traditions (primarily French, though also North American), and a post-1898 period in which the traumas of the US imperial adventures in the Caribbean and Central America ignited a broad turn toward Hispanic poetic and political identity. Though the war itself took place on the islands that remained under Spanish colonial rule, the imposition of US political and economic imperialism in the years following the war—Puerto Rico became a territory in 1898, and Cuba's national sovereignty was severely limited by the Roosevelt-backed Platt Amendment of 1903—sent a shockwave throughout Latin America from the actual theater of conflict in the Caribbean all the way down to the Southern Cone.

The most influential Latin American work to emerge in the aftermath of the war of 1898 was the Uruguayan essayist José Enrique Rodó's *Ariel* (1900). Taking a cue from the French philosopher Ernest Renan's reading of Shakespeare's *The Tempest*, Rodó allegorized the globe as a cultural terrain riven by the opposition between Ariel and Caliban, the spiritual and the physical. Suggesting that the Greco-Roman tradition could provide a bulwark against the materialist instincts fomented in the United States, Rodó appealed to the common value system of European and American countries that shared a "Latin" cultural heritage and an idealist vision of the world.[70] The novelty of Rodó's *Ariel* was to be found neither in its distinctions between Anglo and Latin characteristics, which Torres Caicedo had already delineated in the mid-nineteenth century, nor in any overt political platform it put forward. Its impact stemmed, rather, from its transformation of the trauma of US imperial expansion in Latin America into a simple and eminently appropriable cultural allegory. Providing a language of spiritual kinship that compensated for the perceived fragmentation of Bolivarian territorial aspirations, *Ariel* quickly became a touchstone text for a range of *modernista* and post-*modernista* writers. As Rafael Rojas has written, in the first decades of the twentieth century, appropriations of Rodó's discourse spanned "from liberals to socialists, from the right to the center to the left."[71] Though Rodó himself had stopped short of fully identifying the United States with Caliban and Latin America with Ariel, the subsequent *"arielista"* movement reified these figures into totalizing symbols of a hemispheric geopolitical contest.[72]

Rodó's *arielista* language infuses the most widely read Latin American protest poem of the early twentieth century, Rubén Darío's "A Roosevelt" ["To Roosevelt," 1904], composed as a response to the United States's political maneuvers to secure territory for the construction of the Panama Canal. Darío's poem contests the big-stick-carrying Teddy Roosevelt and his "men with Saxon eyes and barbarous soul" through the voice of a "nuestra América" that melds Hispanic heritage with an indigenous cultural legacy. Darío imagined this tradition as an archive that Latin America could already claim: "But our

América…had poets from the old days of Netzahualcoyotl." Latin America not only has "indigenous blood"; it also possesses the hybridized cultural inheritance of the Aztecs, the Acohluas, Christopher Columbus, and the lost city of Atlantis, "whose name echoes down to us from Plato."[73] Although Rodó and Darío drew from the oppositional tone of Martí's "Our America," they eschewed Martí's rhetoric of the "natural man" in favor of a discourse of Latin cultural inheritance.[74] Here were the first inklings of what would become the twentieth-century Latin American literature of the reader.

The turn to the discourse of Hispanism in Latin America in the early decades after the war of 1898 entailed more than a deepening rift in the literary imagination of the region's most prominent writers. As Darío's poem suggests, it also occasioned a desperate search into the cultural archive for aesthetic models to represent and assert a sense of difference from the United States. This search increasingly revolved around a "return to Spain" and its "classics" as well as contemporary literary traditions. If "To Roosevelt" reunited Spain and its former colonies through the power of metaphor—the Latin American republics are described as "a thousand cubs unleashed by the Spanish Lion"—the actual cooperation between *modernista* writers and the so-called Spanish *generación del '98* was crucial to the development of the Latin American literary field in the first decades of the twentieth century. In *Algunas consideraciones sobre literatura hispano-americana* [Some Considerations about Hispano-American Literature, 1906], Unamuno criticized Spanish attempts to "establish here the metropolis of culture" and insisted that "since Castilian Spanish has spread to lands so wide and separate from one another, it must become the language of all of them, the Spanish or Hispanic tongue."[75] Unamuno cites Darío's influence on contemporary Spanish poetry as evidence of a fertile transatlantic pollination from the Americas to the Iberian Peninsula, a cultural strategy later enshrined in Max Henríquez Ureña's famous description of Darío's poetry as the "return of the [Spanish colonial] galleons" back to their origins.[76]

The spiritualist–materialist distinction that developed in the post-1898 Latin American field had a powerful effect on the avant-garde authors of the 1920s and 1930s who consolidated the position of the Latin American writer-as-reader, as I suggest in the next section. But the *arielista* discourse remained influential in its own right throughout the twentieth century, functioning as what Raymond Williams called a "residual" cultural element, which "has been effectively formed

in the past, but [which] is still active in the cultural process, not only
and often not at all as an element of the past, but as an effective element of the present."[77] Many of the Latin American philosophers and
intellectuals of the mid-twentieth century who attempted to supersede
the *arielist* binary between Latin American spirituality and North
American materialism, such as the Cuban-born Jorge Mañach and the
Mexican Leopoldo Zea, nevertheless tended to assume its starting
point of basic difference. Arguing that the Caribbean should be viewed
as more of a cultural "border" than a battleground between the United
States and Latin America, Mañach's *La teoría de la frontera* [translated
as *Frontiers in the Americas: A Global Perspective*, 1961] nevertheless
insists that it "is obvious that Americans of the North and of the
South—let us speak of them thus for the sake of simplicity—have very
different ways of feeling, of thinking, and of acting."[78] Zea begins "La
cultura de las dos Américas" ["The Culture of the Two Americas,"
1971] with the similar affirmation that "the different cultures of
Anglo-Saxon America and Ibero-America have given rise to several
no less diverse attitudes with regard to the world, nature, and other
beings."[79] Like Mañach, Zea repudiates the distinction between the
"spiritual" Latin America and the "material" as a historical "error."
Yet despite his attempt to prove that the "Ibero-American" is "becoming assimilated with great facility by that world of Anglo-Saxon
culture that used to seem alien to him," Zea ultimately affirms the
nontransferable characteristics of cultural identity: "Today's Ibero-
American, like his ancestors...lives each day as an expression of his
specific personality, both in poverty as in wealth" (67). Zea's "The
Culture of the Two Americas" and Mañach's *Frontiers in the Americas*
exemplify the persistence of the *arielista* binary in the Latin American
cultural field even as both authors advocated for rapprochement
across the North-South divide. As late as the 1980s, the influential
Mexican novelist Carlos Fuentes would insist that "the two cultures
are so different, so dissimilar in their origins, so strange to each other
and therefore so challenging to the comprehension of the other
side....We are different, we are other: North Americans (by which
I mean the citizens of the United States) and Latin Americans."[80]

THE "DEWEY DANGER" (1918–1960)

It was within the context of such widespread debates about the incompatibility of "Anglo" and "Latin" culture that a renewed emphasis

on the practice of reading arose. Indeed, it is far from coincidental that the discourse of writing-as-reading solidified in the Latin American field as literary authors throughout the region grappled with the emerging cultural as well as political hegemony of the United States—a hegemony symbolized in the consecration of US writers in international letters (with five Nobel Prize winners from 1930 to 1952) and the rise of Hollywood film as a global phenomenon. As Sylvia Molloy has observed, the Spanish American practice of "highlight[ing]...the act of reading" can be traced back to the earliest post-Independence works of the nineteenth century.[81] Yet while Molloy's rubric works well for Spanish American writers in the nineteenth and early twentieth centuries, for whom the "desire to show oneself competent, a reader of the canon" responded primarily to what Molloy dubs the "wholesale importation" of European culture and literature (22), her study does not address the geocultural transformation of the second quarter of the twentieth century, during which Latin American writers increasingly set their sights on US literature. The works of writers as diverse as Jorge Luis Borges, José Vasconcelos, Gabriela Mistral, Nicolás Guillén, José Carlos Mariátegui, Roberto Arlt, and Alfonso Reyes furnish evidence of this change. Even Victoria Ocampo, the model of the Francophile author in Molloy's study, would later recall that in the wake of Waldo Frank's visit to Argentina in 1929 (discussed in the next chapter), "our group of writers who had no previous interest in the United States, from the perspective of the arts, began to take contemporary North American literature seriously."[82]

The Latin American reading of US literature was not devoid of recognition, at times explicit and at times implicit, of the new geocultural axis that was reconfiguring the hemisphere. The works of Vasconcelos and Borges, two of the most influential writers of the 1920s and 1930s, reveal the range of strategies that Latin American writers employed to adapt to the growing influence of North American culture and to identify the US literature of experience as its dominant mode. Where Vasconcelos uses a theory of reading to formulate a political and ideological opposition to identity formation through experience, Borges mobilizes an image of the highly intellectualized reader to enact a literary and philosophical critique of an experiential aesthetics. The pairing of these two figures enables me to demonstrate how the overt political tones of Vasconcelos's critique of a Deweyan philosophy of experience, launched from a Hispanist—Latin

Americanist position, were transformed in Borges into a literary creed. Indeed, although the effervescent Latin American *vanguardia* period witnessed numerous forms of artistic experimentation and cultural reorientation, perhaps the most important shift to occur in the Latin American literary field during the 1920s and 1930s was a turn from the *arielista* paradigm of criticizing or rejecting US materialist culture to the reader-oriented paradigm of voraciously consuming and rewriting it. Like nearly all of the Latin American writers who came of age in a post-*modernista* climate still saturated with Rodó's opposition between Caliban and Ariel, Borges reflected the opposition between Latin American spirituality and US materialism in his early writing. Yet part of what gave Borges such staying power among writers and critics as a theorist and practitioner of literature was his simultaneous ability to engage the US literature of experience and offer an alternative aesthetics within the literary realm.

That said, it was the Mexican-born Vasconcelos who was responsible for the most politically motivated engagement with the rise of the aesthetics of experience in US culture. A member of the anti-positivist and anti-Porfirian civil association El Ateneo de la Juventud in the final years of the Díaz government, Vasconcelos would take institutional roles in the Madero and Carranza regimes during the Mexican Revolution. In the early postrevolutionary period, he emerged as the most powerful cultural agent in the Obregón government, serving first as rector of the Universidad Nacional de México in 1920 and later as the head of the newly created Secretaría de Educación Pública. A voracious reader of American literature, he was also familiar with the primary texts of American pragmatism, particularly Dewey's pedagogical writings. In his works of the 1920s and 1930s, he used this knowledge to outline what he described as an existential cultural contest between the United States and Latin America. Vasconcelos laid the foundation for his geocultural politics in *La raza cósmica* [*The Cosmic Race*, 1925], in which he countered the claims of Spencerian racial hierarchies by arguing that hybrid, *mestizo* cultures like the Latin American ultimately triumph over "purer" national compositions such as the North American, with its exclusionary prohibitions on racial interbreeding. Yet it was in his lesser-known pedagogical work *De Robinson a Odiseo: Pedagogía estructurativa* [From Robinson to Odysseus: Structuring Pedagogy, 1935] that this geocultural divide takes the form of an opposition between experiential and readerly cultural formations.

In *De Robinson a Odiseo*, Vasconcelos draws on Rodó's vision of hemispheric relations to reimagine the distinction between a spiritual Latin America and a materialist United States as an opposition between a North American Crusoe, representing a society founded on and motivated by experience and action, and a Spanish American Odysseus, representing a culture founded on adventurous reading and cultural acquisition. In a chapter called "El peligro Dewey" [The Dewey Danger], Vasconcelos criticizes Dewey's experiential pedagogy of "learning by doing," insisting that "[t]he final goal of education is less *to discover* than *to know*."[83] For Vasconcelos, who as the Mexican secretary of education from 1921 to 1924 had experimented with pragmatist pedagogy in the formation of the so-called *escuelas activas*, Dewey's philosophy had degenerated into an uncritical celebration of "useless experiences and arbitrary efforts" (36). Vasconcelos maintains that a return from experiential learning to knowledge acquisition through the reading process is the most pressing concern of child education. In typically biting fashion, Vasconcelos inverts the pragmatist model of "testing" tradition with experience by advocating a test of pragmatism itself: "After so many experiments, why not try putting the child who has learned to read into contact with the works of Plato, Homer, Aeschylus, Dante, Calderón [de la Barca], and Shakespeare?" (24).[84]

Vasconcelos's defense of reading often revolves around a standard classicist or liberal humanist argument about literature as a repository of universal values. Yet his legacy is defined largely by his translation of this argument into a structural opposition between Anglo-American and Latin American culture. Taking Rodó's abstract geographical antithesis as his starting point, Vasconcelos in *De Robinson a Odiseo* reaches an almost Gramscian awareness of the interpenetration of cultural and economic models, as he cautions against the further implementation of Deweyan pragmatism in Latin America:

> Let us suppose that the Deweyan school really took hold in our environment.... [T]he ethic of these schools, *to adapt the student to the environment in which he will live*, would translate for us [in Latin America] into an effort to form a population submissive to the will of the large foreign companies that exploit our land. (26)
>
> [Supongamos que la escuela Dewey llegara a plasmar de verdad en nuestro medio.... [L]a ética de estas escuelas, *adaptar el alumno al medio en que va a vivir*, se traduciría entre nosotros en el sentido de

formar una población sumisa a las conveniencias de las grandes empresas extranjeras que explotan nuestro suelo.][85]

Vasconcelos's crucial gesture was to update Rodó's dichotomy between American materialism and Latin American spirituality by interposing reading and "universal" knowledge as a critical anti-imperialist practice. Even though Vasconcelos eventually turned toward authoritarian answers to the problem of US interventionism, his work of the 1920s and early 1930s functioned as an index of the discursive strategies employed by interwar Latin American intellectuals. As Ignacio Sánchez Prado notes, while Vasconcelos's *mestizaje* discourse has rightly been criticized over the past forty years for its marginalization of indigenous and African cultural traditions, its "attempt to unify politics and aesthetics in a continental concept of the spirit" became the dominant paradigm in many Latin American countries of the interwar period.[86]

On the surface, Borges's articulation of the position of writer-as-reader has little to do with what José Joaquín Blanco describes as Vasconcelos's intellectual and pedagogical mission "to incorporate the book into the vital spaces of society."[87] Yet if Borges's literary trajectory diverged significantly from that of Vasconcelos in the 1930s and 1940s, both writers departed from a common cultural source. Entrenched national literary histories have tended to downplay the Hispanist and pan-Latinist currents in the Argentina of the 1920s and 1930s, as well as the presence in Buenos Aires of committed Latin Americanists such as Alfonso Reyes, Pedro Henríquez Ureña, and Vasconcelos. In fact, at the end of *La raza cósmica*, Vasconcelos remarked that Buenos Aires was the "the center of the Latin continent [del continente latino], the capital of the race."[88] To my knowledge, it has never been observed that upon his return to Argentina from Spain in the early 1920s, Borges's views on the United States largely fell in line with the Hispanist thought of Vasconcelos and Rodó. In his 1921 essay "Buenos Aires," Borges echoes Rodó's disparagement of Latin American *nordomanía* while simultaneously voicing a similar ambivalence toward the principles of American-style democracy: "In the tunnels of our souls leaps a Spanish spirit, but they want to turn us into Yankees, false Yankees, and deceive us with the lukewarm water of democracy and the vote."[89] Although Borges's own public position vis-à-vis the United States would evolve over the next twenty years, *arielismo* remained a key element in his literary formation. Where Vasconcelos and Borges differed was not in their shared belief that hemispheric cultural relations entailed a basic division between expansive US materialism and Latin spirituality, but in the strikingly divergent positions for the writer-as-reader that *arielismo* inspired them to formulate.

In the next chapter, I detail how Borges's aesthetics of reading responded to Waldo Frank's particular variation of the US literature of experience. For now, I will limit myself to one example of the geopolitical thrust of Borges's readerly articulations. Borges's most pronounced defense of the position of the writer-as-reader, as I have suggested, occurs in the 1935 preface to his first work of prose fiction, *A Universal History of Infamy*, where he speaks of reading as a more "intellectual," "civil," and "resigned" activity than that of writing.[90] Beatriz Sarlo's *Borges: A Writer on the Edge* (1993) continues to offer the best overall approach to the *Universal History*, which she describes as the product of secondhand materials reworked "with the freedom of a marginal writer who knows he is writing in the margins."[91] In doing so, however, Sarlo locates Borges on the periphery of European tradition, glossing over the fact that four of his book's original eight stories take place in the United States, the most famous of which, "The Cruel Redeemer Lazarus Morell," is a rewriting of an episode from Mark Twain's *Life on the Mississippi* (1883). As Borges's first attempt to move beyond an analysis of North American poets to a depiction of US society itself, the story suggests an author well attuned to the geopolitical tropes characteristic of the US literature of experience. For instance, where Twain explains the formation of the Mississippi River Delta off the Gulf Coast by stating that "the river annually empties four hundred and six million tons of mud into the Gulf of Mexico," Borges translates and improvises: "más de cuatrocientos millones de toneladas de fango *insultan* anualmente el Golfo de Méjico" ["more than four hundred million tons of mud annually *insult* the Gulf of Mexico," my emphasis] (*OC*, 1.312). As Borges elaborates, rendering Twain's text even more freely, the River Delta not only grows southward but "extends the borders and peace of its fetid empire" (*OC*, 1.312). Twain's simple landscape description acquires a new motivation in Borges's version. It is hard not to see in Borges's "irreverent" translation a clue that he was aware of how the rhetoric of expansion had worked its way into the most seemingly apolitical literary genres, including the US literature of experience.[92]

READING AND UNREADING THE LETTERED
TRADITION (1960–1990)

The generation of Latin American novelists associated with the so-called boom of the 1960s and 1970s was largely responsible for canonizing the aesthetics of reading on a continental scale. This process operated at two related levels. At the level of authorial discourse, the period's four *"grandes"*—Gabriel García Márquez, Mario Vargas Llosa, Carlos Fuentes, and Julio Cortázar—began to position Borges as their own literary precursor and to characterize his work as the very condition of possibility for what Fuentes influentially dubbed the "new Hispano-American novel."[93] At the level of the text, the major boom novels deployed the figures of the archivist, the scribe, and the librarian to an unprecedented degree—from the Borges-like Melquíades in García Márquez's *Cien años de soledad* (*One Hundred Years of Solitude*, 1967) to the meta-author Morelli in Cortázar's *Rayuela* [*Hopscotch*, 1963] and the sixteenth-century bibliophile Valerio Camillo in Fuentes's *Terra Nostra* (1975).

Yet even as Borges and his notion of the "good reader" began to achieve international recognition in the 1950s and 1960s, various cultural actors began to challenge the position of the *lector* and the historical legacy of the Latin American *letrado*. One major challenge came from the emerging decolonial critiques of the new Cuban cultural apparatus, most notably the "Calibanism" of the poet and essayist Roberto Fernández Retamar. In his influential essay "Caliban: Notes toward a Discussion of Culture in Our America" (1971), Fernández Retamar argued that Rodó had correctly identified the "greatest enemy" of Latin American culture (the United States), but had mistakenly cast Ariel as representative of Latin America. For Fernández Retamar, Caliban, the "rude and unconquerable master of the island," was the more appropriate symbol of Latin American identity.[94] Published at a time when several of the boom writers (most significantly, Vargas Llosa and Fuentes) were in the process of withdrawing their support for the Cuban government, the essay's principal target was the historical role that the writer and intellectual had played in Latin America. In Fernández Retamar's account, Borges's aesthetics of reading epitomizes a subservient attitude toward the Western canon that is particularly pernicious for its geopolitical implications: "Borges is a typical colonial writer, the representative among us of a now powerless class for whom the act of writing—and he is well aware of this, for he is a man of diabolical intelligence—is more like the act of reading" (47). Freely borrowing from anticolonial Francophone writers such as Aimé Césaire and Frantz Fanon and anticipating in many ways later postcolonial theories of the 1980s and 1990s, Fernández Retamar reminds his readers that in Shakespeare's *The Tempest*, Caliban and Ariel do not represent opposing factions (as they do in Rodó) but rather two subalterns in thrall to the same oppressive lord, Prospero. Adapting the Gramscian distinction between the "traditional" and the "organic" intellectual to the Latin American cultural terrain, Fernández Retamar situates Borges not as the authentic new voice of Spanish American literature but as the weak and wizened descendant of the ethereal Ariel. Retamar's revised Shakespearean paradigm thus presents the Latin American *arielista*-turned-Borgesian writer with a stark decision: either to serve the Prospero of foreign interests or to "all[y] himself with Caliban in his struggle for true freedom" (62).

A second, related challenge to the authority of the writer-as-reader came through the emergence of a series of novelists from groups that had been historically marginalized from a Latin American field dominated, to an even greater degree than in the United States, by white heterosexual men. Although women poets such as Delmira Agustini and Juana de Ibarbourou participated in the *modernista* movement, and several women writers played crucial roles in the Latin American *vanguardia*—including Victoria and Silvina Ocampo, Julia de Burgos, and Gabriela Mistral—the virtual exclusion of women from the public sphere (and from the literary profession) was one of their constant themes. From the 1960s to the 1980s, however, several Latin American women novelists began to gain substantial readerships: Rosario Castellanos, Elena Poniatowska, Luisa Valenzuela, and Cristina Peri Rossi in the 1960s; Isabel Allende, Gioconda Belli, Carmen Boullosa, Diamela Eltit, and Laura Esquivel in the 1980s. Additionally, the rise of a queer aesthetic in works by José Donoso, Reinaldo Arenas, Nestor Perlongher, and Pedro Lemebel, among others, presented a form of authorship that questioned the masculine subjectivity of the canonical boom writers. Although not all of these works directly attacked the writer-as-reader, they all represented alternatives to the gendered legacy of the *letrado*.

The turn toward Calibanism and the increasing visibility of historically marginalized writers in the Latin American literary field coincided with the rise of the literary genre that most radically altered the cultural landscape of Latin America in the last quarter of the twentieth century: the *testimonio*. The earliest significant example of the genre was *Biografía de un cimarrón* [*Biography of a Runaway Slave*, 1966], the story of Esteban Montejo, a 103-year-old man who had escaped from slavery in the final decades of Spanish colonial rule in Cuba, as told to writer and ethnographer Miguel Barnet. In its most widely disseminated form, the *testimonio* of the 1970s and 1980s was a first-person life history related orally to a professional writer who subsequently transcribed, edited, and published it. Since the majority of these narrators came from historically marginalized populations and possessed little or no formal literary training, they often voiced their suspicion of the traditional Latin American *letrado* and tended to make calculated appeals to personal and group experience as the ultimate grounds of their accounts. As John Beverley argued in a series of influential articles in the late 1980s and early 1990s, such narratives signaled an alternative cultural and political practice to the traditional forms of literary representation in Latin America: "where literature in Latin America has been (mainly) a vehicle for engendering an adult, white male, patriarchal, 'lettered' subject, testimonio allows for the emergence—albeit mediated—of subaltern female, gay, indigenous, proletarian, and other identities."[95]

The most well-known *testimonio* of the period, the Guatemalan activist and indigenous organizer Rigoberta Menchú's *Me llamo Rigoberta Menchú, y así me nació la conciencia* [*I, Rigoberta Menchú: An Indian Woman in Guatemala*, 1983], produced in collaboration with the Venezuelan-born anthropologist Elisabeth Burgos-Debray, provides a paradigmatic example of the genre's radical questioning of the Latin American lettered city and the literature of the reader. At several strategic points in her narrative, Menchú stresses the difference between her own education and the formation of her lettered contemporaries: "I can say, I didn't go to school for my political formation, but instead I tried to turn my own experience into a general situation of all of the people."[96] In a crucial scene describing the government intervention that led to the loss of her ancestral lands, she details how a variety of educated *letrados*, from interpreters and lawyers to landowners and engineers, conspired to force her people to sign documents they could barely understand. Her opening remark that she is providing a "living testimony that I have not learned in a book" (21) therefore becomes legible as a disavowal of the structural position of the writer-reader in Latin American society. Many scholars have pointed out that Menchú and other testimonalists sought to cast their "personal experience" as typical rather than exceptional: hence Menchú's early remark that "the important thing is that what has happened to me has happened to other people too" (21). In its attack on the lettered subject and its affirmation of previously marginalized subjects and collectivities, the *testimonio* signaled an unprecedented reconfiguration of the contours of the Latin American field. Or, to frame the issue in hemispheric terms, we might say that at the same time as postmodern writers in the US literary field challenged the "cult of experience" through an appeal to the writer-as-reader, the *testimonio* contested the Latin American literary field's dominant paradigm of the literature of the reader through the recovery of the experience of oppressed people and accounts of the repression of experience itself.

For all its critical power, however, the *testimonio* attested to the endurance of the urban *letrado* tradition even while explicitly attacking it. Most obviously, nearly all of the *testimonios* canonized in the last decades of the twentieth century were produced in collaboration with interlocutors or *gestores*, typically professional writers, journalists, or anthropologists who transcribed and edited the oral testimony of the narrator. In *I, Rigoberta Menchú*, the tension between oral narrator and lettered transcriber is woven into the very fabric of the text. At the end of her narration, Menchú singles out anthropologists as participants in the politico-juridical complex of anti-indigenous repression: "I continue to hide what I think nobody knows, not even an anthropologist, not even an intellectual, however many books they may have, they don't know how to discern all of our secrets."[97] Yet Burgos-Debray, the transcriber of that line, leaves no doubt in her preface that she sees her role as recoding these secrets into an existing intellectual discourse. Burgos-Debray displays her literary bona fides by ending the preface with a poem from the Guatemalan author Miguel Ángel Asturias, and she includes quotations from the works of the Nobel Prize winner at the beginning of several of the *testimonio*'s chapters. Deploying a well-worn anthropological figure, she positions herself as the literate doppelgänger for her indigenous informant, defining her task as "first to listen and let Rigoberta speak, and then to turn myself into a sort of double of her, in the instrument that would effect the passage from the oral to the written" (18). Doris Sommer has argued that Menchú's reference to the community's "secrets" that can never be revealed to an intellectual outsider are evidence of Menchú's "deliberate textual strategy."[98] Yet the very collaborative structure of the testimonial makes it exceedingly difficult to attribute this strategy to Menchú alone. Indeed, when we approach *I, Rigoberta Menchú* as a hybrid text composed of both its internal narrative and its "framing" device, Burgos-Debray's mediations and Menchú's internal disavowals of those very same strategies seem to represent a kind of controlled polyphony of lettered and antilettered discourse. The conditions of production of the *testimonio* in the Latin America of the 1980s, in other words, remained highly imbricated in the discursive matrix of the lettered city.

We might conclude by emphasizing how distinct the logic of production of *I, Rigoberta Menchú* was from similar testimonial narratives in the US literary field during the same period. Although *I, Rigoberta Menchú* was quickly canonized in the United States after its publication by Verso Books, becoming a lightning rod in the "culture wars" of the 1980s, it remained an anomalous text within the growing multicultural canon within which it was somewhat incongruously placed. Indeed, by the time *I, Rigoberta Menchú* appeared in 1984, a strong tradition of "ethnic" self-writing already existed in the United States, composed mainly by marginalized subjects *writing and publishing under their own names.* Just a few years before the appearance of Menchú's *testimonio* in the United States, Leslie Marmon Silko published *Storyteller* (1981), a hybrid work that blended personal history, oral storytelling, and creation myths in a way not unlike that of Menchú. What distinguished the work of Silko and other writers of the so-called Native American Renaissance from Menchú was not an autobiographical pact that set the conditions for verifiability—no reader would confuse *Storyteller* with eyewitness testimony. The difference, rather, was in the US texts' assumption that the responsibility for molding and withholding personal experience toward narrative ends ultimately rested with the authors themselves. It was indicative of the discrepancies between the Latin American and US literary fields that while Burgos-Debray appeared as the sole author in the Spanish version of the book, in the English-language version Menchú was listed as the author and Burgos-Debray as the editor. The first English translation of *Biografía de un cimarrón* had already employed a similar tactic, rendering *biografía* as "autobiography" rather than "biography," thus shifting the implied agency of the story from the *gestor* (Barnet) to the first-person narrator (Montejo).

Much of the controversy in the United States surrounding the veracity of *I, Rigoberta Menchú* derived from the expectations of a US reading public primed to dissect and evaluate the precise connection between literary production and authorial experience. Alongside the more political concerns unleashed by *I, Rigoberta Menchú*'s incorporation into the US multicultural canon, it was this perceived lack of authorial authority that disconcerted readers in the US public sphere. When American anthropologist David Stoll's *Rigoberta Menchú and the Story of All Poor Guatemalans* (1999) questioned Menchú's account of her life history and of the root causes of the violence in the northern Guatemalan highlands in the 1970s and early 1980s, he took particular issue with Menchú's refusal to clarify the relationship between these two strands of her *testimonio*. Although reactions to Stoll's book tended to polarize along ideological lines, both Menchú "supporters" and Menchú "detractors" seemed to accept the basic belief that the "Menchú-Stoll controversy" existed in part because of the emphasis that the US literary tradition put on experiential writing. Thus, Mary Louise Pratt, a Menchú supporter, suggested that *I, Rigoberta Menchú*'s "American reception is shaped in advance by the historic role that autobiographical writing plays in North American culture," and argued that the *testimonio* should continue to be taught because its "construction as a personal, experiential narrative has the power to break down the distancing strategies that normally govern young Americans' encounters with their racial and economic others."[99] On the other side, the Guatemalan writer Mario Roberto Morales, a Menchú detractor, asserted that this bias toward experiential narrative in the US literary imaginary was precisely the problem: "US academics, starting from the assumption that Menchú had been an eyewitness of the violent events that she narrates, enshrined her version of the conflict as the only true account of the recent history of Guatemala and positioned the Testimonio as the 'true' literary form of subalternity, opposed to the 'false' literary form of 'lettered writers' [escritores 'letrados'] (note the redundancy) such as Asturias, whose versions of the popular they considered to be 'paternalistic.'"[100] Though Morales's comment significantly exaggerates the positions of the US theorists of the *testimonio*, it nevertheless confirms Pratt's assertion that the text's popularity in the United States was due in large part to Menchú's rhetorical appeal to her personal experience and her attempts to distance herself from the "lettered" tradition. In my fifth chapter, I will examine how Latin American writers such as Bolaño have framed the testimonial tradition in relation to the US literature of experience. But before we can begin to understand how contemporary writers have constellated these various traditions, we must first examine how the hemispheric divide crystallized in "inter-American" initiatives and literary texts themselves.

An Inter-American Episode

JORGE LUIS BORGES, WALDO FRANK, AND THE BATTLE FOR WHITMAN'S AMERICA

Very familiar material is not usually that stimulating. [Una materia muy familiar suele no ser estimulante.]
—JORGE LUIS BORGES, *Obras Completas*

The hemispheric divide between the US literature of experience and the Latin American literature of the reader that solidified in the early twentieth century changed how literature was written in the Americas. At the same time, it transformed US–Latin American literary *relations*, that is, the very way in which writers in the United States and Latin America conceived of their participation in something like a transamerican cultural enterprise. Nowhere is this divide more evident than in the works of the US novelist and cultural critic Waldo Frank and the Argentine essayist and short-story writer Jorge Luis Borges, perhaps the two most important proponents of a North–South literary dialogue in the first half of the twentieth century. From his earliest Latin American lecture tours of the 1920s to his official visit to Havana after the Cuban Revolution of 1959, Frank published numerous works on the shared cultures of the Americas and labored tirelessly as a hemispheric literary ambassador. During the same period, Borges became one of the most recognized authorities on North American literature as well as a prominent Spanish-language translator of US authors such as Walt Whitman, Langston Hughes, and William Faukner. Yet while both Borges and Frank envisioned a common literary canon for the Americas, their views of what it should entail developed in strikingly different directions.

This chapter traces the emergence of the discursive split between the US literature of experience and the Latin American literature of the reader through a paradigmatic misencounter between Borges and Frank. Although there is little evidence to suggest that the two men exchanged more than a few words during Frank's several high-profile visits to Argentina from the late 1920s to the 1940s, their enduring textual cat-and-mouse game, scattered across multiple writings and several decades, contributed to entrenching the hemispheric literary divide. Indeed, Frank and Borges's failure to arrive at terms of mutual engagement is the most compelling confirmation of the incompatibility of their frameworks for thinking and writing the hemispheric.

In what follows, I draw from essays, letters, and speeches surrounding Frank's first visit to Argentina in 1929 to reconstruct an implicit debate between Frank and Borges about the source material of Walt Whitman's poetry and his vision of the Americas. Both authors considered Whitman the most indispensable writer in hemispheric literary history, but they held diametrically opposing views about how twentieth-century US and Latin American authors could follow his example. For Frank, Whitman's "message" to writers North and South was that the literatures of the Americas must be grounded on lived experience and real-world "contact" with the American land. He resurrected the "absorption" model of literature Whitman proposed in the 1855 preface to *Leaves of Grass*, extending the poet's injunction to "incarnate" New World geography from the United States proper to the hemisphere as a whole. Borges, on the other hand, cast Whitman as a "man of letters" whose major feat was to convert his readings into a literary portrait of America. Here I will show how Borges revised Frank's experiential framework for interpreting Whitman's poetry, and, in the process, formulated an aesthetics of reading that proved singularly influential to mid- and late twentieth-century Latin American writers. By claiming that Whitman acquired his knowledge of America in the library rather than in endless wanderings through the country, Borges recruited the good gray poet to his own project of mapping the Americas (and particularly the United States).

The Art of Experience

Almost everybody saw Waldo Frank disembark in Buenos Aires on September 23, 1929. The welcoming committee for Frank's visit to

Argentina, the second leg of a whirlwind tour of Latin America in which he lectured on US literature and society and prophesied a new era of inter-American goodwill, was a virtual who's who of the Latin American intellectual establishment of the 1920s. Accompanied on his steamship passage from Montevideo by the writer Alfonso Reyes (then the acting Mexican ambassador to Argentina), Frank was met at the port by a group consisting of the Latin Americanist scholar Pedro Henríquez Ureña, the editor and writer Samuel Glusberg, and the journalist Eduardo Mallea. He was shuttled off to a banquet in his honor, where the Argentine *modernista* poet Leopoldo Lugones delivered opening remarks.[1] Over the next few weeks, amid a series of heavily attended lectures at the Universidad de Buenos Aires and the Amigos del Arte institute, Frank established a strong personal and professional relationship with Victoria Ocampo, with whom he was already discussing the possibility of a literary review that would function as a bridge between the Americas. The cultural network Frank developed during his stay in Buenos Aires was responsible not only for the birth of *Revista Sur*, arguably the most important Latin American little magazine of the first half of the twentieth century, but also for the first sustained twentieth-century effort to translate and disseminate Latin American literature in the United States.[2] Upon his return from Latin America in 1930, an equally impressive group of cultural figures gathered in New York City to honor what an event flyer dubbed Frank's "triumph in Hispano-America." At the Hotel Roosevelt, the audience for Frank's talk "What is Hispano-America to Us?" included Franz Boas, John Dewey, Charlie Chaplin, Lewis Mumford, Maxwell Perkins and Alfred Stieglitz.[3] That such a talk gained such a hearing should alert us to the surprising rapidity of exchanges between the cultural fields of the United States and Latin America in the 1920s and 1930s. Of course, exchange and understanding are not always the same thing.

Who was this man who was generating so much buzz on both sides of the Rio Grande? Born in 1889 into an upper-middle-class Jewish family in New Jersey and raised in New York, Frank spent several years in Europe before returning to the United States in 1911. In 1916, he became the assistant editor of the short-lived but influential magazine *The Seven Arts*; his first novel, *The Unwelcome Man*, would be published the following year. Under the editorship of James Oppenheim, *The Seven Arts* became a collective forum for the so-called Young Americans, a group of left-leaning intellectuals including Frank, Randolph Bourne, and Van Wyck Brooks who merged a belief in anticapitalist leftist politics with a defense of the role of art and literature as a means of national renewal. After the magazine folded in the months leading up to the US entry into the First World War, Frank continued to work as a cultural critic, literary promoter, and novelist, simultaneously championing aesthetic creation and political radicalism. An important advocate for Sherwood Anderson, John Dos Passos, and Eugene O'Neill, he was also the main editor of Jean Toomer's hybrid modernist novel, *Cane* (1923).

Although Frank's literary reputation declined sharply in the early post–World War II period, the scholarship of the past thirty years has brought about a critical revaluation of his cultural labor: he is increasingly recognized as a shaper of modernist institutions in the United States in the 1920s, a precursor to the discipline of American studies, and a cultural ambassador between the United States and Latin America.[4] Frank's 1919 cultural critique *Our America* enjoyed broad popularity among US intellectuals in the immediate aftermath of World War I—Kenneth Burke later hailed it as one of the few books that "had changed our minds."[5] Nevertheless, Frank's celebrity in Latin America far outstripped his status in the US literary field in subsequent decades. By the mid-1920s, Frank had caught the eye of Latin American intellectuals across the ideological spectrum, from Reyes to the leftist politician and essayist José Carlos Mariátegui, who wrote in 1925 that *Our America* was "the most original and intelligent interpretation of the United States yet."[6] It was at Reyes's urging that Frank embarked on his six-month Latin American lecture tour in 1929, speaking to audiences in Mexico City, Buenos Aires, and Lima about US literary and artistic figures from Ben Franklin to Sherwood Anderson and Isadora Duncan. The fanfare with which Frank was met in Latin America is difficult to fathom today. By 1929, Ezra Pound, Gertrude Stein, Sinclair Lewis, T. S. Eliot, Ernest Hemingway, and F. Scott Fitzgerald had all established international reputations. So it might take an effort of the imagination to comprehend how the Peruvian scholar Luis Alberto Sánchez could declare that "in the literatures of America, especially in those of the south, there is no parallel to Waldo Frank."[7] Yet this statement was typical of the hype surrounding Frank's Latin American tour. Newspapers like *La Nación* in Argentina and *El Excelsior* in Mexico wrote glowing accounts of Frank's activities and his lectures, and *El Mundo* in Lima called his trip to Argentina a "unique success." In a memoir published in the early sixties, Ocampo, who as editor of *Sur* for over thirty years frequently collaborated with both Borges and Frank, would go so far as to say that "[f]or some of us (among whom I count myself) we owe Frank the credit for having turned our sights toward the North of our New Continent. Up until then ... with a few exceptions ... we had them fixed on Europe."[8] The remark is telling not only for the protagonist's role it affords Frank in reorienting Argentine culture toward the United States but also for the fact that she attributes this reorientation to Frank at a time when most people in Argentina and abroad would have seen Borges as the person who introduced North America literature to Argentina. Maria Rosa Oliver was one of the many Argentine writers to echo this assessment, stressing that it was Frank who had provided the country's intellectuals with the key to understanding the "dynamism" and "dangers" of the United States and its literature.[9]

From his earliest associations with the *Seven Arts* group, Frank championed a specific politico-aesthetic variant of the US literature of experience. Casey Nelson Blake and Alan Trachtenberg have shown that the Young Americans derived much of their cultural program from a reading of Deweyan pragmatism, leading them to a belief in what Trachtenberg calls "the essential importance of personal experience to any program of cultural renewal."[10] As Blake has argued, the Young Americans were perhaps most influential in the interwar United States for the way they supplemented a Deweyan notion of experience with a Romantic understanding of the power of artistic expression as the basis for radical change. Already in *Our America* (1919), Frank had asserted that experience is "the sole true norm of culture, the sole measure of growth."[11] And in a 1929 letter to Samuel Glusberg, who organized Frank's trip to Buenos Aires and oversaw the Spanish translation of *Our America*, Frank applied this experiential criterion to his relationship to Latin America itself: "the problem today is that of *The* American Culture.... South America is part of it. I feel this. I shall not understand my feeling, however, until I have experienced South America."[12]

As his letter to Glusberg attests, in the decades following the publication of *Our America*, Frank translated the (experiential) nationalist project of the Young Americans into a model for hemispheric cultural production. Indeed, out of all the early twentieth-century writers I study in this book, Frank alone explicitly framed the literature of experience *as* a literature of the Americas. For Frank, the 1929 lecture tour marked a symbolic turn toward this hemispheric theory. On the occasion of the translation of *Our America* into Spanish in Buenos Aires, Frank declared that "[i]n the sense in which I use the word over the course of this book, you are all Americans [vosotros sois americanos]; my America, whose promise is my theme, is also your America. Our America is complete in its full breadth now that the term has become 'Nuestra América' to include you as well."[13] In a 1930 letter to Victoria Ocampo about his travelogue *América Hispana: A Portrait and a Prospect*, (1931), which Frank regarded as the culmination of his Latin American tour, Frank returned to this rhetoric of the (trans-)American experience. Writing in somewhat idiosyncratic Spanish, Frank told Ocampo:

> I've been hard at work on the book. Not writing, of course. But planning and giving it form....I must read a lot—history, etc. to gain mastery over the facts relating to my topic. Only then, gradually, will I begin to write. What frustrates me is that there might be some part of the book that won't be within my experience [que no esté dentro de mi experiencia], in which case I must visit South America again. I cannot write the book unless I am familiar with the material [a menos que conozca bien los temas]. This is a danger and a worry. But if I must return to S.A. perhaps it is my destiny to do so.[14]

Here as elsewhere, Frank predicates the fulfillment of the promise of hemispheric solidarity more on his own firsthand knowledge of Latin America than on traditional forms of US-Latin American cultural exchange. Without denying the importance of reading to his creative process, Frank refuses it ultimate authority, instead implying that his success will depend on his "experience" of the region.

This privileging of experiential contact over literary formation provided Frank with both a principle of composition for his own writing and a program for inter-American cultural exchange. In his acknowledgments to *América Hispana: A Portrait and a Prospect*, Frank outlines the methods he employed for his works of fiction and his national and regional portraits, distinguishing between what he calls his "macrocosmic" narrative of Latin America and more traditional historical treatments, stressing that his aim is not to give "facts or information" but rather "an image of the living organism about which the facts are recorded."[15] Although Frank goes on to list many of the periodicals, books, and articles he has consulted in preparing the work, he concludes by highlighting the vital sources of the book:

"Far more than by any written word, I have been helped to that experience of América Hispana which my book embodies in my friendships, and by my journeys through the land"(xii). Frank's desire to subordinate the past to the present and to capture the restless movement from region to region characterizes the very progression of the book's chapters, which are arranged geographically and typically open with a snapshot of each country as if viewed for the first time from a ship, an airplane, or a locomotive. In "The Andes," we see a cathedral in La Paz in front of which sit "several ragged men and women" (27); in "The Pacific" we find coastal mountains on which even the stealthy "aeroplane" has trouble landing (131); and, in "The Coastal Sea" of Central America and Mexico "we find the dim remains of an archaic people" and "the Maya peasant of today" (103). Each chapter begins in the present tense and only gradually moves backward in time, suggesting that Latin American culture resides more in the places Frank visits and the faces he meets than in national and regional archives.[16] Indeed, the experiential impulse at the core of Frank's literary project helps to explain his paradoxical position as a founding figure of the twentieth-century literature of the Americas: undoubtedly the American writer most well versed in the Latin American literary tradition, he also persistently subordinated this reading to his "experience" of Latin America.

Incarnating the Americas

At the same time that he was preparing *América Hispana: A Portrait and a Prospect* for publication in English in the United States, Frank was also at work on his Spanish-language book *Primer mensaje a la América Hispana* [First Message to Hispanic America]. The book consisted of a series of essays on US literature and culture culled mainly from Frank's lectures in Buenos Aires, which he had delivered in Spanish using translations from the English prepared by the Argentine writer Eduardo Mallea. In *Primer mensaje*, Frank dedicates an entire chapter to the life and poetry of Walt Whitman, "La divina medianía de Whitman" [The Divine Average of Whitman], based on the lecture he had given on October 1, 1929, at the Universidad de Buenos Aires. As Irene Rostagno has written, Frank had begun to champion Walt Whitman as the symbol of American poetry as early as his 1910s affiliation with the Young Americans, who had found in Whitman a harbinger of the latter-day artists who would create a "new collective American consciousness."[17] In the chapter of *Primer mensaje* devoted to Whitman, Frank continues to describe the nineteenth-century poet as a model for contemporary Americans, though here he extends that designation to include Americans both North *and* South. Although there is no concrete evidence that Borges went to the lecture, the general buzz surrounding Frank's visit and the fact that many of Borges's friends, including Alfonso Reyes, were actively participating in the lecture series makes it almost certain that Borges either was at the lecture or read *Primer mensaje* after its release in Argentina in 1931.[18] It will therefore be useful for us to retain throughout this section a mental image of Borges listening in the halls of the Universidad de Buenos Aires as Frank elaborated his vision of Whitman's life and literature.

The signature gesture of Frank's interpretation of Whitman, which draws from an eclectic blend of textual sources and biographical materials, is its repeated reference to Whitman's status as the preeminent US poet of experience. Early in the lecture, Frank exorts his Argentine public to "remember that [Whitman's] book is his life," asserting that Whitman "was not an educated man" and "had been an irregular reader."[19] At these moments, Frank clearly follows Whitman's own tropological moves in *Leaves of Grass*, especially the famous line in "So Long" that fuses the poet's book with his person ("Camerado, this is no book, / Who touches this touches a man"), and the injunction in "Song of the Open Road" to leave the "book / on the shelf unopen'd."[20] Yet Frank also departs from textual analysis in offering a thesis on how Whitman's anxieties of experience fundamentally altered his literary education: Whitman "abandoned, before his thirtieth birthday, his brilliant career as an editor. He returned to the teeming America [América profusa]. He lived with [convivió con] rivermen, coach drivers, prostitutes, and criminals. He traveled to the West; he went to the South. He had many affairs; he worked in many humble professions."[21] Frank shows little desire to bring out Whitman's famous style of "indirection"; instead, Whitman's artistic project is presented as a relentless search for experience, both profound and "profuse." In Frank's account, Whitman seeks to occupy as many employments and subject positions as possible. The signal word in the passage is "convivió"; *convivir* in Spanish literally means "living with," but here it takes on the sense of happy intimacy, as in the etymologically linked English word "conviviality." Frank's Whitman becomes an endless pursuer of the "convivial," the seeker of a fraternal bond that could, through a concerted effort of proximity, solder together the disparate parts of America—or rather, the Americas. "Getting to know the other" is perhaps the clearest formulation of the message that underwrites Frank's trip to Latin America and his lectures on American culture and society.

In speaking of Whitman's contact with the "América profusa," Frank is obviously enacting a biographical reading of *Leaves of Grass*. But his statement does not restrict Whitman's importance to the *fidelity* of his literature to his life (according to the typical demands of literary realism). Instead, it accentuates the *quantity* of life that went into Whitman's literature. In this sense, Frank's critical approach to Whitman represents an important variation on the biographical criticism that had come into vogue in the nineteenth century. Most biographical criticism—the main enemy, as we know, of so many theoretical trends in the twentieth century—sought to retrace the steps back from the author's work to his or her experiences (whether positive or privative), offering an explanatory hypothesis in the form of a psychological etiology. Frank's experiential method for analyzing Whitman, on the other hand, serves as a technique for authorization. America comes to be defined through Whitman's familiarity with it: his ability to absorb each of its features, region by region, occupation by occupation, person by person. One wonders whether Frank is fully aware that his rhetoric of experience distorts the facts of Whitman's actual biography—Whitman had not, after all, been to the West when he celebrated it in "Song of Myself." Only toward the end of his life would he travel to the West, and even then, he did not get further than Colorado. The point for Frank, however, is to stress that Whitman lived the full range of what could be called American experiences—and lived them in a way that pervaded not only his poetic process but his entire mode of existence. Even more than his poetry about the United States, it was Whitman's disposition toward experience that made him the exemplary precursor for the new generation of hemispheric writers that Frank hoped to inspire.

Frank reveals the continuities between his interpretation of Whitman and his own Latin American literary project in his personal essay "Mensaje a la Argentina" [Message to Argentina], which appeared on the front page of *La vida literaria* in November, 1929, just over a month after Frank had left Buenos Aires. It is here that

Frank positions himself most forcefully as Whitman's hemispheric heir, the first US writer to incarnate the entirety of the (trans-) American scene. After reiterating that Whitman is now "our poet, not only the poet of the North," Frank turns abruptly from literary and cultural history to his personal biography: "It's not bad to speak about the Founding Fathers and the American Ideal and our great writers and the contemporary warriors in the modern war of the Spirit. But it is much more pleasurable, at least for me, to speak about myself."[22] What follows is a synthetic autobiographical account that ranges from Frank's childhood growing up in New York City to his realization that his literary and cultural mission is to encounter the "authentic" America. It is a retrospective construction, in other words, of Frank's authorial self.

Frank's literary origin story fits squarely within the imaginary of the US literature of experience, narrating a turn from European bookishness to an appreciation of American people and places. The primal scene of Frank's childhood occurs in his father's library, where "every night we children would gather in the library and my father would read a few pages out loud: and when the page wasn't from the Bible, it was from a European book: and when it wasn't European, it was from an American author like Longfellow or Lowell or Washington Irving, Europeans in all but their names."[23] The trauma of this excessively bookish education—"Books...occupied a special domain and never ventured into the human realm"—leads Frank to his first act of literary defiance, an escape from the library "shelves" into the "world of facts": "My father's house was strict, and early on this instilled in me the habit of escaping from it. New York is a good scene to initiate the life of a modern boy [un muchacho moderno]."[24] Drawing from his description of Whitman as a "wandering young vagabond" in *Primer mensaje*,[25] Frank positions himself as a "modern" equivalent whose experiential curiosity led him into the urban ecology of New York City.

Although the second half of "Mi mensaje a la Argentina" largely repeats the trope of the flight from bookish culture into unmediated experience, it also seeks to validate Frank's experience of Latin America as the culmination of his desire to experience America itself. Sensitive to the possibility that his time in France and Spain could be viewed as contradicting his message, Frank casts his years on the old continent as a preparation for his return to the New World. Admitting that Paris helped to form him and became his temporary "cultural home" [hogar cultural], he nevertheless stresses that his time in Europe only confirmed that he was "not European": "I needed to leave Paris. I knew where to go—I needed to go home...to the heart of America, which was my house."[26] Crucially, the "heart" of this America had now shifted south: "And I then had the first inkling of what would eventually be a great adventure in my life. I felt that those foreigners [I met in Europe] were American, in a certain sense....They came from countries I ignored: I knew not a book, nor a song, nor a painting by them....But all of the Mexicans, Argentineans, and Venezuelans were closer to me than my intimate European friends."[27] Frank's visit to Argentina becomes the final stage in his reincarnation as the writer of the Americas: "My friends, this visit to Argentina, just like my recent visit to Mexico, is nothing more than a stage in my return to America, a stage in my own discovery of America."[28] He closes by describing this "search for America" as the "voyage that is my life" [el viaje que es mi vida]. Given the almost vertiginous pace of Frank's movement—he sent his "message" from Peru, having recently made a series of short stops in Chile and Bolivia—his description of his life as a voyage could hardly have been taken as mere metaphor. His very notion of hemispheric writing was predicated on broad, frequent, and intense cross-cultural travel.

Frank's aesthetics of experience motivated not only his literary production and his lectures on American literary history, but also his overarching cultural program for the hemisphere. As Rostagno demonstrates, Frank's selection of Latin American texts for translation and publication in the United States during the 1930s and 1940s was dictated primarily by how closely these texts adhered to Whitmanian criteria: Frank insisted that he was interested less in the "intrinsic literary value" of Latin American works than in their "portrayal of American life."[29] Just as importantly, these criteria provided the blueprint for the selection of US literary texts for Ocampo's fledgling magazine *Sur*. Frank wrote or commissioned virtually all the essays about US literature in the first years of the magazine's existence—his fellow Young Americans Lewis Mumford and Gorham Munson contributed long articles on US art and literature to *Sur*'s third and fourth issues. And based on the available evidence, it is likely that Frank selected the first US works that Borges translated for the magazine: poems by Langston Hughes and Edgar Lee Masters.[30]

A 1931 exchange of letters between Frank and Ocampo about *Sur*'s editorial policy, reprinted by Ocampo years later, sheds light on Frank's vision for the magazine he believed would become the preeminent hemispheric literary venue. In one letter, Frank advises Ocampo to seek out a few collaborators in each region, "one or two men in the Pacific, in Cuba, and in Mexico that will offer creative help by being close to you personally and becoming your friends."[31] Predictably, Frank's portrait of the ideal collaborator was almost identical to his portrait of the experiential writer: he urged Ocampo to find a team of editors "who are in immediate contact with what is vital in their countries."[32] Of course, Frank himself would be Ocampo's "friend" from the United States, the reliable (trans-) Americanist who would provide her with "vital" material from the north. Although Frank's editorial influence steadily faded as *Sur*'s worldview moved from inter-Americanism toward an Argentine brand of cosmopolitanism, his Whitmanian aesthetics of experience remained its main criterion for selecting, disseminating, and characterizing North American writers.[33] As we will see, this aesthetics of experience also formed the backdrop for Borges's revisionary reading of US literary history.

The Other Whitman

The standard account of Borges's relationship to North American literature is highly conditioned by the Argentine writer's glowing assessments of the United States after his first visit to the country in 1961. In "An Autobiographical Essay," first published in English in the *New Yorker* in 1970, Borges described the United States as the "friendliest, most forgiving and most generous country I had ever visited."[34] And in *Introducción a la literatura norteamericana* [*An Introduction to American Literature* 1967], written collaboratively with Esther Zemborain de Torres, Borges remarked to his Argentine audience that "[o]ur fundamental purpose has been to encourage an acquaintance with the literary evolution of the nation which forged the first democratic constitution of modern times."[35] As Doris Sommer has observed, these were the words of the later "conservative" Borges, the world-renowned author of metaphysical parables whose political gestures included accepting the Grand Cross of the Order of Merit from the Chilean dictator Augusto Pinochet, giving an inscribed copy of Whitman's *Leaves of Grass* to Richard Nixon, and vehemently opposing the Cuban Revolution.[36] One can find inklings of his affinities with North American literature as early as the 1930s, when Borges began to translate works by US writers, write essays on North American literature and film, and compose stories set in the country. Moreover, from the lead-up to World War II to the later decades of the Cold War, Borges, like many Argentine intellectuals opposed to the populist government of Juan Domingo Perón, saw the United States as the main defender of liberal democracy against fascism and socialism.

Yet the gradual recuperation of Borges's writings of the 1920s over the past thirty years—aided significantly by the publication in 1997 of *Textos Recobrados: 1919–1929/Jorge Luis Borges*—has revealed the extent to which the young Borges experimented with various ideological views, from anarchism and Soviet-style communism to the Argentine cultural nationalism of *criollismo*. Scholars such as Graciela Montaldo, Daniel Balderston, and Luis Othoniel Rosa have demonstrated that even as Borges moved toward a purportedly apolitical cosmopolitan literary program in the 1930s and 1940s, his stories and essays continue to be marked by many of his earlier political and aesthetic commitments.[37] Borges's views on the United States were not exempt from this process of experimentation and reversal, and in fact his writings of the 1920s and early 1930s present us with a far more skeptical view of US literary, cultural, and political institutions than his later works would lead us to believe. Rather than working backward from Borges's celebratory remarks about American culture and society in the 1960s and 1970s, I will work forward from his ambivalence toward US culture and the increasing Americanization of Argentina during the interwar years.[38] My basic contention is that Borges's turn toward the aesthetics of the reader—his belief, as his 1935 prologue to the *Universal History* puts it, that reading is a more "intellectual" activity than writing and that "good readers" are rarer and more valuable than "good writers"—was largely the result of his increasing engagement with a wide variety of twentieth-century US literature. More specifically, I aim to show that Borges's highly idiosyncratic depiction of Whitman as the consummate *reader* of the Americas was a response to Frank's uses and abuses of Whitman as the representative poet of the modern (trans-)American "experience."

In 1921 the young Jorge Luis Borges returned to Buenos Aires from a six-year stint in Europe to a cultural environment that was hardly conducive to the appreciation of US literature. As Glusberg remarked to Frank half a decade later, few works by North American writers were available in Argentina at the time ("Aside from Poe, Whitman and Mark Twain, we know nothing about American authors").[39] The main Argentine literary journal, *Nosotros*, did not even have a section on US literature in its monthly bibliography, which was divided into the categories of Argentine, Hispano-American, French, Spanish, Catalan, Italian, and German literature. Significantly, though Borges had been a reader of Whitman since his teenage years in Geneva, he mentions just five North American literary authors in *all* of his writings prior to Waldo Frank's visit to Argentina in 1929: Whitman, Emerson, and Poe (repeatedly); Jack London and Henry Wadsworth Longfellow (in passing). Yet these material obstacles to acquiring books of US literature were not the only factors shaping Borges's view of the United States. As I mentioned in chapter 1, the early twentieth century witnessed the rise in Latin America of *arielismo*, a continent-wide intellectual discourse that posited a supranational Ibero–Latin American identity as a bulwark against US political and cultural hegemony in the hemisphere. Most scholars have argued that the main intellectual current to which Borges responded upon returning to Argentina in the early 1920s was *criollismo*, a nativist discourse popularized by figures such as Leopoldo Lugones, Manuel Gálvez, and Ricardo Rojas in the previous decades. Yet *arielismo* predated *criollismo* in the Argentine literary field, and as Teresa Alfieri has demonstrated, the founding *criollista* figures often infused the rhetoric of *arielismo* into their language of cultural nationalism.[40] A letter from Glusberg to Frank suggests that *arielista* currents continued to eddy through the Argentine cultural world in the late 1920s, when the "Hispanoamericanizers" were still "harping on the odious distinction between Latinism and Yankeeism."[41]

Rarely has it been noticed that when Borges returned to Argentina from Spain in 1921, he drew from many elements of this "odious" *arielista* discourse in his writings. In the 1921 essay "Buenos Aires," which Borges later described as the "abreviatura" or abbreviated essence of his first volume of poetry, *Fervor de Buenos Aires* (1923), he makes a pointed criticism of American influence in Argentina: "In the tunnels of our souls leaps a Spanish spirit, but they want to turn us into Yankees, false Yankees, and deceive us with the lukewarm water of democracy and the vote."[42] Tellingly, Borges's critique of his fellow Argentines' spiritual Americanization, which Rodó had disparagingly labeled *nordomanía*, positions Whitman as a synechdoche for US-style industrialization. Midway through the essay, Borges pauses in the middle of a description of the *porteño* cityscape to remark: "Although a stray skyscraper might occasionally offend our eyes, the total panorama of Buenos Aires is not Whitmanesque."[43] Here, Whitman and his verse appear to stand in for the urbanization of the Argentine capital, the very process that Borges's poems and essays of the early 1920s associate with the eradication of the city's outskirts (*orillas*) and the slow demise of the Argentine way of life.

Even as Borges began to gravitate toward a Whitmanesque aesthetic in his own poetry of the mid-1920s, his essays dramatize the conflict between his appreciation for a select group of US writers—most prominently Whitman and Emerson—and his *arielista*-informed skepticism toward the United States as a politico-cultural entity. This conflict is rendered most acute in his 1926 essay "El tamaño de mi esperanza" ["The Size of My Hope"], which has often been seen as the key to understanding Borges's so-called *criollista* phase of the mid-to-late 1920s. On the one hand, the essay warns against any form of "progressivism" as "subjecting ourselves to becoming almost North Americans"; on the other hand, it borrows its New World vocabulary from the nineteenth-century North American writers Borges esteems.[44] On the one hand, Borges criticizes Sarmiento in xenophobic and racist terms as a "North Americanized wild Indian, a great hater and misunderstander of the criollo"; on the other, he frames his own literary nationalism by quoting from Emerson's "The Poet" and referring to its legacy in Whitman's poetry: "'Yet America is a poem in our eyes [América es un poema en nuestros ojos]; its ample geography dazzles the imagination, and it will not wait long for metres,' wrote Emerson in 1844 in a sentence that is like a premonition of Whitman and that today, in the Buenos Aires of 1925, prophesies once again."[45] This last quotation synthesizes the paradoxical problem around which Borges's 1920s writing about the United States continually revolves: How can the Argentine writer resurrect the Whitmanesque-Emersonian project of capturing "America" while simultaneously resisting the (North) Americanization of Argentina?

Reconstructing Borges's conflicted relationship to Whitman in the 1920s, conditioned as it was by the continental-nationalist discourses that dominated the *porteño* literary world and by his own limited access to twentieth-century US literature, prepares us to recognize the momentousness of Waldo Frank's visit to Argentina in 1929. In all likelihood, Frank's visit represented Borges's first contact with a US writer and his earliest in-depth engagement with a cultural and historical account of US literature. As I have already noted, there is little evidence of substantial exchange between the two writers: Borges's scattered remarks about Frank are vague and largely dismissive, while Frank's *South American Journey* (1943) mentions Borges only to say that although he is "his generation's finest stylist, he brazenly devotes his genius to a literature of fantasy and utter escape."[46] Yet if we return to the context of Frank's first visit to Buenos Aires and his reception in the Argentine literary reviews of the later 1920s, we can trace a sustained if largely implicit debate between Borges and Frank about the figure of Whitman.

In September, 1929, Glusberg's *La vida literaria* published what was likely the earliest Argentine magazine issue devoted exclusively to US literature; introducing the issue, Glusberg affirmed that he planned it to "coincide with Waldo Frank's arrival in Argentina."[47] The issue was, in effect, a celebration of Frank and his vision of hemispheric literature. It advertised the recent Spanish-language translation of *Our America*, and indeed, almost all the US authors included in the issue—Edgar Lee Masters, Robert Frost, Sherwood Anderson, Eugene O'Neill, etc.—played a prominent role in Frank's book. Leopoldo Lugones, Horacio Quiroga, José Carlos Mariátegui, and Guillermo de Torre were among the Latin American contributors. As one would imagine, Whitman was the issue's tutelary figure. Frank's "Whitmanesque Letter" [Carta Whitmaniana], translated into Spanish by Alfonso Reyes, spreads across most of the front page. At the bottom of the third page appeared the very first of Borges's essays dedicated entirely to Whitman, "El otro Whitman" [The Other Whitman]. It is therefore almost impossible that Borges and Frank would have been unaware of each other's schemas for interpreting Whitman's work.

Predictably, Frank's letter begins with a call to writers throughout the hemisphere to "incorporate" Whitman's message into the American experience ("el ser de la experiencia americana").[48] But Borges's essay strikes an entirely different chord. In a line that seems calculated to dispute Frank's trans-American message, Borges specifies that *his* Whitman bears little resemblance to the "cheery and global" [saludador y mundial] image of Whitman enshrined in the twentieth-century imagination, and, indeed, in the rest of the special issue.[49] Significantly, Borges wholly reverses his own earlier endorsement of the Whitmanian-Emersonian project in "El tamaño de mi esperanza," now explicitly criticizing the imitators of Whitman who mimic "the indulgent geographical, historic, and circumstantial enumerations that Whitman strung together to complete a certain prophecy of Emerson regarding the worthy poet of America."[50] Although Borges's essay never directly identifies its antagonist, the context in which it appears—at the end of this special issue—points to Frank. The "other" of its title seems to register a specific complaint against Frank's interpretation of Whitman in addition to its general criticism of the twentieth-century reception of the poet's work.

The evidence of Borges's ongoing efforts to delegitimize Frank's portrait of Whitman as the American poet of experience becomes even stronger in the wake of Frank's 1929 visit. Tellingly, when Borges reedited "El otro Whitman" for his book of essays *Discusión* in 1932, he added two lines to the text: "Almost everything written about Whitman is falsified by two interminable errors. One is the summary identification of Whitman, the pensive man of letters, with Whitman, the semidivine hero of *Leaves of Grass*, just as Don Quixote is of *Don Quixote*; the other, the foolish adoption of the style and vocabulary of [Whitman's] poems."[51] Years later, in his canonical study of the influence of Whitman in Latin America, Fernando Alegría would cite Borges's debunking of the myth of the "semidivine" Whitman as the first time in Latin American history that Whitman's biography was approached with any semblance of critical objectivity. But in the context of Frank's "Carta Whitmaniana," his lectures on Whitman in Buenos Aires, and the chapter of *Primer mensaje* "La 'medianía divina' de Walt Whitman," it seems highly probable that Borges's target in these lines was as much Frank's specific characterization of Whitman as the hero and prophet of the "American experience" as it was "everything that has been written about Whitman."

Borges's separation of Whitman's life and his textual persona serves to undercut the basic premise of the US literature of experience as Frank articulated it in his Latin American journey. And indeed, if we conjure for a moment the Borges that we left sitting in the lecture hall of the Universidad de Buenos Aires, we will almost feel his frustration at each of Frank's interpretive moves linking Whitman's literature to his life. Frank is guilty of all the charges leveled by Borges: he had insisted in his lecture that Whitman's "book is his life," and his very chapter title, "La divina medianía de Walt Whitman," appropriates Whitman's "style and vocabulary" in adopting the poet's self-designation as a "divine average."[52] It would be

hard, however, to call these critical errors, since Frank's stated ambition was to elevate Whitman to the status of *nuestro poeta*, the poetic
model for the Americas, to be emulated in his life as well as in his
literature.[53] In his articles on Frank's visit to Lima, Luis Alberto
Sánchez gives a sense of the degree to which Frank invoked the
figure of Whitman in explaining his own purpose in Latin America.
Clearly alluding to Frank's attempts to position himself as the
modern-day avatar of the Whitmanian poet, Sánchez would write:

> [Frank's] message is his own experience. But this experience adum-
> brates until it is a cosmic one, so that his 'I' merges with the whole,
> and his America becomes the intimate living of every man who
> knows himself and feels his duty and his function. Thus it was that in
> his first lecture in Lima, 'My Message to Peru,' Frank could say in all
> simplicity that the title of his talk concealed a Yankee trick, since his
> message was in reality himself—his person and his life.[54]

Sánchez's words are telling: the "Yankee trick" that Frank puts over
on his Peruvian audience is precisely the Whitmanian illusion of
presenting one's words—one's message—as one's experience.
Sánchez's generally positive portrait cannot quite conceal the implication that Frank's rhetorical performance encoded a more sinister
reminder of the United States' increasing omnipresence in Latin
America, inasmuch as Frank's "America" seeps into the "intimate
being" of everyone who hears or reads him. No wonder Borges felt
that a little critical distance was in order.

One might think the interpretive skirmish between Borges and
Frank would have subsided by the time Borges published his most
famous essay on Whitman, "Nota sobre Whitman" [A Note on
Whitman], in 1947. By this point, having already published *El jardín
de senderos que se bifurcan* (1941) and *Ficciones* (1944) to wide ac-
claim, Borges enjoyed a very different literary status. If Borges's critique in the 1929 North American issue of *La vida literaria* of
the "cheery and global" Whitman barely registered in the broader
Argentine field, now he was speaking from a position of authority.
As the first Spanish-language translator of Faulkner and the most
visible Argentine reviewer of contemporary US fiction arriving in
Argentina from the North, Borges had consolidated his reputation as
an expert on North American literature. Nevertheless, a close reading of the essay suggests that Frank's vision of Whitman as the

American poet of experience continued to rankle Borges all these years later.

After repeating verbatim his own lines from 1932 about the critical problem of conflating the protagonist Whitman with the authorial Whitman, Borges expands in "A Note on Whitman" upon his earlier statement:

> Let's imagine that a biography of Ulysses...indicated that he never left Ithaca. The disappointment, happily hypothetical, that this book would cause is one that all biographies of Whitman cause. To go from the paradisiacal world of his verses to the insipid chronicle of his days is a sad transition. Paradoxically, this inevitable sadness is exacerbated when the biographer attempts to hide the fact that there are two Whitmans: the "friendly and eloquent savage" of *Leaves of Grass* and the poor literary man who invented the book. One never went to California or to Platte Canyon; the other improvised an apostrophe in the latter place ('Spirit that Formed This Scene') and was a miner in the former ('Starting from Paumanok,' I). One, in 1859, was in New York; the other, on December 2nd of that same year, attended the execution of John Brown in Virginia ('Year of Meteors'). One was born on Long Island; the other as well ('Starting from Paumanok') but also in a southern state ('Longing for Home'). One was chaste, reserved, and even taciturn; the other was effusive and orgiastic. To multiply these dissonances is easy; more important is to understand that the happy vagabond presented in the lines of *Leaves of Grass* would have been incapable of writing them.[55]

At first glance, Borges seems to be merely pointing out the biographical fallacy that lies at the heart of Frank's reading: the failure to differentiate between author and speaker, between the limited author Walt Whitman behind "Song of Myself" and the literary character "Walt Whitman" who brazenly proclaims his universality. Borges, however, does not seem particularly keen on suppressing speculation about intentionality or biographical details or limiting his analysis to the "poems themselves." In fact, his purpose in the passage is to propose a theory of inverse correlation between literary invention and life experience. By the end of this paragraph we realize that the real Whitman has gone nowhere: his experience is circumscribed to an area only slightly larger than that of Ulysses's Ithaka, namely the five boroughs of New York City and Long Island. It turns out that Whitman, the poet of America, has never left home.[56]

After several winding passages and translations of Whitman's poems, "A Note on Whitman" culminates by revealing the true inspiration for Whitman's poetry: his *reading*. Borges writes: "Walt Whitman, the man, was the editor of the Brooklyn Eagle, and read his fundamental ideas in the pages of Emerson, Hegel, and Volney; Walt Whitman, the poetic character, extracted them from his contact with America, illustrated by imaginary experiences in the bedchambers [*alcobas*] of New Orleans and the battlefields of Georgia."[57] Here we find not only the centerpiece of Borges's polemic against Frank and the US literature of experience, but the final reversal of his own early flirtation with a Whitmanesque experiential aesthetics. The contrast with Frank's portrait of Whitman as the poet of experience could not be starker. According to Borges, the real Whitman comes into "contact with America" by reading philosophy and editing a daily newspaper, not by incarnating its geography. The "irregular reader" of Frank's 1929 lecture has morphed into a bibliophile.

As scholars informed by the insights of poststructuralism, we might be inclined to side with Borges in his efforts to recuperate the readerly Whitman. But when we examine the passage more closely, it becomes apparent that Borges's portrait of the US poet is no less constructed—and no less exaggerated—than Frank's. His dismissal of Whitman's "imaginary" experiences in a "bedroom" in New Orleans is understandable enough. By long-standing tradition, Whitman's biographers had referred to the poet's supposed love affair with a Creole woman in New Orleans in the early 1850s; this apocryphal story, likely derived from an overly literal reading of a line in Whitman's "Once I Passed through a Populous City" that speaks of a woman "who detain'd me for love of me," was deployed to alleviate early twentieth-century anxieties about the homoerotic content of many of Whitman's poems.[58] Frank recounts the anecdote in his 1929 lecture, claiming to have heard it from the lips of an old man who knew Whitman and could swear to its accuracy. Moreover, Frank mentions the affair as evidence that Whitman had mingled (literally) with the "Latin" population in the United States: "What fertile seed of the Latin tradition did she implant in the misty, generous and prophetic Nordic chaos that existed in the soul of the young Whitman?"[59] For Frank, the story works to highlight how Whitman's appetite for experience and inclination toward Latin culture prefigured his own journey to Latin America. That Borges's refutation almost directly echoes Frank's words at the end of his 1929 lecture ("I want to imagine them together, in some secret bedchamber [alcoba] in New Orleans's Vieux Carré") makes it even more pointed.[60] By characterizing these experiences of Whitman's as "imaginary," Borges effectively undercuts Frank's experiential account of Whitman in his lectures and also, by extension, his self-presentation as a literary experiencer.

But Borges's equally casual dismissal of Whitman's imaginary "experience" on the battlefields of Georgia is less convincing. Here Borges presumably alludes to the war poems in Whitman's 1865 collection *Drum-Taps* that relate important Civil War battles and their aftermath through the eyes of the Union soldiers who fought in them.[61] While Whitman did not participate in the Civil War as a combat soldier, he did in fact witness its action while working as a caretaker in several hospitals around the Washington, D.C. area in late 1862. Whitman's battlefield poems were not all culled from his newspaper work; many of them drew on the war stories of injured soldiers to whom he tended during the more than two years he spent in sickrooms, hospitals, and battle camps. In the section of *Specimen Days* titled "Soldiers and Talks," for instance, Whitman tells of a soldier who "narrates to me the fights, the marches, the strange, quick changes of [the] eventful campaign [of McClellan], and gives glimpses of many things untold in any official reports or books or journals.... The vocal play and significance moves one more than books.... I now doubt whether one can get a fair idea of what this war practically is, or what genuine America is, and her character, without some such experience as this I am having."[62] In this case, Borges's insinuation that Whitman never really left New York belies one of the central—and verifiable—events in the poet's life.

In pinpointing where Whitman's biography departs from his first-person utterances in *Drum-Taps*, Borges engages in shrewd textual exegesis, fleshing out the inherent contradictions of Whitman's texts. But when he classifies Whitman, a few lines later, as one of "those who attribute a doctrine to vital experiences and not to a certain library or tome,"[63] he hardly adheres to an objective critical method. It is one thing for Borges to decouple, in Eliot's words, the "man who suffers and the mind that creates," and quite another for him to *deny* Whitman his eyewitness experience as a nurse in D.C.—that is, to suggest that the poet from Long Island was, in Hemingway's words, "faking it," reading and writing about the war from the comfort of home. In this sense, Frank and Borges come to occupy two untenable extremes in interpreting Whitman: while Frank wants to attribute all of Whitman's poems to his experiences, Borges refuses to countenance the idea that Whitman could have had *any* experience worth writing about. When Borges celebrates Whitman's ability to pawn off his readings as "vital experiences"—the essay's last line claims that Whitman's "victory" was as "vast and almost inhuman" as his efforts (267)—he implicitly calls into question not only the value of experience for writing but the value of experience as such. If literature always trumps life, why would anyone want to "have an experience" at all?

The fact is that the "poor literary man" confined to his native city in "A Note on Whitman" bears a much stronger resemblance to Borges than to the real-life Whitman. Accounts of Borges's cosmopolitan journeys in his later years—to the United States, to Europe, and to Japan—have largely obscured the fact that after returning from Europe to Buenos Aires for the second time, in 1924, Borges did not leave Argentina again (except for a few jaunts to his beloved Uruguay) until 1961, when he went to the United States as a college lecturer. The Borges who wrote on Whitman in 1947 had not yet set foot on North American soil. Like Glusberg, Borges had come to US culture from a distance. His belief that Whitman's ability to poetize his readings as if they were experiences was a virtue rather than a vice—"este procedimiento…no importa falsedad" ["this technique…does not imply falsification"] (266)—takes on added significance when we realize that all of the essays and stories Borges wrote in and about the United States until the 1960s concerned a place that he had literally never experienced.

Eliot may have had the experience but missed the meaning, but at least he *had* the experience; Borges's dilemma in the 1930s and 1940s was how to legitimate his own writings on the United States without having actually visited the country. Rather than formulate a cultural program of resistance, as Rodó had done in *Ariel*, his strategy was to question the very conceptual paradigm of the artist as experiencer that dominated the US literary field in the interwar period. Having flirted with *arielismo* at various points in the 1920s, the Borges of the 1930s began to challenge the aesthetic doctrine of "write what you know" on the level of the aesthetic itself. Instead of participating in a geopolitical rivalry, he offered a paradigm shift.

Write What You Don't Know

Borges's aesthetics of the 1930s have often been studied as a reaction to nineteenth-century psychological realism, Argentine nationalism, Romantic notions of originality and genius, and Eurocentric approaches to the canon. But to the best of my knowledge, there has no been no attempt to study in depth Borges's subversion of the US aesthetic of "writing what you know." Lois Parkinson Zamora and Silvia Spitta argue persuasively that in his essay "Nathaniel Hawthorne" and in *An Introduction to American Literature*, Borges inverts the typical identification of US fiction with realism by referring to an "oneiric" North American literary tradition that "tends more toward invention than transcription, more toward creation than observation."[64] I would add that Borges's hermeneutic inversion is not simply a critical observation but part of a thoroughgoing aesthetic critique of the US literature of experience. Here I am talking not only of Borges's well-known preference for the armchair detective novels of the British tradition over the "worldly" genre of Dashiell Hammett and Raymond Chandler's hard-boilers, nor of his belief, as he put it in 1941, that "the naïve fear of not being sufficiently hardboiled...is one of the most visible and least pleasing signs of North American literature today."[65] I am also referring to his more explicit critiques of the aesthetics of experience among US writers, such as his comments on Ernest Hemingway from *An Introduction to American Literature*: "[Hemingway] was a war correspondent in the Near East and in Spain and a lion hunter in Africa. These varied experiences are reflected in his work. He did not seek out such experiences for literary purposes; they interested him deeply....Overcome by his inability to go on writing, and suffering from insanity, he killed himself in 1961. It grieved him to have devoted his life to physical adventures rather than the pure and simple exercise of the intelligence."[66] This is, I would argue, not merely a criticism of Hemingway's writing style; it is a criticism of his lifestyle—or, better yet, of the way his lifestyle inevitably *becomes* his writing style.

Similar critiques of the US literature of experience abound in Borges's writings of the 1930s and 1940s, where he also availed himself of every opportunity to deconstruct the kind of experiential reading Frank had performed on Whitman. Thus, in an introduction to Bret Harte's stories about the California Gold Rush that provides the epigraph to this chapter, Borges claims that "[t]hose who accuse

[Harte] of not having strictly been a miner forget that if he had been one perhaps he wouldn't have been a writer, or would have preferred other topics, since very familiar material is not usually that stimulating."[67] And in an essay on William James, Borges suggests that James's pragmatist belief that the "elemental substance of what we call the universe is experience" is "closer to idealism than realism."[68] US literature and philosophy offered Borges a seemingly endless supply of theories of experience to critically explore, expand, and explode.

Borges's critique of the literature of experience galvanized both his emerging aesthetic creed and his signature literary strategies. It surfaced in his arguments about the nineteenth-century Argentine tradition of *gauchesca* poetry, which he claimed derived from a group of Europeanized neoclassical writers simulating the oral poetry of the gauchos (*payadores*), rather than from the gauchos themselves. It appeared in his self-constructed origin myth about his own initiation into literature: "For years I have repeated that I grew up in Palermo. I know now that this was mere literary ostentation; the truth is that I grew up on the other side of a large spiked fence, in a house with a garden and the library of my father and my grandparents."[69] And it can be traced in his satirical description of Pierre Menard's "initial method" for composing *Don Quixote*: "To know Spanish well, recuperate the Catholic faith, make war against the Moors and the Turks...to *be* Miguel Cervantes."[70] Menard, that most famous of Borgesian readers, rejects the experiential method not simply because it is *literally* "impossible," but also because it is *culturally* unremarkable: "To be, in some way, Cervantes and to arrive at the Quixote seemed to him less arduous—and therefore less interesting—than to continue being Pierre Menard and arrive at the Quixote through the experiences of Pierre Menard."[71] In a gesture that should be familiar to us at this point, Borges's narrator insists that Menard's version of *Don Quixote* is "infinitely richer" than Cervantes's, precisely because it was written at a distance from Cervantes's own experiences.

Perhaps most significantly, Borges's interpretive battle over Whitman helped motivate his portrayal of US and Hispanic literary figures in his poetry and fiction. The paired sonnets "Emerson" and "Lectores" ["Readers"], collected in Borges's volume *El otro, el mismo* (1964), exemplify this strategy. As Carlos Cortínez has argued, these sonnets establish a contrast between "American" and "Spanish" cultural archetypes in their very first lines, juxtaposing the "tall

American gentleman" (Emerson) with the "sallow, dry-face hidalgo" (Don Quixote).[72] What I would stress is that this contrast instantiates the divide between the US literature of experience and the Latin American literature of the reader in its most paradigmatic form. Whereas Borges's Emerson performs the fundamental gesture of the US literature of experience (he "closes Montaigne's book and goes out / In search of a pleasure worth no less: / The evening exalted by the plains"), his Don Quijote inaugurates the literature of the reader: "It is conjectured of that hidalgo... Perpetually on the cusp of adventure / That he never left his library."[73] Crucially, Borges locates himself in the tradition of Don Quixote. Indeed, as "Lectores" shifts from the third to the first person, the poem turns from an image of Don Quixote inventing his adventures through reading to an image of the young Borges turning the pages of *Don Quixote* and becoming a reader through mimetic desire: "I know that there is something immortal and essential that I have buried in that library of the past / in which I read the story of the hidalgo" [Sé que hay algo / inmortal y esencial que he sepultado / en esa biblioteca del pasado/en que leí la historia del hidalgo] (1.287). The couplet completes this identification, as "The boy [i.e., Borges himself] turns the light pages / and gravely dreams of vague things he doesn't know" [Las lentas hojas vuelve un niño y grave / sueña con vagas cosas que no sabe] (1.287). The poem's conclusion not only inscribes Borges within the modern tradition of the writer-as-reader; it also captures his earliest act of using books to imagine beyond his own experience, his earliest yearnings to write what he doesn't know. It would be hard to overestimate the degree to which this construction of Borges as a compulsive reader who shied away from experience transformed the figure of the author in Argentina and in the broader Latin American literary field.

In any case, we are now in a better position to understand the words that conclude Borges's 1935 prologue to the *Universal History of Infamy*: "Reading... is an activity subsequent to [posterior a] writing: more resigned, more civil, more intellectual."[74] To define oneself as a reader means more than giving priority to one type of intellectual activity; it also entails a mode of constructing the self. This is a lesson that many Latin American writers have taken profoundly to heart, from Manuel Puig in his "readings" of US cinema in *El beso de la mujer araña* [*The Kiss of the Spider Woman*, 1976] to Roberto Bolaño in his reading of African American detective fiction in

"The Part about Fate" in *2666* (2004) to the Argentine novelist
Reinaldo Laddaga's little-known *Tres vidas secretas* [Three Secret
Lives, 2008], which weaves together biographies of Walt Disney,
John D. Rockefeller, and Osama Bin Laden (!) to portray the disso-
nances and contradictions of contemporary US society and life.
With all these writers, the key to literary activity seems to lie in the
double meaning of that quintessentially Borgesian word "subsequent," *posterior*. As Piglia writes in the epilogue to *El último lector*,
citing Wittgenstein: "'In the race of philosophy, the one who wins
is...the one who reaches the finish line last'...The last reader responds implicitly to that program."[75] To write as a reader is not only
to come after a writer of experience with a creative (mis)reading. For
many Latin American writers, enmeshed in a hemispheric debate
whose tone has increasingly been set by the North's rhetoric of the
"American experience," it has also represented their best chance at
having the last word.

Uncommon Grounds

THE REPRESENTATION OF HISTORY IN *ABSALOM, ABSALOM!*, *ONE HUNDRED YEARS OF SOLITUDE*, AND *SONG OF SOLOMON*

They were so different.... One well read but ill traveled.
The other had read only a geography book, but had
been from one end of the country to another.
—TONI MORRISON, *Song of Solomon*

Like many foundational texts of hemispheric literary study, Lois Parkinson Zamora's *The Usable Past: The Imagination of History in Recent Fiction of the Americas* (1997) epitomizes what I have described as the "common grounds" approach to the field. In the book's introduction, Zamora states that her project is "to extend the territory of comparative literary inquiry from its original national parameters in Europe to hemispheric ones in the Americas," excavating a "shared condition" that cuts across the seemingly disparate literary histories of the two Americas.[1] *The Usable Past* identifies this underlying condition as an "anxiety of origins" (5), a peculiarly "American" angst about what Hegel notoriously postulated as the New World's lack of historical consciousness. Drawing on American critics Van Wyck Brooks and Harold Bloom and Latin American writer-theorists Jorge Luis Borges and Carlos Fuentes, as well as György Lukács's seminal study of the historical novel, Zamora makes the hemispheric "American historical imagination" her book's "overarching metaphor" (x). *The Usable Past* convincingly demonstrates that nineteenth- and twentieth-century texts from both the United States and Latin America challenged prevailing notions of the New World as the land of the future by imagining complex and heterogeneous hemispheric pasts. But even while surveying the historical imagination from New

England to Buenos Aires in search of "recognizably American features" (5), the book registers a series of fault lines and fissures. Citing
one of Fuentes's many programmatic contrasts between US and Latin
American culture, Zamora suggests that contiguity does not always
imply continuity. Indeed, she goes so far as to say that the United
States and Latin America have different "conceptions and traditions
of historical process" (19). What from the vantage point of the book's
most panoramic vistas appears to be the shared topography of US
and Latin American literature reveals itself, upon closer inspection,
as a hemisphere divided.

    The Usable Past remains the most insightful study of US and Latin
American historical fiction we have, and by no means do I intend
simply to deconstruct its rhetoric. I begin with Zamora's text, rather,
by way of exemplifying how even those studies in hemispheric literature that establish a comparative framework often manifest an impulse to contrast. The problem it prompts us to formulate is whether
(and when) to subsume ostensible differences across the hemisphere
into broader commonalities. Despite being framed by the caveat that
the United States and Latin America have "different philosophical
lineages and, particularly in the twentieth century, a different historiographic heritage" (19), Zamora's distinctions ultimately resolve
themselves, in *The Usable Past*, into a shared "American" antagonism to
European historical paradigms. Compelled though I am by Zamora's
claim that modern US and Latin American writers have been similarly plagued by anxieties over the "New World's uses of Old World
predecessors" (3-4), I will insist here on a greater differentiation
across the North-South hemispheric divide. If the divergent histories
of the United States and Latin America have caused them to differ in
their historiographic, philosophical, and cultural traditions—as I have
myself contended in chapter 1—it stands to reason that their aesthetic
means for representing history will differ also. Here I adopt what I
take to be the fundamental premise of Lukács's *The Historical Novel*,
namely, that a text's formal means for construing the past are inextri-
cably linked to the historical forces—and the historical paradigms—
that have produced it.[2] To take seriously Lukács's insight about the
relationship between history and the novel, as well as Zamora's com-
plementary assertion that a literary work is a "historical event conditioned by historical circumstances and also conditioning them" (x),
requires us to pursue the distinct hemispheric historical paradigms
within US and Latin American literary texts.

In my first two chapters, I traced the emergence of the US literature of experience and the Latin American literature of the reader
and assessed their impact on hemispheric literary relations from the
early nineteenth to the late twentieth centuries. The present chapter,
by contrast, demonstrates how the divergent histories of the US literature of experience and the Latin American literature of the reader
are recoded in the formal processes of representing history in twentieth-century US and Latin American novels. The three novels I study
here, William Faulkner's *Absalom, Absalom!* (1936), Gabriel García
Márquez's *Cien años de soledad* [*One Hundred Years of Solitude*,
1967], and Toni Morrison's *Song of Solomon* (1977), have been chosen
both for their pattern of influence (Faulkner on García Márquez and
Morrison, García Márquez on Morrison) and their canonicity (all
three writers are Nobel Prize winners). Furthermore, all three address similar questions about the uses of history. The literary bor-
rowings and structural parallels among these writers and novels are
so deeply rooted that they have become something of a critical commonplace in hemispheric and inter-American studies. I return to
these texts, though, not to point to their similarities. Rather, I suggest that we can detect, in the transformation of each precursor novel
by its successor, the distinct gravitational pulls of the US and Latin
American literary fields.

Absalom, Absalom!, *One Hundred Years of Solitude*, and *Song of
Solomon* share formal characteristics at a number of levels. All are
multigenerational novels that revolve around the foundation and
collapse of a family line: the Sutpens, the Buendías, and the Deads.
All three display similar thematic topoi, including incest, twisted genealogies, and alternative temporalities that transcend or confound
what the narrator of *One Hundred Years of Solitude* refers to as the
"order" of "conventional time."[3] The use of "everyday" supernatural-
ism in *One Hundred Years of Solitude* and *Song of Solomon* has led
scholars to link them under the category of magical realism, a literary strain that finds an important (though obviously not exclusive)
precursor in Faulknerian US southern gothic. Perhaps most crucially, all three novels inscribe the personal and family histories they
depict within the *longue durée* of the history of the Americas. They
rehearse narratives of defeat that each author connects, in one way or
another, to US economic hegemony and the rise of industrial capitalism across the Americas. The fall of the Sutpen family functions in
part as a microhistory of the slaveholding US South's destruction in

the American Civil War and the racial tensions of the post-Reconstruction era; the deterioration of the Buendía line coincides with the increasing (North) Americanization of Colombia in the early twentieth century; and "Milkman" Dead's rejection of his family's bourgeois assimilationist tendencies in *Song of Solomon* alludes to tensions within the African American middle class from the beginning of the Great Migration to the end of the civil rights movement. In their attention to broad historical patterns in the Americas as well as in their stylistic similarities and intertextual relationships, *Absalom, Absalom!*, *One Hundred Years of Solitude*, and *Song of Solomon* readily lend themselves to hemispheric analysis.

When this analysis takes the form of a comparative reading, however, significant differences emerge. Where the American works present us with experiential models of transmitting knowledge from generation to generation, a recurring motif in García Márquez's Latin American work makes reading fundamental to knowing the past. This difference is all the more striking given that the main characters in all three novels are obsessed with the recuperation of history, a practice traditionally associated with *both* the investigation of eyewitness testimony and the patient study of written documents. To elucidate the divergence in how the texts represent history and the transmission of knowledge, I concentrate on two characters in each novel: Thomas Sutpen and Quentin Compson in *Absalom, Absalom!*, José Arcadio Buendía and Aureliano Babilonia in *One Hundred Years of Solitude*, and "Milkman" and Pilate Dead in *Song of Solomon*. Assuming a certain familiarity with the basic plot lines of these canonical texts, my interpretation will focus on tracking the migration of formal structures, including the treatment of character, *across* literary fields. Far from obscuring the workings of national and regional cultural systems, this mode of analysis will help delineate those systems' structures in ways that an immanent reading of US or Latin American literature cannot.

The Compson Experience of History

Absalom, Absalom! (1936) begins with a scene of initiation that foregrounds the basic principle of the US literature of experience: knowledge passes most effectively from person to person—and from generation to generation—through physical contact or close proximity, a witnessing with the eye, the ear, even the nose. The novel's opening chapter ends with Thomas Sutpen, the patriarch of the Sutpen family line, forcefully subduing one of his French Caribbean slaves in hand-to-hand combat in front of his children. On one level, this brutal display serves to introduce a central dynamic of the rest of the novel's plot: the ruthlessness of Sutpen's "instinctive will" that propels both his family's spectacular rise and its ultimate decimation.[4] Yet the scene's disturbing gravity depends equally on the affective response the fight provokes in all those present to witness it. Sutpen's purpose in staging this combat—as his wife, Ellen, well understands—is to induct his children and slaves into the social structures of the southern United States, forcing them to experience at firsthand its vicious racializing processes. Sutpen's son Henry emerges from the crowd "screaming and vomiting," and later breaks down in tears (21). But when he eventually kills his part-black brother Charles Bon, we come to see his earlier visceral reaction as a sign that he had taken the lesson of the South's "absolute caste system" to heart, mind, and stomach (276).

So indelibly does the story of Sutpen's fight sear itself into the collective imagination that Quentin Compson, who hears it from Rosa Coldfield at a third remove, responds as if he had actually been there. Indeed, Faulkner's narrative even insinuates that a material trace of the Sutpen incident really does linger in the town of Jefferson, Mississippi: a kind of experiential residue still palpable more than three quarters of a century later. When the second chapter commences amidst the summer of wisteria, Quentin sits "listening" and "hearing" the story of Sutpen, immersing himself in the effusions of a local past that he "already knew, since he had been born in and still breathed the same air in which the church bells had rung on that Sunday morning in 1833" (23). Quentin's knowledge of the fight seems to follow in an unbroken progression from Sutpen's sweaty torso to Henry's frantic screams to Rosa Coldfield's voice, only to be gathered up in the very air Quentin inhales in the summer of 1909. It is an unforgettable contact high, one that will last him the entire novel.

Almost counterintuitively, Quentin Compson's role as regional historian in *Absalom, Absalom!* comes to be defined by this experiential and initiatory mode of knowledge transmission. Beginning with his earwitnessing of Rosa Coldfield's voice, his eyewitnessing of Sutpen's Hundred, and his wisteria-aided olfactory intake of the past, Quentin will soak up as much knowledge of the Sutpen legacy as he can. Drawn to the embodied re-creation of the past, he maintains a distance from the textual archive that might help him better to understand it. Many scholars have focused on Quentin's various modes of recuperating history through acts of narration: by conjuring up ghosts, parsing out family genealogies, following suppressed details, and even inventing motives where existing explanations seem not to cohere.[5] Yet Quentin's sociohistorical reconstructions are just as noteworthy for the methods they neglect as for those they employ. It is remarkable that a character so obsessed with history reads so little of it. Quentin's antibookish inclination is all the more strange in that he makes his greatest effort at retracing the Sutpen line while a student at Harvard University, the very symbol of American knowledge production. In the titillating cold of his campus room, Quentin talks, listens, imagines, and projects—but, as far as we know, he never studies. Even the primary text-within-a-text in the second half of the novel, the letter Mr. Compson mails to Quentin announcing the death of Rosa Coldfield, is freighted with the experiential remainder of Mississippi: the "odor" and "scent" carried "over the long iron New England snow and into Quentin's sitting-room at Harvard" (23). It is a "letter bringing with it that very September evening itself" (142). No less significantly, Quentin's visual and olfactory techniques to (re)produce the presence of the South in the North are exercised against the background of a significant mise-en-scène. For the duration of the last four chapters, a school textbook lies on the sitting-room table, "open" but not functionally available, covered by the letter that Quentin insists on treating less as a linguistic medium than a living thing. He places the letter "at such an angle that he could not possibly have read it" (176) and imagines that by unleashing the envelope's contents "his father's hand could lie on [the] strange lamplit table in Cambridge" (141). Of course, Quentin and Shreve *do* ultimately read the letter. Yet the narrative repeatedly turns on Quentin's attempt to naturalize this activity, both by literalizing the metaphor of "handing down" a tradition (his father's *hand*-writing appears to come to life in his room) and by situating these humanly produced ephemera at the opposite end of the knowledge scale from the more mechanistically (re)produced medium of the book. This desire to substitute the sensory for the scholarly culminates in the memorable moment when Quentin and Shreve's "dreamy and heatless alcove of what we call the best of thought" becomes "filled with violent and unratiocinative djinns and demons" (208). Into the midst of what might have become a campus novel, the experiential lifeworld of Mississippi intrudes.

Although the series of letters that appear throughout *Absalom, Absalom!* have often been interpreted along deconstructive lines as evidence of the textual inscription of the past upon the present, their inclusion serves mainly to highlight Quentin's attempt to access history by alternately circumventing and suppressing the mediating distance implied in the act of reading.[6] In this regard, it is crucial to remember that Quentin's discovery of the most guarded secret of the Sutpen family, Bon's blackness, only becomes possible once he has visited Sutpen's Hundred and received the secret from the lips of the dying Henry. In a novel full of insinuations and ambiguities, Quentin's need for actual testimony about the secret of the divided house is relatively unambiguous: "But I must see too now. I will have to. Maybe I shall be sorry tomorrow, but I must see" (296). His capacity for recognizing the "flaw" in Sutpen's dynastic "design" (Bon to Henry: "So it's the miscegenation, not the incest, which you cant bear" [285]) depends on the novel's deployment of a complex hierarchy of representational modes, according to which immediate sense perception is privileged over heard speech, heard speech over handwritten letters, and handwritten letters over the codified form of the book so conspicuously absent from Quentin's repertoire. Quentin's interior monologue in the first of the "Harvard chapters," during which he recalls his conversations with his father over the Sutpen legacy, spells out this hierarchy quite clearly: "But you were not listening [to Mr. Compson], because you knew it all already, had learned, absorbed it already without the medium of speech somehow from having been born and living beside it, with it, as children will do: so that what your father was saying did not tell you anything so much as it struck, word by word, the resonant strings of remembering" (172). This affirmation of the ultimate power of learning through direct experience leads to an almost Rousseauian description of Quentin's acquisition of knowledge about Sutpen's Hundred, a terrain he had begun mentally mapping as early as his "rambling expeditions of boyhood whose aim was more than the mere hunting of game" (172). Since Quentin has "been here before," he doesn't listen to his father—not because he doesn't care, but simply because he "[doesn't] have to" (173). Quentin maintains this experiential bias even when he is, as often, forced to rely on less reliable (i.e., less direct) modes of knowledge. His desire for immediacy, whatever his means for achieving it, never wanes.

Walter Benn Michaels has influentially argued that US modernist novels, and Faulkner's works in particular, are committed to the "linguistic fantasy" of "making words into things" and the persistent "effort to replace arbitrary or social relations with natural ones."[7] And it is true that many of the characters in *Absalom, Absalom!* are obsessed with the belief that peeling away the layers of social and textual convention will lead them closer to unmediated truth. Yet Quentin's mistrust of mediation does not point primarily to the nativist obsession with racial and cultural difference that Michaels locates at the core of interwar American literature. After all, Quentin is not biologically related to the Sutpens, and, though (Thomas) Sutpen certainly adheres to a "blood is blood" logic, Quentin's project clearly differs from the foundational figure's dynastic design. Quentin can't help but learn *everything* about the Sutpens, including the family secret of miscegenation, and stakes his entire existence on absorbing the full impact of the South's racial and cultural polarities, in a manner beyond good and evil, love and hate ("I don't hate [the South]! I don't hate it!" [303]). Indeed, although Quentin never renders the Sutpen saga into literature, he nevertheless consistently approaches it aesthetically—"aesthetically," that is, in the word's etymological meaning of being *felt* by the senses. Although Quentin disregards Rosa Coldfield's plea in the first chapter that he "write" her story and "submit it to the magazines" (5), he does not shy away from the task of representation. He redefines it. Rather than devote himself to the formal composition of the story so as to "enter into the literary profession as so many Southern gentlemen and gentlewomen too are doing now" (5), Quentin will piece together the narrative of Sutpen and his children in order to relive it. Just as Sutpen had journeyed to Haiti to "make sure" that the rags-to-riches tales of the West Indies were not empty signifiers, resolving "to take any method that came to my hand" to test their validity (196), so too will Quentin obstinately pursue the totality of the southern socioscape beyond the traditional modalities of historical and literary representation. By the time the final chapter of Sutpen's story (and the novel itself) circles back to the opening scenes, Quentin has fully tuned his corporeal senses. Despite being half a country away from Yoknapatawpha, "he could *taste* and *feel* the dust of that breathless (rather, furnace-breathed) Mississippi September night....He could *smell* the horse; he could *hear* the dry plaint of the light wheels in the weightless permeant dust and he seemed to *feel* the dust itself move sluggish and dry across his sweating flesh" (290, emphasis mine). Less *artiste manqué* than committed experiencer, Quentin refigures the representation of history and place as a form of corporeal practice.

Much recent scholarship in visual culture, sound studies, and affect theory has pointed to the depth and variety of Faulkner's exploration of the senses.[8] Yet it is important to keep in mind that the senses in his works tend more toward combination than separation. From Benjy's synesthesia in *The Sound and the Fury* (1929) to Quentin's conflation of the visual, tactile, olfactory, and aural in *Absalom, Absalom!*, these modes of attention often work in tandem to determine characters' engagement with their lifeworld. It is thus no surprise that Faulkner's most iconic statement about his own creative process repurposes these traits as an authorial strategy for capturing local, regional, and national place. Framed as the spoken advice of his erstwhile mentor Sherwood Anderson, who encouraged him to draw his source materials from his "little patch up there in Mississippi," Faulkner's creed suggests that US writers define themselves through repeated acts of experiential immersion: "All America asks is to look at it and listen to it and understand it if you can. Only the understanding aint important either: the important thing is to believe in it even if you don't understand it, and then try to tell it, put it down. It wont ever be quite right, but there is always next time; there's always more ink and paper, and something else to try to understand and tell."[9] The American literary tradition, in other words, resides not in a body of texts but in how the situated body of the author absorbs, transmutes, and transcribes the history and topography of region and country.

The Buendía Family Library

The extent to which Faulknerian narrative, and *Absalom, Absalom!* in particular, privileges this experiential mode of knowledge transmission and sentimental education becomes clearer when we juxtapose the novel with García Márquez's *One Hundred Years of Solitude*. I begin with the observation, at this point well established in comparative studies of the Americas, that *One Hundred Years of Solitude* patterns many of its key moments and characters on *Absalom, Absalom!* As Zamora has shown, the sheer number of structural similarities in the two novels is striking: beginning with the figure of a

New World settler who believes the "future can be molded to his historical design" (Sutpen; José Arcadio Buendía), both novels work through the generational cycles of civil war and economic exploitation, culminating in an apocalyptic ending in which a solitary character (Quentin Compson; Aureliano Babilonia) remains to survey the history of foundation, ascent, decline, and fall.[10] Yet these very similarities make *One Hundred Years of Solitude*'s formal and thematic departures all the more meaningful. Particularly significant, I suggest, are those scenes where García Márquez reformulates the Faulknerian recuperation of history through experience into a model of accessing history through reading.

The first structural transformation of the Faulknerian model occurs near the end of the first chapter of *One Hundred Years of Solitude*. At almost the exact same point in the narrative where Thomas Sutpen initiates his children into the US southern lifeworld in *Absalom, Absalom!*, José Arcadio Buendía, the patriarch of the Buendía family and a foundational figure in the Sutpen mold, stages his own initiation rite in the small Caribbean village of Macondo. Convinced by his wife, Úrsula, that he has neglected his sons Aureliano and José Arcadio for too long, José Arcadio Buendía decides to "dedicate his best hours" to their education:

> In the small separate room, where the walls were gradually being covered by strange maps and fabulous drawings, he taught them to read and write and do sums, and he spoke to them about the wonders of the world, not only where his learning had extended, but forcing the limits of their imagination to extremes. It was in that way that the boys ended up learning that in the southern extremes of Africa there were men so intelligent and peaceful that their only pastime was to sit and think, and that it was possible to cross the Aegean Sea on foot by jumping from island to island all the way to the port of Salonika.[11]

As we quickly recognize, this early scene in García Márquez's text inverts the patriarchal teaching model of *Absalom, Absalom!*: while Sutpen "educates" Henry, Judith, and Clytie through a physical display that the children witness at close proximity, José Arcadio Buendía instructs Aureliano and José Arcadio with mediated representations of people and places that couldn't be more distant from Macondo. Indeed, the very language of the passage emphasizes how the contours of the boys' minds expand through the cartography of their readings. He forces their imaginations to an "extreme" degree (*a extremos increíbles*) so that they might reach the furthest extremes of the globe (*el extremo meriodional de África*). These "hallucinatory" bibliographic sessions "remain . . . printed on the memory of the boys" (15) to such a degree that they rise up in Aureliano Buendía's mind right before the moment (he thinks) he is going to die. Even as members of the family begin to leave home to travel, fight wars, and fall in love, this interior room remains a sanctuary for the Buendía clan to read, write, and speculate about the world outside the village.

In *One Hundred Years of Solitude*, reading appears as both a ritual of initiation into historical knowledge (however extravagant this may be) and an activity defining the movement of the Buendía family through history itself. Over the past thirty years, hemispheric scholars have followed the lead of the major boom authors in arguing that Faulkner's uptake by Latin American writers of the mid-to-late twentieth century owed much to the parallel historical trajectories of Latin America and the US South. Observing that the two "regions share a history of dispossession, socio-economic hardship, political and cultural conflict, and the export of resources to support the development of a 'North,'" Deborah Cohn has argued that Latin American writers were drawn to Faulkner less for his stylistic innovations than for his sustained narrative engagement with what economists of the period called the "development of underdevelopment."[12] It is true that *One Hundred Years of Solitude* lends itself to this interpretation at many points, most notably through its depiction of the US banana company's capitalist transformation of Macondo in the early twentieth century, a process that parallels the industrialization of the US South in Yoknapatawpha decades earlier. Yet the thematic concerns of economic subordination and political defeat that *One Hundred Years of Solitude* shares with *Absalom, Absalom!* should not obscure the different social roles that the Sutpens and Buendías play within the respective historical trajectories of the US South and Latin America. While José Arcadio Buendía and Coronel Aureliano Buendía seem at times to resemble Sutpen as resolute "men of action," they bear an even closer likeness to the nineteenth-century Latin American *letrados* whose political impulses were intimately connected to their literary aspirations. In the early stages of the novel, José Arcadio Buendía acts as what Ángel Rama calls a "projector of cities,"[13] using his maps, experiments, and intellectual formation to design the layout of Macondo, "acquir[ing] such authority among the new arrivals that foundations were not laid or walls built without his being consulted."[14] After Coronel Aureliano Buendía assumes the patriarchal mantle and embarks on a long military career, the novel makes a point of punctuating his exploits with periodic returns to the solitude of the library. Having affirmed his literary inclinations during his brief courtship of the young Remedios by composing "verses without a beginning or an end" (160), he continues to compensate for the frustration of his political projects by reading and writing. While convalescing from one of many assassination attempts, Aureliano studies his poetry with an eye to his own development, evoking "through the reading of the verses the decisive moments of his existence" (239). And when, near the end of his life, the coronel is offered a belated homage by the Conservative government for his services to the country, he responds that he is an "artisan" rather than a "national hero" (325). Finally, whereas the Sutpen library appears in *Absalom, Absalom!* as a backdrop for the human drama that occurs within it (for example, on pages 236 and 257), the laboratory-cum-reading room in *One Hundred Years of Solitude* becomes the scene of self-definition for the majority of the characters.

The last chapter of *One Hundred Years of Solitude* establishes a final structural parallel with *Absalom, Absalom!*, this time between Quentin Compson and Aureliano Babilonia, the last of the Buendía line. Just as Quentin reconstructs the history of the Sutpen family from Thomas Sutpen's arrival in Yoknapatawpha County to the burning of Sutpen's Hundred, Aureliano Babilonia retraces the history of the Buendía family from the founding of Macondo to the biblical hurricane that sweeps the town away in the last lines of the novel. But there is an important difference between the two acts. While Quentin primarily sees, hears, imagines, and invents the arc of his narrative, Aureliano Babilonia primarily *reads* about his. The novel famously concludes with Aureliano poring over the history of Macondo in the cryptic language of Melquíades, first decoding the family's story "down to the most trivial details" (415) and eventually arriving at his own fateful destiny. A polyglot reader who shuttles back and forth between the reading room and the only bookstore in town, Aureliano literally acquires an encyclopedic knowledge. After a long stint in the house, "he discovered that he could understand written English and that between parchments he had gone from the first page to the last of the six volumes of the encyclopedia as if it were a novel" (373). It is no coincidence that Aureliano finds the key to all mythologies in the town bookstore, where he meets both an avatar of the author himself (the young literary aficionado "Gabriel Márquez") and a Catalonian bookseller. One might say that what Aureliano learns in the bookstore is precisely how to functionalize his bibliographic imagination. Whereas Quentin envisions himself as the receptacle of the innumerable stories of the South, a "commonwealth" of voices rather than a single entity, Aureliano connects region, family, and self through the various literal and figurative networks of archival knowledge.

Roberto González Echevarría has convincingly argued that the readerly sanctuary in the Buendía house functions as a figurative manifestation of the weight of the "Archive" in the modern Latin American novel. He documents the presence of such "special abode[s] for manuscripts and books" in a range of mid-twentieth-century novels, and observes that the proliferation of printed texts in these novels often coincides with the "existence of an inner historian who reads the texts, interprets and writes them."[15] One major value of González Echevarría's study is that he traces the evolution of the *letrado* from the colonial period to its manifestation as the figure of the "archivist-writer" in Latin American boom fiction.[16] What I have attempted to show here, however, is that *One Hundred Years of Solitude* represents this evolution by restructuring the Faulknerian historical novel. That is to say, it works through a problem internal to the Latin American tradition *at the same time* that it appropriates and transforms a transnational precursor.

Milkman Dead Anxious to Live

Toni Morrison's 1977 novel *Song of Solomon*, published two decades after she wrote a significant portion of her master's thesis on *Absalom, Absalom!* and seven years after the appearance of Gregory Rabassa's English translation of *One Hundred Years of Solitude*, takes up the central theme of Faulkner's and García Márquez's works: the formation of identity through knowledge transmission and subjective access to history. Critics have often pointed to Morrison's use of "magical realism" in *Song of Solomon* as evidence of her aesthetic affinity with García Márquez, yet I will argue here that her novel's representation of history is far closer to Faulkner's. This is not to insist on *Absalom, Absalom!* as *Song of Solomon*'s only major precursor text. Rather, I suggest that a comparative study can show how despite their many differences, both novels shape and are shaped by the US literature of experience.

Song of Solomon centers on the coming of age of Macon "Milkman" Dead, the youngest member of a bourgeois black family in Michigan who undergoes a self-transformation when he visits his "ancestral home" in Virginia in the early 1960s. The novel's two parts neatly divide Milkman's character formation: trapped in part 1 between his parents' assimilationist values and his best friend Guitar's black separatism, in part 2 Milkman rejects both models of African American identity and travels to the US South. Initially pursuing a family treasure through Pennsylvania and across the Mason-Dixon line, Milkman ends up in rural Virginia, where he reconstructs his family history while simultaneously immersing himself in the "backwoods" of the South, awakening his sensorium ("eyes, ears, nose, taste, touch") for the first time.[17] As Madhu Dubey has observed, the scene in the woods of Shalimar symbolizes Milkman's transition from a "textual to an aural mode of communication."[18] And Morrison herself has suggested that Milkman's southward journey marks "the beginning of his ability to connect with the past and perceive the world as alive."[19] For Milkman, the narrative of his family's historical trajectory only begins to make sense once he recreates it firsthand: "it was being there in the place where it happened that made it seem so real" (231).

The catalyst for Milkman's disavowal of his parents' assumptions about blackness and American life comes primarily from two sources: his reconstruction through oral testimony and vernacular culture of the "real history" of his forefathers and his repeated contact with the family pariah, his father's sister Pilate. Early in the novel Milkman's father (also named Macon Dead) links his materialist faith in "owning things" to an a priori belief in literacy and education as the means to black success in America. Grandson to a slave and son of an uneducated farmer, Macon insists that his own father, the first Macon Dead, lost everything because he was illiterate: "Papa couldn't read, couldn't even sign his name. Had a mark he used. They tricked him. He signed something, I don't know what, and they told him they owned his property.... He should have let me teach him. Everything bad that ever happened to him happened because he couldn't read" (53). Milkman's journey in the second part of the novel, however, compels him to reevaluate his father's cultural assumptions. An encounter just north of the Susquehanna with Reverend Cooper, an old family acquaintance, leads him to question his father's view that his grandfather's illiteracy condemned him to a liminal existence, literally unable to make a name for himself. When the Reverend celebrates the first Macon Dead's practical know-how, Milkman's grandfather comes to seem more like the apex than the starting point of the family's line: "Never mind you can't tell one letter from another, never mind you born a slave, never mind you lose your name, never mind your daddy dead, never mind nothing. Here, this here, is what a man can do if he puts his mind to it and his back in it" (235). Milkman recognizes that his grandfather was as archetypal an American farmer as the archetype itself—an incarnation of the "American Adam," as Valerie Smith puts it, whose prodigious planting abilities made him the envy of the entire town.[20] Morrison seems to one-up Faulkner in her description of Milkman's grandfather, who surpasses even Sutpen with his practical prowess: "He came out of nowhere, as ignorant as a hammer and broke as a convict, with nothing but free papers, a Bible [which he never reads, only points to for the purpose of naming], and a pretty black-haired wife, and in one year he'd lease ten acres, the next ten more" (235). At the level of plot, Milkman's exposure to this alternate history of his grandfather reinforces his growing sense of the vitality of his ancestors despite the ravages of slavery and Reconstruction. At a deeper narrative level, the scene serves to sever the link between literacy and productive black culture that Milkman's father had established at the beginning of the novel.

Of course, the Oedipal dispute over family history between Milkman and his father underscores the highly masculinist assumptions about patrilineal inheritance that the transmission of knowledge— whether experiential or otherwise—has often implied in canonical American fiction. Many scholars have focused on gender difference in *Song of Solomon*, an approach that resonates with Morrison's description of the novel as a "stereotypically male narrative" that marked a "radical shift in imagination" in her own work "from a female locus to a male one" (xii). And indeed, the most obvious casualty in the novel is Milkman's cousin-turned-jilted-lover Hagar, who begins to waste away after Milkman gives in to his "appetite for other streets" (162) and flees the domestic comforts of their quasi-conjugal romance. Yet Morrison's exploration of identity formation is not circumscribed by this gendered binary. It is, in fact, Milkman's aunt Pilate who provides the closest contemporary analogue to the vibrant vernacular culture of his ancestors. Pilate increasingly represents for Milkman an alternative to the materialism of his immediate family, and particularly of his mother, Ruth: "They were so different, these two women. One black, the other lemony. One corseted, the other buck naked under her dress. One well read but ill traveled. The other had read only a geography book, but had been from one end of the country to another. One wholly dependent on money for life, the other indifferent to it" (139). Though the passage goes on to suggest that Ruth and Pilate had "profound" similarities, we later find out that Pilate's expansive travels have allowed her to immerse herself in the varieties of black American experience, while Ruth's educated proprieties function as a hard shell, projecting strength but denying the affective connectivity that Milkman seeks. Pilate's use of her geography book, the "only" book she has read, suggests how the novel literalizes the idea of geo-graphy as writing (and reading) place. Seized by restlessness whenever she thinks about setting down roots, "[i]t was as if her geography book had marked her to roam the country, planting her feet in each pink, yellow, blue or green state" (148). Reading does not lead Pilate to the archive, as it does the characters in *One Hundred Years of Solitude*, but rather serves the limited function of directing her toward experiential travel. Perhaps Pilate's most important lesson for Milkman is that the assimilationist cultural strategies of his parents have mistakenly replaced liberty with literacy—where "literacy" designates not only the ability to read, but also one's responsibility for "civilizing" the black community, along the lines Ruth envisioned for Milkman's liberal-arts-educated sister Corinthians.

Song of Solomon's strategies for representing Pilate and Milkman return us to the question of Morrison's relationship to Latin American "magical realism." Susan Willis was one of the first scholars to describe Morrison's narrative method as a "North American variant" of García Márquez's magical realism; more recently, Wendy Faris has treated the two writers as exemplary figures in a "global" tradition of magical realism that uses repressed folk traditions and mythological wisdom to criticize Eurocentric ideas of rationality and progress.[21] These critics are right to identify correspondences between *Song of Solomon* and *One Hundred Years of Solitude*. There are clear parallels in the two novels' recuperation of popular myth—the birth of an incestuous Buendía baby with a pig's tail; Pilate's birth without a navel—and vernacular miracles: the "flying African" in Solomon/Shalimar's escape from slavery and Milkman's final encounter with Guitar; the ascending virgin in Remedio la Bella's sudden rise into the heavens.

Yet it is just as clear that such magical episodes function within the specific cultural and literary histories of the United States and Latin America from which the novels respectively emerge. *Song of Solomon* routes Milkman's discovery of his gift of flight through the history of American and African American cultural topoi relating to movement: the brutal exodus of the Middle Passage during the colonial period; the turn-of-the-century American "invention" of the airplane and the legacy of Charles Lindbergh; the Great Migration of African Americans during the early to mid-twentieth century; and, finally, the return from North to South embodied in Milkman's journey into the past in Virginia. Some of these mythologies—such as the novels' shared interest in the incest taboo—suggest common cultural roots. More often, however, magical realism is deployed to explore the repressed desires within each particular imagined community. For instance, Aureliano Babilonia's uncanny ability in *One Hundred Years of Solitude* to recite information about distant locales, including "the most hidden corners of [Belgium], which Aureliano knew as if he had spent much time there" (382), suggests a fantasy about encyclopedic omniscience associated with *letrado* culture, while Milkman's "flight pattern" alludes to narratives of migration enshrined in both African American culture, and, as I have argued, the US literature of experience. Indeed, it is in Morrison's effort in *Song of Solomon* "to de-domesticate the landscape that had so far been the site of my work. To travel. To fly" that she articulates both a response to and a restructuring of the US literature of experience (xii). Just as García Márquez adopts a Faulknerian structure to work through the contours of the Latin American lettered city, Morrison adopts magical realism to work through the American cultural geography of expansive movement and "flight." Both uses of magical realism entail a critical gesture, *pace* Faris, but these criticisms are lodged against two *different* cultural systems.

Rereading Morrison's *Song of Solomon* as a deep engagement with the US literature of experience also forces us to revise certain assumptions about Morrison's aesthetics that have become influential in American literary analysis over the past twenty years. Walter Benn Michaels has argued that Morrison's "novels of identity" instantiate a multiculturalist tendency in postwar US literature that privileges "events that are experienced and transmitted rather than represented and known."[22] According to Michaels, Morrison's Pulitzer Prize–winning *Beloved* (1987) is the most canonical example of a prevalent postmodernist sleight of hand that converts history into memory. Referring to *Beloved* along with Art Spiegelman's *Maus* (1986) as "historicist" rather than historical works, Michaels suggests that Morrison's novel about the lingering traumas of slavery offers a misleading sense of continuity between past and present: "it redescribes something we have never known as something we have forgotten and thus makes the historical past a part of our own experience" (137). In Michaels's interpretation, the American reading public's relationship to antebellum history becomes relatively akin to Quentin's relationship to the story of Thomas Sutpen, defined by the understandable but ultimately misguided attempt to embody the past as a means of inheriting it. Rehashing a criticism that originated in his analysis of US modernist literature in *Our America*, Michaels complains that Morrison's narrative efforts to build a bridge between late twentieth-century black subjectivity and the history of slavery elides the actual history that produces the condition of blackness in the first place, namely the formations and transformations of global capitalism. In Michaels's final accounting, Morrison is guilty of a series of postmodern fallacies, replacing class with race, economics with identity, and history with memory. Similarly, Kenneth Warren's analysis of the post–Jim Crow literature of "racial self-affirmation" treats Morrison's works as symptomatic of an idea of "redemption" that is "more spiritual than political, more intuitive than deliberative, more mystical than logical."[23] Both Warren and Michaels take issue with what they see as Morrison's evasion of politics proper in the service of a politics of culture.

At a certain level, Warren's and Michaels's readings of Morrison enact a powerful critique of the essentialist underpinnings of post-1945 literary multiculturalism and identity politics. Ironically enough, however, the most glaring oversight in their evaluations of Morrison's textual economy has everything to do with the status of labor, that is, with the actual *work* involved in the activity of "experiencing." Michaels's emphasis in *The Shape of the Signifier* on the ghost in *Beloved* as the narrative vehicle that compels the "transmission of heritage" from Sethe to Denver is telling (151). If the ultimate source of history and knowledge is natural (or even supernatural—in any case, beyond human agency), then the labor power necessary to acquire it becomes, as Michaels implies, insignificant or null. And indeed, there are moments in *Beloved* when the ghost of the murdered child functions as a kind of magical conduit between the traumatic experience of slavery and its "rememory," allowing the young child Denver to relive the past "through" Beloved: "Feeling how it must have felt to her mother. Seeing how it must have looked."[24]

Yet Milkman Dead's trajectory in *Song of Solomon* shows us that Morrison's texts are equally invested in the *cultural work* that experiencing, remembering, and reconstructing such repressed vernacular history implies. John Brenkman has compellingly argued that the novel's turning point occurs when Milkman's search for his family's treasure, the symbol of inherited material wealth, becomes displaced by his active pursuit of his family's genealogy. By reorienting Milkman from capitalized culture to "oral and transitory culture," Brenkman contends, "Morrison challenges the habit of thinking about cultural heritage in terms of monuments and masterworks.... Such a model is acutely inappropriate for the history of a people whose enslavement denied them literacy and whose oppression in the century since Emancipation denied them the material and institutional means of assembling a monumental culture."[25] Building on earlier work on the role of the militant black nationalist group the Seven Days in *Song of Solomon*, Brenkman describes Milkman's metamorphosis as a response to both his father's materialism *and* his best friend Guitar's embrace of black separatism.[26] As a member of the Seven Days, Guitar anticipates certain strains of late 1960s Black Power and the Black Arts Movement, strains that stressed the homogeneity as well as the autonomy of the "black experience." Guitar's expressions of racial essentialism in *Song of Solomon* ("Not people. White people," 155) echo Amiri Baraka's late sixties assertion that "races are like feelings," just as Guitar's tit-for-tat formula for retributive racial justice functions as a literal rendering of Baraka's notorious line that black artists should create "poems that kill."[27] Milkman finds an alternative to this idea of ontological blackness not only by rejecting Guitar's strategy of combatting systemic structural oppression with random acts of violence, but also, and just as importantly, by redirecting his energies toward exploring the histories of the communities that such politico-artistic movements purported to represent. If, as Brenkman suggests in "Politics and Form," the novel's "literary act of recovery" has a "critical edge" because it suggests that the movements of the 1960s failed to connect with the "everyday life-world" (58), Milkman and Pilate bridge this gap by embarking on experiential journeys: immersing themselves in African American vernacular histories and social lifeworlds, while remaining mobile enough to avoid becoming rooted in identitarian positions. In other words, the novel is far more invested in the work of "experiencing" culture and history than it is in a reified notion of the "black experience."

This desire to articulate active and "productive" practices of experiencing motivates both Pilate and Milkman in *Song of Solomon*. Pilate's trajectory is fueled by her desire to pass through many communities of color rather than stay within any single one: "But Pilate did not want a steady job in a town where a lot of colored people lived. All her encounters with Negroes who had established themselves in businesses or trades in those small midwestern towns had been unpleasant.... Besides she wanted to keep moving" (144). The novel strongly correlates Pilate's desire for geographical coverage ("mark[ing] her to roam the country" [148]) with her cultural politics, which compel her to wrestle during her journey with "the problem of trying to decide how she wanted to live and what was valuable to her" (149). Unlike Ruth, whose lack of exposure to the many layers of African American life narrows her conceptions of family, success, and value, Pilate pushes the "boundaries of the elaborately socialized world of black people" and acquires "a deep concern for and about human relationships" (149). Over the course of the novel, Milkman's own cultural politics gradually shift from his parents' embrace of the spirit of capitalism toward Pilate's experiential model. Only after his immersion in the southern lifeworld does he learn to treat the daily practice of Shalimar's inhabitants—the children's recitation of the "song" of Solomon—as a living document encoding the town's past. This moment, when Milkman finally recognizes that "these children were singing a story about his own people" (304), comes after a lifetime of working to understand his family's past and his own place within it. We might say that what Pilate and Milkman both share with Quentin Compson is the belief that the only way to shatter the mythologies of a self-contained identitarian unit—"the South" in *Absalom, Absalom!*; the "socialized world of black people" in *Song of Solomon*—is ceaselessly to test its on-the-ground realities and absorb its multiple (and often contradictory) histories.

Morrison's 1955 Master's thesis emphasizes exactly this pedagogical labor of investigation and communication in Faulkner's novel: "In *Absalom, Absalom!* Faulkner puts Quentin through a thorough learning process and gives him the task of assimilating, under the eyes of an outsider, Shreve, all that he has been exposed to in the South."[28] Morrison's references to the "learning process" and the "task of assimilating" seem much closer to an antifoundational pragmatist understanding of the constitution of subjectivity than to the identity-based position that Michaels has attributed to both Faulkner and Morrison. Extrapolating from her observation on Faulkner, we might say that *Absalom, Absalom!* and *Song of Solomon* both develop a principle central to the US literature of experience: the very activity of experiencing is a form of "full-time" cultural work requiring geographical coverage (moving), immersion in the history and the reality of a lifeworld (looking, listening, smelling), and the capacity to construct a narrative that captures the particularities and complexities of this "exposure" (telling). Although one could argue that this labor is problematic to the extent that it remains attached to certain presuppositions about its object of study (i.e., that something like "the South" or "the black community" actually exists as a historically continuous whole), such heuristics seem neither more nor less problematic than Warren's and Michaels's distinctions between "political" and "cultural" investments. The important point, at any rate, is that we should make a better effort at understanding the aesthetics of experience in these US writers before we assess them normatively.

A few methodological observations can be drawn from this close textual analysis of *Absalom, Absalom!*, *One Hundred Years of Solitude*, and *Song of Solomon*. First, my analysis calls into question critical approaches that too easily conflate Latin American and US literary representations of history. If, as Zamora has argued, writers from across the Americas have been beset by anxieties over how to create a "usable past" in a hemisphere that has traditionally been associated with newness, we must be attentive to differences as well as similarities in their modes of "historical imagining."[29] Second, it suggests that the fetishization of intertextuality and contact within hemispheric and inter-American studies has led scholars to neglect how literary exchange is often mobilized to work out specific problems within an author's literary field. As I have argued through my readings of this trio of texts, twentieth-century US and Latin American authors not only use distinct strategies for representing history; they also revise and revitalize the historical evolution of their own literary traditions. Having spent the first part of this book establishing that the literature of experience and the literature of the reader developed relationally, I will now turn to an analysis of how they structured the internal logics of the US and Latin American literary fields.

PART II

Literary Fields of the Americas

Full Immersion

MODERNIST AESTHETICS AND THE US
LITERATURE OF EXPERIENCE

> *I want first of all to discover for myself what this country is.*
> *Everybody I meet tells me a different story. Nothing is*
> *for me but to wait, and gather my own account.*
> —KATHERINE ANNE PORTER, *"Mexican Daybook,*
> *Notes, Observations, 1920–21"*

In March 1928, shortly before departing from Paris for the United States, Ernest Hemingway sent a letter to Maxwell Perkins, his editor at Scribner's, explaining why he had abandoned the novel he was in the process of writing. "I know very well I could turn books out when they should come out," he told Perkins, only to remark a few lines later: "But I would like to write a really damned good novel—and if the one I have 22 chap[ter]s and 45,000 words of done doesn't go after I get to America I will drop it and put it away and go on with the other one I am writing since two weeks."[1] The decision to set aside the "one I have" in order to expand the "other one" would prove fruitful; the burgeoning narrative eventually became his iconic war novel *A Farewell to Arms* (1929).

Yet Hemingway apparently had equally high aspirations for the aborted manuscript, tentatively entitled "Jimmy Breen"; he even boasted to Perkins that it could become "a sort of modern Tom Jones" (*SL* 273). Like John Dos Passos's later novel *The 42nd Parallel*, the manuscript of "Jimmy Breen" opens with a railway journey that whisks its protagonist from a small midwestern locale into the brave new world of the industrial United States. But at some point Hemingway decided that he could no longer continue with his American novel. Contrary to what we might expect, though, Hemingway did not attribute his writer's block to a problem of inspiration or style, but rather to a lack of experience: "[T]here is a *very very* good chance that I don't know enough to write ["Jimmy Breen"] yet and whatever success I have had has been through writing what I know about.... I should have gone to America two years ago when I planned. I was through with Europe and needed to go to America before I could write the book that happened there" (*SL* 273–4).[2]

Two years before Hemingway sent this letter to Perkins, and half-way around the world, Katherine Anne Porter made a similar statement about the threshold of lived experience she demanded for her own literary fiction. Back in Greenwich Village in 1926 after spending much of the previous five years in Mexico, Porter was composing a draft of a novel she planned to call "Thieves Market," centered on the Zócalo plaza in Mexico City. Writing to the Mexico-based US novelist and journalist Carleton Beals, she insisted that the project hinged on her ability to return to Mexico for a prolonged period of time: "I have precisely three books planned, outlined, partially written, and whether they are ever finished depends on my being in Mexico for several years more."[3] Like Hemingway, Porter ended up scrapping her manuscript, but she continued to stress the value of firsthand literary source material. Already in her essay "Why I Write about Mexico" (1923), she had parried accusations of her "taste for the exotic" by presenting her Mexican writings as the inevitable product of her personal experience: "The artist can do no more than deal with familiar and beloved things, from which he could not, and above all, would not escape.... All the things I write of I have first known, and they are real to me."[4]

Throughout their writings of the 1920s and 1930s, both Hemingway and Porter expressed variations of these anxieties of experience. They argued that the best literature derived from an author's deep familiarity with places and events, and they warned about the dangers of allowing language to become detached from a concrete relationship to feelings and objects. In their respective letters to Perkins and Beals, however, Hemingway and Porter emphasize not only their need to write from experience already acquired, but also their need for *more* experience of a place before continuing to write. Although the two writers' desired itineraries did not coincide—Hemingway wanted to return to the United States to compose his American novel while Porter wanted to leave it to write books about Mexico—they communicate the same fundamental assumption about the writing process. Both Hemingway and Porter suggest that a novel begins with the deliberate effort to expand one's place-based knowledge through in situ immersion. Although their unshakeable belief in the value of "writing what they know"—or what they *will* know—has struck later critics as exaggerated at best, and at worst disingenuous, their methods for pursuing firsthand knowledge in the 1920s and 1930s were essential in establishing the US literature of experience as a practice as well as a cultural discourse.

A second glance at the geographical circuit of these letters—Paris, New York, Mexico City—reveals an obvious corollary to Hemingway's and Porter's experiential aesthetics. As a matter of both principle and practice, writing from experience meant being international. Since it has become something of a commonplace in contemporary modernist scholarship to remark on the internationalism of the interwar moment, I want to stress that Hemingway and Porter rendered their expansive geographical trajectories into literary form in a specific way. Though they set most of their works outside the United States, they cast their works as "American" precisely because they were filtered through the "felt experience" of a US writer. Although in the global twenty-first century this ambition may strike us as anachronistic—and perhaps even undesirable—Porter and Hemingway expended a great deal of energy and craft trying to reconcile their transnational fiction with the growing demand for a national body of American literature. In this regard, it is telling that Porter's line "All the things I write of I have first known," which so closely resembles the MFA slogan "write what you know," was framed as an explanation of why she wrote about Mexico rather than the United States. We tend to associate the injunction to "write what you know" with a *domestic* logic of literary production, as Mark McGurl points out in *The Program Era: Postwar Fiction and the Rise of Creative Writing* (2009), where he traces the phrase to the pragmatist-inflected creative writing programs of the interwar period. But while McGurl makes a persuasive case for the role US institutions played in inculcating the authority of personal experience during the postwar era, his focus on the self-generating "autopoetic" system of the creative writing program glosses over how the very principle of "writing what you know" was forged in broader geopolitical contexts. Indeed, it should be recalled that the midcentury writers and critics who institutionalized interwar modernism in the United States trained their attention primarily on the international works of "expatriate" writers.

Although Hemingway's centrality to this critical tradition goes without saying, Porter's canonicity during the interwar years might need reiterating, given the relative decline of her reputation in the late twentieth century. Her short stories about Mexico, which began to appear in the *Century Magazine* in the early 1920s and were later collected in *Flowering Judas* (1930), earned her a devoted following among the writer-critics who helped to inaugurate the New Criticism—Robert Penn Warren once described her short stories as "unsurpassed in modern fiction."[5] The only woman writer highlighted in Malcolm Cowley's *Exile's Return* (1934), Porter became an important modernist precursor for Josephine Herbst, Tillie Olsen, and Eudora Welty. Mary McCarthy's campus novel *The Groves of Academe* (1951) gives a sense of how influential Porter and her "Mexican book" remained even in the early postwar years: when the average student at progressive Jocelyn College went to find *Flowering Judas* at the library, "he learned from the librarian that all ten copies were out: Mr. Van Tour, his tutor, was giving it in Contemporary Literature, and several of his other tutees were making it their special interest."[6] If, as McGurl rightly affirms, "it would be hard to overestimate the influence of Hemingway on postwar writers,"[7] my contention here will be that the influence of Hemingway—and of Porter—was inextricable from the expatriate settings of their fictional works.

Two arguments structure this chapter. First, in an era in which the United States was rapidly extending its political and economic reach, US fiction writers began to equate expansive global experience with greater literary authority. And second, Latin America increasingly became the privileged site for US writers of experience. From these two primary arguments, a higher-level claim emerges: that this "experiential" strain of fiction about Latin America was essential to the development of American modernism. Thus while part 1 of this book accounts for the dialectical relationship between the US literature of experience and the Latin American literature of the reader, this chapter revisits the evolution of the literature of experience as a major episode in US literary modernism itself.

As I have already suggested, the rise to dominance of the US literature of experience paralleled similar developments in other cultural fields, such as Dewey's elaboration of a pragmatist theory of art. But whereas Dewey was primarily concerned with establishing a philosophical conception of art *as* experience, the main objective of interwar US modernist writers was to introduce authorial experience as a basic criterion of fictional quality. If Dewey's pragmatist aesthetics held that art originated in the "impulsion" toward "actual life-experience" rather than in the studio or the museum, US modernist writers imbued this principle with literary flesh and blood, engendering a series of narrators, characters, and authorial figures committed to experiential immersion.[8] The introduction to Dos Passos's *USA* trilogy, one of the most widely acclaimed US modernist works, portrays the novelist as a Whitmanesque wanderer whose appetite for experience leads him on a lifelong project to see, hear, and feel as much as humanly possible. With "greedy" eyes fixed upon the changing social scene, the itinerant "young man" endlessly rushes around, possessed by a burning desire to occupy every inch of the globe and every subject position.[9] Dos Passos equates artistic development with full experiential immersion: the young man seeks to "catch the last subway, the streetcar, the bus, run up all the gangplanks of all the steamboats, register at all the hotels, work in the cities, answer all the wantads, take up the jobs, live in the boardinghouse, sleep in all the beds. One bed is not enough, one job is not enough, one life is not enough" (xii). Although the *USA* trilogy is often described as the most "kaleidoscopic" of US modernist works precisely for its multiplicity of perspectives and unobtrusive narratorial persona, it unmistakeably weaves Dos Passos's experiential trajectory into its pages. Indeed, the "Camera Eye" sections, which are drawn primarily from the author's own biography, offer a sort of cumulative guarantee that the disparate material we encounter in the rest of the novel has first been taken in by the writer himself. Before narrating the story of Margo Dowling's disastrous elopement from New York City to Cuba in *The Big Money* (1936), for instance, the novel gives a stream-of-consciousness account of Dos Passos's first trip to Havana in the mid-1920s, where amid the "whirl of sugarboom prices" and the "Augustblistering sun," we find "yours truly tour[ing] the town."[10] These scenes meet all the criteria of the US literature of experience: they depict the writer as an inveterate explorer, they correlate firsthand authorial experience with narrative plot, and they imply that the novelist's transnational trajectory—here instantiated in the hemispheric route from the United States to Cuba—afford him a privileged view of modern life. In the interwar period, US writers not only rehearsed pragmatist arguments about the superiority of material acquired at first hand. Their fiction also increasingly depicted the author as an omnivorous, global experiencer.

Hemingway and Porter stand at the center of this chapter's story about the interwar US literature of experience both for what they have in common and for what differentiates them. Starting their writing careers at the opposite poles of US modernism in the early 1920s—Hemingway in Europe, Porter in Mexico—their development of the discourse of experience over the following decade offers a study in contrasts in geography and gender. However, as the internationalist modernism of the 1920s shaded into the more politicized aesthetics of the mid-1930s, Hemingway and Porter gravitated toward a similar conviction that the literature of experience provided an antidote to "ideological" or "partisan" fiction. Here the Latin American setting of their mid-1930s works proved crucial. Both Porter and Hemingway began to highlight their firsthand knowledge of Latin American political upheaval and the "long experience" of Latin American revolution: for Porter, in Mexico, and for Hemingway, in Cuba. Hemingway's *To Have and Have Not* (1937) and Porter's "Hacienda" (1934) represent the disparity between the lived experience of actual revolution and the abstract ideology of revolutionary writing. The political arguments of these narratives of the Latin American "experience" helped prepare the ground for the growing critical reflexivity about the US literature of experience in the late 1930s and early 1940s, when Philip Rahv and others began to identify a "cult of experience" in US writing and anatomize its distinctive features. Such debates about the relationship between authorial experience and literary production animated the New Critical movement to a surprising degree, with critics such as Robert Penn Warren and Cleanth Brooks redescribing contemporary writers' emphasis on expansive place-based absorption as a question of formal style. As we will see, this "disciplining" of the US literature of experience was one of the major critical acts of the 1940s.

Worldly Experience

Of all the interwar US writers of experience, Ernest Hemingway grabbed the lion's share of the attention, not least because he wrote several articles in the early 1930s about killing lions on African safaris. In the decade spanning the publications of *In Our Time* (1925) and *Green Hills of Africa* (1935), Hemingway set in motion a revolution in literary practice in the United States, reinventing the very idea of what it meant to be an "American writer" through a complex mix of fictional, journalistic, and extratextual strategies. Hemingway formulated his aesthetics of experience most explicitly in an early *Esquire* piece, "Monologue to the Maestro: A High Seas Letter" (1935), where he famously asserted that good writing "will be true in proportion to the amount of knowledge of life that [the writer] has" and that "[t]he more [the writer] learns from experience the more truly he can imagine."[11] Hemingway goes on to specify that this authority of experience did not necessarily imply a rigorous correspondence between objective fact and literary representation—with the benefit of exposure to a range of places and people, the author could extrapolate beyond actual events so that the public would believe that "it all really happened" (215). What the piece insinuates, and what its author's own itinerary of the 1920s and early 1930s attests, is that the success of the Hemingwayesque literary creed depended less on an adherence to the truth about the world than it did on a world of experience. And by 1933, Hemingway was close to achieving that aim. His travels had already taken him to France, Spain, Canada, Germany, Austria, Italy, Turkey, Greece, and Cuba; by the end of World War II, he would also visit Kenya, China, and Peru.

In many ways, Hemingway's collaboration with *Esquire* magazine, where he published a series of nonfiction "letters" and short stories on hunting and fishing from 1933 to 1936, marked the culmination of his efforts to fashion himself as the preeminent US writer of experience.[12] John Raeburn has estimated that Hemingway's *Esquire* letters of the 1930s averaged between 250,000 and 2 million readers a month, such that "no major novelist before Hemingway had ever had so large an audience for so long a period."[13] The magazine thus afforded Hemingway an unparalleled venue for disseminating his literary principles and, so to speak, for putting those principles into action. At the most basic level, Hemingway's *Esquire* pieces allowed him to inform his readers where he had been and to justify visiting new destinations. The headlines of the "letters" typically wedded short alluring descriptions ("Notes on Dangerous Game," "Out in the Stream," "On Being Shot Again") with geographic place names: "Cuba," "Spain," "Paris," "the Gulf Stream," "Africa." And his travels and travel writings generated a feedback loop: Hemingway used the $3,500 advance he received for his first article from editor Arnold Gingrich to purchase the *Pilar*, the legendary fishing vessel that transported him to several of the locations he described in subsequent letters.

But Hemingway also used these *Esquire* pieces to dramatize his voyages as literal and figurative testing grounds for the art of fiction. In "Monologue to the Maestro: A High Seas Letter," for instance, Hemingway's formula for equating the *quantity* of an author's experience with the *quality* of his writing appears in the guise of advice to an "aspirant writer," Mice, who arrives on Hemingway's doorstep in Key West with a twofold request. He implores the famous author to teach him how to write and to show him how to go to sea. Hemingway eventually agrees to take Mice on as a literary apprentice, and promises to carry the itinerant young man on his next expedition to Cuba. The trouble begins at the practical level, for although Mice "worked hard on the boat and at his writing," at sea he was a "calamity": "slow where he should be agile, seeming sometimes to have four feet instead of two feet and two hands, nervous under excitement, and with an incurable tendency toward sea-sickness" (214). Hemingway draws an implicit parallel between Mice's failure to develop as a writer and his inability to find his sea legs. In the cascading logic of the piece, to be inept at rigging a boat is to be unfit for travel, which is to lack physical prowess—all of which make one incapable of producing good literature. Before even turning to the activity of writing (how many hours to spend on a story each day, how to revise, and so on), Hemingway sets forth a standard of worldly experience that every aspiring writer must attain. The "high seas" of the piece's subtitle plays up the latent metaphor in the notion of perfecting the "craft" of fiction. According to Hemingway's formula, learning to right the ship is the best way to learn how to write.

When we take a closer look at *Death in the Afternoon* (1932), the book on Spanish bullfighting in which Hemingway provides his most extended articulation of his literary project, we see that he integrates an argument about fictional craft with a justification of his own efforts to acquire a greater *amount* of experience—in terms of intensity, range, and geography. Many critics have recognized that Hemingway's writings on bullfighting frequently draw analogies between the techniques of the matador and the style of an author. In *The Sun Also Rises* (1925) Pedro Romero inspires Jake Barnes because he "[keeps] the absolute purity of line in his movements and always quietly and calmly let[s] the horns pass him close each time;"[14] and in emphasizing the distinction between "sincere" and "false" bullfighting styles in *Death in the Afternoon*, Hemingway likens good bullfighters to good writers in an even more obvious way. In the early sections of *Death in the Afternoon*, however, Hemingway intimates that he didn't simply use bullfighting as a model for experiential writing; he first traveled to witness the bullfights *because* he was looking for new experiences about which to write. Hemingway asserts that in the aftermath of World War I, "I was trying to write then and I found the greatest difficulty. . . knowing truly what you really felt, rather than what you were supposed to feel,"[15] and he goes on to say that he embarked on his trip to Spain precisely because he thought it would help him become a better writer: "So I went to Spain to see bullfights and to try to write about them for myself" (3). As Hemingway remarked to Perkins, he planned to use this path from ignorance to experience—of Spain, of bullfighting, and of what it taught him about writing—to structure *Death in the Afternoon*: "As it's a thing that nobody knows about in English I'd like to take it first from altogether outside—how I happened to be interested in it, how it seemed before I saw it—how it was when I didn't understand it— my own experience with it, how it reacts on others—the gradual finding out about it and try and build it up from the outside and then go all the way inside with chapters on everything" (SL 234). For Hemingway, as Hugh Kenner put it in his classic study *A Homemade World: The American Modernist Writers* (1974), "the model for the perfection of a style is the perfection of a life."[16]

To isolate these strategies of the experiential writer *only* at the level of style, however, would be to miss some of the most radical aspects of Hemingway's aesthetic. Of course, there is a difference between writing a book about bullfighting and actually attending a bullfight, just as there is a difference between fighting a bull (i.e., being a matador) and watching a bull be killed (i.e., being an aficionado). Yet here and elsewhere, Hemingway's success in equating the description of an activity with the activity itself hinged on his capacity to demonstrate that he himself had *done* the activity in "real" life. Thus it was of incalculable importance that Hemingway himself entered the amateur bullfights (*capeas*) held in conjunction with the bullfighting festivals in Spain, and that he produced various forms of evidence to prove it. In the summer of 1924, after returning from the festival de San Fermín in Pamplona that would provide much of the material for *The Sun Also Rises*, Hemingway wrote to Ezra Pound that "I appeared in the bull ring on 5 different mornings—was cogida [tossed] 3 times—accomplished 4 veronicas in good form and one natural with the muleta, the last morning, received contusions and abrasions in the pecho [chest] and other places" (*SL* 118). Though biographers believe that Hemingway was not actually "gored," as he later claimed, he was most likely in the ring when his friend Don Stewart [Bill Gorton in *The Sun Also Rises*] was charged by a young bull and had two of his ribs fractured. The incident made front-page news in the *Chicago Tribune*, where a story about Stewart and Hemingway was headlined: "Bull Gores 2 Yanks Acting as Toreadors."[17] Such journalistic accounts of his physical participation in the fights contributed to Hemingway's authority as an experiential writer. And to the degree that they magnified a seemingly minor event in his life, they show us how Hemingway used his actions to prepare an American audience for the fiction he would write. Having established his bullfighting bona fides among his friends, in the literary world, and within the US public sphere, Hemingway could turn to a more impersonal statement of the value of amateur bullfighting experience in the text of *Death in the Afternoon*: "It gives enough of a sensation so that there are always men willing to go into the capeas for the pride of having experienced it and the pleasure of having tried some bullfighting manoeuvre with a real bull" (24).

Hemingway's ability to position himself as a conduit for national aspirations and desires abroad fascinated US writers, critics, and casual readers alike during the interwar period. Writing in the *Partisan Review* in 1939, Lionel Trilling remarked that "[p]erhaps no American talent has so publicly developed as Hemingway's: more than any writer of our time he has been under glass, watched, checked up on, predicted, suspected, warned."[18] Tellingly, Trilling goes on to speak of Hemingway's "audience" rather than his readers—a generation that "took from him" not only "new styles of writing," but also a new style "of very being" (62). Trilling's suggestion that Hemingway had created a new subjectivity is surely an overstatement, since this literary "audience" was undoubtedly subject to the same historical and social influences that were molding Hemingway's works themselves, yet it underscores the degree to which Hemingway became, both inside and outside the United States, the most public model for how to live the life of a writer. As Michael Soto observes, "A recurring theme of Hemingway criticism, in fact, has been pinpointing the relationship between Hemingway's novels and his 'true' experiences, and in particular the relationship between his characters and the actual persons on which these are based."[19] However, these guessing games were by no means limited to those who had privileged access to the "seemingly closed-off bohemian enclave" of literary Paris (143), particularly in the 1930s when Hemingway's field of experience had expanded to include such off-the-beaten-path sites as Tanganyika and Cuba. References to Hemingway's itineraries appear in a range of American print sources, from highbrow literary magazines such as H. L. Mencken's the *American Mercury* to more broadly circulating newspapers, including the African American paper the *Liberator* and the dailies of the Hearst publishing empire. Public obsession with what Hemingway was "doing" and where he was doing it rivaled and often outstripped analysis of what he was writing. In the section "Backstage with Esquire," which gave the bios of the magazine's contributors, Hemingway's location was updated from issue to issue: "Ernest Hemingway is in Spain," "Ernest Hemingway is in Paris," "Ernest Hemingway is in Africa." The aura of the Hemingway circuit could even be extended to his fellow American writers. When the editors of *Esquire* purported to "lay our money, in the Great American Novel Sweepstakes" on the still unwritten final novel of Dos Passos's *USA* trilogy, their boosterism did not begin with analysis of his work, but with a description of his itinerary: "John Dos Passos is in Spain with his good friend Ernest Hemingway, having gone there after a summer spent at Antibes [France]."[20]

There was perhaps no biographical detail that did more for Hemingway's literary career than his "experiences" during the Great War. As a member of the Red Cross ambulance corps, Hemingway had been one of the first Americans wounded in Italy, making him an instant celebrity in the American press. Though retrospective critical accounts such as Cowley's tended to make light of Hemingway's injury—he was hit by a burst of shrapnel while delivering cigarettes and chocolates to a group of Italian soldiers—his own obsessive reworking of the incident and its physical and psychological effects in his fiction provided a template for the American writer as experiencer against which other authors were increasingly forced to define themselves. In his review of the Paris edition of *In Our Time*, for instance, Edmund Wilson insisted that Hemingway "has no anti-militarist *parti pris* which will lead him to suppress from his record the exhilaration of the men [in battle]." Instead, Wilson suggested that in his descriptions of the "period of the war," Hemingway "is showing you what life is like."[21] Though Hemingway often fictionally embellished the events surrounding his injury—in *A Farewell to Arms*, for instance, he "promoted" Frederic Henry to a position he himself never held—he later defended the practice by suggesting that he at least knew more than other (American) writers knew: "In Italy, when I was at the war there, for one thing that I had seen or that had happened to me I knew many hundreds of things that I had seen or that had happened to other people who had been in the war in all its phases. My own small experiences gave me a touchstone by which I could tell whether stories were true or false and being wounded was a password."[22] Emphasizing the translatability of his injury to the traumas suffered by soldiers and civilians alike, Hemingway would quickly transform this experiential password into a means for including, excluding, dismissing, or authorizing other writers. In a letter to Wilson in 1923, he complained about the combat scenes in Willa Cather's highly popular war novel *One of Ours*: "You were in the war weren't you? Wasn't that last scene in the lines wonderful? Do you know where it came from? The battle scene in *Birth of a Nation*. I identified it episode after episode. Catherized. Poor woman she had to get her war experience somewhere" (*SL* 105). Though Hemingway initially recognizes the power of Cather's prose, he immediately undercuts her authority, pejoratively feminizing her depiction of the war by "exposing" its derivativeness.

From our contemporary perspective, Hemingway's experiential boasting may very well seem symptomatic of his chauvinist assumptions about literature, and Kevin Maier and David Earle are undoubtedly right to suggest that Hemingway's works of the interwar period—and particularly his travel writings in *Esquire*—articulate a cultural notion of masculinity based on the figure of the man of the world.[23] Yet in emphasizing the importance of direct contact with the subject matter about which one was writing, Hemingway was also engaging in a larger American cultural reflection on the relationship between authorial experience and literary practice. In his preface to a new edition of *The 42nd Parallel*, Dos Passos almost literally took a page from Deweyan pragmatist aesthetics, celebrating the determination of American writers "to test continually slogans, creeds and commonplaces in the light of freshly felt experience."[24] James Weldon Johnson's introduction to the second edition of *The Book of American Negro Poetry* begins with the affirmation that "[a]n artist accomplishes his best when working at his best with material he knows best," and in a satirical piece entitled "How to Be a Bad Writer (in Ten Easy Lessons)," Langston Hughes summed up the experiential creed though the *via negativa*, asserting that the easiest way to become a bad writer is to write about "any place you've never seen and know nothing about."[25] When Gertrude Stein took aim at the public figure of Hemingway in *The Autobiography of Alice B. Toklas* (1932), she not only attacked his self-generated image as the tireless adventurer but also highlighted the gap between his representational strategies and the activities that lay behind them. Writing in the voice of her life-long partner Alice, Stein quipped that Hemingway "writes like a modern and smells of the museums," remarking that she would much prefer "the real story of Hemingway, not those he writes but the confessions of the real Ernest Hemingway."[26] In her quest to position herself at the center of the international modernist movement, Stein does not shy away from taking on Hemingway at his own game, insinuating that even his *afición* for masculine sports was derived from the liter-ary milieu at 27 Rue de Fleuris.[27] For Stein and others in the 1920s and early 1930s, questioning Hemingway's self-fashioning as the pre-eminent US writer of experience did not entail rejecting the equa-tion between worldy experience and literary quality so much as at-tempting to appropriate the experiential aesthetic for themselves.[28]

Throughout the 1920s and early 1930s, Hemingway's writings traced an itinerary of places where one simply had to have gone and things one simply had to have done. Though scholars often take the older Hemingway's theorization of mentally "transplanting yourself" to a remembered place as evidence of his willingness to imaginatively recreate (and distort) his life story, Hemingway's statements of the interwar period consistently play up what might be called the transi-tive rather than the intransitive aspect of his "experience." Of course, much of the power of Hemingway's aesthetic stemmed from the con-stant ambiguity he maintained between the active and passive types of "experience" that went into the writer's craft: the adventure through which one finds "something to write about," and the sedentary, pains-taking, and self-consciously "literary" activity of transmuting that experience into art. One strategy for blurring this line was to fore-ground parallels between practical undertakings and the exacting rigors of what Hemingway referred to as "visual remembrance," a dynamic mental process of problem solving resembling Dewey's notion that "the brain and nervous system are primarily organs of action-undergoing."[29] In his attempt to recall his earlier fishing expe-ditions in Michigan while sleeping in a bunk in Italy during the war, Nick Adams foregrounds the feedback loop between mental recol-lection and the mechanics of fishing: "I would think of a trout stream

I had fished along when I was a boy and fish its whole length very carefully in my mind; fishing very carefully under all the logs, all the turns of the bank, the deep holes and the clear shallow stretches, sometimes catching trout and sometimes losing them."[30] Hemingway's texts and essays obsessively elaborate on the cycle of going out to "have an experience," reconstructing this activity in the mind, and finally writing about it "from the inside."[31]

The poststructuralist trend in academic work over the past twenty years has often led scholars to insist that the adventure narratives in Hemingway's works are largely performative, partaking in what Timo Müller has recently dubbed a "posture of authenticity."[32] Although such critical positions are a welcome departure from earlier studies that tended to take Hemingway's claims to truth-telling at face value, they remain rather narrowly bound by their assumption of an aesthetic that is always already reflexive. For example, in the introduction to their 2012 edited collection *Ernest Hemingway and the Geography of Memory*, Mark Cirino and Mark Ott speak of Hemingway "revisiting," "reimagining," and "transforming" the geographical locations in his writings, implying that his initial encounter with these places had been merely the precondition for a later act of fictionalization.[33] This view downplays the extraordinary energy and resources Hemingway devoted to gaining access to his "source material" (i.e., the places, cultures, and people that would appear in his fiction) in the first place. Several recent studies have begun to advance beyond the limits of this perspective, exploring the relationship between Hemingway's work, travel writing, and the growing tourist industry of the 1920s and 1930s.[34] Yet the continued emphasis on the broad category of Euro-American (and particularly Anglo-American) modernism has tended to occlude the specific role played by Hemingway's merging of the trope of travel with his arguments for the craft of fiction in restructuring the creative process, and the very idea of fiction writing, in the US literary field.

In fact, it is writers from outside the United States who have most clearly recognized how important Hemingway's *actual presence* in these places was for producing his fiction and forging his literary self. This is particularly true of writers in Latin America, where the travel possibilities and types of mobility often taken for granted in the US literary field have often been seen more as a problem than a prerequisite for fiction writing. In a novel that fictionalizes Hemingway's last years in Cuba, *Adiós, Hemingway* (2001), the Cuban author

Leonardo Padura suggests that while biographers and critics have made constant reference to a Hemingway "myth" that "he himself constructed," the "truth was more complicated and terrible":

> [Hemingway] knew that his imagination had always been weak and deceiving, and that the mere telling of those things he had seen and learned in life had allowed him to write books that were capable of exuding that veracity that he demanded of his literature. Without the bohemia of Paris and the bullfights he would never have written *Fiesta* [*The Sun Also Rises*]. Without the wounds at Fossalta, the hospital in Milan, and his desperate love for Agnes von Kuroskwy, he would never have imagined *A Farewell to Arms*.... Without all of those days spent in the Gulf and the marlin he caught and the stories about other huge, silvery marlin told by the fishermen of Cojímar *The Old Man and the Sea* never would have been born.... He knew the truth: he needed to live the life he did to produce his literature, he needed to fight, kill, fish, and live in order to write.[35]

Padura's narrator suggests that contemporary criticism has gotten it exactly wrong. While critics typically treat Hemingway's emphasis on worldly experience as a pretense, the narrator understands that the singularity of Hemingway's fiction was his ability to tether his creative process to real-life events and itineraries, thereby undercutting the idea that imagination and memory alone are powerful enough to create great literature. Padura's portrait of Hemingway is, of course, itself a textual rendering, but this does not make his relationship to the US writer a matter of prose style alone. Writing in 2006, long after Cubans had been prohibited from leaving the island without permission from the Castro government, Padura cannot have seen the possibility of culling one's source material from foreign adventure as a question of simple (or even complex) mental reconstruction.

Her Own Account of Mexico

Hemingway's route—global, frenetic, and expensive—represented the most visible pathway for the US literature of experience in the interwar period, but it was not the only one. The career of Katherine Anne Porter, who was born in Texas in 1893 and spent much of the 1920s and early 1930s in Mexico City, represented an important alternative trajectory. Whereas the works of Hemingway and other writers of the "lost generation" embodied the transatlantic itinerary often associated with US modernist literature, Porter's interwar writings helped launch an important genre that would become increasingly prominent in the postwar period: the fictional narrative about the US expatriate in Mexico.

When Porter crossed the border into Mexico in late 1920, she was embarking on the same path that many US writers had taken before her. They had come, like Stephen Crane, Jack London, and John Kenneth Turner, during the thirty-year dictatorship of Porfirio Díaz; they had come, like John Reed, Lincoln Steffens, Carleton Beals, and Langston Hughes, during the tumultuous decade of Revolution. And they would later come, like Alma Reed, John Dos Passos, Anita Brenner, Waldo Frank, Archibald MacLeish, and Hart Crane, during the agitated postrevolutionary period of social transformation and artistic innovation. As scholars such as Helen Delpar, John Britton, and Rachel Adams have shown, during the 1910s and 1920s a wide array of intellectuals, journalists, and novelists traveled to Mexico to witness the Revolution and its aftermath, fueling debates about the conflict's main actors and political programs that filled the pages of mainstream and radical magazines alike.[36] For those on the left, this journey across the Rio Grande in the midteens held a special appeal. Mexico offered what the United States lacked: a massive popular uprising linked to demands for land redistribution, anti-imperialism, and grassroots political changes. For more than a decade, Mexico therefore occupied a role that Russia, Cuba, China, and a few other countries would serve over the course of the twentieth century: a place for US journalists, writers, intellectuals, and activists to experience firsthand the political and social revolution they envisioned for the United States. Indeed, by the mid-1910s, as Mexican forces began to coalesce around popular revolutionary figures such as Pancho Villa, Emiliano Zapata, and Venustiano Carranza whose political "plans" increasingly began to attract the American left, the appeal to on-the-ground experience became something of an industry standard for articles on Mexico. For instance, an editorial note in *Everybody's Magazine* preceding Lincoln Steffens's 1916 article "Into Mexico—and Out" not only trumpeted the leading muckraking reporter's "record in digging the truth out of complicated situations" but also specified that "[f]or five months Mr. Steffens has been traveling in Mexico with Carranza."[37] As US journalists attempted to parse the complex factionalism of the Revolution, giving a "balanced viewpoint" entailed seeking out firsthand contact with the various contenders in the revolutionary struggle as well as entertaining competing versions of events.

Porter's writings of the early 1920s suggest that she was aware of the competition among US writers to capture the most unfiltered view of the upheaval occurring across the border—and that she was eager to compete. Shortly after her arrival in Mexico City in 1920, Porter met Steffens, whom she dubbed the "follower of revolutions," stating in her notebook: "I mean to write fully some day the inside story of this show. It is more improbable than a legend, and more amusing than Lincoln Steffen's [*sic*] stories, and more tragic than any Golgotha ever dreamed of."[38] Over the course of her Mexican travels from 1920 to 1931, as the combat phase of the Revolution gradually receded into the past, Porter became increasingly ambivalent about not only the Revolution's aims, but the ways that foreign writers— and particularly US ones—depicted it. If Porter attributed these writers' failures to a variety of errors and biases, her major concern was to prove that writing about the transformations of 1920s Mexico required prolonged immersion in the country rather than hasty impressions of it. Her concern was as much aesthetic as ethical and political. In another notebook entry of 1920, she wrote:

> Why not story on impossibility of writing a story at short notice on Mexico. Maybe I shall write a few, but curiously enough—It may be five years before I can really write about Mexico. I am not one of those amazing folk who can learn people or countries in a fortnight.... I want first of all to discover for myself what this country is. Everybody I meet tells me a different story. *Nothing is for me but to wait, and gather my own account.* (emphasis mine)[39]

Here we encounter in embryo many of the strategies that Porter would eventually employ in her fiction and journalism about Mexico. In addition to offering a program for acquiring material for her work through a kind of slow distillation of her personal experience of Mexico—perhaps five years, she says, to fully "gather her own account"—she also signals that her fiction might function as a critique of non-Mexican stories about the country written "at short notice," and suggests how reflexive literary techniques (the "story on the impossibility of writing a story") could help her differentiate between superficial and profound accounts of Mexico among foreign observers. Mauricio Tenorio-Trillo convincingly situates Porter among those foreign writers who "claimed to be authentic discoverers of Mexico, as opposed to either fake idealizers or insurgent bashers of Mexico."[40] Rather than judging Porter for these claims, though, I want to explore how she turned them into literary techniques: how her vision became, in many ways, *the* US modernist vision of postrevolutionary Mexico.

Perhaps the most noteworthy feature of Porter's Mexico stories of the 1920s and 1930s is that they are nearly all versions of the roman à clef, narratives that represent real-life people and events in fictional form. "The Martyr" (1923) is a thinly veiled satire of Mexican muralist Diego Rivera and his model and wife, Lupe Marín; "That Tree" (1934) models its protagonist on Carleton Beals; and, as Thomas Walsh has shown, "Flowering Judas" (1930) uses composite portraits of US journalists Alma Reed and Mary Doherty and well-known Mexican radicals Samuel Yúdico and Luis Morones to create the characters of the American Laura and the Mexican revolutionary Braggioni. In 1943, Porter remarked of her composition process for "Flowering Judas": "All the characters and episodes are based on real persons and events, but naturally, as my memory worked upon them and time passed...the order and meaning of the episodes changed, and became in a word fiction" (*CS* 716). Commenting on this assertion and Porter's later claim that "my fiction is reportage, only I do something to it," Walsh argues that "'Flowering Judas' is not historical fiction that fixes on a specific time in Mexican history, but intentionally obscures and rewrites history to make it conform to fictional needs."[41] Yet this seems to miss the point that by modeling the vast majority of her characters on real-life figures in the contemporary Mexican scene—and repeatedly saying she was doing so—Porter was in a way inviting this very confusion between her fiction and her biography. As Sean Latham observes, the "roman à clef ultimately depends for definition on...the introduction of a key that lies beyond the diegesis itself,"[42] a verification process that forces the reader from internal plot dynamics to the historical people and events the narrative encodes. That Porter was writing first-person essays and articles for many of the same US magazines in which her stories appeared—as in the pairing of "Why I Write about Mexico" and "The Martyr" in the *Century Magazine*'s July 1923 issue—made a conflation between what she had experienced and what she had invented all the more probable. Judging from reviews of *Flowering Judas and Other Stories*

(1935), readers did in fact have trouble separating Porter's fiction about Mexico from her experience of it. Edith Walton's review of the expanded edition in the *New York Times* provides a typical example of this conflation: "Apparently Miss Porter is thoroughly familiar with the raggle-taggle of American radicals, artists, and writers who haunt Mexico City."[43] Porter's variation on the roman à clef entailed realigning the relationship between fact and fiction along a geographical axis: her US audience would have to seek the extradiegetic key to her texts in their Mexican contexts.

Taken as a whole, Porter's Mexican writings articulate a literary mode that we might call the expatriate roman à clef. It was a mode that allowed her both to *authenticate* her firsthand knowledge of Mexico—on the principle that "all the things [she] wrote of [she had] first known"—and *authorize* her "own account" of postrevolutionary Mexico against the narratives of other US writers and journalists. Nowhere does this appear more clearly than in "That Tree." The story is ostensibly about a typical maladjusted expatriate American in Mexico City: a journalist who longs to be a poet, a student of revolutions who gets the jitters when he hears explosions, a potential lothario who cannot find the means to break away from his narrow-minded midwestern wife back home. Porter later wrote, "That Tree has for its hero something like ten thousand wistful American boys who have been brought up in dull ways and dull surroundings, and are infected with the notion that romance and glory lie in other places, and in a different occupation."[44] Yet the breadth of this statement—"something like ten thousand wistful American boys"—belies the specificity of the unnamed protagonist in the story's opening lines: "an important journalist, an authority on Latin-American revolutions and a best seller" (CS 72). In fact, the only plausible candidate for this description was Porter's erstwhile friend Beals, who had by the time of the story's publication become perhaps the most prominent US journalist writing on Latin America, the author of numerous nonfiction books on Mexico, Nicaragua, and Cuba. This interplay of fact and fiction, universality of motive and particularity of experience, was crucial to contemporary readings of "That Tree": John Chamberlin remarked in the *New York Times* review that "[o]ne rather guesses that it was suggested by the life of Carleton Beals,"[45] and Walton surely had the story in mind when she touted Porter's familiarity with the "American radicals, artists, and writers who haunt Mexico City." As these contemporary readers grasped, Porter's story was less an allegory about idealistic "American boys" than a commentary on the specific practices of US idealist writers in the Latin America of the 1920s and 1930s.

The correspondence that Porter establishes between Beals and the protagonist of "That Tree" serves not only to highlight her experience of expatriate life in postrevolutionary Mexico, but also to undercut Beals's own position as an "authority on Latin-American revolutions." The narrative tone toward the protagonist is negative throughout, casting a harsh light on his lifestyle in Mexico as well as his writings on Latin America. We find out that though the protagonist is known as an "important journalist," the reason "he had come to Mexico in the first place" was "to be a cheerful bum lying under a tree in a good climate, writing poetry" (CS 72). His romantic views on life in Mexico damage everyone around him, and his writings present a highly sentimentalized portrait of Latin American revolution to his US audience. At one point in the story, the narrator reveals that the protagonist's "sympathies happened to fall in exactly right with the high-priced magazines of a liberal humanitarian slant which paid him well for telling the world about the oppressed peoples" (CS 84). What the text everywhere implies, but never explicitly states, is that the reality of interwar Latin America appears not in the sentimental stories Beals tells the world but in the backstory of his situation in Mexico we are reading, a sort of literary equivalent to behind-the-scenes filmmaking. By showing the gap between the reality of Mexico and Beals's portrayal of it, Porter stakes a claim to a more penetrating vision of the country than that of the most famous US journalist writing about Latin America. "That Tree" thus functions both as a document of the failure of US writers like Beals to produce a literature of experience about postrevolutionary Mexico, and an argument for why Porter's own work exemplifies precisely this kind of experiential literature.

But if Porter's strategies for styling herself a writer of experience in Mexico often hinged on disqualifying or undermining other expatriate writers, they must also be seen as part of her larger effort to combat the exclusionary principles with which the US modernist canon was beginning to be constructed in the interwar period. As influential critical accounts like Edmund Wilson's *Axel's Castle* and Cowley's *Exile's Return* cemented the idea that Paris and London had been the proving ground of "modern" literature for US as well as European writers, Porter continued to insist on the importance of

Mexico as the scene of her own cultural formation. Even after she finally traveled to Europe in the early 1930s and began to turn to other geographies in her fiction, Porter wrote several essays that offered correctives to US- and Eurocentric biases in critical accounts of the interwar period. In these postwar essays, Porter disputed the assumptions about both geography and gender in the dominant narratives of US literature of the 20s and 30s—or, perhaps more precisely, the way geography itself was gendered. One of the major claims of Cowley's *Exile's Return*, reinforced by his own biography as well as by the itinerary and writings of Hemingway, was that the "common experience" of volunteer military service in Europe during the First World War had produced the structure of feeling shared by the chief American writers of the 1920s (6). Yet this was not the world Porter inhabited at all: having grown up in Texas, she felt a stronger connection to Mexico than to Europe; having come of age as a woman in radical New York, she sought to distance herself from the narratives of masculine sacrifice and loss associated with "the Fitzgerald-Hemingway crowd in Paris."[46] To have gone to Mexico was, in an important sense, to have avoided a specific exile and a specific exilic return. Cowley's transatlantic account in *Exile's Return* must have seemed particularly distorted to Porter, since she herself had acted as travel guide to Cowley during his visit to Mexico in 1930, introducing him to a very different "narrative of ideas" from the one he had imbibed in Europe.

When Porter wrote to Cowley in 1965, "I wish I had a true place in [*Exile's Return*], but of course, I haven't" (*SL* 307), she was therefore referring to "place" both literally and figuratively. Cowley's diminution of Mexico was, in Porter's eyes, indicative of his overall diminution of her "place" in the 1920s canon, as the one woman writer who (as he put it in revised editions of *Exile's Return*) had received "as much praise or critical attention as half a dozen men of the same age" (315). In this sense, Porter's rejection of Cowley's cursory mapping of her (literal) waywardness of the twenties resembled a similar critique she made of Hemingway in his role as the representative US writer of experience. In an extraordinary 1964 essay recalling her one and only meeting with Hemingway in Sylvia Beach's famous bookstore in Paris in 1934, Porter lampoons Hemingway's efforts to build himself up as the supreme man of adventure, mocking how the "*beau garçon* who loved blood sports, the dark-haired sunburned muscle boy of American literature" would immediately remove his socks and shoes when entering Shakespeare and Company, "showing Sylvia the still-painful scars of his war wounds got in Italy" (CS 676–677). Yet Porter does not end by deconstructing Hemingway's attempts to prove he had always been in the line of fire; to the contrary, she plays up her own experiential credentials. Midway through the essay, Porter subjects Hemingway's ostentation of his battle wounds and his penchant for blood sports to a swift and definitive reversal: "It was not particularly impressive. . . . I had seen all the bullfights and done all the hunting I wanted in Mexico before I ever came to Paris" (CS 677). Porter not only insists that she had witnessed danger in Mexico before going to Europe but also insinuates that she had found Latin America before Hemingway did—a significant claim given that Hemingway had begun to position himself as a Cuba-based novelist in the mid-1930s.

Taken as a whole, Porter's essay seems to make the simple but necessary point that the Hemingwayesque version of the literature of experience was itself a kind of masculine performance. Her 1955 essay "St. Augustine and the Bullfight," ostensibly about Porter's own relationship to bullfighting in Mexico in the 1920s, also offers an oblique commentary on Hemingway's famous notion of the "moment of truth" from *Death in the Afternoon*. As I have already noted in the introduction, Porter's essay hinges on differentiating "real experience" from "mere adventure." Thus, she writes, "adventure is something you seek for pleasure, or even for profit, like a gold rush or invading a country; for the illusion of being more alive than ordinarily, the thing you will to occur; but experience is what really happens to you in the long run; the truth that finally overtakes you" (CS 808). Repurposing her earlier argument that experiential writing required prolonged immersion in a place rather than hasty impressionism, she implicitly contrasts her definition of "real experience" with the thrill-seeking adventurism Hemingway had embodied in the 1930s. If the essay ends with Sylvia Beach bringing the two together in a sort of ritual of literary matchmaking—"'Katherine Anne Porter . . . this is Ernest Hemingway . . . Ernest, this is Katherine Anne, and I want the two best modern American writers to know each other!'" (CS 677)—Porter leaves no doubt that the "two best modern American writers" knew very different things. Though Porter and Hemingway were both advocates of a literature of experience, they defined "experience" in markedly contrasting ways.

True Testimony in Latin America

Throughout the 1920s and early 1930s, Hemingway and Porter opposed their experiential writing to various other kinds of literature— romantic, idealistic, bookish, feminine (in Hemingway's case), and masculine (in Porter's). But by the mid-1930s, Porter and Hemingway began to converge in their criticism of one particular literary strain they viewed as antithetical to the literature of experience: partisan or ideological fiction. The timing of their objection was not coincidental. In the United States, the onset of the Great Depression had made a deep impression on the literary field, and by the early thirties the "proletarian" novel was gaining momentum. Critics such as Wilson and Cowley joined the editors of the *New Masses* in advocating for more overtly politicized writing, pointing to Soviet realism as the most advanced current in contemporary literature. And as Michael Denning and others have shown, the formation of the Popular Front in 1934 brought a growing number of intellectuals, activists, poets, playwrights, and novelists into its orbit. Yet even as many US writers began to radicalize, both Porter and Hemingway became increasingly skeptical about the propagandistic uses of art. As Darlene Unrue notes, Porter's disillusionment with the legacy of the Mexican Revolution deepened when she returned to the country for sixteen months in 1930–1931,[47] and she was discouraged by the extent to which the Depression-era cultural logic in the United States reminded her of arguments she had heard in Mexico in the 1920s. In an autobiographical fragment of 1934, she rejected the basic claim of the US literary left (along with that of other leftist writers from Mexico to the Soviet Union) that art should serve an ideological function: "Politically my bent is to the Left. As for esthetic bias, my one aim is to tell a straight story and to give true testimony" (*CS* 1008). For his part, Hemingway grew increasingly agitated with what one of his correspondents dubbed the "leftward turn" in US literature. In a 1932 letter addressing the purported shift in ideological sympathies among US writers, Hemingway insisted that while his political orientation was anarchist and anticapitalist, there is "no left and right in writing. There is only good and bad writing" (*SL* 363). In the mid-1930s, both Hemingway and Porter began to adapt their aesthetics of experience to expose what they saw as the inherent danger of literature derived from ideological positioning as opposed to firsthand eyewitnessing.

It is no coincidence that Latin America was the setting for Hemingway's and Porter's most significant texts of the mid-1930s: *To Have and Have Not* (1937), Hemingway's first "Cuban" novel (and the only novel he would publish in the 1930s), and "Hacienda" (1934), Porter's last work to take place exclusively in Mexico (and her longest story up to that point). I have already suggested that Mexico was the primary testing ground for US writers to gain firsthand knowledge of revolutionary activities in the early twentieth century. For those writers who missed the decade-long fighting in Mexico, the Cuban Revolution of 1933—a student-led insurgency that briefly brought the left-leaning university professor Ramón Grau into office—presented a second "opportunity" to witness political upheaval in the hemisphere. John Gronbeck-Tedesco has recently argued that first-hand documentation of the 1933 Cuban Revolution and its aftermath became a sort of talisman for US writers and intellectuals in the midst of a broad cultural swing to the left in the United States: "To travel and bear witness to Cuba's revolution was to create a distinct set of experiences in left phenomenology. Authors were seen in a new light because of their perceived level of dedication, their writing measured to be testimony of the conditions 'as they were' that invited readers to engage with 'real' and 'authentic' revolutionary occurrences."[48] While Gronbeck-Tedesco rightly underscores the importance that the "experience" of Latin American revolution held for US writers of the period, his account focuses almost exclusively on works produced by the literary left within the context of what he calls the "brief and explosive period of rebellion" that marked the Revolution's most exhilarating phase. For Hemingway and Porter, however, the most important lesson of the Latin American revolutions of the 1920s and 1930s was not their initial promise of revolt but their eventual failure. In their method of composition and their strategies of representation, Hemingway and Porter suggested that an accurate portrayal of revolution required prolonged exposure to its temporal unfolding and a willingness to document *all* of its phases. Whereas writers on the radical left typically subordinated their "experiences" of Mexico and Cuba to their political commitments, Porter and Hemingway used the aesthetics of experience to illuminate the problem of positing ideology as the basis for art.

Both *To Have and Have Not* and "Hacienda" are romans à clef that draw on living figures and real historical circumstances. The plot of Hemingway's novel is simple enough. Harry Morgan, the struggling

American captain of a fishing boat, turns to rum running and human trafficking to Cuba in order to support his family in Key West, before losing his life in a plot connected to the Cuban Revolution of 1933. In order to understand how Hemingway shaped the story according to his experiential aesthetics, however, we first need to understand how he transmuted his actual journeys to Cuba from 1932 to 1936 into fictional form. From 1932 to 1936, he made four separate visits to the island, spending a total of more than six months in Havana and the surrounding coast. His final visit was a week-long trip in December 1936: after sending a letter to *Esquire* editor Arnold Gingrich in which he claimed that he needed to return to Havana to "see some places again" before completing the novel, he arrived back in Key West eight days later and wrote to Maxwell Perkins: "I got what I needed in Cuba and am back here now to not move again until I finish the novel."[49] Hemingway's program of repeatedly revisiting Cuba during the process of writing *To Have and Have Not* finds a formal analogue in the novel's tone, which opens on a note of easy familiarity that invokes the author/narrator's sustained exposure to the island: "You know how it is there early in the morning in Havana."[50] The line's second-person address creates a particular rhetorical effect: those of "us" who have been to Cuba just "know" how it feels.

The novel's address to the reader conveys the impression not only of firsthand knowledge of the physical and social environs of 1930s Havana, but also of the lived experience of the various phases of the 1933 Cuban Revolution itself. Although most Hemingway biographers have claimed that deep-sea fishing was the primary reason he traveled to Cuba in the early 1930s, he was in Havana from April to early August, 1933, when a series of strikes, mobilizations, and assassination attempts paralyzed the Machado regime, and on May Day, 1934, he returned to the capital city with Dos Passos to witness a series of mass demonstrations. To a certain degree, Hemingway's nonfiction writings of the mid-1930s would have prepared readers of *To Have and Have Not* for its depiction of revolutionary violence in Cuba. In *Green Hills of Africa*, Hemingway tells big-game hunter Philip "Pop" Percival that he had seen the Cuban Revolution "from the start," and continues, "It's very hard to get anything true on anything [about revolutions] you haven't seen yourself."[51] One method that Hemingway employed in the novel to play up his firsthand knowledge of revolution was to transpose and repurpose scenes from his nonfiction work. For example, in *Green Hills of Africa* Hemingway gives the following description of an outbreak of violence in 1933 from the perspective of his wife, Pauline: "I was crouched down behind a marble-topped table while they were shooting in Havana. They came by in cars shooting at everybody they saw" (132–133). A similar passage appears in the first chapter of *To Have and Have Not*, retold and intensified by Harry, who witnesses the deaths of a group of Cubans associated with a revolutionary plot: "I saw a closed car come across the square toward them. The first thing a pane of glass went and the bullet smashed into the row of bottles on the showcase wall to the right. I heard the gun going and, bop, bop, bop" (6).

Hemingway's methods for transposing these firsthand "experiences" of revolution into *To Have and Have Not* were motivated, in this case, by his ongoing argument with the literary left. In the years leading up to the novel's publication in 1937, many critics in the United States—including several like Cowley and Wilson whom Hemingway respected—contended that *Death in Afternoon* and *Green Hills of Africa* signaled his evasion of the most pressing concerns of the Depression era. They argued that Hemingway's adventure writings had left him detached from the actual concerns of workers and the "American people," not to mention of US-based writers and readers. In a 1935 review of *Green Hills of Africa* in the *New Masses*, for instance, Granville Hicks asked, "Would Hemingway write better books if he wrote on different themes?" Hicks argued that Hemingway should write a book about a strike, "not because a strike is the only thing worth writing about, but because it would do something to Hemingway. If he would just let himself look squarely at the contemporary American scene, he would be bound to grow."[52] Hemingway's response to his leftist critics was to point to the gap between their ideology and their actions, between their experience of violence (which was nil) and their violent revolutionary belief system. This attack was by no means entirely accurate—many of these writers *had* visited the Soviet Union and others had been involved in street fights that erupted between police officers and workers in the massive strikes of the early thirties. But it was rhetorically effective. By dramatizing the link between his own experience of the 1933 Cuban Revolution and his fictional material, Hemingway could lay claim to more experience of "actual" revolution than the literary revolutionaries themselves. Indeed, Hemingway had already made this point explicit in a 1935 essay: "If the men who write editorials for the New Republic and The Monthly Review, say, had to take an examination on what they actually know about the mechanics, theory, past performance and practice of actual revolution, as it is made, not as it is hoped for, I doubt if any one of them would have one hundredth part of the knowledge of his subject that the average sensible follower of horses has of the animals."[53]

In *To Have or Have Not*, the representative of this kind of literary leftist, rich in theories of revolution but poor in knowledge of its practice and mechanics, is Richard Gordon, an embittered social novelist who functions in the novel as a foil to Harry Morgan. Scholars have pointed out that Gordon figures as an exaggerated portrait of Dos Passos, the mid-1930s lion of the literary left whose fictional counterpart has, according to his wife, "changed [his] politics to suit the fashion" (186). Less commented upon, however, is the extent to which Gordon's failings are specifically linked to the gap between the material of his proletarian literature and his trajectory as an established bourgeois writer. Midway through the text, for instance, the novel depicts Gordon comfortably ensconced in his middle-class home in Key West at the same time that he composes a novel about a "strike in a textile factory" (176). In this scene, which seems like a deliberate rejoinder to Hicks's comment in his 1934 review of *Green Hills of Africa* that Hemingway should write about a strike, it is Gordon's desire to compose a proletarian novel from his bourgeois perch that seems evasive. This point is brought home by the implicit contrast between the literary politics of Gordon and the actual experience of Harry, who first witnesses—and then falls victim to—Cuban revolutionary violence. In *Green Hills of Africa*, Hemingway responds to Pop's question about how the 1933 Cuban Revolution "was" with an epigram about revolution itself: "Beautiful. Then lousy. You couldn't believe how lousy" (132). In *To Have and Have Not*, Gordon epitomizes the literary leftist who idealizes the beauty of revolution with little or no exposure to real violence, while Harry embodies the "people" who actually suffer the consequences of revolutionary activity once it becomes "lousy."

It is Harry's immiseration by the economic conditions in Key West—and thus his status as a member of the precariat that Gordon purports to represent—that leads him to assist the misguided Cuban revolutionaries, a decision that ultimately kills him. And in one of the novel's final twists, these very revolutionaries seem unaware that their actions on behalf of the Cuban cause are motivated less by an actual knowledge of the underlying conditions of economic exploitation than by a kind of ideological puritanism. Crucially, one revolutionary insists to Harry that his fellow conspirator engages in indiscriminate violence solely because he finds himself at a particular juncture of the revolutionary process: "You know he doesn't mean to do wrong. It's just what that phase of the revolution has done to him" (165). In the end, this particular logic of revolution seems to receive the heaviest criticism in *To Have and Have Not*: among political actors, the reification of a particular phase of the revolutionary process without a perception of the long view; and, concomitantly, among writers and critics, the romantic description of this phase of rebellion without prolonged exposure to the revolution's aftermath. In its practices of composition as well as in its strategies of representation, Hemingway's novel advocates for a literature that depicts the full range of experiences of the revolutionary process. For Hemingway, this entailed coming to terms not just with the failures of revolution but also with failed revolution itself.

The broader message of *To Have and Have Not*, however, was not that all radicals are hypocrites, or that all writers who touch on social issues are condemned to misrepresentation. Indeed, when fighting broke out in Spain in 1936 between the Republican government and Fascist forces, Hemingway was quick to join the effort on the side of the Republicans. Rather, what *To Have and Have Not* ultimately underscores is that a writer's obligation during times of political strife is not simply to transmute historical event into literature but actively, persistently, and repeatedly to seek to experience it. Hemingway's fallout with Dos Passos over the Spanish Civil War has been discussed from innumerable angles. Yet it is helpful to recall that when Hemingway, who continued to support the Republican cause until the end, sent a letter to Dos Passos in March 1938 effectively severing their friendship, his rationale touched as much on the writer's relationship to politics as on politics itself. After lambasting Dos Passos for mistakenly having referred to a Polish general as a Russian (i.e., Soviet), Hemingway suggested that if Dos Passos was intent on attacking the communist presence in the Spanish Civil War, "I think you should at least try to get your facts right" (*SL* 463). Hemingway's advice to Dos Passos about the latter's reporting on Spain turns on the concept of full immersion: "The thing is that you don't find out the truth in ten days or three weeks and this hasn't been a communist run war for a long time. When people read a series of articles running over six months and more from you they do not realize how short a time you were in Spain and how little you saw" (*SL* 463–464). Here again Hemingway's criticism was couched in the language of authorial experience. The place had changed, the situation was different, and the ideological axes were now reversed. What remained the same was Hemingway's aesthetic program.

Hemingway composed his critique of "ideological" literature in *To Have and Have Not* only a few years after a revolutionary uprising that had itself lasted just over a few months. Katherine Anne Porter's anti-ideological project in "Hacienda," however, was formulated nearly fifteen years after her first visit to Mexico and nearly twenty years after the start of the Mexican Revolution. "Hacienda" is Porter's longest and most complex story about postrevolutionary Mexico, and an analysis of the text (and its contexts) allows us to see how it incorporates many of the tropes of Porter's earlier Mexican fiction while developing new strategies of representation for the literature of experience. The event that catalyzed the story was the Russian film director Sergei Eisenstein's visit to Mexico in 1930–1932 to shoot his (never-completed) film *Que Viva México!* Produced by a Hollywood group headed by Upton Sinclair, shot with a Russian film crew, and advised by artists and functionaries associated with the governing PNR (Partido Nacional Revolucionario), the film promised to be the most international artistic work of Mexico's postrevolutionary period. Yet Porter's story about the filming, based on a nonfiction piece published in the *Virginia Quarterly Review* about the three days she spent on set with Eisenstein and his crew in July 1931, tells of nothing but unmitigated disaster. Though conceived as a paean to the combined victories of the Mexican and Russian Revolutions, the thinly disguised stand-in for *Que Viva México!* in Porter's story hinges on an irony that becomes the central theme of the story. The setting for this film about social and political changes in contemporary Mexico is a colonial hacienda and pulque factory that has not changed hands since the Revolution and, even worse, continues to exploit its indigenous workers. The task of Eisenstein (Uspensky in the story), as the Russian assistant puts it, is to film the present-day conditions of the hacienda *as if* they were the historical conditions of the Díaz era that had been entirely "swept away by the revolution." This he says "without cracking a smile or meeting my eye" (*CS* 152).

As with Porter's earlier expatriate romans à clef, the characters in "Hacienda" are clearly identifiable: Eisenstein becomes Uspensky, his codirector Grigory Alexandrov becomes Andreyev, the American producer Hunter Kimbrough (Sinclair's brother-in-law) becomes Kennerly, and Porter's erstwhile friend Adolfo Best-Maguard becomes the Mexican artist Betancourt. A fictional commentary on the contradictions of the political and social revolution in Mexico after its institutionalization in the late 1920s, Porter's account took on particular force because the historical actors were so readily discernible. Yet Porter departs from the narrative technique she had employed in stories such as "Flowering Judas" and "That Tree" by focalizing "Hacienda" through a first-person narrator, an American woman writer clearly identified with Porter herself. If her earlier stories about Mexico frequently make her expatriate US protagonists into object lessons in how not to write about the country, "Hacienda" offers a more positive model for how the literature of experience should be composed. In the story's opening paragraph, the narrator-protagonist establishes both her familiarity with Mexico's social customs ("'Ah, it is beautiful as a *pulman!*' says the middle-class Mexican when he wishes truly to praise anything" [CS 142]) and her sustained firsthand knowledge of the country's political and cultural evolution: "Now that the true revolution of blessed memory has come and gone in Mexico, the names of many things are changed, nearly always with the view to an appearance of heightened well-being for all creatures" (CS 142). Indeed, though "Hacienda" owes much to classic travel literature, since the time of its narrative overlaps entirely with the length of the narrator's trip, the text also frequently makes reference to the narrator's prior impressions of Mexico. We are given to understand that the narrator's prolonged immersion in the country is precisely what enables her to chronicle the gap between ideology and lived experience in the postrevolutionary period.

Although the story's characterization of the failures of the revolution has been much discussed—the continued presence of rapacious American business interests in the country; the propagandistic drive of the Russian crew and the Mexican advisers to whitewash the still profound inequities of 1930s Mexico—Porter's strategy for authorizing her own version of the Mexican scene *against* these agents of distortion deserves a closer look. Robert Brinkmeyer has observed that the presence of a faded fresco on the wall of the hacienda detailing the legend of pulque functions for the narrator as a sign of "the trivialization of Aztec myth by educated Mexicans, the transformation of a living faith into a textbook entry" (65). Yet the ossification of the living Mexico into a static representation is not limited to the

Mexicans; rather, it seems to be the goal of every character in the story *except for the narrator*. In her reviews of the 1920s, Porter had excoriated American tourists who acted like "self-appointed prophets" when they crossed the border, eager (and under contract) "to stuff it all down in a hurry and rush back with a book while the racket is still good" (*CS* 997). In "Hacienda," Kennerly assumes this role of the impetuous American traveler, announcing that he is " 'going to write a book about [Mexico]' " (*CS* 149), despite the fact that he has been in the country for only a few months and lacks even the most rudimentary knowledge of Spanish. And Uspensky, whom the narrator espies "directing a scene which he was convinced could be made from no other angle" (*CS* 164), operates the camera as the very mechanism of selective vision, a perpetual voyeur in a country he does not even remotely understand. Indeed, both the opportunistic American and the revolutionary Russian film crew fall into the same trap, using aesthetic expertise to promote the aims of an increasingly doctrinaire Mexican government that "wanted to improve this opportunity to film a glorious history of Mexico, her wrongs and sufferings and her final triumph through the latest revolution" (*CS* 153). In the end, this glorious history proceeds less through intensified vision than through sins of omission. As the Russian crew and American producer travel throughout the country,

> Dozens of helpful [Mexican] observers, art experts, photographers, literary talents, and travel guides swarmed about them to lead them aright, and to show them all the most beautiful, significant, and characteristic things in the national life and soul: if by chance anything not beautiful got in the way of the camera, there was a very instructed and sharp-eyed committee of censors whose duty it was to see that the scandal went no further than the cutting room. (*CS* 153)

With all of these "professional propagandists" hovering around the hacienda impatient to use their medium of choice to fix a particular— and particularly narrow—version of Mexico, the only character who refuses to cut any of this disturbing footage is the narrator herself.

The contrast between the various ideological arts of the Russians, Americans, and Mexicans and the narrator's aesthetics of experience ultimately emerges as the central narrative conflict in "Hacienda." When Kennerly remarks on the coincidence between an accidental shooting death on the premises of the hacienda and a similar scene that had been shot for the film, he marvels at the fact that "'the same thing has happened to the same people in *reality!*'" (*CS* 171). Shortly afterward, he repeats the exclamation, "'*Reality!*'" and "lick[s] his chops" (*CS* 171). Over the course of Kennerly's lengthy disquisitions on the coincidence between fiction and reality—at one point, he suggests the cameraman could have simply shot the accidental death and incorporated it into the film to give the footage more authenticity—we realize that he has no qualms about subordinating the on-the-ground conditions of Mexico to the cinematic needs of the film. Indeed, the significance of the film for the narrator seems to reside in the way that several different ideological groupings—the corporatist and imperialist Hollywood perspective of Kennerly, the revolutionary triumphalism of Uspensky, and the institutional leftism of the Mexican state and its artists—have conspired to produce a narrative about contemporary Mexico that captures everything but what is *actually* happening. The text develops an elaborate parallel between the type of filmic "arrangement" this distorted image demands (preparatory photographs, cutting, and montage) and the more political and economic types of "fixing" that allow for the hacienda to remain a site of exploitation under the very noses of those who profess to be chronicling its demise:

> The workers in the vat-room began to empty the fermented pulque into barrels, and to pour the fresh maguey water into the reeking bullhide vats. . . . The white flood of pulque flowed without pause; all over Mexico the Indians would drink the corpse-white liquor, swallow forgetfulness and ease by the riverful, and the money would flow silver-white into the government treasury; don Genaro and his fellow-hacendados would fret and curse, the Agrarians would raid, and ambitious politicians in the capital would be stealing right and left enough to buy such haciendas for themselves. It was all arranged. (*CS* 175)

Not coincidentally, this political and economic "arrangement" is happening right *and* left. Uspensky/Eisenstein's technique of dialectical montage comes across as one more component of aesthetic ideology that elides the depressing reality of postrevolutionary Mexico. It is this reality—the "real reality"—that the narrator alone perceives.

In its narrative progression and its treatment of character, "Hacienda" inexorably leads the reader toward the conclusion that no existing ideological system can provide an adequate foundation for an aesthetic mode of representation. Thus, while Porter diligently traces the etiology of economic exploitation, suggesting (as in the passage on *pulque* above) the systemic logic through which such exploitation takes place, the text deliberately forestalls the possibility that art can and should serve the sole purpose of transforming this system. The narrator's greatest criticism of Eisenstein/Uspensky is that he has a "monkey attitude towards life" that "saved explanation" (*CS* 161), instinctively producing images of transformation even where transformation has not occurred. We see in Porter's depiction of Uspensky's filmic style a condensation of her mistrust of the emerging proletarian aesthetic in the United States as well: one of the accusations against Uspensky is that "American communists were paying for the film" (*CS* 152), and Porter's use of Sinclair's brother-in-law as the model for Kennerly indicates her desire to further flesh out the relationship between US leftist culture and the exoticizing of Mexico that she had begun to delineate in "That Tree." What "Hacienda" ultimately proposes, then, is not a solution to the contradictions of postrevolutionary Mexican life, but rather an aesthetic program for exposing and understanding them. Against the backdrop of a US literary scene in which writers were increasingly advocating for revolutionary change, Porter insisted on the need for a literature of experience to portray and evaluate the changes that the revolution had (and had not) actually brought about.

When Porter first conceptualized the article that became "Hacienda" in July 1931, she pitched it to Cowley with an assurance that the "names and such [would be] disguised." In appealing to the assistant editor of the *New Republic* in this way, she communicated the urgent need for journalistic and literary work to evince a deep, prolonged, and unideological take on the events in Mexico. A few years earlier, she had been more explicit in offering Cowley one of her "political" articles. "I promise not to write as an authority on Mexico," she insisted, "nor apologist, nor propagandist, nor enemy, but as an observer putting two and two together in the probable but distant hope of getting four out of it."[54] As usual, Porter's words could not quite be taken at face value. She certainly believed in her ability to put events together, at least much more than others did, just as surely as she was convinced that she was as qualified as any US writer to say something about the country. Yet the prohibitions she lays out for writing on Mexico—it ought not be done as propagandist, enemy, or apologist—function as a kind of short list of the commandments for the

US writer. What she was advocating was not quite realism, nor partisan or committed literature; she was advocating for a literature of experience.

In the end, posterity was not particularly kind to Hemingway's and Porter's mid-1930s Latin American texts. "Hacienda" remains far less anthologized than either her earlier Mexico story "Flowering Judas" or her short novels of the late 1930s, and Howard Hawks's 1944 film adaptation of *To Have and Have Not*—a Bogart-Bacall romance set in wartime Martique rather than revolutionary Cuba—has had a longer afterlife than Hemingway's novel. But even though these texts (with all their geographical specificity) eventually receded from the US cultural imaginary, their political arguments proved crucial to the critical debates of the 1930s and 1940s. We can begin to trace this lineage in Philip Rahv's iconic essay "The Cult of Experience in American Writing," which first appeared in the *Partisan Review* in 1940.

As I stated in my introduction, Rahv's "The Cult of Experience in American Writing" was the fullest contemporary exploration of the US literature of experience. Predictably, Rahv cited Hemingway's work as the primary example of the contemporary American novel's "intense predilection for the real…as a vast phenomenology swept by waves of sensation and feeling."[55] Yet Rahv's essay was not concerned with the "cult of experience" exclusively as an aesthetic phenomenon; he also highlighted how the literature of experience had shaped the representation of politics and revolt within the US novel. In fact, one of Rahv's strongest claims was that the political, economic, and cultural shifts that came in the wake of the crash of 1929 had masked a continuity in the realm of aesthetics between the 1920s and 1930s: "Though the crisis of the nineteen-thirties arrested somewhat the progress of the experiential mode, [the cult of experience] nevertheless managed to put its stamp on the entire social-revolutionary literature of the decade" (17). For Rahv, this meant that Hemingway and "American left-wing" writers such as John Steinbeck shared far more than one might expect: "What does a radical novel like The Grapes of Wrath contain, from an ideological point of view, that agitational journalism cannot communicate with equal heat and facility? Surely its vogue cannot be explained by its radicalism. Its real attraction for the millions who read it lies elsewhere—perhaps in its vivid recreation of a 'slice of life' so horrendously unfamiliar that it can be made to yield an exotic interest" (17). Contrasting the thirties strain of the literature of experience with the protocommitted

European novels of André Malraux and Ignazio Silone, Rahv claimed that US writers had depicted the experience of economic exploitation without addressing its structural causes.

Denning's work on the writers, intellectuals, and workers of the Popular Front has demonstrated that radical thinkers in the United States of the 1930s were far more deliberate and effective in their "cultural labor" than previous scholars had suggested, while Americanist scholarship of the past few decades has indicated the shortcomings of Rahv's assessment of the impact of radical thought on the writing during this decade.[56] Yet we should not entirely dismiss Rahv's comments about how deeply the experiential discourse continued to mark US literature in the 1930s, even as economic woes, labor disputes, and political strife increasingly radicalized American intellectual life. In "I Was Marching," published in the *New Masses* in 1935, Meridel Le Sueur draws heavily from the anaphoric sentence structure of Hemingway's style as she catalogues the physical sensations of participating in the 1934 Minneapolis general strike.[57] And the fear of producing lifeless dogmatic literature was just as acute among writers of the left as it was for Hemingway and Porter. James Agee prefaced *Let Us Now Praise Famous Men* (1939) by opposing his documentary account of tenant farmers in the South to a "safely dangerous" book that could be neatly categorized as "'scientific' or 'political' or 'revolutionary,'" insisting that "in the immediate world, everything is to be discerned, for him who can discern it, and centrally and simply, without either dissection into science, or digestion into art, but with the whole of consciousness, seeking to perceive it as it stands."[58] Looking back on the overall climate of the thirties in his memoir *American Hunger* (1944, 1977), Richard Wright remarked on the leftist magazines's "passionate call for the experience of the disinherited,"[59] a phrase that can be taken as alluding not only to the ideological bent of the decade's writing—populist, proletarian—but also to the dominant form it took: that is, a literature *of* experience.

Even more importantly for our purposes, though, is the degree to which Rahv's "The Cult of Experience" affirms the key rhetorical strategy of *To Have and Have Not* and "Hacienda." In spite of his frequent avowals of the limitations of the literature of experience, Rahv nevertheless maintains that its most positive attribute has been its anti-ideological thrust: "the primacy of experience in late American literature…conferred certain benefits upon it, of which none is more bracing than its relative immunity from abstraction and otherworldliness.

The stream of life, unimpeded by the rocks and sands of ideology, flows through it freely" (19). If Rahv explicitly recognized Hemingway as a proponent of this type of experiential aesthetics, the statement also reflects an awareness of the strategies of representation Porter had employed in works like "Hacienda." In fact, Rahv might very well have drawn on Porter's response to a *Partisan Review* questionnaire the year before his essay appeared, where she claimed that her "whole attempt has been…to make a distillation of what human relations and experiences my mind has been able to absorb," adding that as the "[p]olitical tendency since 1930 has been to the last degree a confused, struggling, drowning-man-and-straw sort of thing… I hope we shall have balance enough to see ourselves plainly" (*CS*, 706).

While Rahv's statements about the anti-ideological character of US literature and thought have often been characterized as the very substance of American ideology, they represented the unfolding of a specific cultural argument within a specific historical moment. When taken in the context of Hemingway's and Porter's evolving aesthetics of the 1920s and 1930s, "The Cult of Experience" begins to seem less like a series of bird's-eye pronouncements than a concrete intervention in the US literary field—indeed, an important inflection point in the way the "experiential mode" in US writing was conceptualized. At once channeling the narrative tropes of interwar writers such as Porter and Hemingway and naming what up to that point had been a series of loosely connected cultural arguments spread across the domains of fiction, poetry, philosophy, and political thought, Rahv's essay created an interpretive matrix for understanding the literature of experience as a dominant discourse. And in fact, the belief that there was a particularly American literature of experience motivated several critical operations of the 1940s and the early postwar period.

Disciplining the Literature of Experience

As US ascendancy on the global stage reached a high point with the Allied victory in World War II, and as American literature became consecrated through the awarding of the Nobel Prize to Faulkner and Hemingway in 1949 and 1954 respectively, the US literature of experience began to reach a worldwide audience. No doubt bolstered by the steady exportation of Hollywood adaptations of the novels of the interwar modernists—such as the 1932 film version of *A Farewell to Arms*, starring Gary Cooper as the unflappable Frederic Henry—writers outside the US literary field started to describe the literature of experience as a specifically American cultural phenomenon. In the next chapter, I detail how Latin American writers of the post-1945 period responded to and reshaped the US literature of experience. But the idea that the US literary tradition promoted a particular attitude toward experience circulated well beyond the hemisphere. Already in the 1930s, Cesare Pavese, one of the best-known Italian writers of the mid-twentieth century and an important translator of American fiction, dedicated a series of essays to the US literature of experience. In an essay on Herman Melville that anticipates the broad themes of Rahv's "Cult of Experience," Pavese claims that "the whole literary tradition of the States, from Thoreau to Sherwood Anderson, consciously or unconsciously tends [toward] . . . the creation of powerful individuals who spend a good number of years in uncultivated pursuits, experiencing and absorbing, and who then devote themselves to culture, reelaborating the experienced reality in reflections and images."[60] In the early postwar years, European writers of various stripes weighed in on the aesthetic value and influence of that experiential tradition. French feminist Simone de Beauvoir spoke of a generation of French writers who held that in "the American novels we like so much . . . Life is revealed in all its truth," while Italo Calvino claimed that he and his Italian contemporaries recognized in Hemingway a nonphilosophical "American philosophy, linked . . . to a milieu of activity and practical concepts."[61]

Even as the US literature of experience was being read and debated abroad, the "cult of experience" was domesticated—and institutionalized—in the postwar US university. As McGurl suggests, the rapidly proliferated creative writing–MFA program became the laboratory for much of post-1945 fiction, as well as the official workshop for "writing what you know." McGurl alludes to the prominence of Hemingway's statements on the writing process in the development of the creative writing program, yet Porter's incorporation into the postwar US institutions of higher education was equally dramatic. This was not only because she taught creative writing (she had several stints as a writing instructor) but also because her literary aesthetic was treated with growing admiration both in the academic classroom and the creative writing workshop. Beginning in the 1930s, Porter befriended several writers associated with the Southern

Renaissance—Allen Tate, Robert Penn Warren, and Cleanth Brooks—who later formed the core of the New Critical movement that swept through academia in the 1940s and 1950s. Tate and Brooks both wrote essays celebrating Porter's work, and Warren published a seminal article that began with the assertion that Porter "belongs to that relatively small group of writers…who have done serious, consistent, original, and vital work in the form of short fiction—the group which would include James Joyce, Katherine Mansfield, Sherwood Anderson, and Ernest Hemingway."[62] By the early 1950s, Porter could be mentioned alongside Hemingway as one of the US authors who had so permeated the American university that, as McCarthy's narrator playfully put it, advocates of modern poetry aimed to displace those writers who were identified by their "flaccid, prosy devotions to K.A.P., Hemingway, Lardner, [and] Saroyan."[63] During these midcentury decades, a range of important writers and critics sought to articulate, historicize, and critique the rise to dominance of the US literature of experience, from New York Intellectuals such as Rahv and McCarthy to New Critics such as Warren and Brooks.

This literal institutionalization of the US literature of experience, however, masked a more subtle way in which the New Critics brought Porter's and Hemingway's work into the academic fold: by corralling their notion of writing from expansive personal experience into the confines of the text itself. Although the antihistorical, antibiographical bent of the New Criticism and its analytical methods has been much documented, the relationship between the New Criticism and the "cult of experience" has rarely, if ever, been fully explored. At times, New Critical analysis would take a normative stance toward the writer as experiencer, as in Brooks and Warren's assessment of Hemingway's stories in their introduction to "The Killers": "The figures which live in this world, live a sort of hand-to-mouth existence perceptually, and conceptually, they hardly live at all. Subordination implies some exercise of discrimination—the sifting of reality through the intellect. But Hemingway has a romantic anti-intellectualism which is to be associated with the premium which he places upon experience as such."[64] Yet if the experiential thrust in the works of Hemingway (and Porter) was problematic for Brooks, Warren, and Tate, the way these writers invoked a creed of "tell a straight story" (Porter) or "write it how it is" (Hemingway) to call into question the validity of ideological literature appealed enormously to the New Critics, who were steadily moving toward a separation of literature from politics in the 1930s and early 1940s.[65]

Warren's analysis of "Flowering Judas" in "Katherine Anne Porter: Irony with a Center" (1942) sheds light on how Porter's experiential aesthetics was recast by the New Critics as exemplary modernist style, that is, how the emphasis on personal experience in Porter's writings was transformed into a question of purely literary technique. In Warren's reading, "Flowering Judas" becomes an exercise in verbal irony rather than a commentary on the lived irony of the postrevolutionary period in Mexico. "We have here a tissue of contradictions," he writes about the text's treatment of the "skilled revolutionist" Braggioni, "and the very phraseology takes us to these contradictions. For instance, the word *yearns* involves the sentimental, blurred emotion, but immediately afterward, the words *sideways* and *oily* remind us of the grossness, the brutality, the physical appetite."[66] In passage after passage, the revolutionary's betrayal of the cause is framed in the language of "irony," "paradox," "contradiction," and "ambiguity," critical terms that would become central to the New Critical vocabulary. In fact, it is not difficult to trace how "Katherine Anne Porter: Irony with a Center" served as a kind of test run for the process of literary criticism anatomized in Warren and Brooks's *Understanding Fiction*, the standard New Critical textbook for literary fiction first published in 1943. In their introduction, Warren and Brooks identify irony, the literary technique of producing a "vindictive opposition" and a conflict in the "alignment of judgments and sympathies on the part of the author," as the very characteristic that distinguishes good fiction from the "merely dogmatic and partisan vilification" of writers who see the world in terms of right and wrong.[67] Though these dogmatic and partisan authors go unnamed in the textbook, Warren and Brooks point to Hemingway's work as an example of the kind of complex fiction they reproduce in their anthology, fiction that attends to the inherent contradictions of political, social, and personal situations rather than deploying abstract values: "we may recall that...in Hemingway's *For Whom the Bell Tolls* the scene of greatest brutality is that of the massacre of Fascists by Loyalists, or that the book closes with the distant figure of the Young Fascist lieutenant (whom Hemingway has previously presented as a sympathetic character) caught in the gunsights of the hero" (xix). If Warren and Brooks sought to distance themselves from Hemingway's and Porter's experiential creeds, they adopted almost wholesale these authors' belief that good politics cannot be the basis for good literature.

Although Warren's essay on Porter seeks to locate the theme of ideological betrayal primarily at the textual level, this does not necessarily mean that his interpretation significantly warps the sense of Porter's work. In fact, one is struck by how closely his reading tracks the critique of ideology I have already analyzed in "Hacienda." When Warren reaches his conclusion in "Irony with a Center"—that Porter's work affirms "the constant need for exercising discrimination, the arduous obligation of the intellect in the face of conflicting dogmas" (62)—we realize that Porter's representational strategies are conducive to Warren's New Critical approach in part because they have produced it. Similarly, when Warren and Brooks anthologized "The Killers" in *Understanding Fiction*, they revised their earlier comments about Hemingway's fiction by suggesting that his compositional techniques were fully consonant with the New Critical approach to literature, since his "style of direct experience" was actually a "dramatic device" rather than a deeply held aesthetic principle (311). Thus while Porter and Hemingway found the key to their defeat of ideology in full immersion, the New Critics would transfer the "inherent contradictions" of the political, social, and personal from the lived experience of the author to the text itself. Although Hemingway himself insisted to his reader midway through *Death in the Afternoon* that "it is necessary that you see a bullfight yourself" (63), Warren's essay on Porter in "Irony with a Center" implies that the textual rendering of "incident and implication" (62) is all a critic needs. An intelligent critic, in other words, can get the meaning without having had the experience.

Warren's New Critical interpretation of Porter's work demonstrates in miniature a critical operation I would call the "disciplining" of the US literature of experience. When one reads the essays, textbooks, and articles by New Critics such as Warren, Tate, and Brooks in the 1930s and 1940s, one encounters not only reminders of the "intentional fallacy" linking an author's intent to the meaning of a text, but also, and perhaps more insistently, an assault on the idea that the scope, place, or intensity of a writer's personal experience is material to the production and consumption of a literary text. As the New Criticism became the dominant scholarly trend in postwar academia, the line between literary critics and fiction writers would increasingly be defined in terms of their stance on the relationship between authorial experience and creative writing.[68] Only at this point, I would argue, did McGurl's story about the "sneering war between creative writers and scholars in the university" truly commence.[69] It was a war, I might add, that was waged in literal and conceptual territories that extended far beyond the campus. Where was the authority of literature located? Was it in the author's life experience, the places, events, and peoples with which he or she has come into contact? Was it in the transmutation of these experiences into art? Or was it always already inside the text, subject to the extracting devices of the best tools of interpretation?

Although these arguments eventually shaded into debates about how race, gender, and class "experience" affected literary production, they continued to undergird many of the major debates in the US literary field in the 1960s and 1970s. In his 1966 foreword to the second edition of *The Philosophy of Literary Form*, Kenneth Burke summarized this entire period of US literary history in the following way: if the 1930s represented the emergence of a greater emphasis on politics and "Ideology" among US writers and critics, the postwar period signaled a shift toward a "'Beatnicist' ferment" that "more closely resembles the stirrings of the twenties than the thirties."[70] I have suggested in this chapter that Hemingway's and Porter's works maintained a twenties aesthetic predicated on full immersion and "practical world experience" in the face of the "political turn" of the 1930s, offering in effect a defense of the US literature of experience that linked the modernist moment with the arguments against "ideological" fiction that gained ground among New Critics and New York intellectuals alike in the 1940s and 1950s. In the late 1950s and 1960s, the Beat writers would again take up the mantle of the literature of experience, and again turn to Latin America, though this time within a different hemispheric context. It is to this context that we will turn in the next chapter.

Voracious Readers

THE LATIN AMERICAN LETTERED CITY AND THE US
LITERATURE OF EXPERIENCE

*I went from being a cautious reader to a voracious reader.... I wanted
to read everything.*

—ROBERTO BOLAÑO, *Entre Paréntesis*

When the Uruguayan critic Ángel Rama died in a plane crash in
1983, he left behind an incomplete manuscript, *La ciudad letrada*
[*The Lettered City*, 1984], a grand yet unfinished narrative of Latin
American intellectual history. Published posthumously the following
year, the book traces the relationship between literature and politics
in the region from the colonial period forward, arguing for a long-
standing complicity between the state and the *letrado*—a culturally
specific term that Rama employs to capture the various roles of the
Latin American writer-intellectual as scribe, lawyer, novelist, and
journalist. According to multiple sources, Rama planned to conclude the book with a chapter on the legacy of the *letrado* tradition
in his own generation, formed during the tumultuous decade of the
1960s. Having reconstructed the cultural history of the "lettered city"
from Hernán Cortés's remodeling of Tenochtitlán in 1520 to Oscar
Niemeyer and Lúcio Costa's "inauguration" of Brasilia in 1960, Rama
apparently intended to update his work to reflect the evolving contours of Latin American cultural production in the second half of the
twentieth century. It is no coincidence that Rama selected 1960 as his
historiographic cut, a Janus-faced year that simultaneously marked
the founding of the most recent Latin American lettered city and the
possibility of a new cultural formation in the wake of the Cuban
Revolution of 1959.

Writing less than ten years after Rama's death, John Beverley spoke approvingly of the "new cultural and political practices" precipitated by the Cuban Revolution and the guerrilla movements of the 1960s, 1970s, and 1980s, practices that challenged the position of the Latin American "lettered subject" as it traditionally had been defined.[1] In his influential study *Against Literature* (1993), Beverley argued that the genre of the *testimonio*—that is, nonfiction works narrated from the perspective of previously marginalized populations—was already displacing the so-called *nueva narrativa latinoamericana* as the dominant form of written work produced in Latin America. As I mentioned in my first chapter, the Cuban poet and essayist Roberto Fernández Retamar lambasted Jorge Luis Borges in 1971 as the archaic "representative among us of a now powerless class for whom the act of writing… is more like the act of reading"; later in the essay, he indicts Carlos Fuentes, the main architect of the *nueva narrativa*, as "a spokesman for the same class as Borges."[2] Though Rama himself did not dismiss Fuentes or the *nueva narrativa* in such categorical terms, he pressed for greater recognition of the *testimonio*, helping to create an annual prize for the genre under the auspices of Fernández Retamar's revolutionary cultural organization and publishing house Casa de las Américas. This new paradigm seemed to augur a significantly reduced role for the activity of reading and the figure of the writer-as-reader in Latin American literature. We might surmise that had Rama lived to complete the chapter, he would have described many of these literary forms poised to supplant the Latin American *letrado* tradition in the 1970s and 1980s.

By the first decade of the twenty-first century, however, Beverley's prediction about the wholesale replacement of literary fiction with the *testimonio* had not come to pass, even as the "pink tide" of progressive governments began to dismantle many elements of the old order that Beverley had linked to the lettered city. Not only did the figure of the writer-intellectual remain a powerful political force in Latin America;[3] equally significantly, Latin American writers increasingly turned to the reader in their fiction as the privileged subject position from which to represent politics. The list of canonical post-boom works with writer-reader protagonists could very well pass for a survey of the Latin American political novel from 1980 to 2010: Ricardo Piglia's *Respiración artificial* [*Artificial Respiration*, 1980] and *Prisión perpetua* [*Perpetual Prison*, 1988]; Luis López Nieves's *Seva* (1983); Sergio Pitol's *El desfile del amor* [*The Love Parade*, 1984];

Fernando Vallejo's *La virgen de los sicarios* [*Our Lady of the Assassins*, 1994]; Roberto Bolaño's *Estrella distante* [*Distant Star*, 1996], *Los detectives salvajes* [*The Savage Detectives*, 1998], and *2666* (2004); Cristina Rivera Garza's *Nadie me verá llorar* [*No One Will See Me Cry*, 1999], *La cresta de Ilión* [*Ilion's Crest*, 2002], and *La muerte me da* [Death Comes to Me, 2007]; Juan Villoro's *El testigo* [The Witness, 2004]; Horacio Castellanos Moya's *Insensatez* [*Senselessness*, 2005]; Pola Oloixarac's *Las teorías salvajes* [*Savage Theories*, 2008]; and Rodrigo Rey Rosa's *El material humano* [Human Matter, 2009]. The veritable explosion of reader protagonists in the early twenty-first century demonstrates the extent to which the activity of reading became almost the zero degree of identity formation in the contemporary Latin American novel.

Borges is unquestionably the precursor to this literary constellation, both as acknowledged influence and as the kind of retroactively agglutinating signifier that the Argentine author himself explored in "Kafka and His Precursors." Yet we still lack a convincing account of how a writer so frequently criticized for his conservatism and retrograde aesthetics from the 1950s to the 1980s became the primary inspiration for the Latin American literary avant-garde at the turn of the twenty-first century. If, as Idelber Avelar and others have effectively argued, the most powerful (and canonical) works of postdictatorial Latin American fiction have mourned the defeat of the radical left by returning to its supposedly superseded political and cultural horizons, how did Borges—rather than, say, Neruda—become the literary model for this generation? For evidence of this transformation, we need look no further than the writings of Fernández Retamar, perhaps the most visible late-twentieth-century spokesperson for the Latin American institutional left. Although Fernández Retamar had unabashedly attacked Borges's bookishness in the 1970s as the mark of a "typical colonial writer," by the end of the 1990s, he had almost entirely reversed his earlier view. In the significantly titled essay "Como yo amé mi Borges" [As I Loved My Borges, 1999], he redefines the Argentine writer's literary internationalism as "postcolonial" rather than "colonial."[4] Offering his best Borges impression, Fernández Retamar details his obsession with the Argentine writer's works in the years leading up to the Cuban Revolution: "I didn't only read everything written by [Borges] in the magnificent library of that university and others in the country, including materials in weird magazines, but also, since his name had not yet become international. . . .

I acquired first editions of his books in out-of-the-way bookstores, in Spanish-language publications."[5] Discarding his earlier portraits of the artist as rugged revolutionary, Fernández Retamar's self-fashioning here seems (almost literally) to take a page from the scholar quests of Borges's "Tlön, Uqbar, Orbis Tertius" or "The Library of Babel." Framed as an homage to the modern writer who best understood the quiet complicity between saints and heretics, heroes and traitors, Fernández Retamar's essay provides a fitting if ironic ending to an important chapter in Latin American literary history. While Fernández Retamar's discursive reversal with respect to Borges could be attributed to a change in personal taste or simply to political cynicism, I would argue that his comments reflect a continent-wide literary transformation.

Just as Fernández Retamar altered his portrait of Borges in the late twentieth century, so too did postboom writers reshape the image of the Borgesian reader in the Latin American literary field. The most basic strategy of this generation was to recast the reader as an underground exegete of the state-sponsored violence of the Latin American dictatorships, a role that Piglia's and Bolaño's alter egos (Emilio Renzi and Arturo Belano, respectively) assume in numerous fictional works. At the same time, these writers also reached back into the Latin American cultural archive, reinterpreting those figures of the left least associated with the *letrado* tradition. Piglia's study of Che Guevara in *El último lector* [The Last Reader, 2005] exemplifies the process by which the icons of the Latin American guerrilla movements were refashioned as poet-warriors. Underscoring references in Guevara's diaries and testimonies to his voracious appetite for literature even in the most dangerous moments of his guerrilla campaigns, Piglia writes, "[r]eading persists as a remnant of the past, in the middle of the experience of pure action, of dispossession and violence, of guerrilla warfare, of the hills."[6]

In the first decade of the twenty-first century, this dual project of radicalizing the reader and reinjecting reading into the Latin American radical tradition became an even more urgent project for writers who did not conform to the image of the white male Creole author typically associated with the *letrado*. Craig Epplin has described how in the aftermath of the Argentine financial crisis of 2001, a number of small presses emerged in Buenos Aires that challenged the "modern book culture" epitomized by Borges and subverted the distribution tactics of contemporary transnational publishing houses.

As Epplin shrewdly notes, though the writers associated with these presses alternated between "exalting" and "debasing" conventional literary forms, they remained almost uniformly committed to the persistence of a culture of reading in one capacity or another.[7] In the early years of this century, Washington Cucurto, cofounder of the Eloísa Cartonera press, went so far as to recommend that the Argentine state adopt the famed *cartonera* practice of printing Latin American literary works on recycled cardboard: "Zero investment and you change Argentine culture. Who wouldn't buy a book on the street for a peso and a half?"[8] Cucurto is one of the many contemporary Latin American authors who have imagined a future for the writer-as-reader outside of (but not necessarily isolated from) the traditional confines of the lettered city. Furthermore, as we will see, Cristina Rivera Garza's novels and critical works have insistently questioned the gendered tropes inherent in the position (and nomenclature) of the *letrado*, recuperating a tradition of twentieth-century Latin American women reader-writers while creating a space for the *lectora* within the contemporary Latin American literary field. Thus while the readers we encounter in Latin American novels of the twenty-first century draw from the representational strategies of earlier "lettered" discourse, they bear little resemblance to the *letrados* of previous eras.

This transformation of the writer-as-reader in Latin America has not, however, been merely an internal phenomenon. For Latin American authors of the end of the twentieth century, to define oneself as a voracious reader also meant defining oneself in relation to the US literature of experience. As I observed in my introduction, the most influential postboom Latin American writer-readers largely converge in their belief that the injunction to write from experience structures the US literary field: Bolaño writes of the "North American classics who concentrated their efforts on the observation of life and experience"; Piglia refers to "the myth, so typically North American, of lived experience [*de la experiencia vivida*]"; and Villoro asserts that the North American literary tradition begins with the "invitation... to go out into the world in search of experience."[9] Indeed, it was this generation of writers of the 1980s, 1990s, and the 2000s that first made the interaction between Latin American readers and US experiencers a central dynamic of their literary works. A 2007 conversation between Piglia and Villoro about Bolaño clarifies the scope of this hemispheric dynamic. Responding to Villoro's question about the correlation of "reading," "action," and "detective work" in *Los detectives salvajes*, Piglia observes:

> I'm very interested in how Bolaño works with the figure of the reader. There's always an intrigue surrounding a text whose meaning is never fully captured or understood, and here I believe we can think of a certain tradition. That tension between "arms and letters" or "how to leave the library" always appears as a problem, as if the library were isolated from life.... The Beat generation might be one of the examples—one of the last examples that I know of—that offers a response to this problem: to go out on the road [salir al camino], the experience of Kerouac, the experience of Allen Ginsberg.[10]

Tellingly, Piglia inscribes the "problem" of reading and experience within a broader consideration of US–Latin American literary relations, represented here by Bolaño's appropriation of the Beat generation. That Piglia merely alludes to the US literature of experience rather than defining it—as he had done in many of his texts of the 1980s and 1990s—only confirms the degree to which he takes the (North) Americanness of the modern experiential "tradition" for granted.

In this chapter, I demonstrate how Piglia's, Bolaño's, and Rivera Garza's late twentieth- and early twenty-first-century works reinvigorated debates about the role of reading in contemporary literature by staging a series of fictional misencounters between Latin American readers and US experiencers. This theorization of the structural relationship between the Latin American literature of the reader and the US literature of experience should force us to rethink several influential strains of Latin Americanist criticism over the past few decades. Scholars such as Avelar and Beatriz Sarlo have used the work of Walter Benjamin and the Frankfurt school to locate an anti-experiential impulse in contemporary Latin American fiction that offers an alternative to what Avelar refers to as "naive realisms and testimonialisms of various sorts." Employing the Benjaminian language of the modern "crisis of experience," Avelar has insisted that Piglia is among those contemporary writers who have "confront[ed] the epochal crisis of storytelling and the decline of the transmissibility of experience."[11] Sarlo too, so different from Avelar in other ways, has championed a strain of Argentine fiction that challenges the *testimonio* by "think[ing] *outside* of experience [*desde afuera* de la experiencia]."[12] Although I agree that the rhetoric of the "crisis of experience" thoroughly permeates the contemporary Latin American field, I argue that the target of this antiexperiential impulse is as much the US literature of experience as the Latin American *testimonio*. For Latin American writers of the turn of the millenium, to engage with the "literature of experience" has not only entailed responding to a regional or local phenomenon or to a diffuse characteristic of global modernity; it has also meant naming a specific US–Latin American literary relationship. The debate about *testimonio* has thus been inscribed within a broader hemispheric dynamic in which Latin American reader-writers have simultaneously admired and competed with the US literature of experience. Although Piglia's *Prisión perpetua* reveals the ambivalence of this relationship most explicitly, it surfaces in various guises in nearly all of the Latin American writers I examine.

My account of the relationship between contemporary Latin American readers and US experiencers also contests Beverley's argument about US–Latin American cultural politics in his most recent book, *Latinamericanism after 9/11* (2011). Analyzing the rise of a twenty-first-century strain of "neo-Arielist" writing that defends the power of "literature as such," Beverley convincingly shows that hemispheric relations have had a deep effect on contemporary Latin American cultural production and that a variety of writers have deployed strategies of representing the United States that hark all the way back to Rodó's *Ariel*.[13] But his argument falls short in two respects. The first is that the contemporary Latin American writers and critics Beverley studies engage with US cultural traditions to a far greater degree than he acknowledges. Alongside what Beverley correctly describes as mistrust of institutional US multiculturalism, we also find an abiding fascination with the US counterculture from the Beats to the Black Power movement. The second is Beverley's marked propensity to oppose this "lettered" generation to the leftist governments that emerged in the first decade of the twenty-first century in Latin America. His book sets up a false opposition between "organic" intellectuals of the left such as García Linera and the (naively) utopian or (disingenuously) neoliberal ideologues of neo-Arielism. While this opposition may hold for a few unabashedly antiprogressive writers like the later Vargas Llosa, the most important writer-intellectuals of the turn of the twenty-first century generally supported (though by no means unreflexively) the leftward turn in Latin American politics. This is as true of Piglia as it is of Hugo Achugar, one of Beverley's main examples of the "neo-Arielist" critic, who in fact served as national director of culture for the left-leaning administration of Uruguay's José Mujica. Thus, although the (geo)political orientation of these writers will be crucial to my account, I will resist the temptation to offer a hemispheric narrative of progressive heroes versus reactionary villains.

It is important to reiterate here that the primary goal of this study is to track the crystallization of cultural dominants in US and Latin American literature rather than to celebrate or condemn them. My analysis hinges on the recognition that literary works that take an oppositional role in the political, social, and economic realms may *at the same time* begin to function as dominant forms in the cultural realm, forms that can overshadow and even inhibit the production of literary alternatives. Kerouac's *On the Road* (1957), for example, is at once a profound expression of US counterculture and a work that reentrenched the US literature of experience in the postwar period, just as Bolaño's *The Savage Detectives* is simultaneously an attack on the Mexican literary hierarchy and a reterritorialization of the Latin American lettered city on other grounds. I do not mean to imply that no alternatives to such works exist, but rather that they emerge in a literary field whose changing landscape has been shaped by these dominant forms. Before we examine the characteristics of these dominant forms, however, we must first attend to the broader material relations between the United States and Latin America that have conditioned the development of these literary strains over the past forty years.

Reading, Experiencing, and the Politics of Movement

The characters in Bolaño's fiction often travel between the United States and Latin America. The Americans Oscar Fate and Albert Kessler cross the US-Mexican border in *2666* (2004), the Mexican poet Rafael Barrios relocates to California in *The Savage Detectives*, and numerous other figures make hemispheric journeys north and south. Nevertheless, as I mentioned at the beginning of this book, Bolaño never once set foot in the United States. In a 2002 interview with the Chilean writer Javier Campos, Bolaño, who was born in Chile and spent nearly ten years in Mexico City in the 1960s and 1970s, said that he had no intention of "heed[ing] the call of Uncle

Sam."[14] In the interview, Bolaño gave a surprising reason for never having been to the country:

> No, I don't have plans to travel to the United States....Maybe when I was younger it would have been interesting to live in Arizona or California or New York, which I suppose are places full of energy....Honestly, I don't think that they would have given me a visa to enter the United States when I was young. They only give visas to rich people and terrorists. Of course I could have entered as a wet-back, but in Mexico I already lived like a wetback, so in the United States I would have been a double wetback. Or a wetback and a wet chest, which would have been even worse.[15]

Although Bolaño's typically sardonic tone may leave us in doubt as to his true motives for refusing the call of "Uncle Sam," his comments nevertheless point to a very real dynamic in the US–Latin American politics of movement. The time Bolaño spent in Mexico City from 1968 to 1977 coincided with major shifts in US policy toward Latin American migration. Beginning in 1954 with Dwight Eisenhower's Operation Wetback—a name that alluded to would-be immigrants who crossed the shallow waters of the Rio Grande River to enter the country—the US government initiated a federal campaign to increase security measures to control the southern border and deport undocumented immigrants to Mexico. Almost simultaneously, the US state retooled its visa policy to drastically limit the number of legal tourists and immigrants coming across the southern border. Bolaño was thus probably justified in concluding that, as a lower-middle-class immigrant from Chile, he would not have received a visa to visit the United States in the 1970s. The sociologists Mark Purcell and Joseph Nevins argue that the 1970s witnessed a generalized fear in the United States in which state actors began to see the US-Mexican border as a "grossly under-resourced line of defense against what were framed as invading hordes from Mexico and other points in Latin America."[16] As I write these words in the aftermath of the 2016 US presidential election, it seems all too clear that such nativist tropes remain deeply entrenched in the US cultural imaginary.

These collective fears about Latin American immigration to the United States have emerged in tandem with increased material obstacles to free movement for Latin Americans. As Steffen Mau and Heike Brabandt argue in their study *Liberal States and the Freedom of*

Movement: Selective Borders, Unequal Mobility (2012), theories of globalization that point to high levels of cross-border activity as a sign of a "borderless" or "seamless" world overlook the fact that the general rise in mobility over the last thirty years has been accompanied by unparalleled efforts to select and control the *kinds* of people who are allowed to enter and leave certain countries.[17] Their study demonstrates that national visa policies are the primary factor in determining the freedom of movement for people around the world, and that wealthy liberal democracies like the United States have access to a broader range of global terrain than poorer, authoritarian, and troubled nations (as of 2010, the United States had visa-free arrangements with ninety-two other countries, while Iraq and Afghanistan had visa waivers with only two other countries). Although the United States has negotiated visa-free reciprocal agreements with nearly all of the countries in the European Union over the past twenty-five years, visa-free accords have been reached with just three Latin American nations: Argentina (1996), Uruguay (1998), and Chile (2014)—and the accords with Argentina and Uruguay were quickly rescinded in the wake of 9/11 and the financial crisis that hit the River Plate countries in 2001–2002.

For a generation that came of age during a period of brutal dictatorships in Latin America (Bolaño was twenty when Augusto Pinochet took power) and at the height of the Cold War, forced migration and exile not only uprooted writers and intellectuals from their home countries but often severely limited their overall freedom of movement. Though the rise of neoliberal governments in several Latin American countries in the late 1980s and 1990s contributed to an easing of travel restrictions, Latin American writers' access to foreign countries continues to fluctuate based on internal economic and political conditions as well as diplomatic relations with the United States. The problem of access to the United States is the theme of one of the best-known contemporary Bolivian novels, Juan de Recacoechea's detective thriller *American Visa* (1994), which tells the story of a high school teacher from a small town in Bolivia who risks his life in order to acquire a visa to visit his son in Miami. For the majority of Latin American writers in the second half of the twentieth century, trips to the United States were often authorized and financed for a specific cultural function: conferences, readings, literary fairs, or teaching positions. It is telling that the two most recognized Mexican literary figures in the United States in the twentieth century, Octavio Paz and Carlos Fuentes, were from diplomatic families and had prolonged stints as state ambassadors. I do not wish to dispute that Latin American writers have played a formative role in the construction of global literary networks during this period. Rather, I want to highlight that inter-American and transnational scholarship of the past twenty years has not adequately studied the broader cultural implications of this seismic change in the hemispheric politics of movement. Thus, to take seriously Jean Franco's exhortation to examine Bolaño's relationship to exile, we must begin to explore US–Latin American literary dynamics in terms of the complex symbolic effects of this change. This requires more than simply tracking trans-American immigration patterns; it necessitates an understanding of the structural ways in which different kinds of transnational movement have been narrativized within the literary field. We might begin by making a basic distinction between the cultural imaginaries surrounding the *voluntary exile* typical of US-born writers in the hemisphere and the *forced exile* of Latin American writers, which, though stretching back to the early post-Independence years in the nineteenth century, became a major topos of the literary works of the last decades of the twentieth century.

In earlier chapters, I discussed the emergence of the figure of the American writer as experiencer in the interwar US literary field. Yet despite the sanctification of Hemingway as the iconic American adventurer, it wasn't until the postwar era that the cultural type of the American writer as explorer of the outer latitudes of experience would become fully consecrated, largely through the works of the Beat generation. Combining openness to mind-bending "trips" on hallucinatory drugs with a penchant for the bizarre, the far out, and the exotic, the Beats both obsessively crisscrossed the United States and made frequent journeys beyond its geographical borders. Jack Kerouac and Allen Ginsberg took career-altering trips to Mexico; Leroi Jones (later Amiri Baraka) wrote his influential essay "Cuba Libre" (1960) after a pilgrimage to the Sierra Maestra; Jane and Paul Bowles spent most of their adult lives in Tangiers in Northern Africa; and William Burroughs, the most experiential (and experimental) of them all, began a twenty-year, four-continent-long odyssey after fleeing from a drug charge in New Orleans. In his classic biography of the Beat generation, *Naked Angels* (1976), John Tytell identified this "Beat affinity for the road" as "the symbol of an attitude toward experience that braves anything as long as movement is encouraged."[18] If in Kerouac's *On the Road* Sal Paradise and Dean Moriarty end up exhausting the American road and careening down the "Pan-American highway" to Mexico City, the global scope of the Beat "attitude" is perhaps best illustrated by the other classic of this generation, Burroughs's *Naked Lunch* (1959). Composed over nine years in Mexico City, the Amazon regions of Colombia and Peru, Morocco, Paris, and Copenhagen, the novel frequently unleashes series of paractic place names (i.e., "In Yemen, Paris, New Orleans, Mexico City, and Istanbul…") that surpass even Whitman in their geographical reach.[19]

The Beat writers were hardly unaware that the global terrain they traversed was subject to increasing prohibitions on the freedom of movement. Burroughs's works repeatedly thematize the significance of passports, visas, and other forms of identification, all of which he dismissively groups under the informal rubric of "papers." In Annexia, the dystopian city of *Naked Lunch*, for example, every citizen "was required to apply for and carry on his person at all times a whole portfolio of documents. Citizens were subject to be stopped in the street at any time; and the Examiner, who might be in plain clothes, in various uniforms, often in a bathing suit or pyjamas, sometimes stark naked except for a badge pinned to his left nipple, after checking each paper, would stamp it" (19-20). This absurdist projection of a system in which everyone needs permission to go anywhere can be read as a critique of the extreme bureaucratic control of international movement in the postwar era. Yet in his epistolary novel *The Yage Letters* (1963), it becomes clear that Burroughs—through his alter ego William Lee—tended to view Latin American travel laws as annoyances rather than real obstacles. Having been stopped and briefly imprisoned in the Putumayo region of Colombia because of an error in the dating of his passport, Lee sounds off on the "stupidity" of the Colombian system: "Travel in Colombia is difficult even with the soundest credentials. I have never seen such ubiquitous and annoying police."[20] The difficulty is resolved, however, by a simple meeting with the Commandante, who "shook hands pleasantly, looked at my papers, and listened to my explanation" before announcing, "This man is free" (22). In the next letter Lee reveals just how quickly his status as a US citizen could be turned in his favor when he is mistaken for a representative of the Texas Oil Company: "free boat rides, free plane rides, free chow; eating in the officers' mess, sleeping in the governor's house" (24). An initial hindrance gives way to the fullest freedom (and luxury) of movement.

The experiential trajectories of the Beats, coupled with their critique of the strictures and conformity of postwar US society, found sympathetic audiences in many parts of Latin America. A number of Beat-inspired movements arose in the 1960s and 1970s, including the Mexican Onda, the Argentine Grupo Opium, and the *infrarrealista* movement that Bolaño created in Mexico City with his best friend, Mario Santiago. These Latin American writers began to equate the Beats (and the US counterculture in general) with the idea of experience *as* artistic experimentation, an interpretation that was bolstered by the fact that the verb *experimentar* can mean both "to experience" and "to experiment" in Spanish. This is the verb Bolaño employs when describing Burroughs as an American classic: "He traveled throughout the world...and experimented with [*experimentó con*] all kinds of drugs....He loved weapons."[21] Burroughs's capacity for full immersion becomes the signature of a lifestyle defined by its openness to all forms of experience: "They say he had all of the vices in the world, but I believe he was a saint, approached by all of the vices in the world because he had the delicacy and imprudence to never shut his door."[22] In his writings, Bolaño treats the multilingual, transcontinental, and bisexual Burroughs as the personification of the US experiential writer.

Although Bolaño claims that Burroughs was open to nearly everything, he mentions reading as the one activity in the US writer's oeuvre that is associated with a lack of freedom: "When he talked about his readings one had the sense that he was remembering vague periods of his life in jail."[23] This association of the activity of reading with constriction in Burroughs's work, so at odds with a US critical tradition that has celebrated Burroughs's "cut-up method" as one of his most significant literary contributions, can partially be explained by the different conditions of reception of Burroughs's work in the United States and Latin America. Like Porter, Burroughs wrote his first works in and about Mexico, and Latin American writers have often been quick to identify the importance of Mexico to Burroughs as a place of escape from literature as well as from US society. Recalling Burroughs's first published novel, *Junkie* (1953), much of which takes place in Mexico City, the Mexican writer Jorge García-Robles has observed:

> Burroughs wrote alone in Mexico. Without wanting to be cultural, without looking for literary circles, much less academic or intellectual ones. WSB was never interested in modern Mexican culture; he never exchanged a word with a single national luminary of the period; he never attended a conference or went to a play. It's quite possible that he never bought a book written by a Mexican. Forty years later, he had never heard of Octavio Paz, Carlos Fuentes, or Juan Rulfo. He might have caught a glimpse of the walls of the Palacio de Bellas Artes or the Hotel del Prado, without particularly liking them. Burroughs remained oblivious to Mexico's cultural fireworks. He had other interests.[24]

Though García-Robles's description of Burroughs's apathy toward Mexican literature and culture might seem negatively charged, for the most part the US writer's antibookishness fills García-Robles with perverse relish. One of the founders of the Mexican Onda movement, García-Robles claims that he wrote the book "moved by the passion that William S. Burroughs's destiny inspires in me."[25]

Yet even such Beat-inspired Latin American writers could not help but perceive the distance between the antiliterary aesthetic of Burroughs's Mexican works and their own literary production. In the paragraph after García-Robles notes Burroughs's ignorance of Mexican culture when the two writers met in the early 1990s, he muses on the irony that Burroughs's time in the country coincided with the heyday of Mexican literature. He unleashes a Borges-like list of all the literary events in Mexico that Burroughs failed to notice: "He wasn't even aware that during those years Paz published *Libertad bajo palabra*, *El laberinto de la soledad*, and *Águila o sol*, that José Revueltas brought out *Los días terrenales*, that José Ortiz de Montellano, Xavier Villaurrutia and José Clemente Orozco died."[26] Burroughs's ignorance of Mexican literature, in other words, awakens García-Robles's desire to display his own mastery of the Mexican literary scene. The passage sheds light on the asymmetry in cross-cultural representation between two writers who ostensibly share the same artistic code. It also suggests the extent to which broad cultural stereotypes about US and Latin American literature have remained deeply ingrained—and perversely productive—well into the twenty-first century.

The Latin American Engaged Reader

While American writers of the early postwar period traveled mostly to Mexico and the Caribbean, the *figure* of the American experiential writer begin to spread across Latin America through literary translation. Even as many of the most influential Latin American writers remained staunchly critical of the Cold War interventionism of the US government, particularly after the 1959 Cuban Revolution, they were highly receptive to US cultural production. The literature of the Beat generation circulated alongside older works by Hemingway and Faulkner, and the American hard-boiled novel started to gain in popularity in the region. What all of these US genres shared, in spite of their obvious thematic and formal differences, was a commitment to the principle of experiential immersion. This at least was the thesis of Ricardo Piglia, whose writings of the 1970s and 1980s interrogated the position of the US writer of experience at the same time that they constructed a new paradigm for the Latin American writer-as-reader.

As I suggest in the second chapter, Borges was the most influential Latin American writer to challenge the US discourse of experience in the early twentieth century. For many Latin American writers of the early post–World War II era, however, the problem with taking Borges as a literary model was that his defense of the writer-as-reader seemed intimately linked to his political conservatism. The belief that Borges's cosmopolitan bookishness and literary "escapism" were source and symptom of a right-wing tendency became common-place on the radical left. The militant Argentine writer and historian Jorge Abelardo Ramos wrote that Borges had been a reactionary since his family "shut him up in a marvelous library full of English fantasy literature."[27] And, as I have mentioned above, Fernández Retamar rehearsed the standard *vendepatrias* complaint when he claimed that for Borges "the creation par excellence of culture is a library; or better yet, a museum—a place where the products of culture from abroad are assembled" (47). For these leftist intellectuals, Borges was a selfish, solitary writer whose bibliophilia was a means of evading social responsibility and political action.

This view changed in the final decades of the twentieth century. As I argue in the first part of the book, the initial signs of this shift surfaced in the works of writers associated with the Latin American boom: Gabriel García Márquez, Julio Cortázar, Fuentes, and Vargas

Llosa. Yet the more fundamental transformation came through the efforts of a generation of leftist writers and critics in Argentina, including Piglia, who began to look past Borges's overt political statements of the 1960s and 1970s. Recuperating an alternate view of Borges's legacy that centered on what might be called, to put a slight spin on the Sartrean formula, a practice of Borgesian *engaged reading*, Piglia reconstructed Borges's affinities with the early twentieth-century anarchist writer Macedonio Fernández and foregrounded Borges's deep commitment to Argentine literature and history in stories like "The South" and "A Biography of Tadeo Isidoro Cruz."[28] In his early essays and fiction, Piglia also developed Borges's analogy of the reader as detective and used it as a lens to analyze other literary and cultural traditions.[29] Although constantly in dialogue with the readerly aesthetics of such European writers as Italo Calvino and Umberto Eco, Piglia differentiated himself from a line of ludic Borgesian reader-writers by insisting on a geopolitical approach to reading that entailed a profound engagement with historical, cultural, and social formations.[30]

The recovery of this Borgesian practice of engaged reading occurred alongside another cultural phenomenon in Argentina: the discovery of Walter Benjamin and the Frankfurt School's theorization of modernity as a continual "crisis of experience." Though numerous poststructuralist critiques of "lived experience" can be traced throughout Europe and the Americas in the late 1960s and 1970s, in Latin America—and especially in Argentina—Benjamin's rejection of the cultural claims of "immediate felt experience" [*Erlebnis*] was particularly influential. As Sarlo has written, the appearance of Benjamin's works in translation in Buenos Aires in the late sixties and early seventies marked the beginning of a veritable "Benjamin phenomenon" in Argentina.[31] Perhaps the most compelling of Benjamin's theses for this generation of Argentine intellectuals was his notion that the violent conditions of modern life have made us "unable to assimilate the data of the world around [us] by way of experience." In Benjamin's "Experience and Poverty," published in 1933 as the Nazis were rapidly consolidating their power, the German critic insisted that the writers of the future would compose from an acknowledged state of experiential poverty: "[this must] not be understood to mean that [they] are yearning for new experience. No, they long to free themselves from experience; they long for a world in which they can make such pure and decided use of their poverty…that it will lead to something respectable."[32] This Argentine generation found in Benjamin's vivid account of experience "checkmated at every turn" by the rise of European fascism a powerful analogue to its own situation under the late twentieth-century military dictatorship.

Piglia's *Artificial Respiration*, released in 1980 at the height of Argentina's "dirty war," recasts Benjamin's impoverished writer as a contemporary Argentine intellectual disenchanted with the waning of experiential possibilities in a country steadily moving toward total authoritarian control. "There are no longer any experiences," Piglia's alter ego Emilio Renzi remarks midway through the novel, "just illusions. We all invent different stories (which in the end are always the same) to imagine that something has happened in our lives."[33] Although Renzi's words initially appear to describe the universal condition of all modern writers, he goes on to detail the specific sense of paranoia and loss of a generation encircled physically and intellectually by the dictatorship. Speaking in the allegorical key that permeates the novel as a whole, Piglia-as-Renzi muses on the disenchantment of the Argentine writer for whom the typical modernist itinerary increasingly seems like an unattainable goal. In a letter to his uncle Marcelo, whom we later find out has been disappeared by the state, Renzi explains his predicament:

> Sooner or later, I used to think, I'm going to become a great writer; but first, I thought, I have to have adventures. And I thought that everything that happened to me, however ridiculous it was, was a way of contributing to that fund of experiences from which great writers, so I supposed, constructed their great works. At that time, when I was 18 or 19, I thought that once I got to be 35 I would have exhausted every kind of experience and I would also have a solid body of work, work that was so diverse and of such quality that I could go to Paris for four or five months to live it up.... But my life now, in keeping with the tone of your last letter, seems, when I have time to think about it, pretty senseless. I go to the paper to write bullshit (even worse, bullshit about literature) and then I come here and shut myself up to write.[34]

This sense of claustrophobia, of the "experience" of not having experiences, becomes the major key of the novel.

Artificial Respiration explores the habitus of the Southern Cone writer-as-reader under the dictatorship through the Benjaminian concept of the loss of communicable experience in modernity. Piglia's next work of fiction, *Prisión perpetua* [Perpetual Prison, 1988], reframes the dialectic between experience and reading within a hemispheric context. "En otro país" [In Another Country], the novella that opens *Prisión perpetua*, functions as a sort of exemplary tale of the misencounter between the US experiencer and the Latin American writer-as-reader. The novella tells of the meeting in the 1950s between the teenage Emilio Renzi and an American novelist, Steve Ratliff.[35] Hewing closely to Piglia's personal biography, the exchange between Renzi and Ratliff takes place in the Argentine city of Mar del Plata, where Renzi's family has settled after his father was released from prison for having resisted the military coup against Juan Domingo Perón. The description of Ratliff, a once-famous New York writer who wanders through the narrator's provincial city drinking gin and telling stories, captures at a stroke the main outline of the US experiential writer: "He was an American. He wanted to submerge himself in the flow of experience to distill the art of fiction."[36] The novella is rife with intertextual references to the US literary tradition—the title is taken from James Baldwin's *Another Country* (1962) and Hemingway's short story of the same name; and Ratliff's preferred bar, Ambos Mundos, alludes to Hemingway's favorite hotel in Havana. Yet if Ratliff determines, like Hemingway, to immerse himself fully in Argentina in order to produce his literary art, Renzi feels hopelessly constrained in his attempt to imitate the American writer. "Nothing ever happened to me," he recalls, "nothing ever really happens but at that time it worried me. I was naive; I was always seeking extraordinary adventures."[37] Renzi ultimately hits upon the solution of keeping a personal diary—a diary not of his own experiences but the experiences of others: "Then I began to steal experiences from the people I knew, personal histories I imagined they lived when they weren't around me."[38] Eventually, this hobby of collecting foreign experiences centers on Ratliff, whose wild tales about the United States begin to fill the pages of the young narrator's notebooks, and then the very narrative we are reading. As Renzi incorporates Ratliff's experiences into his prose, the text itself takes on the paratactical geographical mode I have already noted in Whitman, Porter, Hemingway, García, and Burroughs: "There once was a woman, in Trenton"; "There once was a woman in Arizona"; "There once was a convict who had recently gotten out of jail."[39]

More than anything else, Ratliff affords Renzi access to a US life and culture that Renzi himself could not have acquired in person: an America, as Renzi says at one point in reference to New York, that is radically different from the one "he had seen in the movies" (19). At the level of content, Ratliff's stories cover the quintessential topoi of the US literature of experience. For instance, Ratliff relates a passionate affair with a woman he meets in Greenwich Village that leads to a rollercoaster road trip: the couple "traveled throughout the country and stayed in hotels in the ghetto and bought drugs from the police" before finally ending up in Havana.[40] At the level of style, Ratliff adheres to the basic Hemingwayesque formula that the quality of one's writing is proportional to the amount of life one has lived. "Narration is easy," Ratliff explains to Renzi at one point, "if one has lived enough to capture the order of experience."[41] Ratliff's impulsive drive to full immersion reinforces the vertiginous stakes of the US literature of experience, in which "a narrator must be able to create a hero whose experience is greater than that of all of his readers."[42] It's not so much that Ratliff hasn't read—in fact he introduces Renzi to a range of US authors, from Faulkner, F. Scott Fitzgerald, and Henry James to Hortense Calisher and Robert Lowell (19)—but rather that Argentina represents for him a place beyond literature, an opportunity to accumulate experiences whose quantity and intensity will determine the very value of his writing.

Over the course of "En otro país," it becomes apparent that Renzi's poverty of adventure and Ratliff's experiential overflow, though representative of divergent modes of access to literary source material, result in a strange type of transcultural exchange. If, as Renzi claims, stealing Ratliff's experiences transformed him from a literary naïf into an actual author—"Without him I wouldn't be a writer; without him I wouldn't have written the books I wrote"[43]—this novelistic expropriation does not come without a cost. As Renzi continues to acquire stories, anecdotes, and experiences, he arrives at the conclusion that Ratliff uses him as much as he uses Ratliff: "He practiced friendship as exploitation."[44] It turns out that as Renzi was vamping Ratliff's experiences, Ratliff was busy molding Renzi into the perfect interlocutor for his novel:

> He determined that I should learn English because he needed at least one reader to gauge his novel while he was writing it. Sometimes I think he made me read the books that he needed to read and prepared

me to understand clearly what he was seeking, albeit without losing
that ingenuousness that Steve considered indispensable for a reader
of fiction.... He talked to me about the novel, read me what he had
been writing, showed me versions and variations, and discussed plot
alternatives with me; I was a kind of private reader who sat there, at
the table of Ambos Mundos by the window of Rivadavia, waiting for
the story to continue.[45]

Giving a geocultural turn of the screw to the idea of a reader-oriented
aesthetics, the narrator locates the relationship between the US writer
of experience and the Argentine reader somewhere between symbi-
osis and mutual parasitism. Ratliff cannot fully organize his experiences into a coherent narrative, so he delegates them to his "private
reader," Renzi, to make meaning of them; Renzi, on the other hand,
lacks access to the sheer expansiveness of experience that Ratliff
possesses and therefore appropriates Ratliff's life stories as his
own. This writerly codependency results in two divergent claims
about the author's relationship to source material. Where Ratliff sub-
merges himself in the "flow of life" in Argentina, Renzi constructs
his version of the United States at a readerly distance. To borrow
a term from Fredric Jameson, the novel dramatizes the conditions of
possibility for two different kinds of "cognitive mapping" of the
Americas, two distinct modes of writing about "another country."
Ratliff's literary project demands Renzi's cooperation as a literal
instantiation of what narrative theory calls the "ideal reader,"
while Renzi's growth as a writer depends on systematically "stealing"
Ratliff's experiences.

Though framed in the texts themselves as the idiosyncratic reflections of Piglia's semiautobiographical Renzi, Piglia's conceptual arguments in *Artificial Respiration* and *Prisión perpetua* helped to
construct a new paradigm for the Latin American writer. In the 1980s
and 1990s, a growing number of Latin American novels and stories
turned to the engaged reader to document the historical imbrication
of culture and politics. By the 1980s, one can already begin to trace
the rise of the researcher-detective as the major protagonist in Latin
American literature, with the ubiquitous National Library as the literal and symbolic site for the contestation of historical narratives.
Sergio Pitol's *El desfile del amor* (1984) opens with the historian
Miguel del Solar leaving Mexico City's Biblioteca Nacional while
contemplating his tendency to spend "so much time buried in

archives and libraries."[46] Luis López Nieves's *Seva: Historia de la primera invasion norteamericana de la Isla de Puerto Rico ocurrida en mayo de 1898* [Seva: A History of the First North American Invasion of the Island of Puerto Rico in May 1898, 1983] tells the tale of a crusading history professor who unearths an alternative narrative of the US invasion of Puerto Rico by scouring Puerto Rico's National Archives, the Library of Congress in Washington, and the colonial archives in Spain. These texts clearly draw from earlier narrative strategies in the Latin American literature of the reader, following the pattern set by Borges's "Tlön, Uqbar, Orbis Tertius," in which an initially minor archival discovery leads to an all-consuming bibliographic search. The literary sleuths of Borges's story, who "comb...through the libraries of both Americas and Europe" (1.464–465) are the obvious precursors to *Seva*'s scholar hero, who announces midway through his inquiry that "there are few libraries on the [Iberian] peninsula that I haven't scrutinized shelf by shelf, drawer by drawer, inch by inch."[47] And *El desfile del amor* has an obvious boom antecedent in Fuentes's *Aura* (1962), which similarly focuses on a young Mexican historian obsessed with resurrecting a forgotten episode in the country's past. Yet unlike "Tlön" and *Aura*, the narrative solutions in Pitol's and López Nieves's texts do not depend on the codes of fantastic literature or magical realism, but rather on their ability to imitate and co-opt the project of historical research itself—an ambition that succeeded so dramatically in the *War of the-Worlds*–style reception of *Seva* in Puerto Rico that it altered the island's historiographic tradition. The legacy of Piglia's engaged reader can also be seen in many of the earliest works of the Mexican "Crack" generation, such as Jorge Volpi's *A pesar del oscuro silencio* [*In Spite of the Dark Silence*, 1993] and Pedro Ángel Palou's *En la alcoba de un mundo: Una vida de Xavier Villaurrutia* [In the Bedroom of the World: The Life of Xavier Villaurrutia,1992], which similary deploy the writer-as-researcher to resurrect the lives and texts of forgotten avant-garde precursors.

To trace the emergence of this experience-wary engaged reader in the Latin American literary field of the 1980s and 1990s is to call into question a narrative of postdictatorial literature advanced both by scholars who have championed the *testimonio* (Beverley, Doris Sommer, George Yúdice, etc.), and by those who have criticized the genre's experiential basis (such as Sarlo and Avelar). Despite their divergent opinions on the efficacy of the *testimonio*, both of these critical views downplay the persistence of role of the *letrado* in laying the groundwork for the postdictatorship literary field. Already in the early 1980s, as the *testimonio* began to gain significant mainstream popularity, writers such as Piglia and López Nieves countered the idea that the *testimonio* was the only option for the Latin American literary left by politicizing the figure of the writer-as-reader. Ironically, though also somewhat predictably, the protagonists of these readerly fictions bore less of a resemblance to the unlettered and marginalized subject of the *testimonio* than to the *gestor* who acted as cultural mediator, establishing and framing the spoken word—"a kind of a double, the instrument that would convert the oral into the written," as Elisabeth Burgos-Debray put it in the introduction to the narrative of Rigoberta Menchú.[48] Crucially, these readerly texts implicitly compared the experientialism of the *testimonio* to the "cult of experience" in US literature. The protagonist of *Seva*, the renegade scholar Víctor Cabañas, is exemplary in this respect. In order to establish the "truth" about the US invasion of Puerto Rico, he must parse both the testimony of the last survivor of the massacred Puerto Rican population (a traumatized witness, like Rigoberta Menchú; a runaway slave, like Esteban Montejo of *Biografía de un cimarrón*) and the diary of the commander of the US forces, General Nelson Miles, a document meant to recall the entire tradition of "experiential" writings about the Spanish-Cuban-American War from Teddy Roosevelt to Richard Harding Davis and Stephen Crane. Cabañas's heroism resides not in his ability to transmit his own experience of violence but rather in his role as researcher and editor. In this way, late twentieth-century Latin American engaged readers borrowed many of the narrative strategies of the *testimonio* and the US literature of experience, even as they distanced themselves from the claims to experiential authority represented by both of these literary strains.

Merging the Reader and Experiencer

Roberto Bolaño's self-fashioning undoubtedly participates in the strategies of engaged reading common to many Latin American writers of the 1980s and 1990s. Indeed, reading is the main activity through which Bolaño's characters understand the historical, political, and social contexts in which they live and write. In the foreword to *Distant Star*, the first of an extraordinary series of fictional works that Bolaño produced from 1996 until his death in 2003, the narrator announces this readerly strategy with a reference to Borges's urtext, "Pierre Menard, Author of the Quijote." After defining his role as "preparing drinks" and "consulting a few books," the narrator invokes the "increasingly lively ghost of Pierre Menard" to testify to "the validity of reusing many paragraphs."[49] Ostensibly justifying the novel's cannibalization of Bolaño's earlier *Nazi Literature in the Americas*, the line also hints at the late twentieth-century resurgence of the Borgesian practice of fictionalizing history through textual rewriting, a practice that, along with Menard's ghost, grows more and more apparent every day [*cada día más vivo*, 11]. In works of the late 1990s such as *Distant Star*, *The Savage Detectives*, and the short story "Sensini," Bolaño draws on Piglia's formula for mapping the history of the dictatorship and postdictatorial periods through a reading of literary tradition. The analogy between the reader and the detective governs the narrative logic of *Distant Star*, where the semiautobiographical protagonist Arturo Belano finds the poet-assassin Carlos Wieder largely by reading forgotten literary reviews.

Unlike Piglia and the other writer-readers of the 1980s and 1990s, however, Bolaño reinvests the category of experience with significance by exploring primarily the continuities, rather than the gaps, between life and literature. The frenetic routines of the visceral realists in *The Savage Detectives*, who spend equally inordinate amounts of time reading, drinking, traveling, and—in the young García Madero's words—*cogiendo*, are only the most obvious examples of the Bolañian character for whom literature is a spur to experience, and experience a spur to literature. In one of his more programmatic affirmations in 2003, Bolaño insisted: "I write from experience, my own personal experience, that is, as well as my bookish or cultural experience, which over time have merged [se han fundido] into a single thing."[50] And he ends one of his final essays, "Literatura + enfermedad = enfermedad," with an insight supposedly gleaned from Kafka: "journeys, sex, and books are all paths that don't lead anywhere, but they are paths along which you must travel and get lost, to find yourself, or to find something: a book, a gesture, an object you lost; to find whatever it is, maybe a method."[51] This essay, originally delivered as a lecture in Barcelona less than a year before Bolaño's death, when he was frantically finishing his twelve-hundred-page novel *2666*, can be seen as a kind of final manifesto in which his literary "method" is defined as a blend of two experiential

modes (travel and sex) with the activity of reading. Just as importantly, Bolaño developed his method for merging the discourses
of reading and experience in part by staging a series of fictional
(mis)encounters between US and Latin American characters.

The most archetypal confrontation between a US experiencer and
a Latin American reader in Bolaño's oeuvre appears in the middle
section of *The Savage Detectives*. Amid the polyphony of voices that
recreate Belano's and Ulises Lima's itineraries in the Mexico City
of the 1970s, the narratives of the Mexican poet Manuel Maples
Arce and the American expatriate Barbara Patterson mark a clear
contrapuntal movement. Placed in consecutive order in the text, the
two narrative segments repeatedly play off one another, offering a
sustained cross-cultural contrast.[52] To the aging avant-garde poet
Maples Arces, Patterson comes off as the typical antiliterary *gringa*:
"The American looked me in the eyes and nodded. I doubt she knew
Borges well. I doubt she knew my work at all, even though I was
translated by John Dos Passos. In fact, I doubt she knew much about
John Dos Passos."[53] To the exhuberant, profanity-prone Patterson,
Maples Arce comes off as the typical Mexican intellectual, one of the
"old fuckers festering in their memories and literary quotations," an
irredeemable *letrado*:

> That mother-fucking hemorrhoid-sucking old man, from the begin
> ning I saw the bad faith in those beady, bored little monkey eyes, and
> I said to myself this bastard will take any chance he can get to spit on
> me, the son of a whore. But I'm stupid, I've always been stupid and
> naïve and I let down my guard. And then it happened—what always
> happens. Borges. John Dos Passos. Vomit casually splattered on
> Barbara Patterson's hair. And on top of all this the fucker looked at
> me with pity, as though he were thinking these guys brought me this
> pale-eyed *gringa* just so I could shit all over her, and Rafael also
> looked at me and that midget asshole didn't even budge, like he was
> already used to every fart-stinking old man insulting me, every con
> stipated old man of Mexican letters.[54]

Here, as in *Prisión perpetua*, the narrative conflict arises from a clash
between a US experiencer and a Latin American reader. Yet if the
first passage tempts us to side with Maples Arce in his dismissal of
Patterson, her words force us to reinterpret the entire scene in light
of her invective against the violence, sexism, and conservatism of his
letrado discourse. And in fact, though Maples Arce and the rest of the

estridentistas elicit a certain respect from Belano and Ulises Lima as alternatives to the literary world dominated by Paz, Patterson's critique of the traditional *letrado* also becomes a recurring theme of the novel. It anticipates the visceral realists' search for Cesárea Tinajera as the most liminal participant in the *estridentista* movement (and the only woman associated with it), as well as their decision to detach themselves permanently from Latin America's oldest lettered city, replete with old men (and young ones too) "constipated" by Mexican literature. Patterson's critique of the *letrado* tradition, in other words, gets incorporated into the very raison d'être of the novel's protagonists.

The Savage Detectives's return to the Mexican avant-garde scene of the 1970s must thus be considered, among other things, as a means of reconciling the cultural practices of the Latin American literature of the reader and the US literature of experience. It is well known that the manifesto announcing the formation of infrarrealism, the real-life counterpart to the visceral realist movement in the book, takes its cue from Kerouac's *On the Road* in encouraging the group's poets to "[l]aunch themselves on the roads to discover something new." In fact, the desire to assimilate the aesthetic of the Beats—in Piglia's mind, the last generation to hold a commitment to "pure experience"—remained a part of Bolaño's project until well into the 1990s. In a 1998 interview that coincided with the publication of *The Savage Detectives*, Bolaño recalled, "The voyage [el viaje], in my generation's imaginary, was the voyage of the Beatniks. And that remained the case for many years after, even when I traveled through Europe."[55] This does not mean, of course, that Bolaño was unaware of the cultural and historical distance that separated the Beat generation from his own—in a 2003 conversation, he playfully claimed: "I don't want to become the Jack Kerouac of the Third World."[56] Instead, his interest resides in how cultural discourses originating in the United States were translated, adapted, and repurposed in the Latin American literary field.

In this sense, the US literature of experience provided a specific literary strategy for Bolaño to convert his personal trajectory into literary form. This strategy can be seen most clearly in Bolaño's reworking of the most important "experience" in his life (and his writing career): his firsthand witnessing of the Chilean military coup of September 1973. Bolaño's repeated evocations of this harrowing ordeal, refracted in *Distant Star*, *The Savage Detectives*, and *Amuleto* [*Amulet*, 1999] through the character of Arturo Belano, present the

incident not only as the primal scene of trauma but also as the starting point for an epic odyssey. It is true, as a number of critics have
argued, that Bolaño's work obsessively probes the geographical,
physical, and emotional wounds of the violent Latin American military dictatorships of the 1970s and 1980s.[57] Yet unlike many postdictatorial works that dwell on the lingering effects of trauma and the
denunciation of the crimes of the past, the majority of Bolaño's characters peer into the abyss with eyes wide open, pressing forward for
better angles and even deeper stimulation. In a controversial essay
on literature and exile, Bolaño lambasted the "sad song of exiles... in-
toned by Latin Americans and also by writers from other impoverished or traumatized zones [who] insist on nostalgia and a return to
their country of birth."[58] And in a 2002 conversation with the
Spanish critic Ignacio Echevarría, after voicing his general admiration for Piglia, Bolaño distanced himself from the Benjaminian
trope of the exhaustion of experience woven throughout *Artificial
Respiration* and *Prisión perpetua*. Alluding to the affirmation in
Prisión perpetua that "[t]he modern novel is a carceral novel. It narrates the end of experience," Bolaño says, "what I can't subscribe to
in Piglia's work... is the idea that literature, or the novel, or narration, is a prison, the most faithful reflection of the prison."[59] In his
essays and novels, Bolaño appropriated the tropes of the US literature of experience to counter the narrative of the exhaustion of
experience in Piglia and other postdictatorial Latin American writers of the 1980s and 1990s. At the same time that Bolaño stressed the
aesthetic and political value of moving on, his fiction systematically
transmuted stories of trauma into travel narratives.

The intertwined discourses of reading and experience find
their deepest articulation in *2666*. The novel brings together Latin
American writers who use their bookish backgrounds to make sense
of the world beyond the lettered city and US writers who rethink
their reliance on experience in the context of a political tragedy that
requires a turn to the historical archive. The five parts of the sprawling novel revolve around the violent murder of hundreds of women
in the US-Mexican border town of Santa Teresa, a fictionalized version of Ciudad Juárez described in the novel as a "black hole" whose
centripetal force sucks in even the most distant people and events.
2666 also dramatizes the struggle of writers, critics, journalists, intellectuals, and detectives—those whose very livelihood hinges on the
principles of hermeneutic understanding—to find an interpretive

framework that can account for the scale and scope of the crimes. If, as Ignacio Echevarría has suggested, the basic figure in Bolaño's work is the poet, the first parts of 2666 diverge from this model in centering on professionalized readers who are torn from their institutional landscapes and forced to use their literary training to decode a reality that impinges on and then overwhelms the books, reviews, and cultural establishments that form their readerly habits. Though the material for much of the book did not come from Bolaño's experience, the passage from reading to experience clearly delineates the narrative arc of nearly all of the parts of 2666. This structural element is reinforced by the first and last lines of the novel, which lead inexorably—and, over the course of nearly twelve hundred pages, almost interminably—from a scene of reading ("The first time that Jean-Claude Pelletier read Benno von Archimboldi") to an experiential journey ("Soon afterward [Archimboldi] left the park and the following morning he left for Mexico").[60] The novel's opening part, "The Part about the Critics," narrates the winding trajectory of a group of four European comparative-literature professors who come together (and fall apart) over the reading of the German writer Benno von Archimboldi, ending up on a track not to tenure but to Santa Teresa, where they hope to locate Archimboldi but are instead faced with the brute violence of the femicides.[61] The novel works almost like a *Künstlerroman* in reverse: life does not lead to art; rather, literary formation becomes life preparation. As an old writer tells Archimboldi toward the end of the novel: "I won't tell you that experience can't be obtained by continuous contact with a library, but experience will always be above and beyond the library."[62]

The most conspicuous example of the reader turned rebel in 2666 is Sergio González, the journalist for the Mexico City–based daily newspaper *La Razón*, who begins to investigate the femicides while on assignment for a human-interest story in Santa Teresa. To a certain degree, the character of González can be understood by analogy to the role of the detective as a reader of the social scene. Yet Bolaño literalizes the analogy in the case of González, since we learn early in "The Part about the Crimes" that he is actually—that is, professionally—a reader: "Normally he wouldn't have accepted the job [of investigating a crime in Santa Teresa], because he wasn't a police reporter but a journalist in the culture section. He reviewed philosophy books."[63] At the same time that the journey to Santa Teresa awakens González to the brutality of the femicides and the precarity of those living on the border, it also displaces him from the cultural establishment in Mexico City, where his writer friends "probably didn't care a lot about what was happening in that distant corner of the country."[64] Just as significant as the textual presence of González the character is the fact that Sergio González Rodríguez was a real-life Mexican writer and journalist whose nonfiction book on the femicides, *Huesos en el desierto* [Bones in the Desert], was published in 2002. As Marcela Valdes has shown, Bolaño read the manuscript version of the book shortly before its publication, and whole passages in "The Part about the Crimes" are lifted nearly verbatim from González Rodríguez's book.[65] Bolaño's inclusion of González Rodríguez in the novel was more than just homage. Since Bolaño himself never traveled to the north of Mexico, in *2666* González supplants the semiautobiographical Belano as the representative reader-experiencer, both a voracious consumer of books and an important metatextual intermediary between the Spain-bound novelist and the on-the-ground events on the US-Mexico border.

"The Part about Fate," the third part of *2666*, is Bolaño's most sustained attempt to work through the conventions of the US literature of experience. This part focuses on Oscar Fate, a reporter for the African American magazine *Amanecer Negro* who arrives in Santa Teresa to cover a boxing match, only to become embroiled in a series of misadventures seemingly connected to both the femicides and the city's drug cartels. In the house of a rich businessman, Fate vaguely senses that a young student, Rosa, risks becoming the next victim. The second half of "The Part about Fate" tracks Fate's and Rosa's paths through Santa Teresa as they flee from their pursuers while simultaneously trying to untangle the logic of the violence that has suddenly ensnared them. During the period when he wrote *2666*, Bolaño was reading the works of the African American detective novelist Walter Mosley, and I would argue that the narrative motor of the "The Part about Fate" comes from absorbing, at least temporarily, the codes and language of Mosley's version of the US literature of experience. In a review of the Spanish translation of Mosley's *Gone Fishing* [*De pesca*, 1997], published in 1999, Bolaño analyzes the narrative world of Easy Rawlings, the protagonist in Mosley's mystery novels:

> Because Easy Rawlings is not really a detective but just an intelligent guy who occasionally solves problems, searches for missing persons, and tries to settle little disputes that inevitably turn into life-or-death

matters after a few pages. The problems get so big that they become unmanageable, the machine of reality starts working [la máquina de la realidad se pone en funcionamiento] and everything leads the reader to believe that Easy won't come out alive, among other things because he is black and poor and has no political or religious power behind him, a guy who has nothing going for him except a bit of physical strength and a large dose of intelligence. But Easy always survives the dead ends into which Mosley puts him.[66]

Bolaño's description of the "machine of reality" in Mosley's novels bears a striking resemblance to the machinery of violence in Santa Teresa that slowly engulfs Fate, turning his journalistic assignment into an existential encounter with what Bolaño elsewhere dubs the "secret of evil."

But if "The Part about Fate" opens with a concentrated effort, as Bolaño puts it, to stick to "the observation of life and experience," this hard-boiled narrative mode is interrupted in the middle. Right before he arrives in Santa Teresa, Fate travels to Detroit to write an article on Barry Seaman—a fictional version of one of the real-life founders of the Black Panthers, Bobby Seale. Fate's interview with Seaman, which recalls Belano and Ulises Lima's brief conversation with Cesárea Tinajero in *The Savage Detectives*, functions similarly as an exploration of a marginalized cultural tradition—in this case with the legacy of radical African American thought. Yet where one might expect that Seaman's discourse would center on the "black experience" of the post–Jim Crow era in the United States, he focuses instead on a different message. In a talk in a small church in Detroit witnessed by Fate, Seaman speaks to the all-black audience about the importance of reading, a practice he developed while serving a prison sentence:

> What I'll say to you is that you have to read books. . . . And all of you who are so nice will probably be asking yourselves: what did Barry read? I read everything. But more than anything else I remember a book I read in one of my most desperate moments that restored my tranquility. What book was that? . . . That book was called *The Selected Compendium of the Works of Voltaire* and I will tell you that it's very useful or at least was of great use to me.[67]

Though Seaman imparts these words in a playful tone, his views on literature and reading echo Bolaño's own authorial discourse in his

essays and interviews. Seaman reiterates Bolaño's defense of omnivorous reading ("I read everything") and, in his seemingly random reference to Voltaire's compendium, uses almost the exact same phrase
that Bolaño did in his last interview when underscoring the kind of
audacious reader he admired: "I'm moved by no-nonsense readers,
those who still dare to read Voltaire's *Philosophical Dictionary*, which
is one of the clearest and most modern books I know."[68]

The full scope of Seaman's message remains incomplete, however,
until we parse the passage's implicit engagement with the black radical archive. As we might recall, in his essay on Burroughs, Bolaño
remarks that "When he talks about his readings one has the sense
that he was remembering vague periods of his life in jail." In the Beat
literary tradition, the American prison system often appears as the
one place where reading temporarily substitutes for experience, a
pause between adventures not unlike the university in its logic of
confinement. Seaman's emphasis on the importance of his prison
reading to his identity formation, however, points to an alternative
strain of US literature, a black intellectual tradition that encompasses Malcolm X, George Jackson, and Chester Himes (Bolaño
makes reference to Himes's prison novel, *Yesterday Will Make You
Cry*, in *Between Parentheses*). Jackson, for instance, became a vital
voice of the Black Panthers without ever leaving San Quentin Prison,
interspersing his political and social writings with readings of Marx,
Lenin, and Gramsci. Thus, when Seaman advises his audience: "Read
books by black (male) authors. And by black (female) authors [auto-
ras negras]. But don't just stop there,"[69] he is both proposing a politics of voracious reading and drawing from a tradition of radical
black intellectuals who advocated reading beyond the black
experience.

Seen in this light, Seaman's "sermon" on reading prefigures Fate's
interrogation of the logic of identity politics after his arrival in
Mexico. After identifying as "American" [*Soy americano*] to a Mexican
cashier, Fate muses about his motives for defining himself by nationality rather than race: "Why didn't I say African American. Because
I'm outside of the country? ... Does that mean that in some places I
am American and in other places African American and in other
places, by the sheer force of logic, that I am no one?"[70] Beginning
to view his identity as situational rather than fixed, Fate finds a new
purpose in his journey to Santa Teresa. Although he had initially
come to cover the fight because a black boxer was involved, he

gradually realizes that the femicides are the more urgent story: they speak to the broader cycle of violence, economics, and displacement into which Fate himself has been drawn. When Fate proposes a "great story" about the murders to his editor at *Amanecer Negro*, the following argument ensues:

> —Oscar—the section editor said to him—you are there to cover a fucking boxing match.
> This is better—said Fate—the fight is an anecdote, what I'm pitching you is much more.
> —What are you pitching me?
> —A portrait of industrial conditions in the Third World—said Fate—an aide-mémoire of the current situation in Mexico, a panorama of the border, a mystery drama of the first order, for fuck's sake.[71]

Fate's editor responds by defending the putative autonomy of the black American experience—"How many fucking brothers are involved?" ["¿Cuántos putos hermanos están metidos en el asunto?", 373]—but Fate's curiosity demands that he continue to unravel the many loose ends of the Santa Teresa crimes. This scene takes on added significance when we recognize that the story Fate proposes to his editor resembles the story Bolaño himself will write: a border mystery set in contemporary Mexico that addresses the global (post)industrial conditions of the twenty-first century. The question Fate's editor puts to him thus becomes a question for the author behind *2666*: why write about something you don't know, something beyond the scope of your own experience? The answer is one that, as I have suggested, Bolaño articulates in *2666* and beyond: a politics and a praxis of voracious reading that is formulated not only on the various narrative levels of the text but also in the book's paratexts: the essays, interviews, and authorial statements that Bolaño disseminated in the years spanning the novel's composition. Moreover, it is a politics inherent to Bolaño's praxis, that is, his method of gathering source material to write a novel set in multiple places he had never been.

Bolaño's combination of this politics of voracious reading and a renewed discourse of experience came to define an important position in Spanish-language literature of the early part of this century. With the posthumous publication of *2666* in Spanish in 2004, Bolaño became the most important literary model for Latin American writers.

His attempt to merge the positions of the reader and experiencer has rapidly become the cultural dominant in the Spanish-speaking world: characters like Belano and Fate who embark on experiential journeys in search of literary precursors now populate the fiction of authors from Mexico to Argentina. Though there is a growing wariness among more established writers about a perceived proliferation of Bolaño acolytes (what the Chilean writer Alberto Fuguet wryly refers to as the rise of the "Bolañitos"), some of the most compelling novels of the first decade of the twenty-first century worked from a Bolañian paradigm to explore the imbrication of literature, history, politics, and daily life. The Mexican writer Juan Villoro's *El testigo* (2004), for example, interrogates Mexican political history in the wake of the PAN's historic 2000 victory by returning to the works of early twentieth-century poet Ramón López Velarde. Commenting on the book's relationship to *2666*, Villoro has said: "I am interested...in the moment when the researcher no longer interprets only texts and books, in how they take him to other experiences and places in life."[72] Here we detect the central principle of Bolaño's work: that reading should enhance one's ability to interpret the world and its contemporary social formations.

Gendering the Lettered City

In an oft-cited introduction to a Spanish-language translation of *The Adventures of Huckleberry Finn*, Bolaño alludes to the formal possibilities opened up by the nineteenth-century US literature of experience: "All American novelists, including authors in the Spanish language, catch a glimpse at some point in their lives of two books on the horizon, two paths, two structures, and, above all, two plots. Occasionally two destinies. One is Herman Melville's *Moby Dick*; the other is Mark Twain's *The Adventures of Huckleberry Finn*."[73] In a 2011 text, the Mexican novelist, essayist, poet, and short story writer Cristina Rivera Garza commented on this pronouncement:

> It's clear that the horizon Bolaño speaks of here is what we might call the "universal" North American novel, and the period he refers to is undoubtedly the nineteenth century, which is another way of naming the origins of modernity. But in this symmetrical bifurcation, with all

its neatness and its appearance of seeming natural or inevitable, Bolaño forgot the uncomfortable, the unclassifiable, the frequently unsettling third way. He overlooked the third book, or, to put it in his terms, the third plot and the third destiny. He forgot Emily Dickinson. Yes, Emily Dickinson, the poet who rarely left home and whose portraits often depict her dressed in black and with her hair set tightly in a bun. The inhabitant of a room in Amherst—where she read everything she could and should read, by the way. The unpublished one. We must remember that no map of North American literature of the time would be complete without the poet who considered "no" the most savage word in existence.[74]

Faced with the seeming inescapability of these two male-centered North American literary routes—Twain's journey through the heartland; Melville's voyage across the seven seas—Rivera Garza signals a third way: Emily Dickinson the reader, Emily Dickinson the woman, Emily Dickinson the poet—as lost to the Latin American male novelists of the turn of the twenty-first century as she was to her nineteenth-century US contemporaries.

Rivera Garza's commentary on Bolaño's formula for the "universal" American novel speaks to two separate but related literary concerns in her novels, stories, and criticism of the previous decade. First, it points to her efforts to recuperate a series of writers—most of them women—marginalized or effaced by dominant national and linguistic literary traditions, while at the same time reconstructing the mechanisms by which these traditions come to "seem natural or inevitable." In this vein, Rivera Garza's description of how Dickinson's "uncomfortable" and "unclassifiable" poems disrupt Bolaño's teleological account of nineteenth-century US literature reproduces the thematic concerns of two of her own novels, *La cresta de Ilión* [The Crest of Ilion, 2002] and *La muerte me da* [Death Comes to Me, 2007], which use the texts and figures of earlier Latin American women writers to interrogate the gendered construction of the Mexican literary tradition and the Latin American lettered city respectively. Second, by signaling Dickinson's notoriously hermitlike existence and her propensity to read rather than travel, Rivera Garza's commentary on Bolaño's text outlines an alternative course for reconstructing US literary history that does not pass through the literature of experience; it dispels the Beat-inspired notion that the pathways of American literature should be likened to actual routes of transit (*caminos*). Here, she extends a line of inquiry that winds through many of her essays, newspaper columns, and blog posts, in which she repeatedly highlights twentieth-century North American writers-as-readers who went against the grain of the US literature of experience, from Muriel Rukeyser and Charles Reznikoff to David Markson and Kathy Acker.[75] We might say that whereas Bolaño attempted to merge the traditions of the US literature of experience and the Latin American literature of the reader through an aesthetics of excess—to read everything, to experience everything—Rivera Garza has attempted to deconstruct the very terms of the opposition, seeking, through a paradigmatically poststructuralist practice, to recuperate those figures who fall outside the cultural dominants of the US experiencer and the Latin American *letrado*.

In the early twenty-first century, Rivera Garza has emerged as the most prominent of a number of contemporary Latin American writers who have challenged the masculinist code implicit in the analogy of the reader and the investigator. The Latin American voracious reader, like the *letrado*, has traditionally been male. And the avatars of the reader-experiencer in Bolaño's works are almost uniformly men, including Arturo Belano and Ulises Lima of *The Savage Detectives*, who replay a stereotypical "hunt" for the texts and the body of Cesárea Tinajero. In the first decade of the twenty-first century, writers such as Rivera Garza, Pola Oloixarac, and Guadalupe Nettel began to articulate gendered critiques of the figure of the voracious reader, attempting to create a space for women reader-experiencers within the Latin American lettered city. Although their critiques often borrow from the *testimonio*'s ethos of resistance, these writers have not disavowed the lettered subject (as we have seen was the case with Rigoberta Menchú) so much as they have appropriated—and exaggerated—its typical gestures. Oloixarac, for instance, has observed that her novel *Savage Theories* "has sparked verbal violence and a sexist uproar precisely because it doesn't deal with the issues that are traditionally associated with 'women's literature,' but instead contains a sociological critique that is both intelligent and satirical, which are apparently traits solely reserved for men."[76] These twenty-first-century novels of the *lectora*, as I would call them, maintain a close but often tense relationship to the Latin American literature of the reader as it developed from the mid-twentieth century to the early twenty-first. Oloixarac's *Savage Theories*, with its unmistakable allusion to *The Savage Detectives*, not only transposes the intellectual energy and sexual fury of Bolaño's novel from Mexico City to

Buenos Aires; it also contains a "sociological critique" of how the *porteño* intelligentsia reacts when the cultural "savaging" is done by a woman rather than a man.[77] This critique of the lettered city also registers in Rivera Garza's work. What makes Rivera Garza particularly compelling for hemispheric literary study is that her interrogation of *letrado* discourse takes the form of a sociological analysis of the historical relationship between the Latin American literature of the reader and the US literature of experience.

In this sense, Rivera Garza's first and best-known novel, *No One Will See Me Cry* (1999), can be read as an exploration of how the Latin American *letrado* and the US experiencer have typically operated as two male agents struggling for control over the female narrative and body. A historical novel that draws from Rivera Garza's doctoral dissertation about the early twentieth-century Mexican insane asylum La Castañeda, *No One Will See Me Cry* reimagines the life of one of La Castañeda's patients, Matilda Burgos. Claudia Parodi has shown how the novel uses the Foucauldian insights of Rivera Garza's dissertation to describe the way early twentieth-century Mexican institutions and discursive regimes discipline Matilda's body and her words, and Brian Price has argued that by choosing to focus on a figure who exists at the margins of the military and political theaters of the Mexican Revolution, Rivera Garza undercuts the masculinist epos of the Revolution spanning from the early postrevolutionary novels of Mariano Azuela and Martín Luis Guzmán to the best-selling late twentieth-century fiction of Fuentes and Ignacio Solares.[78] It is worth adding, however, that the novel's interrogation of gendered narratives extends beyond the Mexican national tradition. The two most prominent male characters in the novel, Joaquín Buitrago, a Mexican photographer who falls in love with Matilda, and Paul Kamàck, Matilda's expatriate American husband, seek to gain mastery over Matilda's life—and her life story—by occupying, almost stereotypically, the positions of the Latin American reader and the US experiencer respectively.

Early in *No One Will See Me Cry*, Joaquín's desire for Matilda leads him to the Biblioteca Nacional, where he embarks on an ambitious project of reconstructing her past and her entire genealogical line. Having illegally procured Matilda's file from a doctor at La Castañeda, Joaquín enters the library's reading room convinced that researching her history is the first step toward conquering her heart: "every piece of information brings him a little closer to her."[79] Not only does

Joaquín "feel safe among books" since "[t]he order of the stories guides him in the mystery of the world";[80] he also fantasizes, through an image that superimposes Borges's "The Library of Babel" onto Rama's *The Lettered City*, that "[i]f the city were a library he would be happy."[81] As Joaquín begins to assume the traditional role of the *letrado*—"the photographer reads all the books"[82]—the library reveals itself to be one more institution of social order and gender control. Even though Joaquín is more decadent artist than moralizing hygienist, and hence stands in contrast to the doctors who literally confine Matilda during her time in the asylum, he too usurps Matilda's agency over her own narrative, first by stealing her medical file (i.e., her personal archive) and then by scouring the library for information to hold over her. If Joaquín hopes that his research-informed version of the talking cure will bend Matilda to his will—"He wants Matilda to grow docile and flexible like a reed"[83]—her ultimate response will be to deny him this knowledge-power: "I alone will find the way to escape, Joaquín. No one will save me."[84]

In the second half of the novel, Joaquín's desire to possess Matilda through his reading finds a counterpoint in Paul's campaign to woo Matilda when he encounters her in the Mexico City brothel La Modernidad. While Paul initially arrives in Mexico as a Porfirian-era American engineer who dreams of building a vast mining system outside the town of Real de Catorce, he returns to the country not as a successful capitalist but as a US experiencer: "He arrived...without any goal in mind...and if he had decided to return to Catorce it was less for the desire to make his fortune and more for the lunar landscape to which he had once yielded."[85] Though not himself a literary author, Paul indexes an entire tradition of US writers of experience in Mexico. Like Burroughs in García-Robles's and Bolaño's accounts, he sees Mexico as a site for exploration rather than intellectual inspiration: "he ignored everything that had to do with the artists and intellectuals of the period."[86] Like Hart Crane, he comes to Mexico seeking rejuvenation and ends up committing suicide. Finally, like Ambrose Bierce, perhaps the historical figure most similar to Paul, he disappears without a trace into the Mexican countryside. Matilda watches him depart almost as if from the perspective of one of the Beat wives: "the masculine figure crosses the threshold of the door and, from there, the woman watches how his body moves forward and shrinks into the distance."[87] Although Joaquín and Paul pursue Matilda using opposite means—Joaquín with the books in the library and Paul with the experiencer's tool kit of an "explorer's backpack, a compass, and a pair of lemons to quench his thirst"[88]—their textual function is strikingly similar: they seek to wrest control of her life (and her life history) by subjecting her to their own cultural dramas and desires. *No One Will See Me Cry*'s closing line, "Let me rest in peace" ["Déjenme descansar en paz" [259]], indicts not only the modern Mexican state apparatus and its normalizing impulse, but also the parade of men in the novel who use their social position to regulate and control Matilda.

Although one might expect from *No One Will See Me Cry*'s descriptions of the coercive power of the book that Rivera Garza would abandon the position of the writer-as-reader in subsequent works, her twenty-first-century writings remain committed to finding noncanonical, marginalized, and oppositional figures of the reader within the Latin American and US literary traditions. The novels and stories Rivera Garza has published since *No One Will See Me Cry* experiment with different cultural models of the reader, often with the purpose of subverting the gendered profile of the *letrado* subject as traditionally defined. *La cresta de Ilión* begins with a mysterious woman "interrupting [the] reading and [the] leisure" of a male narrator.[89] After revealing her identity as the relatively little known real-life Mexican short story writer Amparo Dávila, the woman destabilizes the reader-narrator's gender by referring to him with feminine pronouns. In the story "La ciudad de los hombres" ["The City of Men," 2008], a woman journalist visits a city composed exclusively of men in order to write a travel narrative from "a female perspective"—only to find out that she is the latest in a line of women reporters in the city who have been been prohibited from either publishing or leaving.[90] In *La muerte me da* (2007), meanwhile, Rivera Garza reflects on the murders in Ciudad Juárez and the growing drug violence in northern Mexico, an inverted *novela negra* in which a female informant works with a female detective and a female journalist to investigate a string of murders committed by a female assassin. In all of these fictional works, Rivera Garza seeks to defamiliarize the deeply ingrained masculinist modes of thinking, speaking, and representing that cut across the Latin American public sphere and its literary tradition. In *La muerte me da*, for instance, after seeing the first castrated male corpse, the narrator remarks: "I thought about...the term 'serial killing' [asesinatos seriales] and I realized that it was the first time that I connected the word to the male body.

And I thought…it was interesting that, at least in Spanish, the word 'victim' [víctima] is always feminine."[91] Later, she links the gendered violence in the language of criminality with the gendered violence of Latin American literature itself: "I also couldn't help but notice that on the very surface of the name Cortázar the words *cortar* [to cut] and *azar* [luck] were hiding, menacingly—two words that, at that moment, lacked all innocence."[92]

La muerte me da represents the culmination of Rivera Garza's ambitious endeavor to recuperate a tradition of *lectoras* in the heart of the "city of men." The main precursor here is the mid-twentieth-century Argentine poet Alejandra Pizarnik, whose texts appear on the corpses of the murdered men throughout the novel. In a 2006 interview, Rivera Garza said that the novel's working title was *Las lectoras de Pizarnik* [Pizarnik's Readers] and that "in many ways [the novel] has to do with my ideas of what reading is."[93] In the novel itself, Rivera Garza associates Pizarnik with the practice of reading at two narrative levels. At the diegetic level, multiple characters insist that in order to solve the murder mystery the detective must first learn to decode Pizarnik's texts: "Without reading [Pizarnik], without reading her well, you'll never find the killer."[94] At the metadiegetic level, the fourth part of the novel takes the form of an academic essay published by a "Doctor Cristina Rivera Garza" that examines Pizarnik's readerly practice in relation to her legendary text *La condesa sangrienta* [*The Bloody Countess*, 1971]. Perhaps the best-known rewriting of a foreign source text in twentieth-century Argentine literature after Borges's *A Universal History of Infamy*, *The Bloody Countess* is a grim retelling of the masochistic and systematic slaughter of young women by the sixteenth-century countess Erzsébet Báthory, appropriated almost entirely from the French surrealist Valentine Penrose's *Erzsébet Báthory la comtesse sanglante* (1962). In the essay, the Rivera Garza character describes Pizarnik's rewriting of Penrose with the following words: "Alejandra Pizarnik turned the stories of others [el relato ajeno] into a sort of refuge."[95] The phrasing here has a double rhetorical effect. On the one hand, it unmistakably evokes Borges's famous lines in the 1954 prologue to *A Universal History*, in which he describes himself as a "timid man" who "falsified and manipulated…other people's stories [ajenas historias]."[96] On the other hand, attributing this aesthetic breakthrough to Pizarnik rather than to Borges aligns Rivera Garza's own practice of writing-as-reading with the former rather than the latter. The Rivera Garza character later

writes of Pizarnik: "In Spanish, she herself said, nobody could serve
as a model for her. Not Paz, not Cortázar, not Borges."[97] The line
underscores the novel's overall characterization of Pizarnik's work as
a disruption of the masculine modality of the lettered city and its
male-dominated literary tradition. At the same time, as the self-
reflexive formulation of an academic who shares her name with
the author, the line alludes to the possibility that Pizarnik—and perhaps Rivera Garza herself—can "serve as a model" for twenty-first-
century *lectoras*.[98] This, at least, is how the Puerto Rican novelist Mayra
Santos-Febres characterized *La muerte me da* in a 2008 blog post,
referring to the novel as a "rereading" of the "entire canon of twentieth-
century women writers" that was also "a book for those of us women
who voraciously read other women." A voracious reading that
produces voracious readers, in other words—though here the identity and temporality of the reader have completely changed. "I am
Pizarnik," Santos-Febres knowingly concludes, "reading Cristina
Rivera Garza."[99]

Although *La muerte me da* does not explicitly invoke US literary
tradition to the same degree as does *No One Will See Me Cry*, the
novel sets up a number of implicit dialogues with the US "citational"
writers mentioned in Rivera Garza's essay collection *Los muertos indóciles: Necroescrituras y desapropiación* [The Disobedient Dead:
Necrowriting and Disappropriation, 2014].[100] In her introduction to
the collection, Rivera Garza refers to the theoretical writings of
Kenneth Goldsmith, Vanessa Place, and Robert Fitterman in describing twenty-first-century conceptual poetry as "a series of strategies
that…proposed forms of appropriation that dynamited conservative (and often retrograde) notions of authorship and the lyrical
'I'…transforming the writer into a manipulator of signs and a cura-
tor of contemporary language."[101] In *La muerte me da*, this transfer
of authority from author to reader surfaces both in the way the novel
intersperses the poems of Pizarnik as clues to the identity of the
killer and in the related appeal to the reader to take responsibility for
the interpretation of the text: "It will be up to the readers…to involve
themselves, if necessary, in the resolution of the enigma."[102] Yet if
Rivera Garza claims in *Los muertos indóciles* that Goldsmith and
Craig Dworkin's *Against Expression: An Anthology of Conceptual
Writing* is "required reading for anyone who wants to write in and
with the now,"[103] this does not mean that there are no differences
between Rivera Garza's aesthetic and US conceptual poetics. Whereas

Goldsmith and Dworkin largely attribute contemporary "strategies of copying and appropriation" to the rise of digital technology and developments internal to the cultural world—Dworkin celebrates Borges's Pierre Menard as a precursor to the "figure of the uncreative writer" for his stylistic achievement of textual transposition[104]—Rivera Garza's work repeatedly foregrounds the geopolitical as well as formal dimensions of the writer-as-reader. Here Rivera Garza's connection to Bolaño, Piglia, and the long tradition of the Latin American literature of the reader is crucial, helping to explain not only the citational techniques she employs in her work but also the degree to which her protagonists remain committed to the activity of reading as a means of mapping social, political, and cultural cartographies.

At the same time that Rivera Garza's work can be seen, like Bolaño's, as a complex reflection on the US literature of experience and the Latin American literature of the reader in the twentieth century, it also anticipates several important trends in US–Latin American literary relations in the second decade of the twenty-first. As a transnational author born on the Mexican side of the US–Mexico border, Rivera Garza writes in English as well as Spanish, and has spent most of her professional career in the US academy. Several critics have suggested that Rivera Garza's deconstruction of gender and genre norms must be understood within the context of her position between the US and Latin American fields, linking her work to other border writers of the late twentieth century and early twenty-first century.[105] But Rivera Garza's practice represents more than an alternative narrative about the border or even the geographical spaces of the US and Mexico. It also points to a broader contemporary reformulation of literary strategies among authors on both sides of the North-South divide.

After Bolaño

TOWARD A CONTEMPORARY LITERATURE
OF THE AMERICAS

But whatever the reason, I soon found myself director of
a newly created section called Poetry of the Americas.
—ANA MENÉNDEZ, *Adios, Happy Homeland!*

In her 2009 introduction to the twenty-fifth anniversary edition of *The House on Mango Street* (1984), subtitled "A House of My Own," Sandra Cisneros writes of the conditions that led her to create her iconic coming-of-age story about a young Mexican-American girl in Chicago and her trajectory after the book's initial publication. A picture of Cisneros's twenty-three-year-old self, taken while she was in the midst of writing the novel, occasions a reflection on her transformation from an aspiring creative writer to arguably the most prominent Latina/o author of the late twentieth and early twenty-first centuries. But the introduction can also be read as a different kind of portrait, a rendering of the shifting relationship of the US and Latin American literary fields over this same twenty-five-year period. The Cisneros of these pages no longer finds her place in the small but recognizable abode of Chicana literature; instead, she inhabits a transnational house of fiction spanning the two spacious wings of the US and Latin American traditions. Indeed, Cisneros credits Latin American women writers with changing the way she conceived of her role as an author, even as she acknowledges that she produced *The House on Mango Street* without many of the influences that would later come to define her authorial persona. Addressing herself to friend and editor Norma Alarcón, Cisneros insists that she had few "literary models" until Alarcón introduced her to "the Mexican writers Sor Juana Inés de la Cruz, Elena Poniatowska, Elena Garro,

Rosario Castellanos. The young woman in the photograph was looking for another way to be—'*otro modo de ser*,' as Castellanos put it."[1]
The introduction concludes with a wry comparison between Cisneros
and Isabel Allende, perhaps the most famous Latin American woman
novelist in the English-speaking world. After hearing from her mother
that Isabel Allende has a "HUGE desk and BIG office" (xxv), Cisneros
proudly shows her mother her new home in San Antonio with a working space that rivals that of the Chilean author. Twenty-five years after
writing about the cramped physical and spiritual quarters of the rented
house on Mango Street, Cisneros finally has a room—indeed, a whole
property—of her own. The major subtext that runs through the introduction is that she has also gained possession of a new literary tradition that encompasses writers from both sides of the hemisphere:
women as well as men, marginal as well as canonical, Latin American
as well as American and Latina/o.

   One of the main rhetorical strategies of "A House of My Own," then,
is to cast Cisneros as a reader of Latin American literature whose
cultural knowledge of the region owes as much to the archive as to
her personal experience. But we should not lose sight of the fact that
the introduction was written retrospectively in 2009, at a significant
distance, both temporally and culturally, from the actual composition of *The House on Mango Street* in the early 1980s. Indeed, "A
House of My Own" marks a crucial shift in Cisneros's strategies of
representation. From her earliest story cycles to the sprawling novel
Caramelo (2002), Cisneros tended to shy away from "high" literary
references to Latin American authors, preferring, like Katherine
Anne Porter, to identify Latin American (and particularly Mexican)
culture with its popular forms: folk tales, *corridos*, and oral history, as
well as the *telenovelas* that function for Cisneros as a rough equivalent to the public Mexican muralism that Porter had championed
over half a century before her. Whereas Cisneros's earlier fiction had
rendered her Chicana subjectivity and the bridge between the United
States and Latin America in terms of "lived experience," as I argue in
chapter 1, her introduction makes visible the ways in which she has
crossed both the boundaries of literary tradition and the physical
borders of the North and South. The primary literary figure Cisneros
claims here as an influence on *The House on Mango Street* is telling:
Jorge Luis Borges, upon whose genre-defying *Dreamtigers* (1964)
"the young woman in the photo is modeling her book-in-progress"
(xvi). It might come as something of a surprise that the author of

what has often been seen as a classic example of American ethnic self-writing would so readily identify with the consummate Latin American writer-as-reader. But Cisneros's image of her younger self reading Borges indicates the significant reconfiguration of US, Latin American, and Latina/o literary discourse in the early years of the twenty-first century.

This shift in contemporary Latina/o fiction toward a reader-oriented relationship to Latin American culture appears nowhere so prominently as in the Cuban-American novelist and short story writer Ana Menéndez's *Adios, Happy Homeland!* (2011). Menéndez's story cycle, presented as an anthology of twentieth-century Cuban literature collected by an Irish immigrant librarian named Herberto Quain, displays the full range of narrative strategies employed by Roberto Bolaño and other Latin American voracious readers. In addition to lifting her frame narrator from Borges's story "An Examination of the Work of Herbert Quain," Menéndez has Quain introduce the anthology as the culmination of a lifetime spent in the "quieter pursuits of reading an imaginary world."[2] The anthology itself is a mishmash of hemispheric writing on Cuba: it contains Google "translations" of Gertrudis Gómez de Avellaneda and José Martí, cites Victoria Ocampo and Ricardo Piglia, and even offers a pastiche of Hemingway's *The Old Man and the Sea* in a story by "Ernesto Del Camino" ("If it were in a book, you couldn't say the boy lived in Matanzas because it would be too ridiculous. But he did" [24]). *Adios, Happy Homeland!*, in other words, stamps its knowledge of literature from and about Latin America on nearly every one of its pages, repeatedly letting us know just how much it knows.

What ultimately separates Menéndez's book from Cisneros's 2009 introduction to *The House on Mango Street*, though, is not simply the force with which it stakes its claim to a cultural inheritance that includes both Latin American and US literature. It is the fact that while Cisneros's self-inscription into a hemispheric literary tradition appears as a paratext, a retrospective gloss on a novel that does not itself take up such concerns, the question of literary belonging—what one has read and what one has not read—forms the thematic core of *Adios, Happy Homeland!* That the frame narrator holds the occupational title of director of a "newly created section" of the Cuban National Library called "Poetry of the Americas" (11) alerts us early on to the degree to which the appellative "American" literature will be put to the test in the pages that follow. Indeed, in what seems like a clear nod to Bolaño's hemispheric pseudoencyclopedia *Nazi Literature in the Americas*—a joke, as one of Bolaño's characters remarks in a different context, but a joke to be taken seriously— Menéndez's book internalizes and makes visible the very critical arguments I have been discussing in this study. It becomes a reflection on what it means to "really" know a place—and this reflection centers on the relationship between reading and experience.

Over the past decade, I contend here, the US and Latin American literary fields have grown significantly closer, merging several of the most important tropes and conventions of the US literature of experience and the Latin American literature of the reader. If the idea of a hemispheric literature remained an aspiration or projection for most of the nineteenth- and twentieth-century authors I have discussed, in our own contemporary moment we may be witnessing the birth of something that may truly be called *a* literature—as opposed to the plural literatures—of the Americas. This does not mean that the linguistic, political, and cultural divisions I have described throughout this book have disappeared. Rather, as US authors read Latin American literature now more than ever, and Latin American authors write more frequently about their "experience" of the United States, these transpositions have produced a literature at once more intertwined and intertwinable. To substantiate this claim, I will analyze contemporary works by three different groups of writers: Latina/o writers composing in English in the United States (such as Francisco Goldman, Menéndez, and Junot Díaz), non-Latina/o US writers (such as Ben Lerner and Kenneth Goldsmith), and Spanish-language writers living in the United States (such as the Mexican novelist Valeria Luiselli and the Puerto Rican poet Mara Pastor).

One manifestation of these writers' reconciliation of the US literature of experience and Latin American literature of the reader is, somewhat predictably, a degree of self-consciousness about the merger. In Ben Lerner's *Leaving the Atocha Station* (2011), the expatriate American writer-narrator confesses he has few prospects for acquiring experience aside from "the experience of experience sponsored by [his] fellowship";[3] in Valeria Luiselli's *Los ingrávidos* [*Faces in the Crowd*, 2011], a Mexican writer living in New York satirizes the US reading public's suddenly insatiable demand for the "foreign pearls" of Latin American literature, referring to the new "Latin American boom" in the United States after "Bolaño's success in the gringo market."[4] While such self-reflexive moments could plausibly be

attributed to casual postmodern irony—an American writer paro-
dying the journey to have a "real experience"; a Mexican writer cari-
caturing gringo publishers who have suddenly discovered Latin
American literature—they read more convincingly as the textual and
authorial anxieties of writers struggling to reformulate US–Latin
American literary relations. The inability of Lerner's protagonist to
master the Spanish-language canon and the refusal of Luiselli's protagonist to offer up her "foreign pearl" to the American publisher are,
I will argue, textual reminders of the material and symbolic difficulties of creating a truly responsive and reciprocal hemispheric literary
tradition. In presenting themselves simultaneously as readers *and*
experiencers of the Americas, these contemporary authors help to
shed light on the entrenched assumptions of their respective literary
fields. At the same time, they offer a glimpse of a possible rapprochement between the US and Latin American literary fields in our contemporary moment. This merging of the position of the reader and
experiencer remains an ongoing process, one that has no single etiology but must be traced to a number of interrelated shifts in the
demographic, cultural, and literary relationship between the United
States and Latin America.

Prolegomena to an American Bolaño

Where should we begin tracing this twenty-first century merging of
the US literature of experience with the Latin American literature of
the reader? The first and most obvious shift has been the exponential
growth in the United States of the Latina/o population, defined here
in US census terms as persons "of Cuban, Mexican, Puerto Rican,
South or Central American, or other Spanish culture or origin regardless of race." This demographic expansion—according to the
US census, Latinas/os went from 6 percent of the US population in
1980 to an estimated 17 percent in 2013, not including undocumented immigrants[5]—has led to an increase in the absolute number
of Spanish speakers in the United States and also an increased
awareness of the role of Latin America and Latina/o immigrants in
national life. Kirsten Silva Gruesz has persuasively argued that contemporary mainstream debates about Latino "emergence" tend to obscure both the earlier cultural contributions of Spanish speakers in
the United States and the continued presence of undocumented (and

therefore uncounted) Latin American immigrants.[6] Still, it is important to recognize that this changing demography has motivated self-conscious reformulations of literary practice among Latina/o writers. As Lawrence Buell has suggested, with Latinas/os now constituting the United States' largest minority, we might well anticipate that novels addressing cultural divides in the United States will continue to move away from the white-black "polarities" of the twentieth century.[7] What I want to stress here is that contemporary novelists have portrayed this cultural split as one rooted as much in the implicit codes and conventions of the US and Latin American literary fields as in what Buell dubs the "ethnoterritorial" divides of region and race.

The most powerful literary-critical effort to account for this shift in the cultural imaginary of US–Latin American relations has come from a generation of writers and critics associated with the "borderlands" territories of the US Southwest—in particular, the Rio Grande Valley immediately north of the US border with Mexico. Building on the pioneering studies of Américo Paredes from the late 1950s forward, the works of Rolando Hinojosa, Gloria Anzaldúa, Nicolás Kanellos, Ramón Saldívar, and José David Saldívar have contested the binary logic of the US and Latin American literary-field imaginaries through a cultural politics emphasizing the bilingual, hybrid, and antiassimilationist nature of the borderland peoples between the United States and Mexico. This generation's pursuit of what Kanellos dubs "counterhegemonic" political and cultural narratives has often been studied. Beginning in the 1970s and 1980s, however, the work of the borderlands writers and critics also implied a more specific revision of literary practices across the hemispheric divide, particularly as these related to reading and experience. As the founder of Arte Público Press and the head of the Recovering the US Hispanic Literary Heritage project at the University of Houston, Kanellos has framed his labors of archival recovery as a corrective to the "Chicano movement's notion that populations in the Southwest were bereft of a written tradition and literature and therefore the academy needed to focus on the collecting and study of oral lore."[8] Hinojosa's trajectory from a student (and later professor) of Spanish literature with a master's thesis on *Don Quixote* to the foremost Latina/o novelist of the US-Mexico border underscores the degree to which the merging of the US and Latin American literary fields motivates his novelistic project. Hinojosa has repeatedly stated that his Klail City Death

series about the Rio Grande Valley was conceived as an amalgama-
tion of the Hemingwayesque and Faulknerian creed of "writing what
you know" ("I write about what I assume other writers write about:
that which they know") with a lifetime of reading the Hispanic literary tradition and identifying as a reader ("I am now convinced that I
am a reader who decides to write until the opportunity to read again
becomes available").[9] Hinojosa's ability to move between the US and
Latin American fields—he won the influential Casa de las Américas
fiction prize for *Klail y sus alrededores* in 1976—established an important precedent for later writers who moved across the hemispheric literary divide. A particularly significant contribution of this
generation was to make available the *concept* of the "literature of
the Americas" to writers and critics alike. Hinojosa ends his essay
"Chicano Literature: An American Literature with a Difference" with
the affirmation: "Chicano Literature is a United States literature, but
it is also a literature of the Americas, as Martí so clearly saw and la-
belled the New World."[10] With Hinojosa, the notion of a "literature
of the Americas" began to appear in the US literary field as what
historians dub an actor's category (i.e. as a term that writers themselves used to describe their own work) at the same time that it was
being formulated as a critical term within the academy.

The expansion of the "border" concept—and the contemporane-
ous emergence of the "literature of the Americas" as a literary and
critical category—owes much to major interventions in the late 1980s
and 1990s by the feminist poet-scholar Gloria Anzaldúa and the
critic José David Saldívar. Anzaldúa's influential *Borderlands/La
Frontera: The New Mestiza* (1987) can be seen as a radicalization of
the borderlands thesis developed in the work of Paredes and his
heirs, insofar as the text uses the geographical liminality of the US–
Mexican borderlands as a metaphor for the transgression of "psychological," "sexual," and "spiritual" boundaries "not particular to the
Southwest."[11] Linking her own bilingual queer Chicana subjectivity
to the "vague and undetermined" (25) status of all those who exist
between two cultures, Anzaldúa argues that the concept of the borderlands works to deconstruct a series of commonly held binaries:
English and Spanish, Anglo and indigenous, American and Mexican,
male and female. A key component of Anzaldúa's antidualist model
is the term *mestiza*, which she adopts from José Vasconcelos's concept
of *mestizaje* and glosses as a theory of "inclusivity" that opposes the
"policy of racial purity that white America practices" (99). As I noted

in chapter 1, Vasconcelos subsequently added to his culturo-biological theory of *mestizaje* an argument for the activity of reading as an alternative to the Deweyan pragmatist creed of "learning by doing." Anzaldúa's practice of citing a range of authors from the Americas— from Bernardino de Sahagún and the mythical Huitzilopochtli to Vasconcelos and Violeta Parra—thus actualizes Vasconcelos's reader-oriented aesthetics in performing its *textual* hybridity. Anzaldúa's more expansive understanding of the "borderlands" and its relevance for moving toward an inclusive "literature of the Americas" was paralleled by Saldívar's hypostatization of the "border" concept in his influential studies *The Dialectics of Our America; Genealogy, Cultural Critique, and Literary History* (1991) and *Border Matters: Remapping American Cultural Studies* (1997).

Yet as central as the theory and practice of textual hybridity have been to the academic landscape and the rise of the "New Americanist" studies, it is worth emphasizing that until recently the cultural politics of voracious reading has not been a majority view among Latina/o writers. These literary "borderers" (as Hinojosa dubbed them) came from a particular geographical location in the Rio Grande Valley of South Texas, and nearly all of them—including Hinojosa and Anzaldúa—could trace their roots back to the Spanish occupation of the present-day Southwest before the region was annexed by the United States in the mid nineteenth-century. In the ever-expanding canon of Latina/o literature produced in the wake of the Chicano movement of the 1960s, the difference in aesthetic aims between these "native" authors and "mainstream" English-speaking authors such as Cisneros, Cristina García, and Oscar Hijuelos is significant. For these latter authors, Latin American culture continued to be experiential and popular: what one absorbed in person, heard on the radio, or saw on TV.

The argument that Latin American textual hybridity was at the core of Latina/o literary practice did not itself go "mainstream" until the mid-1990s, with the publication of the Mexican-born writer-critic Ilan Stavans's *The Hispanic Condition: Reflections on Culture and Identity in America* (1995). Unlike earlier works on borderlands culture, Stavans's book emphasized primarily the positive characteristics of what he dubbed the "Hispanization of the United States, and Anglocization of Hispanics," offering an avowedly millenarian vision of what the United States would look like as the Hispanic population moved "from periphery to center stage."[12] Critics were quick to point out that Stavans's triumphant appropriation of the discourse of Hispanic *mestizaje*—his description of New World history as a "fiesta of miscegenation" and his avowal that "[m]any of us Latinos already have a Yankee look" (13, 8)—downplayed many of the ongoing economic and social struggles of the Latina/o community. Yet one of the book's major virtues was that it provided an argument for how Latina/o writers could use the US cultural apparatus to "promote a revaluation of things Hispanic" (16) and a direct appeal to Hispanic literary tradition as the agent of that transformation. In *The Hispanic Condition*, and even more so in Stavans's later memoir *On Borrowed Words* (2001), Borges becomes both the Virgilian guide for his navigation of Latin American literature and the constant reference point for the possibilities of cultural translation across the hemispheric divide.[13] Of course, prominent US postmodern writers such as John Barth and Thomas Pynchon had championed Borges as a guiding spirit as early as the 1960s, and Cisneros herself began to mention Borges's influence on *The House on Mango Street* in interviews of the early 1990s. But Barth's references to Borges in his iconic essay "The Literature of Exhaustion," where the "Argentine master" is positioned at the leading edge of an international avant-garde including Beckett and Robbe-Grillet, were indicative of a general tendency in the US literary field to recognize Borges's aesthetic achievement while largely omitting its relationship to his Argentine and Latin American context. As a writer who immigrated to the United States when he was already in his early twenties, Stavans made his oscillation between Spanish and English, and between the Latin American and US literary fields, the central theme of his work. Rereading Borges back into a Hispanic literary tradition, and at the same time frequently appealing to the Borgesian aesthetics of the reader, Stavans provided an important model for later Latina/o writers such as Goldman, Díaz, and Menéndez who came to Latin American literature later in life. Finally, as the general editor for the *Norton Anthology of Latino Literature* (2010), Stavans established a blueprint for Latina/o literary tradition that incorporates Spanish-language texts typically confined to the Latin American canon—from the colonial writings of Bartolomé de las Casas to the novels of the late twentieth-century Puerto Rican writer Luis Rafael Sánchez—that will likely have a major effect on the way Latina/o fiction is written as well as read in the twenty-first century.

All of these factors help to shed light on the so-called "Bolaño boom" in the United States over the past half decade. We cannot begin to understand the effect of Bolaño's work without taking into account the increased circulation of Latin American literary works in the United States, the self-conscious engagement between US and Latin American writers in contemporary fiction, and the visibility of US Latina/o authors who (to paraphrase Borges) feel free to draw irreverently from the Latin American tradition. In this regard, it is crucial to note that Goldman was the first person to recommend Bolaño to Barbara Epler at New Directions, the US publisher of all of Bolaño's works except for *The Savage Detectives* and *2666*, as well as that Goldman and Stavans were two of the earliest and most fervent reviewers of his novels.[14] For a variety of reasons both historical and literary, Bolaño's work (and his reception in the United States) has allowed English- and Spanish-language writers alike to reflect on their own literary practice. It is to that practice—and the crossing of the hemispheric literary divide that it constitutes—that we will now turn.

The Bolañian Turn in Contemporary Latina/o Fiction

The literary careers of three of the most influential contemporary Latina/o writers—Francisco Goldman, Junot Díaz, and Ana Menéndez—mark an inflection point in the relationship between the US and Latin American literary fields. In their twenty-first-century fiction, we can detect a fundamental shift in the representation of Latin America: the region becomes a literary field to be *reconstructed* and *read* as well as a physical place to be absorbed and experienced. Not only do the major works of these writers foreground Latin American historical, intellectual, and literary traditions; they also create textual figures of the reader whose research "projects" about Latin American culture drive the plots of their novels. For all of these writers, the encounter with Bolaño's work has been a major catalyst of their authorial transformation. Since Bolaño offers, as I have suggested, a geopolitical mapping of Latin American literary history and a privileged role for the "voracious reader," these writers have found in his oeuvre a guide to Latin American literature and a canonical model for fashioning themselves as readers of it. This "Bolañian turn" in US Latina/o literature can be traced in a number of works of the past fifteen years, including Goldman's *The Divine Husband* (2004) and *Say Her Name* (2011); Díaz's *The Brief Wondrous Life of Oscar Wao* (2007); and Menéndez's *Loving Che* (2003) and

Adios, Happy Homeland! (2011). In many ways, this literary line represents the most nuanced and provocative exploration of US–Latin American relations in contemporary US fiction.

Goldman's trajectory over the past thirty years is emblematic of a broad shift in contemporary US literary strategies for depicting Latin America. Born to a Guatemalan mother in the United States in 1954, Goldman spent many years as a journalist in Central America and Mexico. In addition to the four novels he has published since the early 1990s, he has written numerous articles and reviews for mainstream publications such as *Harper's*, the *New Yorker*, and the *New York Times*. Scholars have often viewed Goldman as a "hemispheric writer" whose work moves beyond the traditional boundaries of US fiction. Rodrigo Lazo, for instance, situates Goldman's *The Ordinary Seaman* (1997), a novel about a group of migrant Central American workers in New York, at the heart of a contemporary tradition of hemispheric American novels that track transnational flows of people and goods in order to contest dominant US political and cultural discourses in the Americas.[15] And yet, though compelling as an interpretation of this single novel, Lazo's reading fails to account for the trajectory of Goldman's career, and thus, of his evolving relationship with the US and Latin American literary fields. A new set of aesthetic issues emerges when this larger framework is considered. Although his later works continue to explore hemispheric economics and politics, Goldman increasingly filters his concerns through the prism of US-Latin American literary relations. Set more than a century apart, the historical novel *The Divine Husband* and the fictional memoir *Say Her Name* both intervene in a US literary field in which Bolaño's reader-experiencers increasingly represent a viable paradigm. Goldman's works enact this paradigm by foregrounding the hermeneutic activity of reading in various settings and periods— whether that be nineteenth-century Guatemala or twenty-first-century New York—and by repeatedly returning to the problematic of reading and experience within a hemispheric literary context, much as Latin American writers such as Bolaño, Piglia, and Rivera Garza have done.

On the very first page of *The Divine Husband*, the narrator—a semiautobiographical character later referred to as "Paquito," the diminutive of Goldman's nickname "Paco"—announces his turn to a readerly aesthetic: "What if we read history the way we do love poems, or even the life stories of sainted Sacred Virgins?"[16] This line, whose full meaning is not revealed until we reach the end of the novel, can be seen as an anticipation of the compositional principle underlying the book. As we make our way through *The Divine Husband*, we realize that its main plot line—the "historical" encounter between José Martí and the young Guatemalan-born María de las Nieves Moran, who later moves to the United States—has been spun from an obsessive, almost Nabokovian reading of Martí's verse. Taking as its primary source material one of Martí's most iconic love poems, "La niña de Guatemala," and contextualizing it through translations of Martí's diaries, political writings, and *crónicas* of New York, the novel imagines a fictional backstory to Martí's real-life journey to Guatemala in the 1870s—and a connection that links Martí, María de las Nieves, and the narrator himself. In the epilogue, the narrator's decision to make Martí's corpus the aleph through which to "unearth" the story of María de las Nieves acquires further relevance, as it is implicitly linked to Goldman's own literary trajectory. Paquito reveals that his hemispheric historical "project" began as an investigative report into early twentieth-century immigrant Guatemalan laborers in his hometown in Massachusetts. This fictional assignment recalls Goldman's early journalism for *Harper's* and the migrant focus of *The Ordinary Seaman*. Insofar as it intersects with a genealogical interest on the part of Paquito ("Some members of my own family may be partly descended from those workers" [452]), it also recalls the quest for identity that plays a central role in Goldman's first novel, *The Long Night of the White Chickens*. But Pacquito veers away from these journalistic and genealogical leanings when he comes across the writings of Martí, whom he emphatically describes on the first page as "one of Latin America's greatest poet-heroes not just of the nineteenth century but *of all time*, for ever and ever" (3). The entry of Martí's texts into the story—and into the narrator's life—thus comes to symbolize the narrative's preoccupation with the way that reading literature and reconstructing literary history changes our notions of history proper. Immediately before the narrator's hypothesis about how history looks when read as literature, he informs us that he will be telling us a story (in reality, a series of stories) that "would not only influence the history of that small Central American Republic [of Guatemala] but also alter the personal lives of some of our American hemisphere's most illustrious men of politics, literature, and industry" (3). In *The Divine Husband*, and in Martí's legacy as the novel reconstructs it, literature becomes inseparable from the questions of "politics" and "industry" that have motivated Goldman since early in his career.

If for the narrator of *The Divine Husband* reading signifies an alternative mode of unearthing and writing hemispheric history and identity, for the rest of the characters it signals the key to their identity formations. The second part of Paquito's opening question—what if we read history the way we do "the life stories of sainted Sacred Virgins" (3)—alludes to the self-fashioning of María de las Nieves, whom we first meet as a nun's apprentice who can barely contain her "bookish enthusiasm and habits" (20). In the cloister library, María de las Nieves discovers the *vida* of Sor María de Agreda, a seventeenth-century Spanish nun famous for her reputed ability to cross geographical boundaries through bilocation, that is, the physical habitation of two different places at the same time. Likening María de las Nieves's reading of Sor María's life story to this mystical practice, the narrative ruminates on how the young apprentice's absorption of a textual narrative distant from her both spatially and temporally functions as both a substitute for and an impulse toward experience:

> In her meditations, interior prayers, and as she lay awake at night, she lost herself in methodically narrated adventures and inner dialogues inspired by the mystical travels of the Spanish nun. These imagined flights were becoming so vivid that in her high excitement she sometimes wondered if they might not be the anteroom to the actual experience, as the antechoir was to the upper-choir (46).

When the liberal government declares the decloistering of the country's Catholic Church, María de las Nieves finds a secular equivalent to the cloister library in a "reading room kiosk" (213) in the center of the capital city, where she continues her quixotic practice of "methodically" narrating her life through textual materials. The reading room becomes perhaps the most significant setting of the novel's later chapters: a space where María de las Nieves not only reads newspapers and books about the outside world, but also forges relationships with Martí and her future husband Mack. By depicting Latin America's emergence into modernity through the passage from the cloister library to the public reading room, Goldman highlights the mechanisms of the Latin American lettered city in ways that previous US writers had rarely done.

In this sense, the entire novel may be seen as an attempt to retool the dominant methodologies for approaching Latin America in contemporary Latina/o literature, insofar as it predicates an awareness of current political and economic exploitation in the Americas on immersion in the Latin American cultural archive. Paquito's gradual transformation from someone who "had never heard of José Martí" (452) into a reader-researcher of Latin America—a narrative arc that enfolds the story of Martí and María de las Nieves—dramatizes the process by which the Latina/o writer comes to define himself or herself within a "hemispheric" as opposed to merely US literary tradition. In fact, "hemispheric" becomes a keyword in the novel: in addition to its early mention of the illustrious figures of the "American hemisphere," the spread of the Martí myth across the Americas is likened to a "hemispheric cloud of pigeons" (103), and the transatlantic journeys of Teresa de Avila's family are invoked as proof that the Spanish saint is "ubiquitous in our hemispheric DNA" (146). Most tellingly, in the novel's epilogue, the narrator mentions Martí's coverage of the infamous Panamerican Conference of 1890, which the burgeoning revolutionary "considered a ploy by the United States to extend economic control over all the compliant states of the Americas, at the expense of building hemispheric consensus for the cause of Cuban independence" (457). The novel's historical impulse is to activate this dormant sense of the "hemispheric" as a category of thought and political action. It does so in part by reconstructing Martí's network and itineraries through Central America, New York, and the Caribbean, and in part through a kind of Whitmanesque impulse to name the very "America" it seeks to conjure into existence, one that is now hemispheric rather than national. It hardly seems coincidental, then, that the novel's acknowledgments section recognizes several scholarly works on Martí that have been foundational to the contemporary field of hemispheric studies, including those of Doris Sommer, Julio Ramos, Rafael Rojas, and Susana Rotker-Martínez.

Goldman's "fictional memoir" *Say Her Name* (2011) transports this exploration of hemispheric literary production from the late nineteenth century into the present, filtering US–Latin American literary dynamics through a personal narrative about Goldman and his real-life spouse Aura Estrada. Alongside the history of Goldman's traumatized response to tragedy—Estrada died after a swimming accident off the coast of Mexico in 2007—the memoir details Estrada's attempts to transform herself from a graduate student in Latin American literature at Columbia University into an English-language novelist, at the same time that Goldman immerses himself in the cultural ecology of Mexico City. In an essay written in 2008, three years before *Say Her Name* was published, Goldman spoke about the revelation he and Aura shared when reading Bolaño for the first time: "he wrote about the worlds we'd lived in."[17] Goldman's essay clearly spells out Bolaño's deep effect on his writing:

> For several months after Aura's death I couldn't read fiction, but then, when finally I could, pretty much the first thing I really yearned to read were the passages about Archimboldi's lover Ingeborg's death in the last book of *2666*, "The Part about Archimboldi." Like I've said, I read the novel on our week-long honeymoon on the Pacific [coast of Mexico]. I nearly finished it; I tore through it, astounded and enthralled.... I suppose this makes it sound as if all we did on our honeymoon is read, which isn't really true, though so what if it was?

And indeed, Goldman's memoir repeatedly turns on a structural trope that inverts the arc of the characters in Bolaño's *2666*: a journey of experience and desire that ends in compulsive reading.

Moreover, for Goldman (the narrator), the position of voracious reader provides the fulcrum for his reflections on love and loss more explicitly in *Say Her Name* than it does for Paquito in *The Divine Husband*. During the confusion following Estrada's death, he says, "I look for answers where I usually do, in books."[18] Earlier in the memoir, the erotic energy between the US-born, English-speaking Goldman and the Mexico-born, Spanish-speaking Estrada migrates from the bedroom to their exchanges of reading materials. Their elective affinity for Borges ignites an insatiable desire for literary cross-pollination that morphs into a Bolañian hunger for books: "I wanted to read.... Aura had finished reading a Fabio Morábito collection of stories the day before—she loved it—and was now restlessly switching between Silvina Ocampo and Bruno Schulz..." (313–314). Of course, these lists of primarily Latin American (and little-known) writers are meant to challenge a US audience's horizon of expectations, a practice whose possibility was opened up by the unprecedented receptivity in the United States to Bolaño's work.

The restless Bolañian alternation between experience and reading described in *Say Her Name* might cause us to revisit what Lazo refers to, in relation to *The Ordinary Seaman*, as Goldman's "Central American connection" (1084). By what calculus can we reconcile these two Francisco Goldmans: the one who composes a novel that demarcates, in Lazo's words, "a relationship between New York as the economic capital of the United States and…a [Central American] region that has been ravaged by the effects of US-funded wars" (1084), and the other who reveals in his memoir that he lives in a gentrifying neighborhood of Brooklyn and spent his honeymoon reading (and not reading) in a Mexican tourist hot spot? It is hard not to see in *Say Her Name* at least an unconscious recognition that the only way Goldman could map the hemispheric routes of exploitation in *The Ordinary Seaman* was to have had privileged access to an experiential trajectory reminiscent of those of Hemingway and Porter. The memoir speaks of Goldman's ten years on assignment for the *New York Times* in Nicaragua and Guatemala, his frequent and unfettered travel, and the apartment that he keeps in the heart of Mexico City. It becomes clear, in other words, why an ordinary Nicaraguan seaman could not have written *The Ordinary Seaman*. On the other hand, *Say Her Name* develops an emergent position for the contemporary US Latino writer that incorporates not only a plastic use of English and Spanish but also the full scope of the Latin American and US literary traditions. Allusions to Borges, Ocampo, Juan Rulfo, and Juan Carlos Onetti appear alongside references to Emerson and the poems of Bob Dylan. Thus, whatever one's appreciation for the sentiment behind Lazo's call for "a hemispheric approach rather than a presumptuous designation of a new field that would include all novels published in the Americas" (1086), it might be countered that the desire to incorporate (nearly) all of the novels of the Americas is precisely the ambition of the contemporary writers that Lazo analyzes. This is not to suggest that Goldman has merely been "influenced" by Bolaño, but rather that the literal and cultural translation of Bolaño's work in the United States (to which Goldman has substantially contributed) has helped create what Pierre Bourdieu calls a new "space of possibles" in the US literary field.[19]

The slow shift toward the figure of the voracious reader in Goldman's fiction can also be tracked in the works of two of the most celebrated Latina/o writers of a younger generation: Junot Díaz and Ana Menéndez. Scholars have demonstrated the various ways in which Díaz's *The Brief Wondrous Life of Oscar Wao* (2007), with its singular idiom of Spanish-inflected English prose and a narrative arc that spans the history of the Caribbean diaspora, challenges the geographical and linguistic expectations of its US-based audience.[20] We might also note that although *The Brief Wondrous Life of Oscar Wao* carries forward Díaz's preoccupation with cross-cultural representation established in his short-story cycle *Drown* (1996), its depiction of the *longue durée* of hemispheric history draws on literary strategies that significantly diverge from those of his earlier work. Whereas the characters in *Drown* are defined primarily through their lived experience of migration between the United States and the Dominican Republic, in *Oscar Wao*, reading itself becomes a form of cultural and geographical transit. The most obvious reader in the novel is the eponymous protagonist, Oscar, whose immersion in the worlds of genre fiction functions as an escape from the daily turmoil of his life as a "ghetto nerd" growing up in New Jersey. But it is the novel's main narrator, the equally genre-obsessed Yunior, who channels Oscar's sci-fi and fantasy "bibliomania" and tries to reorient it toward the historiographic and literary traditions surrounding the Dominican Republic. Alongside quotations from *The Lord of the Rings* and *The Fantastic Four*, the novel includes citations from and references to Mario Vargas Llosa's *The Feast of the Goat*, Jesús Galíndez's *La era de Trujillo*, and Bartolomé de las Casas's *A Short Account of the Destruction of the Indies*.[21] If Díaz's work "reflects a turn in American letters toward a hemispheric…literature and culture," as Monica Hanna, Jennifer Harford Vargas, and José David Saldívar put it, that turn itself reflects the broad shift toward the practices of voracious reading inaugurated by Bolaño's introduction into the US literary field.[22] In a blurb for *The Divine Husband*, Díaz refers to Goldman as "the greatest American novelist of our generation," and, more recently, he has described Bolaño as "[o]ne of our greatest writers, a straight colossus.…Latin American letters (wherever it may reside) has never had a greater, more disturbing avenging angel than Bolaño."[23] Here we find Díaz subtly but insistently redrawing the literary map of the Americas: Goldman and his novels of Central Americans and Cubans become the guiding light of contemporary "American" fiction, just as the itinerant Bolaño becomes the avatar of an increasingly deterritorialized Latin American literature.

Both *The Brief Wondrous Life of Oscar Wao* and Díaz's extratextual comments about its genesis indicate his growing concern with his place in the history of US–Latin American literary relations. In an interview with Edwidge Danticat, for example, Díaz responded to a question about *The Brief Wondrous Life of Oscar Wao*'s connection to other books about the Dominican Republic with the following explanation: "I'm book-obsessed and I wrote about a book-obsessed protagonist. The narrator too: book-obsessed. You better believe that I was fucking with other books written about the Dominican Republic."[24] At the most basic level, the comment suggests a continuity between Díaz's own self-fashioning as a voracious reader and Oscar's and Yunior's reading practices in the novel. In the interview, Díaz singles out Peruvian writer Vargas Llosa's *The Feast of the Goat*, a dictator novel about Trujillo, as the principal novel he was "fucking with." And indeed, the two references to *The Feast of the Goat* in the novel are critical: in one, Yunior complains about Vargas Llosa's "sympathetic" treatment of Trujillo-confidante-turned-Dominican-president Joaquín Balaguér; in the other, he insinuates that Vargas Llosa's narrative use of the common Dominican trope of "The Girl Trujillo Wanted" merely reifies a catchall explanation for the political problems on the island (90, 244). Rewriting this trope becomes a major plot line in *Oscar Wao*, which not only borrows from Vargas Llosa the theme of the prominent Dominican patriarch called upon to offer up his daughter to Trujillo, but also adds a self-reflexive touch by giving Oscar's Dominican family the same surname (Cabral) as the main character in *The Feast of the Goat*. This operation of repurposing Vargas Llosa's plot line is presented as a conscious discursive act by Yunior, whose narrative management often entails negotiating between Oscar's preferred genres of fantasy and science fiction and the more politically minded Latin American dictator novel as exemplified by *The Feast of the Goat*. If the Yunior of *Drown* struggles to find meaning beyond the brutal experience of migration between the United States and the Dominican Republic, the Yunior of *Oscar Wao* begins to seek answers in a cultural archive that expands his narrative purview both temporally and geographically.

However, the bifurcation of the figure of the reader between Yunior and Oscar in *The Brief Wondrous Life of Oscar Wao* complicates the geopolitical thrust of the practice of voracious reading as Goldman and Bolaño had developed it. Despite Díaz's claim in his interview with Danticat that Oscar and Yunior are equally "book-obsessed," in the novel itself Oscar's "commitment to the Genres" outpaces Yunior's commitment to the hemispheric cultural archive. The most obvious expression of Yunior's failure to master the codes of cross-cultural representation appears in one of the novel's many footnotes, where Yunior claims that he initially made a factual error in his description of a Dominican coastal city: "In my first draft, Samaná was actually Jarabacoa, but then my girl Leonie, resident expert in all things Domo, pointed out that there are no beaches in Jarabacoa" (132). This casual destabilizing of Yunior's narrative authority about the Dominican Republic, I would argue, dramatizes a larger anxiety about Latin American culture that haunts Díaz's writings. Within the Spanish-speaking world, several writers and critics have pointed out that although Díaz's texts incorporate a significant number of Spanish words, Díaz's own ability to read and speak Spanish is limited; a recent polemical text by the Santo Domingo–based Puerto Rican writer Pedro Cabiya, for example, has referred to Díaz's "feeble to nonexistent competence in Spanish."[25] Though it would be impossible fully to address here the complicated linguistic politics involved in such a statement, we might nevertheless acknowledge that in comparison to Goldman's *The Divine Husband* and *Say Her Name*, the scope of *Oscar Wao*'s Spanish-language literary references is relatively narrow. I would venture that one reason why the novel remains so committed, like Oscar, to the practices of reading genre fiction is that fantasy and sci-fi offer a literary terrain whose every contour is familiar to the protagonist, the narrator, *and* the author. It is no coincidence, therefore, that at the end of *Oscar Wao* Yunior symbolically entrusts his narrative to a figure who will presumably depart from what Yunior refers to in *Drown* as his "busted-up Spanish" (145). He imagines that Isis, the daughter of Oscar's sister Lola, who "speaks Spanish and English" and "is a little reader too," will eventually compose a master narrative incorporating Yunior's stories and her tío's books: "she'll take all we've done and all we've learned and add her own insights and she'll put an end to it" (331). While Yunior might at times seem capable of knitting together the experience of Caribbean migration and the US and Dominican cultural archives, the novel ultimately defers this responsibility to the next generation.

If Goldman's and Díaz's novels experiment with various figures of the Latin American reader-experiencer, Ana Menéndez's trajectory offers the most dramatic example of the dissolution of the hyphenated experiencer into the hemispheric archivist. From her linked short-story collection *In Cuba I Was a German Shepherd* (1999) to *Adios, Happy Homeland!* (2011), Menéndez's three Cuban-themed works present an evolving portrait of the Cuban-American authorial figure as she transitions from documenting the passage from the United States to Cuba to voraciously reading and rewriting both of these countries' literary traditions. The final story of *In Cuba I Was a German Shepherd*, Menéndez's first fictional work, introduces us to a young narrator whose life story mirrors the author's own: a Cuban-American journalist "born in Miami, two years after the revolution."[26] Titled "Her Mother's House," the story tells of the narrator's journey to absorb—and eventually write about—her firsthand impressions of the Cuba her family left behind. The story's arc largely follows the model set by García's *Dreaming in Cuban*: the trip to the island allows the narrator to move beyond her mother's ideological vision of postrevolutionary Cuba ("The people had been kind. The police hadn't followed," 212) to establish a balanced, if still ambivalent, view of the "actual experience" of the "homeland." Menéndez's next work of fiction, *Loving Che* (2003), picks up where "Her Mother's House" leaves off, with a young Cuban-American reporter who has "settled in a small beach town north of Miami" after making several trips to Cuba, "supporting myself by writing short articles about the places I visited."[27] But while in "Her Mother's House" the protagonist's journey to her mother's (erstwhile) house in Cuba helps her to establish affective connections with the island, *Loving Che* withholds the possibility of a place-based solution, replacing it with a hermeneutic puzzle to be solved. When the narrator receives a package of letters and photographs from a Cuban artist who claims to be the narrator's mother and tells her that Che Guevara is her biological father (!), she is compelled to embark on a "research project" about Cuba to reconstruct her mother's story through the historical archive: "I gave myself over to the research, eventually collecting two shelves' worth of books on Che Guevara and Cuban history" (163). When, toward the end, the narrator finally meets with her former Cuban history professor, she has already begun to develop an expertise in Cuban culture: noticing that the historian's shelves "were stacked with books, every one of them, as far as I could tell, about Cuba," she recognizes "quite a few" of them "from [her] own growing collection" (172).

The "research project" that animates much of the last section of *Loving Che* prepares us for the final manifestation of the figure of the author in Menéndez's work: the reader-anthologizer Herberto Quain of *Adios, Happy Homeland!* As I have mentioned previously, both the (pseudo)anthology's structure and Quain as a figure highlight for a general US audience Menéndez's appropriation of the narrative strategies associated with the Latin American literature of the reader. But for those already familiar with Menéndez's earlier work, the prologue to *Adios, Happy Homeland!* also dramatizes a decade-long shift in her conception of what a book about Cuba should be. The fantasy of *In Cuba I Was a German Shepherd* is that of a totalizing narrative of the "Cuban experience," a mosaic of subjective accounts of the lives of Cubans on the island and abroad; here, however, the Borgesian compendium serves as the governing trope. Presented as an anthology of Cuban literature edited by the protean librarian Quain, the book opens with a prologue that describes the Irish bibliophile's initial exposure to Cuban verse at a transatlantic remove. Referring to his discovery of the encyclopedic *A Brief History of Cuban Poets*, Quain writes: "In the early evenings, after my chores and my lessons, I would wind my way through the house back to the library.... It was on one such day, in early winter, that I came across a curious book.... In that book I learned of a place where there is good sun, and water of foam and sand so fine" (7–8).[28] Even when he arrives in Cuba and finally gets a chance to explore the place that fired his imagination, he opts to "present himself at the National Library" (10), spending the "happiest years of [his] life immersed in Cuban verse" (11), rather than in the Cuban lifeworld that had obsessed Menéndez's earlier protagonists. And indeed, since the pseudoanthology rewrites many Cuban literary classics, from Gómez de Avellaneda's "Al partir" ["On Leaving," 1836] to Alejo Carpentier's "Viaje a la semilla" ["Journey Back to the Source," 1963], the very legibility of the collection's stories depends on a detailed knowledge of Cuban literature and literary history. In a final narrative twist that seeks to eradicate any associations we might continue to draw between the book's author and on-the-ground conditions in twenty-first-century Cuba, the "Contributors' Notes" section at the novel's close includes Ana Menéndez as "the pseudonym of an imaginary writer and translator, invented... to offer [the collection] the pretense of contemporary relevance." *Adios, Happy Homeland!* thus moves to the far end of the readerly spectrum, imagining a narrative universe in which authorial experience is entirely proscribed.

On the Superiority of Latin American Literature

In April 2010, I attended a symposium at Princeton University entitled "Poetry of the Americas," a one-day event convened to consider the viability of a trans-American poetics. In addition to the many Americanist, Latin Americanist, and inter-Americanist academics who participated, the US poet Kenneth Goldsmith was invited to give a reading and take part in the discussion. Over the course of the day, it became clear that Goldsmith, a prominent figure associated with the conceptual poetry movement, considered Borges to be an important precursor to his notion of "uncreative writing." But it also seemed clear to me that Goldsmith had little familiarity with Latin American literature and culture beyond the work of a few old masters. My suspicion was heightened during Goldsmith's reading performance, which included a verbatim recitation of Salvador Allende's radio announcement delivered shortly before his death in 1973, reproduced (by Goldsmith) entirely *in Spanish*. Hearing the heavily aspirated h's and excessive gringo intonations, and knowing Goldsmith's penchant for self-dramatization, I assumed he was trying to caricature his own ignorance of the language. Goldsmith's reading of Allende's speech simultaneously performed his ignorance and made of it a literary act. At the time, the reading struck me as sensationalist, self-aggrandizing, and tone-deaf. Yet I also must admit that after witnessing a number of far more earnest attempts at hemispheric cultural exchange in the years since, Goldsmith's performance has stayed with me as a vivid demonstration of the extent to which the Hispanic world's language, literature, and culture remains beyond the grasp (and the tongue) of so many Anglo-American writers. The symposium's ostensible aim was to establish a hemispheric dialogue, but Goldsmith's performance forcefully demonstrated that we couldn't even rely on a common language. Was this how we should be talking when we talk about the literature of the Americas?

The sense that US writers miss something significant by failing to engage with Latin American literatures and languages is itself nothing new. The mainstream US literary establishment's "discovery" of Borges and the boom writers in the 1960s and 1970s led to numerous admonitions against overlooking writers from the South. What changed in the last decade of the twentieth century and the first decade of the twenty-first, however, was the degree to which US writers began to suggest that contemporary Latin American literature was, in its totality, more interesting and important than literature produced in the United States. One of the more surprising proponents of this view was David Foster Wallace, who frequently accompanied his diagnoses of the maladies of postmodern American literature with

prescriptions for reading more literature from the rest of the hemisphere. In a 1994 article on Zbigniew Herbert, he blasted the "whole
spectrum of American poetry—from the retrograde quaintness of
the Neoformalists and New-Yorker-backyard-garden-meditative
lyrics to the sterile abstraction of the Language poets" while arguing
that "only writers from Eastern Europe and Latin America have succeeded in marrying the stuff of spirit and human feeling to the pa-
rodic detachment the postmodern experience seems to require."[29] At
a time when twenty-first-century US fiction has increasingly been
criticized by mainstream and academic critics for failing to engage
with other linguistic and national traditions—"too insular, too isolated," as Swedish Academy secretary Horace Engdahl controversially
put it in 2008; "improperly worlded," in the influential definition of
Bruce Robbins—the command of multiple literatures displayed by
many contemporary Latin American writers has begun to seem like
a distinct advantage. After a long period during which Latin America
(and the Spanish-speaking world in general) figured in the US literary imagination as a region of cultural sparseness, we may now be
witnessing a paradigm shift in which American novelists and poets
not only recognize the broad merits of Latin American literature but
also feel an acute sense of *inferiority* vis-à-vis writers in the Spanish-
speaking world. This phenomenon, which might be termed "Bolaño
envy," has manifested itself in various ways, from preemptive gestures meant to demonstrate some familiarity with Hispanic culture
to a self-conscious fictional thematization of the lack of reciprocity
between Latin American and US writers. In the midst of what Caren
Irr has identified as the rise of the US geopolitical novel in the
twenty-first century, Bolaño's work is not the only model, but it may
be the most influential one.

   The strongest sense of cultural inferiority to Latin America has
appeared, I would argue, in the works of a group of mostly white,
male, and Ivy-educated contemporary US writers and critics who see
themselves, either explicitly or implicitly, as belonging to the main
currents of American literary history. The persistent discourse about
what Bolaño and other Spanish-language writers "offer American
readers" in literary magazines such as *n+1* speaks to this urgency to
transcend the boundaries of the US literary field. The trajectory of
n+1 founding member Benjamin Kunkel, whose *Indecision* (2005)
was hailed by many as a generation-defining novel, is indicative of a
writerly milieu in which Latin America increasingly figures as the

scene of cultural awakening. In *Indecision*, the protagonist's epiphany that neo-conservatism and neoliberalism are the same thing occurs as he ingests mushrooms in the rainforests of Ecuador—a trope that fits squarely within the US literature of experience. Yet Kunkel's post-*Indecision* explorations of Latin American literature and culture have been more substantial. Several years after moving to Buenos Aires as a form of "self-imposed exile," Kunkel produced a long essay on Argentina's bicentennial that ended with his assertion that he was happy to be outside the United States as its institutions crumbled.[30] Kunkel's preference for Latin America over the United States has so far been voiced in primarily politico-economic rather than literary terms: he saw the rise of the Kirchners in Argentina and of other left-ist governments in twenty-first-century Latin America as infinitely preferable to the US neoliberal order. Yet if Kunkel has publicly stated that he took time away from fiction to concentrate on his in-troduction to contemporary political theory, *Utopia or Bust: A Guide to the Present Crisis* (2014), it seems likely that his next work of fic-tion will entail a mode of incorporating Latin American literature similar to that of Goldman, Díaz, or Menéndez.

The strenuous effort to imbibe Hispanic literary tradition per-vades *Leaving the Atocha Station* (2010), the picaresque first novel by the New York–based writer-poet Ben Lerner. A semiautobiographi-cal account of the year Lerner spent on a Fulbright Fellowship in Madrid in 2004, it tells the story of the charming yet flat-footed poet Adam, whose time in the city coincides with the horrific March 11 attacks on the Atocha train station. It might seem strange to include *Leaving the Atocha Station* in a discussion about the relationship be-tween the United States and Latin America, since it takes place almost entirely in Spain, but I analyze it here in part because of an extraor-dinary interlude midway through the novel about American writers in Mexico. The scene, related in the form of an instant messenger exchange between the Madrid-based Adam and his friend Cyrus back home, describes a trip to Mexico taken by Cyrus and his girl-friend, Jane. In the words of the narrator, "they'd driven to Mexico in her pickup with little money and no real plan in order to acquire experience, not just the experience of experience sponsored by my fellowship [in Spain]" (68). The trip to Mexico turns tragic when Cyrus and Jane witness the accidental death of a young Mexican girl—but the strangest part of the episode is that Jane, an aspiring writer, "seemed excited" by the tragedy because it certified that she "had had a 'real' experience" (77). As Cyrus puts it to Adam: "I had this sense...that the whole point of the trip for her—to Mexico—was for something like this, something this 'real' to happen. I don't really believe that, but I felt it, and I said something about how she had got some good material for her novel" (77). Through its knowing recapitulation of the tropes of the US literature of experience in Mexico, the scene suggests an alternative literary trajectory that Adam himself might have followed. This scene, and Adam's subsequent declaration, "I hate new experience" (69), highlights the degree to which the novel we are reading presents the US literature of experience as an exhausted paradigm, a dead end for the American writer in the Spanish-speaking world. If for Burroughs the experience of Latin America was the catalyst for his writerly transformation, for Lerner's Adam, that experience promises nothing but literary bad faith.

In an interview about *Leaving the Atocha Station* from 2013, Lerner claimed: "I am sure Spanish language writers like Javier Marias, Roberto Bolaño and José Camilo Cela are important influences for me, but I'm not sure I could pinpoint how."[31] I believe, however, that we can pinpoint the novel's relationship to Bolaño's work, not only in how it takes up the Bolañian formula of novelizing the life of the avant-garde poet but also in the way it represents the Madrid of the early twenty-first century as a hyperliterary urban metropolis rather than an exotic ecology. Hemingway's valiant matadors and earnest peasants are nowhere to be seen: the *madrileños* meet in galleries, watch *Citizen Kane*, and compare the narrator's poetry to Spanish writers exiled during the Franco years. Adam's near complete ignorance of Spanish-language literature, however, precludes him from following through on the fellowship project that had brought him to Spain in the first place: a "research-driven" poem about the influence of the Spanish Civil War ("about which I knew nothing") on a generation of Franco-era writers ("few of whom I'd read," 23). The specter of this alternative academic-sounding project continues to haunt him until the final scene of the novel, when he confuses the names of the famous Spanish poets Antonio Machado and Juan Ramón Jiménez at a heavily attended conference on literature and politics, proving, in the most egregious way, that "[t]he celebrated American fellow cannot get four names deep into the list of the most famous Spanish poets of the twentieth century" (177). At the diegetic level, the scene exemplifies Adam's failure to relate culturally, as opposed to merely touristically, to the Spanish literary world. At the extradiegetic level, the scene becomes a kind of *apologia* for the novel we are in the process of reading, a novel that not only doesn't relate Spanish literature to the Spanish Civil War but also cannot really deliver on its implicit promise to give us some insight into the Atocha bombings themselves. Here is where Lerner parts company with Bolaño, whose novels are charged with precisely this desire to trace the complicated and often sinister strands connecting literature, history, and politics.

A blurb on the back of Lerner's book touts him as a "homegrown version" of Bolaño, but I would describe him as a prototypical example of the contemporary American writer who is attuned to all the reasons he *cannot* be Bolaño. Lerner's novel assumes a sort of humility—not unmixed with resentment—toward the Spanish and Latin American writer who reads everything and can still view literature as a matter of importance and even of life and death. The power of *Leaving the Atocha Station* arises from the way Adam's linguistic and cultural failures compel the narrator—and the novel itself—to revisit the idea of experiential immersion that dominates the US literature of experience from Hemingway, Porter, and Hughes through Kerouac and Burroughs. The instant-message interlude about the reality-seeking US writer who goes to Latin America for "experience" is the most poignant reminder of the literary expectations Adam cannot meet. At times he believes he can pull together the experiential demands of the US literary field and the bookish demands of the Hispanic literary tradition: "reading, instead of removing me from the world, intensified my experience of the present" (89). Yet the novel ultimately rests on failures rather than successes, failures that may in part be strategies of representation, but which also speak to anxieties that go beyond the written page. If Adam makes clear that a Hemingwayesque sense of adventure no longer suffices for a description of the Hispanic world, he also leaves us wondering whether he himself is up to the task.

The United States of Spanish America

The first issue of the New York–based Spanish-language literary magazine *Los Bárbaros*, published in March 2014, opens with the following declaration:

We have been waiting for too long.

New York was taken over by Borges's labyrinths decades ago. Today it is populated by detectives who traverse the city's streets and replicate with the following code inscribed on their foreheads: 2666.

The circle has closed.

Language departments in the United States used to house a small group of savages called Spanish. They grew, and, surviving multiple literary currents, demonstrated what many of us now know. The Hispanic world has conquered the heart of the city. The barbarians are in control.[32]

The insurgent tone of this declaration, composed by Peruvian writer and *Los Bárbaros* editor Ulises Gonzáles, draws much of its force from its linguistic register, the millenarian urgency typical of a Latin American literary avant-garde tradition that runs from Vicente Huidobro's *creacionista* manifestos of the 1910s to the 1973 infrarrealist manifesto of Bolaño and Mario Santiago. Yet two new elements can be discerned in the declaration of *Los Bárbaros*. First, it claims as its protagonist a figure that has hitherto been marginalized in the Latin American literary field: the Spanish-speaking writer who lives in the United States, teaches in the US academy, and writes about US American life. Although he acknowledges the historical presence of Spanish-language writers in the United States, Gonzáles insists that we are currently witnessing a paradigm shift: only now has *el mundo hispano* begun to take control of New York literary life. Second, the declaration attributes this paradigm shift to a specific literary constellation that begins with Borges and ends with Bolaño—the labyrinths of *Labyrinths* spawn a virtual New York in which Bolañian detectives proliferate. As if to provide a visual corroboration of this somewhat unlikely periodization of Spanish-language writing in the United States, the issue's cover, illustrated by Manuel Gómez Burns, depicts a New York subway car in which two Borgeses sit side-by-side: the first, looking very much the old master of his later years; the second, a much younger version of the Argentine writer, reading an English-language copy of Bolaño's *The Savage Detectives*. You might recognize this image from the cover of *Anxieties of Experience*.

The dense verbal and visual iconography of the inaugural issue of *Los Bárbaros* speaks to the complex discursive mechanisms that have shaped twenty-first-century Spanish-language writing in the United States. At first glance, the selection of Bolaño and Borges as tutelary figures for twenty-first-century Spanish-language writers in New

York City seems puzzling. The issue might very well have featured other major Latin American authors—Martí, for instance—whose residence in New York and literary treatment of the city offer more concrete examples of the kind of transnational writing the magazine aims to offer. But it quickly becomes clear that Bolaño and Borges function less as guides for capturing the particularities of New York—or even for "making it" in the gringo market—than as models for a specific literary practice. The manifesto culminates in a collective portrait of US-based Spanish-language authors as eager "parasites" nourished by the long tradition of the Latin American literature of the reader: "attached to New York, sucking the blood of literature written in English, transforming it into the vital liquid that feeds visceral realists, the swords and libraries of Babylon, and the leaf storm" (5). English-language literature becomes the lifeblood of the Bolañian visceralist as much as of the Borgesian bibliophile, and even the boom-inspired García Márquez fan can get his or her fill. The only difference is that these Latin American writers are here rather than there: in New York rather than in Mexico City, Buenos Aires, or Aracataca.

The rhetorical thrust of the early issues of *Los Bárbaros*, in short, is to imagine what happens when the voracious Latin American reader undergoes the (stereo)typical "American experience." The opening text of the third issue makes this aim explicit, when Gonzáles refers to the "range of voices" that comprise the new "barbarians":

> Theirs is the language of provincial men who, after a flea-ridden life of reading Reyes, Paz, and Borges, came here to better understand Salinger, Whitman, Faulkner, and also Foster Wallace. The barbarians cannot watch a sunset over the Hudson or a boat crossing Upper Bay at sunrise without an image appearing in some part of their memory that requires the words of Martí, Onetti, and Arguedas; the verses of Pizarnik, Vallejo, and Lorca; the wisdom of Parra.[33]

What Gonzáles articulates is not an entirely new literary subjectivity—Latin American writers have, after all, been living and publishing in US territory since the early nineteenth century—but rather a new cultural syntax for the US-based Spanish-speaking writer. Relying upon material changes in the US public sphere—the Bolañian "boom" in translated Latin American literature, the increased importance of Spanish-language literature in the United States—Gonzáles renders this transformation into a poetic language of insurgency. *Somos los bárbaros, señores: hemos llegado*—"We are the barbarians, gentle-men: we have arrived" (5).

The vast majority of the Spanish-language writers included in the early issues of *Los Bárbaros* are, as Gonzáles suggests, associated in some way with institutions of higher education in the United States. In fact, many of the most powerful twenty-first-century Latin American literary works written in the United States have been produced—and often set—within the ubiquitous departments of Spanish (or Romance languages, as the case may be) that have traditionally integrated humanistic inquiry and language study in the American university. There is, of course, a long history of Latin American writers and intellectuals who have been affiliated with US universities. In the early twentieth century, Pedro Henríquez Ureña taught at Harvard and José Vasconcelos at the University of Chicago, and, following Borges's highly publicized stints as a visiting professor at the University of Texas-Austin and Harvard during the 1960s and 1970s, Latin American writers such as José Donoso, Ricardo Piglia, Diamela Eltit, Tomás Eloy Martínez, Cristina Rivera Garza, and Edmundo Paz Soldán have held long-term positions in American universities. Yet aside from a few notable exceptions, such as Borges's *fantastic* story about meeting his double on the Charles River while teaching at Harvard, "The Other" (1972), and Donoso's *Donde van a morir los elefantes* [Where the Elephants Go to Die, 1995], Latin American writers composing in Spanish have often elided or downplayed their position as US academics when addressing themselves to national or regional literary audiences. In the post-Bolaño era, however, Latin American writers are increasingly situating their fictions within the United States and acknowledging the role of the US academy in initiating a northern migration. As I mentioned in the last chapter, several scenes in Rivera Garza's *La muerte me da* [Death Comes to Me, 2007] are set in the US academy, and Piglia's campus novel *El camino de Ida* [Ida's Way, 2013], unlike his previous works, takes place almost entirely in the United States. However, as Gonzáles implies in his introduction, it has been Bolaño's posthumous canonization both North and South that has most clearly motivated the Latin American turn toward representations of the United States. Ironically, though Bolaño never visited the United States, his depiction of the country in *2666* and *The Savage Detectives* has galvanized Latin American writers to filter their works through the United States to a far greater degree than had been possible in the twentieth century.

Los ingrávidos [*Faces in the Crowd*, 2011], the first novel by the Mexican writer and former Columbia University graduate student Valeria Luiselli, functions both as an example of and a reflection on the migration of the Latin American reader-experiencer to the United States. The novel centers on a young Mexican writer-academic in the midst of composing a novel about her early days in New York as a translator and researcher for a small Manhattan-based publishing house. In so doing, the novel enacts a series of transpositions of the Bolañian model. While the main characters in *The Savage Detectives* try to reconstruct the poet Cesárea Tinajero's relationship to the Mexican *estridentista* movement of the 1920s, the narrator of *Faces in the Crowd* reenvisions the forgotten American years of Gilberto Owen, a member of the *Contemporáneos* group that formed the nucleus of Mexico's historical avant-garde. Whereas Belano and Ulises Lima scour the municipal libraries of northern Mexico to find evidence of Cesárea's literature and her life, Luiselli's narrator spends her time combing through Owen's correspondence with fellow *Contemporáneos* poets Xavier Villaurutia and Salvador Novo in the Casa Hispánica at Columbia University, speculating on the poet's two-year stint in Harlem during the 1920s and his final days in Philadelphia after World War II. As the narrator contemplates her marital life with two young children, her mind roams back to a time when her days alternated between translation, reading, and an exploratory sex life that differs dramatically from her current domestic situation. Eventually, the *relato ajeno* of Owen's life culled from his letters begins to encroach on the narrator's story, and much of the novel's second half is told from the perspective of Owen, who recounts a (mostly invented) saga of his bohemian adventures in New York—from his liaisons with prostitutes to his turbulent before-they-were-stars encounters with Federico García Lorca, Louis Zukofsky, and Nella Larsen.

If this readerly recuperation of an overlooked literary predecessor sets the tone for many of the scenes in *Faces in the Crowd*, perhaps the most interesting aspect of the novel is its interrogation of the Bolañian *habitus* that the narrator herself often seems to occupy. Even as the narrator weaves her own fictionalized account of Owen's passage through New York during the roaring 1920s and the heyday of the Harlem Renaissance, the novel questions both the institutionalization (through the academy) and the commodification (through the literary market) of the Bolaño model. The catalyst for this critique is the narrator's erstwhile employer, an American literary editor named White who runs a small New York publishing house dedicated, as the narrator sardonically puts it, to recovering "foreign pearls" still hidden from the US reading public. Early on, the editor predicts that "after the success of Bolaño in the gringo market...there would be another Latin American boom"; later, he asks the narrator if she has an interview with or a letter from Bolaño—"anything we can publish."[34] The narrator's relationship with White begins to unravel once she realizes that the only way to convince him of the relevance of a Mexican writer like Owen is to insinuate falsely that Owen was a friend and collaborator of Zukofsky, the founder of the American objectivist poetry movement: "This is how literary success works, at least to a certain degree."[35] The narrator's suspicion of the editor's agenda is confirmed when White eagerly accepts a book of Owen's poems supposedly translated by Zukofsky but really rendered into English by the narrator herself. By the time she admits to the fraud, the buzz surrounding Owen has reached a fevered pitch: "The Department of Hispanic Letters at the University of Texas-Austin created an 'Owen Archive'; the articles that Owen had written for *El tiempo* in Bogotá in the thirties and forties appeared, edited by a professor who published them in Mexico City in a volume by [the publishing house] Porrúa, after which they were translated immediately for Harvard University Press."[36] This satire of the publishing and academic worlds concludes with a premonition about how the US culture industry will anoint its next Latin American literary star: "Owen would become, without a doubt, the new Bolaño."[37] In Luiselli's novel, as in Sarah Pollack's critical account, Bolaño's works operate as a (distorted) "prism through which other works of Latin American narrative are read, selected, appreciated, and brought to readers in the United States."[38]

Pollack's focus in "After Bolaño" on the US literary market's "new commodified forms of reading Latin America" (661) helps us to understand the politics behind the translation of Latin American fiction into the United States that Luiselli also exposes. But it would be a mistake to believe that the problems surrounding Bolaño's canonization are entirely due to his US reception. Indeed, the unresolved tension in *Los ingrávidos* between the Bolañian literary model the narrator *employs* and the Bolaño publishing boom the narrator *condemns* indicates the extent to which Bolaño's legacy has become a contested issue within contemporary Latin American literature itself. What remains to be seen is whether the figure of the reader-experiencer will

continue to have the same critical power in Latin American literature that it has generated over the last twenty years. If Bolaño's protagonists inhabit the voracious reader's outsider status in relatively
unproblematic ways, Luiselli's narrator often vacillates at the very
moment when we would expect a historical, social, or cultural critique to be launched. "I spent the night...flipping through a boring
anthology of Mexican poets, all friends of Octavio Paz, that had been
translated into English," the narrator remarks at one point, only to
conclude, "maybe there's an *ergo* somewhere here, but I'm not sure
where to put it."[39] Belano, of course, would have known exactly what
should follow: a lengthy harangue against the insiderism of the
Mexican cultural world. Yet one can sense Luiselli's realization that
the very novel she is writing, like those of so many writers of her
generation, might come to be seen as a kind of anthology of or coda
to the work of Bolaño. "Did you hear that?" White remarks to an assistant editor at one point, "We have the honor of working with the
only Latin American who wasn't friends with Bolaño."[40] At times
consciously and at times unconsciously, Luiselli's novel contemplates
the exhaustion of the Bolaño paradigm.

This struggle to think US-Latin American relations "beyond"
Bolaño (to adapt the influential formulation of Héctor Hoyos) has
become a major feature of contemporary Spanish-language literature
produced in the United States.[41] I have already suggested that for
Gonzáles, Bolaño represents a model for US-based Latin American
writers to emulate—and, for Luiselli, a marketing ploy to avoid.
But some of the most compelling appropriations of the Bolaño paradigm in contemporary Latin American literature have come from
writers whose work is less preoccupied with what Bolaño signifies
as an emblem of contemporary Latin American literature than
with what it means to write Latin American literature after Bolaño.
Paralleling recent critical interventions by Francisco Carrillo
Martín and Oswaldo Zavala, which have situated Bolaño's oeuvre
at the end of a Latin American literary-historical period spanning
the rise and fall of the revolutionary left and the eclipse of Latin
American modernity, these writers have been as sensitive to the
historical conditions of Bolaño's work as to its aesthetic qualities.[42]
In the wake of the global financial crisis of 2008, a number of
Spanish-language writers in the United States have interrogated
the role of the voracious reader in the context of a new hemispheric
cultural, political, and economic order.

Mara Pastor's poetry volume *Candada por error* [Mistakenly Locked Up, 2009], published while the Puerto Rican author was a graduate student in Spanish at the University of Michigan, weighs the risks and rewards of reading Bolaño—indeed, of reading in general—within the US academy after the 2008 crisis. The volume's first poem, "El otro día nos volvimos a ignorar," reveals a speaker plagued by the thought that her literary ambitions have guided her straight into the confines of the ivory tower—or, more likely in this case, into a graduate apartment building—from which there is no escape:

Literature	La literatura
has spoiled the life I imagined	me ha podrido la vida que
as a girl	soñé de niña
and has made it into a window-	y le ha hecho una casa
less house,	sin ventanas,
literature has taken me hos-	la literatura me tiene de
tage, looking	rehén mirando
toward the house, complaining.[43]	hacia la casa, lamentándome.

If the first part of the collection details the daily travails of the speaker, who feels herself, as the title indicates, "mistakenly locked up," the second part introduces a new subject, Manuel, who seems to find his sense of self in the extreme literary practices that the speaker despises. Manuel, of course, is a voracious reader of Bolaño:

I've known Manuel	Conozco a Manuel
since he began to read Bolaño	desde que lee a Bolaño
every time I see Manuel	siempre que he visto a Manuel
we've talked about Bolaño	hemos hablado de Bolaño
Manuel reads Bolaño all day	Manuel lee a Bolaño todo el día
and all night because	y toda la noche porque
Manuel never sleeps.[44]	Manuel no duerme.

Though we never find out exactly *why* Manuel reads only Bolaño, we might surmise that he is seeking sort some of literary initiation like those of Arturo Belano and Ulises Lima—"all day and all night" presumably referring to the fact that he not only reads a lot but defines himself, fundamentally, as a reader. Yet the reference to the windowless house of literature in the earlier poem leads us to wonder whether Manuel's academic reading of Bolaño will lead to the practice of the academics in works such as *2666*, who use their literary training as a spur to experience.

In a review of *Candada por error*, Pastor's fellow Puerto Rican novelist and critic Luis Othoniel Rosa has pointed to her use of the figure of Bolaño as a way of suggesting that her poetry increasingly revolves around the question of the function and value of literature itself—"literature, that is, not as an intellectual tradition, but as an activity, a way of life that conditions one's economic, domestic, emotional, and geographic situation."[45] And indeed, Pastor's later volume *Poemas para fomentar el turismo* [Poems to Promote Tourism, 2011] continues to inquire into the relationship between what one reads and how one lives, though here the geopolitical scope of the inquiry has expanded considerably. Dedicated to the "300,000 Puerto Ricans who emigrated between 2005 and 2009," the volume paints a series of portraits both intimate and monumental of an entire generation of Puerto Ricans—many of them writers and artists—who left the island because of an economic crisis that began in 2006. One of the major personal and political ironies the volume addresses is the fact that a large number of these émigrés—Pastor included—came to the United States to escape the Puerto Rican crisis, only to encounter the US financial crisis shortly after arriving. "I have touched down so many times," the speaker observes at one point, "but I never thought I'd traffic/ in global crises."[46]

The collection's most ambitious and celebrated poem, "Los estudiantes" [The Students], is an extended meditation on the precarity of Pastor's generation of intellectuals—both those who went to the United States on scholarships and fellowships and those who remained in Puerto Rico in the embattled university system. If "Conozco a Manuel" drew upon Bolaño as the symbol of a reading practice that remained largely intramural, here the Bolañian trope of using one's reading to spur one's actions acquires new force. The poem begins with an epigraph by Bolaño's self-proclaimed poetic master, Nicanor Parra—"The professors made us crazy"—and, at one point, the speaker returns to the image of a literary education behind closed walls: "They sat us down in a lie about things / Which was an uncomfortable place to be" [Nos sentaron en la mentira de las cosas / que resultó un asiento muy incómo, 69]. Yet almost immediately the speaker finds answers, literally—

> from which we arose with answers
> read behind the backs of creative writing teachers
> and with poems by Parra in the Biblioteca Lázaro
> where the striking students made a garden.[47]

Composed in the crucible of the Occupy moment in the United States and shortly after the largest student occupation in the history of the Universidad de Puerto Rico, the poem culminates in a call to put these answers to work:

> Meanwhile, occupy.
> Meanwhile, occupy.
> The young took off their wings
> with an unexpected grace.[48]

What we find in "Los estudiantes," in other words, is less an invocation of Bolaño as spiritual guide than a dramatization of how a kind of Bolañian education works, moving from reading to action, poetry to praxis.

In her introduction to the 2012 Mexican edition of *Poemas para fomentar el turismo*, Nicole Cecilia Delgado convincingly refers to the "politicization of [Pastor's] discourse" evident in the poems, as well as a "growing critical acumen that allows her to observe and share the social reality that surrounds her."[49] What I have tried to emphasize here is that this politicization occurs by means of an encounter—at times oblique, at times direct—with the figure of the Bolañian voracious reader, and that Pastor's growing critical acumen derives not only from a changing social reality but from an interrogation of the literary repertoire one must draw upon to capture it. Othoniel Rosa has spoken even more explicitly about the ethical dimensions of Bolaño's literary economy, despite the evident commercialization of his work in both the English- and Spanish-speaking worlds. Characterizing Bolaño's creed as a variation on the "politics of metaliterature"—"it's not that I give birth to my literature, my literature gives birth to me"—Othoniel Rosa describes his own literary practice as "be[ing] an 'I' figuring out a way to live."[50] In interviews about his first novel, *Otra vez me alejo* [Departing Again, 2012], Othoniel Rosa has connected Bolaño's "politics of metaliterature" to the Occupy movement itself. Referring to the academic origins of many of Occupy Wall Street's organizers, he writes that "it is an interesting movement or displacement, because before now the US academy was the campus, a total ivory tower—literally a campus, with walls and everything. And suddenly, the academic who was protected in this bubble is once again on the street—we need to understand or relearn our place in society."[51] As Othoniel Rosa puts it in his review of *Candada por error*, Bolaño's lesson here is less aesthetic than practical. It's about finding the right use for one's literary education in a specific historical situation.

This current generation of Spanish-language writers in the United States includes many of my colleagues in the US academy, and also many of my friends. I began this book by invoking my formation as an English-speaking American who returned to US literature through Latin America. As I come to the book's end, I recognize that one of my primary motivations for undertaking it was to understand better how my Latin American friends and contemporaries wrestled with US literary traditions and the cultures that engendered them. To no small degree, this study took the shape it did because of my relationship with these writers and their work—which is to say, because of my experience and my reading.

{ NOTES }

Introduction

Unless otherwise noted, all translations from the Spanish are my own.

1. Sarah Pollack, "Latin America Translated (Again): Roberto Bolaño's *The Savage Detectives* in the United States," *Comparative Literature* 61 (Summer 2009), 353.

2. Ricardo Piglia, *El último lector* (Barcelona: Anagrama, 2005), 21: "[P]ara ellos, la lectura no es sólo una práctica, sino una forma de vida."

3. Roberto Bolaño, *Entre paréntesis* (Barcelona: Anagrama, 2004), 20, 318: "Soy mucho más feliz leyendo que escribiendo"; "[P]asé de ser un lector prudente a ser un lector voraz... Quería leerlo todo."

4. Javier Cercas, *Soldados de Salamina* (Barcelona: Tusquets Editores, 2001), 146: "Yo leo hasta los papeles que encuentro por las calles."

5. Jorge Luis Borges, *Obras completas* 4 vols. (Buenos Aires: Emecé, 1989), 1.305: "[L]os buenos lectores son cisenes aun más tenebrosos y singulares que los buenos autores."

6. Ángel Rama, *La ciudad letrada* (Montevideo: Arca, 1998), 63.

7. The most influential post-1960s critique of the discourses of the lettered city is John Beverley's *Against Literature* (Minneapolis: University of Minnesota Press, 1993); George Yúdice and Ileana Rodríguez have similarly argued that a range of postboom Latin American cultural practices, from the *testimonio* to the literature of marginalized women, sought to undermine the representational strategies of the traditional Latin American *letrado*. At the same time, a number of scholars have criticized Rama's cultural and historical framework. Gonzalo Aguilar has argued that Rama's concept of the lettered city fails to account for diachronic shifts in the Latin American metropolis ("Ángel Rama y la ciudad letrada o la fatal exterioridad de los intelectuales," in *Estrategias del pensar: Ensayo y prosa de ideas en América Latina siglo XX* [Mexico City: UNAM, 2010], 225–257), and Lois Parkinson Zamora has taken issue with Rama's sharp distinctions between high literature and popular forms of visual culture (*The Inordinate Eye: New World Baroque and Latin American Fiction* [Chicago: University of Chicago Press, 2006]). Though these studies argue for a more careful periodization of the various historical stages of the "lettered city," to my mind they do not negate Rama's fundamental insight about the importance of the writer-intellectual to the development of the Latin American public sphere.

8. Bolaño, *Entre paréntesis*, 148: "La literatura, de la que vivió durante los últimos treinta años, le interesaba, pero no demasiado, y en eso fue semejante a otros clásicos norteamericanos que concentraron sus esfuerzos en la observación de la vida o en la experiencia."

9. Juan Villoro, "El 'Quijote', una lectura fronteriza," in *De eso se trata: Ensayos literarios* (Barcelona: Anagrama, 2008), 53: "Una invitación al viaje... salir al mundo en busca de experiencia."

10. Roberto Bolaño, *Bolaño por sí mismo* (Santiago, Chile: Universidad Diego Portales, 2006), 57: "El viaje, en el imaginario de mi generación, era el viaje de los beatniks."

11. Roberto Bolaño, "Jim," in *El gaucho insufrible* (Barcelona: Anagrama, 2003), 11.

12. Ernest Hemingway, "Monologue to the Maestro: A High Seas Dialogue," in *By-line: Ernest Hemingway; Selected Articles and Dispatches of Four Decades*, ed. William White (New York: Scribner, 1967), 215.

13. For reevaluations of the cultural importance of experience in the United States after the neopragmatist turn in philosophy, see Martin Jay's *Songs of Experience: European and American Variations on a Universal Theme* (Berkeley: University of California Press, 2005) and Joan Richardson's *A Natural History of Pragmatism: The Fact of Feeling from Jonathan Edwards to Gertrude Stein* (New York: Cambridge University Press, 2007). Recent scholarly works that address the discourse of experience in relation to US literary production include Mark McGurl's *The Program Era: Postwar Fiction and the Rise of Creative Writing* (Cambridge, Mass.: Harvard University Press, 2009), Walton Muyumba's *The Shadow and the Act: Black Intellectual Practice, Jazz Improvisation, and Philosophical Pragmatism* (Chicago: University of Chicago Press, 2009), Paul Grimstad's *Experience and Experimental Writing: Literary Pragmatism from Emerson to the Jameses* (New York: Oxford University Press, 2013), and Lisi Schoenbach's *Pragmatic Modernism* (New York: Oxford University Press, 2012). The best overview of contemporary scholarship on the relationship between pragmatism and US literature is Nicholas Gaskill's review essay, "What Difference Can Pragmatism Make for Literary Study?" *American Literary History* 24 (Summer 2012), 374–389.

14. Raymond Williams, *Marxism and Literature* (New York: Oxford, 2009), 119.

15. I adopt this term, "misencounters," from Julio Ramos's work in *Desencuentros de la modernidad en América Latina: Literatura y política en el siglo XIX* (Santiago, Chile: Cuarto Propio, 2003) on the *desencuentros* created by unequal modernities within Latin America. I argue that the literary and cultural "misencounters" produced by the heterogeneity of global modernity that Ramos has located *within* Latin America also can be seen in the divergence *across* the Americas.

16. Jay, *Songs of Experience*, 1.

17. The linguist Anna Wierzbicka has argued that we should distinguish the English word *experience* from its cognates in other European languages, since it does not have an exact semantic equivalent in any other language. Demonstrating that the English *experience* and the French *experiénce* have different meanings along both synchronic and diachronic lines, she writes that "the semantic history of experience is linked with important developments in Anglo culture and Anglo ways of thinking" (*Experience, Evidence and Sense: The Hidden Cultural Legacy of English* [New York: Oxford University Press, 2010], 31).

18. John Dewey, "The Development of American Pragmatism," in *John Dewey: The Later Works, 1925–1953*, vol. 2: *1925–1927* (Carbondale: Southern Illinois University Press, 1984), 12.

19. John Dewey, *Art as Experience* (New York: Penguin, 2005), 265.

20. It should be noted that the American pragmatist movement of the late nineteenth century and early twentieth century comprised several different strains. Although virtually all of the so-called classical pragmatists believed themselves to be participating in a critique of Cartesian mind-body dualism and of the British empiricist tradition's correspondence theory of truth, the opposition of "lived experience" to abstract philosophizing and linguistic mediation was stronger in Dewey and James than in figures such as Charles Sanders Peirce and George Herbert Mead. My book focuses primarily on Dewey and James for two reasons: first, because they clearly posited experience as the ultimate horizon of

pragmatist epistemology and aesthetics; and second, because they had a far greater influence—both direct and indirect—on the development of US literature than any other figures associated with the movement. My decision to approach pragmatism primarily as a cultural movement rooted in the development of nineteenth- and twentieth-century US society rather than as a philosophical mode or school in the strictest sense owes much to Cornel West's *The Evasion of Philosophy: A Genealogy of Pragmatism* (Madison: University of Wisconsin Press, 1989), which argues that pragmatism emerged as a "specific historical and cultural product" in the United States through a "particular set of social practices" (4).

21. Waldo Frank, *Our America* (New York: Boni and Liveright, 1919), 28.

22. Katherine Anne Porter, "My First Speech," in *Collected Stories and Other Writings*, ed. Darlene Unrue (New York: Library of America, 2008), 691. Hereafter I refer to this volume as *CS*.

23. W. E. B. Du Bois, "An Essay toward a History of the Black Man in the Great War," *Crisis* 18 (June 1919), 72.

24. Philip Rahv, "The Cult of Experience in American Writing," in *Image and Idea: Fourteen Essays on Literary Themes* (New York: New Directions, 1949), 8.

25. For accounts of the antiessentialist strain in American pragmatist aesthetics regarding identity and race, see Ross Posnock's *Color and Culture: Black Writers and the Making of the Modern Intellectual* (Cambridge, Mass.: Harvard University Press, 1998) and Bill Lawson and Donald Koch's edited volume *Pragmatism and the Problem of Race* (Bloomington: Indiana University Press, 2004).

26. Porter, *Collected Stories and Other Writings*, 148.

27. Letter from Waldo Frank to Samuel Glusberg, Aug. 9, 1926, Buenos Aires: CeDinCi: Fondo Samuel Glusberg, number 1114/series 5.

28. Letter from Samuel Glusberg to Waldo Frank, Dec. 14, 1927, Buenos Aires: CeDinCi, Fondo Samuel Glusberg, number 1212/series 5: "Qué dichoso usted que puede viajar. Yo todavía estoy aquí sin poder moverme y lo peor es que no sé hasta cuando.... No basta ser judío para ser errante."

29. Nicolás Guillén, "Conversación con Langston Hughes," in *Nicolás Guillén: Prosa de prisa, 1929–1972* (Havana: Editorial Arte y Literatura, 1975), 17: "Después de haber estudiado un año en Columbia, me lancé a recorrer el mundo, libre de todas las trabas, al margen de todos los convencionalismos.... He visitado Dakar, Nigeria, Luanda.... Por aquellas tierras se me fortaleció el alma en el sentimiento de amor a los negros, que ya no habrá de abandonarme. En contacto con esa dulce gente... yo comprendí que era necesario ser su amigo, su voz, su báculo: ser su poeta."

30. The full Spanish version of these lines runs: "De seguro a ti / no te preocupa Waldo Frank / ni Langston Hughes / (el de 'I, too sing America')."

31. Ricardo Piglia, *Crítica y ficción* (Barcelona: Anagrama, 2001), 89: "Era un hombre culto y refinado seducido por el mito, tan norteamericano, de la experiencia vivida, se embarcó para conocer el mundo y anduvo navegando cerca de un año y tuvo una trágica historia con una mujer en Buenos Aires y ya no se fue de la Argentina."

32. Leonardo Padura, *Adiós, Hemingway* (Barcelona: Tusquets Editores, 2006), 38, 39: "[Hemingway] sabía que su imaginación siempre había sido escasa y mentirosa, y sólo contar las cosas vistas y aprendidas en la vida le había permitido escribir aquellos libros capaces de rezumar la veracidad que él le exigía a su literatura... Él sí lo sabía: debía hacerse de una vida para hacerse de una literatura."

33. This is a hypothesis that finds support in recent work in cultural linguistics. The revival of cultural theories of language, displaced in the latter half of the twentieth century by Chomskyan Universal Grammar, has been one of the most powerful scholarly currents in linguistics and semiotics over the past forty years. This culturalist orientation grounds a number of seminal works from George Lakoff's and Mark Johnson's *Metaphors We Live By* (Chicago: University of Chicago Press, 1980) and Anna Wierzbicka's *Semantics, Culture, and Cognition: Human Concepts in Culture-Specific Configurations* (New York: Oxford University Press, 1992) to John Gumperz's and Stephen Levinson's *Rethinking Linguistic Relativity* (New York: Cambridge University Press, 1996). Taking on Noam Chomsky's assertion that "the conceptual resources of a lexicon are largely fixed by the language faculty," Wierzbicka points to a vast amount of research that suggests that "cross-linguistic and cross-cultural variation are not minor but colossal" and that this "lexical variation" helps to institute distinct social realities in different places (Wierzbicka, *Semantics, Culture, and Cognition*, 5, 19).

34. See Franco Moretti's "Conjectures on World Literature," *New Left Review* 1 (Jan.–Feb. 2000), 54–68. Moretti cites Itamar Even-Zohar on Hebrew poetry: "There is no symmetry in literary interference. A target literature is, more often than not, interfered with by a source literature which completely ignores it" (56).

35. Irene Rostagno, *Searching for Recognition: The Promotion of Latin American Literature in the United States* (Westport, Conn.: Greenwood Press, 1997); Helen Delpar, *The Enormous Vogue of Things Mexican: Cultural Relations between the United States and Mexico, 1920–1935* (Tuscaloosa: University of Alabama Press, 1992).

36. Gustavo Pérez Firmat, "Introduction: Cheek to Cheek," in *Do the Americas Have a Common Literature?*, ed. Gustavo Pérez Firmat (Durham, N.C.: Duke University Press, 1990), 5. This approach derives from the "shared histories" theory of the Americas first elaborated by the historian Eugene Bolton in the early twentieth century. As Antonio Barrenechea explains in "Good Neighbor/Bad Neighbor: Boltian Americanism and Hemispheric Studies" (*Comparative Literature* 61 [Summer 2009], 231–243), Bolton's research on the Iberian presence in what is now the US Southwest led him to formulate a hemispheric rather than national approach to American history. Bolton's hemispheric approach "treated contested lands without imposing isolationist paradigms and recognized historical parallels that appear all the more radical for having been neglected for so long" (233).

37. Lois Parkinson Zamora and Sylvia Spitta, "Introduction: The Americas, Otherwise," *Comparative Literature* 61 (Summer 2009), 192.

38. Stephanie Kirk, "Mapping the Hemispheric Divide: The Colonial Americas in a Collaborative Context," *PMLA* 128 (October 2013), 977. Kirk points out that hemispheric analyses often draw their inspiration from other transnational fields such as Atlantic studies with far richer traditions of historical encounters. According to Kirk, this frequently leads hemispheric scholars to posit a model of cross-cultural contact that is not always present in their objects of study. Kirk's argument builds on Ralph Bauer's observation that transnational American literary anthologies frequently assume a basic continuity between literary historical periods in the United States and those of the rest of the Americas, "at times run[ning] the risk of subsuming the hemisphere within the literary history of the US, rather than the US within the literary history of the hemisphere" ("Early American Literature and American Literary History at the 'Hemispheric Turn,'" *American Literary History* 22 [Summer 2010], 255). For an early critique of the reliance on Bolton's thesis for hemispheric literary scholarship, see Kirsten Silva Gruesz's *Ambassadors of Culture: The Transamerican Origins*

of Latino Writing (Princeton, N.J.: Princeton University Press, 2002), which advocates a shift from the analysis of "shared historical 'themes' " to a comparative literary study of the "complex imbrications of power and influence in the Americas" (9).

39. Pierre Bourdieu, *The Field of Cultural Production: Essays on Art and Literature*, ed. Randal Johnson, trans. Claud DuVerlie (New York: Columbia University Press, 1993), 181, 164.

40. My own method borrows more from Bourdieu's thesis about the specificity of literary fields than his argument about *how* they reproduce other systems, since I believe that his somewhat rigid description of the reproduction of capital often obscures the complexity of the relationship between literature and language, culture, and geopolitics.

41. Moretti, "Conjectures on World Literature," 56. It is worth making clear that this study does not aspire to a total picture of the global literary system in the twentieth century or even of the hemispheric half of that system. I rely far more upon the specific insights of Moretti's attention to the relationship between geography and literary history than the quantitative research associated with his notorious "distant reading" model. The questions posed throughout these pages will return almost obsessively to the same concern: why certain works were written in a certain time and a certain *place*. Here, Moretti's description of literary evolution as both a temporal and geographical process is simply invaluable. This model of literary history permits us to ask why some forms flourished in the United States and not in Latin America (and vice versa), and why various permutations of these forms rose to dominance in each of these respective literary fields. Contrast is therefore given as much space as similarity in this study, since I often seek to explain why one feature appears in a particular work and not in another.

42. See Ignacio Sánchez Prado, "Hijos de Metapa: Un recorrido conceptual de la literatura mundial," in *América Latina en la "literatura mundial"* (Pittsburgh: Instituto Internacional de Literatura Latinoamericana, 2006), 7–46. Sánchez Prado synthesizes this argument in a comment on the absence of Borges from Moretti's and Casanova's models: "The example of Borges is helpful here because it allows us to identify something that remains unclear in the debate about world literature: the difference between Europe's perception of Latin American literature and the place that this literature actually occupies in the world" [El ejemplo de Borges es muy instructivo aquí porque permite discernir algo que no queda claro en el debate de la literatura mundial: la diferencia entre la percepción que Europa tiene de la literatura latinoamericana y el lugar que esta literatura ocupa, de hecho, en el mundo] (33). In a similar vein, Héctor Hoyos has advocated a "Latin American-inflected" approach to world literature to counteract the "American-inflected take on world literature" dominant in the US academy (*Beyond Bolaño: The Global Latin American Novel* [New York: Columbia University Press, 2015], 9).

43. See Josefina Ludmer, *Aquí América latina: Una especulación* (Buenos Aires: Eterna Cadencia, 2010).

44. Although I gesture toward the longer *dureé* of this hemispheric dynamic at various moments, I largely leave aside the broader implications of the relationships between, for example, the US literature of experience and British empiricism and the Latin American literature of reading and the Spanish colonial discourse of the *letrado*.

45. On McKay's relationship to the black international tradition, see Brent Hayes Edward's *The Practice of Diaspora: Literature, Translation, and the Rise of Black Internationalism* (Cambridge, Mass.: Harvard University Press, 2003) and Michelle Stephens's *Black Empire: The Masculine Global Imaginary of Caribbean Intellectuals in the United States, 1914–1962*

(Durham, N.C.: Duke University Press, 2005). On McKay's relationship to Soviet internationalism, see Kate A. Baldwin's *Beyond the Color Line and the Iron Curtain: Reading Encounters between Black and Red, 1922–1963* (Durham, N.C.: Duke University Press, 2002).

46. Claude McKay, *Home to Harlem* (Boston: Northeastern University Press, 1987), 153–154.

47. Wayne Cooper, *Claude McKay: Rebel Sojourner in the Harlem Renaissance* (Baton Rouge: Louisiana State University Press, 1987), 235.

48. Quoted in Cooper, *Claude McKay*, 235.

49. Langston Hughes to Claude McKay, March 5, 1928; W. E. B. Du Bois, "The Browsing Reader: Review of Home to Harlem," *Crisis* 35 (June 1928), 202.

Chapter 1

1. Walter Mignolo, *The Idea of Latin America* (Oxford: Blackwell, 2005), x, xiv.

2. Mignolo builds substantially on Edmundo O'Gorman's notion of the Americas as a historical "invention" of Europe. See O'Gorman's *La invención de América: El universalismo de la cultura de Occidente* (Mexico City: Fondo de Cultura Económica, 1958).

3. The term is from Anna Brickhouse's *Transamerican Literary Relations and the Nineteenth-Century Public Sphere* (New York: Cambridge University Press, 2004). See also Kirsten Silva Gruesz's *Ambassadors of Culture: The Transamerican Origins of Latino Writing* (Princeton, N.J.: Princeton University Press, 2002), Iván Jaksić's *The Hispanic World and American Intellectual Life, 1820–1880* (New York: Palgrave Macmillan, 2007), and Rodrigo Lazo's "'La Famosa Filadelfia': The Hemispheric American City and Constitutional Debates," in *Hemispheric American Studies*, ed. Caroline Levander and Robert Levine (New Brunswick, N.J.: Rutgers University Press, 2008).

4. Martin Jay, *Songs of Experience: European and American Variations on a Universal Theme* (Berkeley: University of California Press, 2005), 19–23.

5. See Jim Egan, *Authorizing Experience: Refigurations of the Body Politic in Seventeenth-Century New England Writing* (Princeton, N.J.: Princeton University Press, 1999).

6. Ralph Waldo Emerson, "The American Scholar," in *Essays and Lectures*, ed. Joel Porte (New York: Library of America, 1983), 70.

7. On the role of intertextual reference in Emerson's writings, see Eduardo Cadava's *Emerson and the Climates of History* (Stanford, Calif.: Stanford University Press, 1997), Wai-Chee Dimock's "Deep Time: American Literature and World History," *American Literary History* 13 (Winter 2001), 755–775, Michael Soto's *The Modernist Nation: Generation, Renaissance, and Twentieth-Century American Literature* (Tuscaloosa: University of Alabama Press, 2004), and Paul Giles's *The Global Remapping of US Literature* (Princeton, N.J.: Princeton University Press, 2011).

8. Walt Whitman, *Poetry and Prose* (New York: Library of America, 1996), 14; Walt Whitman, "Walt Whitman and His Poems," *The United States Review* 5 (September 1855): 205–12, whitmanarchive.org, accessed 7/9/14.

9. Whitman, *Poetry and Prose*, 297, 307.

10. In "Post-Colonial Emerson and the Erasure of Europe," in *The Cambridge Companion to Ralph Waldo Emerson* (Cambridge: Cambridge University Press, 1999), ed. Joel Porte and Saundra Morris, 192–217, Robert Weisbuch notes a performative indifference to British culture in American Renaissance figures like Emerson and Whitman that he interprets as

the mark of a "deliberate cultural strategy" rather than a lack of interest or familiarity with European traditions. Both Weisbuch and Lawrence Buell ("American Literary Emergence as a Post-Colonial Phenomenon," *American Literary History* 4 [Autumn 1992], 411–442) argue that the unequal relationship between US and European writers in the mid-nineteenth century should be understood as a postcolonial literary dynamic.

11. For Americanist studies of the relation between aesthetics and ideology in Whitman, see Henry Nash Smith's chapter "Walt Whitman and Manifest Destiny," in *Virgin Land: The American West as Symbol and Myth* (Cambridge, Mass.: Harvard University Press, 1950), Quentin Anderson's *The Imperial Self: An Essay in American Literary and Cultural History* (New York: Knopf, 1971), and Betsy Erkkila's *Whitman the Political Poet* (New York: Oxford University Press, 1989). For a detailed political analysis of Whitman's stance on the Mexican-American War, see Mauricio González de la Garza's polemical but well-documented *Walt Whitman: Racista, imperialista, antimexicano* (Mexico City: Colección Málaga, 1971).

12. Gretchen Murphy, "The Hemispheric Novel in the Age of Revolution," *The Cambridge History of the American Novel*, eds. Leonard Cassuto, Claire Eby and Benjamin Reiss (Cambridge: Cambridge University Press, 2011), 553–570.

13. See David Reynolds, *Walt Whitman's America: A Cultural Biography* (New York: Alfred A. Knopf, 1995).

14. See Bruce Kuklick's *The Rise of American Philosophy: Cambridge Massachusetts, 1860–1930* (New Haven, Conn.: Yale University Press, 1976), Louis Menand's *The Metaphysical Club: A Story of Ideas in America* (New York: Farrar, Strauss, and Giroux, 2001), Joan Richardson's *A Natural History of Pragmatism: The Fact of Feeling from Jonathan Edwards to Gertrude Stein* (New York: Cambridge University Press, 2007), and Paul Grimstad's *Experience and Experimental Writings: Literary Pragmatism from Emerson to the Jameses* (New York: Oxford University Press, 2013).

15. Henry James, *Daisy Miller: A Study*, in *Major Stories and Essays* (New York: Library of America, 1999), 27.

16. Richard Harding Davis, *Soldiers of Fortune* (New York: Scribner's, 1919), 350.

17. Amy Kaplan, "Black and Blue on San Juan Hill," in *Cultures of United States Imperialism*, ed. Amy Kaplan and Donald Pease (Durham, N.C.: Duke University Press, 1993), 219–236.

18. Willa Cather, "When I Knew Stephen Crane," in *Stories, Poems, and Other Writings*, ed. Sharon O'Brien (New York: Library of America, 1992), 938.

19. On the relationship between the boom of mass-circulation newspapers in the 1880s and 1890s and the development of Crane's "realist literary practice," see Michael Robertson, *Stephen Crane, Journalism, and the Making of American Literature* (New York: Columbia University Press), 150. In *The Politics and Poetics of Journalistic Narrative: The Timely and the Timeless* (New York: Cambridge University Press, 1984), Phyllis Frus draws a broad connection between turn-of-the-twentieth-century US realism and increased American military involvement around the world: "Although there is some evidence to support a causal relationship between the writing of journalism and realistic fiction, most of it shows journalists' experience being broadened and their attitudes toward the world affected by covering...wars and other international events that lure them abroad" (57).

20. William James, "Philosophical Conceptions and Practical Results," in *William James: Writings 1878–1899*, ed. Gerald Myer (New York: Library of America, 1992), 1078.

21. Deborah Whitehead, *William James, Pragmatism, and American Culture* (Bloomington, Ind.: Indiana University Press, 2015), 70.

22. Alexander Livingston, *Damn Great Empires! William James and the Politics of Pragmatism* (New York: Oxford University Press, 2016).

23. John Dewey, "America in the World," in *John Dewey: The Middle Works*, ed. Jo Ann Boydston, vol. 10 (Carbondale: Southern Illinois University Press, 1980), 71.

24. See, for example, Walter Benn Michaels and Donald Pease's edited volume *The American Renaissance Reconsidered* (Baltimore: Johns Hopkins University Press, 1985) and Pease's *Visionary Compacts: American Renaissance Writings in Cultural Context* (Madison: University of Wisconsin Press, 1987). For a detailed study of the Melville Revival and its cultural politics, see Brian Yothers's *Melville's Mirrors: Literary Criticism and America's Most Elusive Author* (Rochester, N.Y.: Camden House, 2011).

25. Carl Van Doren, *The American Novel* (New York: Macmillan, 1921), 72.

26. D. H. Lawrence, *Studies in Classic American Literature*, ed. Ezra Greespan, Lindeth Vasey, and John Worthen (New York: Cambridge University Press, 2003), 157.

27. Ernest Hemingway, *The Sun Also Rises* (New York: Scribner, 2006), 151.

28. Influential discussions of the relationship between the New Negro Renaissance and modernist literary currents of the 1920s can be found in Houston Baker's *Modernism and the Harlem Renaissance* (Chicago: University of Chicago Press, 1987) and Ann Douglas's *Terrible Honesty: Mongrel Manhattan in the 1920s* (New York: Farrar, Straus, and Giroux, 1995). For studies of the historical and conceptual links between New Negro writer-philosophers and classical pragmatism, see Cornel West's *The American Evasion of Philosophy: A Genealogy of Pragmatism* (Madison: University of Wisconsin Press, 1989), George Hutchinson's *The Harlem Renaissance in Black and White* (Cambridge, Mass.: Belknap Press of Harvard University Press, 1995), and Nancy Frasier's "Another Pragmatism: Alain Locke, Critical 'Race' Theory, and the Politics of Culture," in *The Revival of Pragmatism: New Essays on Social Thought, Law, and Culture*, ed. Morris Dickstein (Durham, N.C.: Duke University Press, 1998), 157–175.

29. Jean Toomer, *Cane* (New York: W.W. Norton, 1988), 84.

30. Nella Larsen, *Quicksand and Passing* (Blacksburg, Va.: Wilder Publications, 2010), 7.

31. Langston Hughes, *The Big Sea* (New York: Hill and Wang, 1993), 3.

32. Frederick Douglass, *Narrative of the Life of Frederick Douglass* (New York: Oxford University Press, 1999), 39.

33. James Weldon Johnson, *The Autobiography of an Ex-Coloured Man* (New York: Vintage, 1989), 42.

34. In this vein, see Robert Stepto's "Distrust of the Reader in Afro-American Narratives," in *Reconstructing American Literary History*, ed. Sacvan Bercovitch (Cambridge, Mass.: Harvard University Press, 1985), 300–322.

35. John Dewey, *Art as Experience* (New York: Penguin, 2005), 150.

36. Rachel Adams, *Continental Divides: Remapping the Cultures of North America* (Chicago: University of Chicago Press, 2009), 105. On Porter's relationship to Mexican art and culture, see Darlene Unrue's *Truth and Vision in Katherine Anne Porter's Fiction* (Athens: University of Georgia Press, 1985) and *Katherine Anne Porter: The Life of an Artist* (Jackson: University Press of Mississippi, 2005), Thomas Walsh's *Katherine Anne Porter and Mexico: The Illusion of Eden* (Austin: University of Texas Press, 1992), Robert Brinkmeyer's *Katherine Anne Porter's Artistic Development: Primitivism, Traditionalism, Totalitarianism* (Baton Rouge: Louisiana State University Press, 1993), Ruth Alvarez's " 'Royalty in Exile': Pre-Hispanic Art and Ritual in 'Maria Concepción,'" in *Critical Essays on Katherine Anne*

Porter, ed. Darlene Unrue (New York: G. K. Hall, 1997), and José Limón's *American Encounters: Greater Mexico, the United States, and the Erotics of Culture* (Boston: Beacon Press, 1998).

37. Katherine Anne Porter, *Collected Stories and Other Writings*, ed. Darlene Unrue (New York: Library of America, 2008), 869.

38. Katherine Anne Porter, "Mexican Daybook, Notes, Observations, 1930–31," series 2, box 12, folder 17. Katherine Anne Porter Papers, Special Collections, University of Maryland Libraries.

39. The only references to twentieth-century Spanish-language Mexican writers I have been able to locate in Porter's unpublished writings of the 1920s and 1930s are brief mentions of Amado Nervo, Salvador Novo, and Martín Luis Guzmán. It is true that Porter wrote essays on the nineteenth-century soldier-novelist José Joaquín Fernández de Lizardi and the colonial poet Sor Juana Inés de la Cruz, and published translations of their work in her name. Yet Walsh has shown through epistolary evidence that the translation of Lizardi's *El periquillo sarmiento*, published as *The Itching Parrot* in 1942, was in fact the work of Porter's then husband Eugene Pressly (*Katherine Anne Porter and Mexico*, 196–197). And a note to Porter's boyfriend Francisco Aguilera in 1923 suggests that, at least at that time, her Spanish was not good enough to translate Spanish-language texts without significant assistance.

40. Helen Delpar, *The Enormous Vogue of Things Mexican: Cultural Relations between the United States and Mexico, 1920–1935* (Tuscaloosa: University of Alabama Press, 1992), 182. Delpar further remarks that in the midst of the "Mexican vogue" of the twenties and thirties, only two Mexican novelists were translated into English: Mariano Azuela and Martín Luis Guzmán.

41. Katherine Anne Porter, "Parvenu," in *Collected Stories and Other Writings*, ed. Darlene Unrue (New York: Library of America, 2008), 998–999.

42. Quoted in Irene Rostagno, *Searching for Recognition: The Promotion of Latin American Literature in the United States* (Westport, Conn.: Greenwood Press, 1997), 53.

43. See Jeffrey Lawrence, " 'I Read Even the Scraps of Paper I Find on the Street': A Thesis on the Contemporary Literatures of the Americas," *American Literary History* 26 (Autumn 2014), 545.

44. William Carlos Williams, *In the American Grain*, ed. Rick Moody (New York: New Directions, 2009), 109.

45. Vera Kutzinski, *Against the American Grain: Myth and History in William Carlos Williams, Jay Wright, and Nicolas Guillén* (Baltimore: Johns Hopkins University Press, 1987), 12.

46. Williams, quoted in Kutzinski, *Against the American Grain*, 36.

47. Williams, quoted in Moody, introduction to Williams, *In the American Grain*, xi.

48. Quoted in James Mellow, *Hemingway: A Life without Consequences* (Boston: Houghton Mifflin, 1992), 314.

49. Soto, *The Modernist Nation*, 149.

50. John Dos Passos, *1919* (Boston: Mariner Books, 1991), 4.

51. Raymond Chandler, *Later Novels and Other Writings* (New York: Library of America, 1995), 681–683.

52. Langston Hughes, *Selected Poems of Langston Hughes* (New York: Alfred A. Knopf, 1959), 49.

53. In critiquing how US writers and Americanist scholars alike have privileged a nationalist "vernacularism," Jonathan Arac has advocated the recuperation of a "polyglot, cosmopolitan" tradition within American literary history ("Babel and Vernacular in the Empire of Immigrants:

Howells and the Languages of American Fiction," *Boundary 2* 34 [Summer 2007], 2, 4). But like so many of the current scholarly heuristics that sharply differentiate national and transnational impulses in US literary production, Arac's model fails to register the degree to which non-English idiomatic expressions were constitutive of canonical works of US literature from the mid-nineteenth to the late twentieth century. Far from running counter to the dominant literary trend, the use of foreign idioms helped define it.

54. Thomas Pynchon, *Slow Learner: Early Stories* (Boston: Little, Brown, 1998), 21–22.

55. *The Norton Anthology of Latino Literature*, ed. Ilan Stavans (New York: W.W. Norton and Co., 2010), 1461–1469.

56. Sandra Cisneros, *The House on Mango Street* (New York: Vintage, 2009), 17–18.

57. Sandra Cisneros and Marcienne Rocard, "An Amphibian: An Interview with Sandra Cisneros." *Revue française d'études américaines* 66 (November 1995), 585–586.

58. Sandra Cisneros, *Woman Hollering Creek and Other Stories* (New York: Vintage, 1991), 17.

59. Cristina García, "At Home on the Page: An Interview with Cristina García," in *Latina Self-portraits: Interviews with Contemporary Women Writers*, interviews by Bridget Kevane and Juanita Heredia (Albuquerque: University of New Mexico Press, 2000), 70.

60. Ángel Rama, *La ciudad letrada* (Montevideo: Arca, 1998), 43.

61. See John Phelan, "Pan-Latinism, French Intervention in Mexico (1861–1867), and the Genesis of the Idea of Latin America," in *Conciencia y autenticidad históricas*, ed. Juan A. Ortega y Medina (Mexico City: Universidade Nacional Autónoma de México, 1968), 279–298, Arturo Ardao, *Génesis de la idea y el nombre de América Latina* (Caracas: Centro de Estudios Latinoamericanos "Rómulo Gallegos," 1980), Mónica Quijada, "Sobre el origen y difusión del nombre 'América Latina' (o una variación heterodoxa en torno al tema de la construcción social de la verdad)," *Revista de Indias* 214 (1998), 595–615.

62. Doris Sommer, *Foundational Fictions: The National Romances of Latin America* (Berkeley: University of California Press, 1991), 55.

63. José Mármol, *Amalia* (Buenos Aires: Colección Austral, 1978), 504.

64. James Sanders, "The Vanguard of the Atlantic World: Contesting Modernity in Nineteenth-Century Latin America," *Latin American Research Review* 46 (2001), 112–113.

65. On Martí's debt to US constitutional republicanism, see Rafael Rojas, "Otro gallo cantaría: Essay on the First Cuban Republicanism," in *The Cuban Republic and José Martí: Reception and Use of a National Symbol*, ed. Mauricio Font and Alfonso Quiroz (Lanham, Md.: Lexington Books, 2006), 7–17. On Martí's early liberalism, see Ericka Beckman's *Capital Fictions: The Literature of Latin America's Export Age* (Minneapolis: University of Minnesota Press, 2013).

66. José Martí, "El poeta Walt Whitman," 102, 104, and "Emerson," 62, in *Escenas norteamericanas* (Caracas: Biblioteca Ayacucho, 2003).

67. José Martí, "Nuestra América," in *Obras Competas*, vol. 6 (Havana: Editorial Nacional de Cuba, 1996), 17: "el libro importado ha sido vencido en América por el hombre natural. Los hombres naturales han vencido a los letrados artificiales."

68. On the importance of displaced "foreign correspondents" such as Martí and Rubén Darío to the rise of newspapers like *La Nación* in Argentina, see Julio Ramos, *Desencuentros de la modernidad en América Latina: Literatura y política en el siglo XIX* (Santiago, Chile: Cuarto Propio, 2003), 115. For Ramos, the political and economic precariousness of the *modernista* generation reflects the "uneven modernization" of Latin America at the turn of the twentieth century.

69. Arcadio Díaz Quiñones, "Pedro Henríquez Ureña (1884–1946): La tradición y el exilio," in *Sobre los principios: Los intelectuales caribeños y la tradición* (Bernal: Universidad Nacional de Quilmes Editorial, 2006), 167–254.

70. José Enrique Rodó, *Ariel* (Madrid: Ediciones Cátedra, 2004), 196.

71. Rafael Rojas, "El lenguaje de la juventud: En diálogo con Ariel, de José Enrique Rodó," *Nueva sociedad* (Mar.–Apr. 2012), 31.

72. On the uses and abuses of Rodó's figure of Ariel, see Arturo Ardao's "Del mito Ariel al mito anti-Ariel," in *Nuestra América Latina* (Montevideo: Ediciones Banda Oriental, 1986).

73. Rubén Darío, *Antología poética*, ed. Francisco Nebot (Mexico City: Biblioteca Edaf, 2015), 145.

74. As numerous studies have shown, an important strain of Whitmanesque naturalism remained influential for twentieth-century Latin American poets such as Pablo Neruda and Octavio Paz. Yet relatively little attention has been devoted to examining the equally strong *arielista*-inflected anti-Whitman currents that coursed through Latin American literary reviews of the early twentieth century. In the Argentine journal *Claridad*, for example, the poet Aníbal Diaz published a sonnet titled "Walt Whitman" that opens with the line "This booming, magnificent Whitman tires me," and goes on to describe this "colossus with his verses of steel" as the symbol of a "nebulous, heavy, hateful country, / where nothing is a dream and there is no beautiful impossible" [de un país nebuloso, pesado, aborrecible,/ donde nada es un sueño ni hay un bello imposible] (*Claridad* 1 [July 1926], 43). Even many of the *modernista* writers who held favorable views of Whitman, such as Leopoldo Lugones and Darío, tended to read his work within an *arielista* framework. See Enrico Mario Santí's "The Accidental Tourist: Walt Whitman in Latin America," in *Do the Americas Have a Common Literature?*, ed. Gustavo Pérez Firmat (Durham, N.C.: Duke University Press, 1990) for a reading of the "repressed elements" and "open misunderstandings" in Whitman's twentieth-century reception in Latin America (158).

75. Miguel de Unamuno, *Algunas consideraciones sobre literatura hispano-americana* (Madrid: Espasa-Calpe, 1947), 93: "establecer aquí la metrópoli de la cultura…desde que el castellano se ha extendido a tierras tan dilatadas y tan apartadas unas de otras, tiene que convenirse en la lengua de todas ellas, en la lengua española o hispánica."

76. See Max Henríquez Ureña, *El retorno de los galeones y otros ensayos* (Mexico City: Ediciones Galaxia, 1963).

77. Raymond Williams, *Marxism and Literature* (New York: Oxford University Press, 1977), 122.

78. Jorge Mañach, *Frontiers in the Americas: A Global Perspective*, trans. Philip H. Phenix (New York: Columbia's Teacher's College, 1975), 48.

79. Leopoldo Zea, "The Culture of the Two Americas," in *Looking North: Writings from Spanish America on the US, 1800 to the Present*, ed. and trans. John J. Hassett and Braulio Muñoz (Tucson: University of Arizona Press, 2012), 56–67.

80. Fuentes, *Latin America: At War with the Past*, 9.

81. Sylvia Molloy, *At Face Value: Autobiographical Writing in Spanish America* (New York: Cambridge University Press, 1991), 17.

82. Victoria Ocampo, "Posdata (Waldo Frank y *Sur*)," in *Testimonios: Series sexta a décima* (Buenos Aires: Editorial Sudamericana, 2000), 94: "un grupo de escritores a quienes los Estados Unidos nos tenían sin cuidado, desde el punto de vista del arte, empezamos a tomar en serio la literatura norteamericana contemporánea."

83. José Vasconcelos, *De Robinson a Odiseo: Pedagogía estructurativa* (Mexico City: Trillas, 2009), 26: "[e]l fin final de la educación no es tanto *descubrir* como *saber.*"

84. This theoretical argument built upon Vasconcelos's actual policies as head of the Ministry of Education in the early twenties, when he launched an ambitious publishing initiative under the auspices of the Departamento Editorial. The department printed and distributed twenty thousand to twenty-five thousand copies of a select group of "classics" that included the works of Homer, Euripides, Dante, Plato, and Goethe. His other initiatives included the construction of new libraries in small towns and rural areas and the deployment of scores of cultural emissaries and teachers, among them the Chilean poet and pedagogue Gabriela Mistral.

85. In formulating this critique of the relationship between Deweyan pragmatism and US industrialism, Vasconcelos was surely aware of Lewis Mumford's influential account of the "pragmatist acquiescence" mentioned in chapter 2.

86. Ignacio Sánchez Prado, "El mestizaje en el corazón de la utopía: La raza cósmica entre Aztlán y América Latina," in *Intermitencias americanistas: Estudios y ensayos escogidos (2004–2010)* (Mexico City: Universidad Nacional Autónoma de México, 2012), 166.

87. José Joaquín Blanco, *Se llamaba Vasconcelos: Una evocación crítica* (Mexico City: Fondo de Cultura Económica, 1983).

88. José Vasconcelos, *La raza cósmica* (Mexico City: Editorial Porrúa, 2007), 113.

89. Jorge Luis Borges, *Textos recobrados: 1919–1929*, vol 1 (Buenos Aires: Emecé, 1997), 103.

90. Jorge Luis Borges, *Obras completas*, 4 vols. (Buenos Aires: Emecé, 1989), 1.305 (hereafter cited as *OC*).

91. Beatriz Sarlo, *Borges: A Writer on the Edge* (New York: Verso, 1993), 28.

92. For a more in-depth analysis of Borges's translation and adaptation of Twain's *Life on the Mississippi*, see Jeffrey Lawrence, "An American History of Infamy," *Variaciones Borges* 31 (2011), 160–179, and Sergio Waisman's *Borges and Translation: The Irreverence of the Periphery* (Lewisburg, Pa.: Bucknell University Press, 2005).

93. See Carlos Fuentes, *La nueva novela hispanoamericana* (Mexico City: Cuadernos de Joaquin Mortiz, 1969), 26.

94. Roberto Fernández Retamar, "Caliban: Notes toward a Discussion of Culture in Our America" (1971), trans. Lynn Garafola, David Arthur McMurray, and Robert Márquez, *Massachusetts Review* (Winter–Spring 1974), 15.

95. John Beverley, *Against Literature* (Minneapolis: University of Minnesota Press, 1993), 98.

96. Rigoberta Menchú and Elisabeth Burgos-Debray, *Me llamo Rigoberta Menchú, y así me nació la conciencia* (Mexico City: Siglo Veintiuno Editores, 1985), 144: "Yo puedo decir, no tuve un colegio para mi formación política, sino que mi misma experiencia traté de convertirla en una situación general de todo el pueblo."

97. Menchú and Burgos-Debray, *Me llamo Rigoberta Menchú*, 271: "Sigo ocultando lo que yo considero que nadie sabe, ni siquiera un atropólogo, ni un intelectual, por más que tenga muchos libros, no saben distinguir todos nuestros secretos."

98. Doris Sommer, "Rigoberta's Secrets," *Latin American Perspectives* 18 (Summer 1991), 36.

99. Mary Louise Pratt, "I, Rigoberta Menchú, and the 'Culture Wars,'" in *The Rigoberta Menchú Controversy*, ed. Arturo Arias (Minneapolis: University of Minnesota Press, 2001), 39.

100. Mario Roberto Morales, "Introducción: El debate académico más allá de la simple diatriba," in *Stoll-Menchú: La invención de la memoria* (Guatemala City: Consucultura, 2001), 4: "los académicos en Estados Unidos, partiendo de que Menchú había sido testigo ocular de los hechos de violencia que relata, instauraron su versión como la única verdadera acerca de la historia reciente de Guatemala y postularon al Testimonio como la forma literaria 'verdadera' de la subalternidad, opuesta a la forma literaria 'falsa' de los escritores 'letrados' (valga la redundancia) como Asturias y demás, cuyas versiones de lo popular fueron consideradas 'paternalistas.'"

Chapter 2

1. See Miguel Rodríguez Ayçaguer's *Visitas misionales: Waldo Frank en Argentina* (Buenos Aires: Impresiones Buenos Aires, 2007) for a more detailed description of events and a list of participants in Waldo Frank's Buenos Aires tour.

2. See Irene Rostagno, *Searching for Recognition: The Promotion of Latin American Literature in the United States* (Westport, Conn.: Greenwood Press, 1997), 1–30.

3. M. J. Benardete, in *Waldo Frank in America Hispana* (New York: Instituto de las Españas en los Estados Unidos, 1930), 241.

4. See Rostagno's *Searching for Recognition*, Rodríguez Ayçaguer's *Visitas misionales*, Casey Nelson Blake's *Beloved Community: The Cultural Criticism of Randolph Bourne, Van Wyck Brooks, Waldo Frank, and Lewis Mumford* (Chapel Hill, N.C.: University of North Carolina Press, 1990), Michael Ogorzaly's *Waldo Frank: Prophet of Hispanic Regeneration* (Lewisburg, Penn.: Bucknell University Press, 1994), Walter Benn Michaels's *Our America: Nativism, Modernism, and Pluralism* (Durham, N.C.: Duke University Press, 1995), and Horacio Tarcus's *Mariátegui en la Argentina: O las políticas culturales de Samuel Glusberg* (Buenos Aires: Ediciones El Cielo por Asalto, 2001).

5. Quoted in Rostagno, *Searching for Recognition*, 5.

6. Quoted in Tarcus, *Mariátegui en la Argentina*, 28.

7. Sánchez, quoted in Benardete, *Waldo Frank in America Hispana*, 122.

8. Victoria Ocampo, *Testimonios: Series sexta a décima* (Buenos Aires: Editorial Sudamericana, 2000), 95: "Algunos (entre los que me cuento) le debemos a Frank el haber vuelto la mirada hacia el Norte de nuestro Nuevo Continente. Hasta entonces—salvo raras excepciones...—la teníamos fija en Europa."

9. María Rosa Oliver, *La vida cotidiana* (Buenos Aires: Editorial Sudamericana, 1969), 257. The full quote runs: "con una sensibilidad en todo afín a la nuestra, [Frank] fue dándonos, tanto en el aula magna de la Facultad de Filosofía y Letras como en Amigos del Arte...un panorama en hondura, sin complacencia ni pesimismo, de la vida cultural y social de los Estados Unidos, ligándola a la economía. Esto era nuevo para mí y sumamente esclarecedor: me entregaba una clave para comprender el dinamismo de aquel país, los peligros que lo acechaban y las causas por las cuales sus estructuras básicas tendrían fatalmente que modificarse."

10. Alan Trachtenberg, introduction to Blake's *Beloved Community*, xii. The Young Americans eventually broke with Dewey over his support for US involvement in the First World War, and later argued that his defense of instrumentalism had veered into an "acquiescence" to the dogmas of US industrial capitalism and modern imperial warfare.

Nevertheless, they continued to accept the Deweyan emphasis on the philosophical value of personal experience and engaged in a decades-long debate with Dewey on the role of experience in political, social, and artistic life. For more on the "pragmatic acquiescence," see Lewis Mumford, *The Golden Day: A Study in American Literature and Culture* (New York: W.W. Norton and Co., 1926).

11. Waldo Frank, *Our America* (New York: Boni and Liveright, 1919), 28.

12. Frank to Glusberg, August 9, 1926, Buenos Aires: CeDinCi, Fondo Samuel Glusberg, number 1114/series 5.

13. "Un mensaje inédito de Waldo Frank, el buen americano," *La vida literaria* 1.12 (July 1929), 1: "En el sentido en que empleo la palabra, en el curso de este libro, vosotros sois americanos; mi América, cuya promesa es mi tema, es también vuestra América. Our America se cumple en su extensión, ahora que el término ha venido a ser Nuestra América, para incluiros a vosotros."

14. Frank, quoted in Victoria Ocampo, *Autobiografía* (Buenos Aires: Ediciones Fundación Victoria Ocampo, 2005–2006), 209–210: "He estado trabajando duro en el libro. No escribiendo, por supuesto. Pero planeando y dando forma.... Y debo leer muchísimo—historia, etc. para obtener maestría en los hechos de mi tema. Y entonces, gradualmente, encararé la composición. Lo que me molesta es que pueda haber cierta parte que no esté dentro de mi experiencia, en cuyo caso debería visitar nuevamente Sudamérica. No puedo escribir el libro a menos que conozca bien los temas. Esto es un peligro y una molestia. Pero si debo volver a S.A. quizá sea mi destino hacerlo."

15. Waldo Frank, *América Hispana: A Portrait and a Prospect* (New York: Charles Scribner's Sons, 1931), ix.

16. As an early twentieth-century travelogue in the tradition of Alexander von Humboldt, *América Hispana* clearly participates in what Mary Louise Pratt has described as the long-standing practice of naturalizing the Latin America socioscape (*Imperial Eyes: Travel Writing and Transculturation* [New York: Routledge, 1992]). Yet Frank's book marks a departure from earlier travel writings on the region in the way it carefully structures its content around the dual imperatives of demonstrating extensive coverage of the entire breadth of Hispanic America and in-depth firsthand immersion in its urban and rural environments.

17. Rostagno, *Searching for Recognition*, 3.

18. The most conclusive evidence I have been able to find of a personal encounter between the two is from an invitation to a celebration in late September 1929 organized by the literary review *Nosotros* in honor of Frank's visit. The invitation is addressed to Frank and Borges is listed as an attendee.

19. Waldo Frank, *Primer mensaje a la América Hispana* (Madrid: Revista de Occidente, 1930), 204, 196–197. "Recordad que su vida es su libro;" "[N]o era un hombre educado. Había leído irregularmente."

20. Walt Whitman, *Poetry and Prose* (New York: Library of America, 1982), 611, 307.

21. Frank, *Primer mensaje*, 78–79: "Abandonó, antes de los treinta, su brillante carrera de editor. Volvió a la América profusa. Convivió con los hombres del río, con conductores de ómnibus, con prostitutas, con criminales. Viajó por el Oeste, fue al Sur. Tuvo muchos amoríos, ocupó muchos empleos humildes."

22. Waldo Frank, "Mensaje a la Argentina," *La vida literaria* 2.16 (Nov. 1929), 1: "nuestro poeta, no tan solo el poeta de América del Norte.... No está mal el hablar de los Padres

Constituyentes y del Ideal Americano y de nuestros grandes escritores y de los guerreros contemporáneos en la moderna guerra del Espíritu. Pero es mucho más grato, al menos para mí, el hablar de mí mismo."

23. Frank, "Mensaje a la Argentina," 1: "Cada noche nos recogíamos los hijos en la biblioteca y mi padre leía en voz alta alguna página: y cuando la página no era de la Biblia, era una página europea: y cuando no era europea, era de algún autor americano como Longfellow o Lowell o Washington Irving, europeos en todo salvo el nombre."

24. Frank, "Mensaje a la Argentina," 1: "Los libros…ocupaban un especial dominio desde el que no se aventuraron nunca hacia el acto humano.…La casa de mi padre era estricta, cosa que me infundió pronto el hábito de escaparme de ella. Nueva York es un buen escenario para iniciar la vida de un muchacho moderno."

25. Frank, *Primer mensaje*, 197: "errante y joven vagabundo."

26. Frank, "Mensaje a la Argentina," 2: "Necesitaba dejar París. Sabía adonde ir—debía ir a casa…a las entrañas de América, que eran mi casa."

27. Frank, "Mensaje a la Argentina," 2: "Y tuve entonces la primera sugestión de lo que había de ser en mi vida una gran aventura. Sentí que esos extranjeros eran americanos, por modo cierto.…Venían de países que yo ignoraba: ni un libro, ni una canción, ni un cuadro suyo conocía.…Pero todo mejícanos, esto argentinos, estos venezolanos, estaban más cerca de mí que mis íntimos amigos europeos."

28. Frank, "Mensaje a la Argentina," 2: "Amigos míos, esta visita a la Argentina, lo mismo que mi visita reciente a Méjico, no es más que una etapa de mi regreso a América, una etapa de mi propio descubrimiento de América."

29. Quoted in Rostagno, *Searching for Recognition*, 15.

30. See Ocampo, *Autobiografía III*, 213. In *The Worlds of Langston Hughes: Modernism and Translation in the Americas* (Ithaca: Cornell University Press, 2012), Vera Kutzinski also speculates that Borges came into contact with Hughes's poetry through Frank (96).

31. Quoted in Ocampo, *Autobiografía, III*, 222: "Uno o dos hombres en el Pacífico, en Cuba, en México, que te servirían creativamente por estar personalmente cerca tuyo como amigos."

32. Quoted in Ocampo *Autobiografía III*, 224: "hombres que están en inmediato contacto con lo que es *vital* en sus países."

33. In 1944, a special issue of *Sur* devoted to North American literature opened with an introduction by Ocampo that reiterated Frank's earlier assertions that a Whitmanesque aesthetics should be the main criterion of selection for US literary works in the review. In presenting such contemporary US writers as Katherine Anne Porter, Hart Crane, Wallace Stevens, Robert Penn Warren, and Eudora Welty, Ocampo writes that "to familiarize oneself with nineteenth-century North America and recognize what it would impart to the twentieth century, the reader should procure…a few pages of Whitman" ("Para conocer la Norteamérica del siglo XIX y reconocer la que de ella surgiría en el siglo XX, dése al lector…unas páginas de Whitman"). *Sur* 113 (Mar.–Apr. 1944), 8. Fittingly, the issue leads off with Whitman's "Poets to Come" ["Poetas del porvenir"] (1860).

34. Jorge Luis Borges with Norman Thomas Di Giovanni, "An Autobiographical Essay," in *The Aleph and Other Stories: 1933–1969* (New York: E.P. Dutton, 1978), 255.

35. Jorge Luis Borges, in collaboration with Esther Zemborain de Torres, *An Introduction to American literature*, ed. and trans. L. Clark Keating and Robert O. Evans (Lexington: University of Kentucky Press, 1971), 4.

36. Doris Sommer, "Freely and Equally Yours, Walt Whitman," in *Proceed With Caution, When Engaged by Minority Writing in the Americas* (Cambridge, Mass.: Harvard University Press, 1999), 56.

37. For Borges's relationship to *criollismo*, see Graciela Montaldo's "Borges: Una vanguardia criolla," in *Literatura argentina siglo XX: Yrigoyen entre Borges y Arlt (1916–1930)*, ed. David Viñas (Buenos Aires: Paradiso, 2006), 176–191. On Borges's early verse celebrating the pro-Soviet revolutionary spirit of the early 1920s, see Daniel Balderston's "Políticas de la vanguardia: Borges en la década del '20," in *Innumerables relaciones: Cómo leer con Borges* (Santa Fe, Argentina: Ediciones Universidad Nacional del Litoral, 2010). On Borges's lifelong engagement with anarchist philosophical and aesthetic principles, see Luis Othoniel Rosa, *Hacia una estética anarquista: Borges con Macedonio* (Santiago, Chile: Cuarto Propio, 2016).

38. In *Invisible Work: Borges and Translation* (Nashville: Vanderbilt University Press, 2002), Efraín Kristal argues persuasively that Borges's writings on Whitman reflect a transition from a theory of literature as autobiographical expressionism in the 1920s to a more dialectical theory of reader-oriented aesthetics in the 1930s, and a similar transition from nationalism to cosmopolitanism over this same period. Whereas Kristal sees Borges's turn away from nationalism as the impetus for his shifting relationship to Whitman, I contend that Borges's reading of Whitman (and US literature in general) helped him to work through his changing views on nationalism.

39. Glusberg to Frank, Dec. 23, 1925, Buenos Aires: CeDinCi, Fondo Samuel Glusberg, number1207/series 5: "Después de Poe, Whitman y Mark Twain nada sabemos de autores americanos."

40. Alfieri notes that in the Argentine nationalist works of the period there are "countless textual marks of *arielismo*" ("La identidad nacional en el banquillo," in *Historia crítica de la literatura argentina: La crisis de las formas*, vol. 5, gen. ed. Noe Jitrik, vol. ed. Alfredo Rubione [Buenos Aires: Emecé, 2006], 527). Alfieri quotes Manuel Gálvez's *Diario de Gabriel Quiroga* (1910), which defined Argentine identity as the first of a series of concentric circles that spans from the national to the pan-Latin: "We are Latins, but before that Spaniards, and even before that Americans, and before all that Argentineans [Somos latinos, pero antes españoles, pero antes aún americanos y antes de todo argentinos] (527).

41. Glusberg to Frank, Apr. 1927, Buenos Aires: CeDinCi, Fondo Samuel Glusberg, number 1209/series 5: "los hispanoamericanos están haciendo una cuestión odiosa de latinismo y yanquismo."

42. Jorge Luis Borges, *Textos Recobrados: 1919–1929* (Buenos Aires: Emecé, 1997), 1.103: "En los subterráneos del alma nos brinca la españolidad, y empero quieren convertirnos en yanquis, en yanquis falsificados, y engatusarnos con el aguachirle de la democracia y el voto."

43. Borges, *Textos Recobrados*, 1.103: "Aunque a veces nos humille algún rascacielos, la visión total de Buenos Aires no es whitmaniana."

44. Jorge Luis Borges, *El tamaño de mi esperanza*, (Buenos Aires: Seix Barral, 1993), 14: "someternos a ser casi norteamericanos."

45. Borges, *El tamaño de mi esperanza* 13–14: "norteamericanizado indio bravo, gran odiador y desentendedor de lo criollo"; " 'Sin embargo, América es un poema ante nuestros ojos, su ancha geografía deslumbra y con el tiempo no han de faltarle versos,' escribió Emerson el cuarenta y cuatro en sentencia que es como una corazonada de Whitman y que hoy, en Buenos Aires del veinticinco, vuelve a profetizar."

46. Waldo Frank, *South American Journey* (New York: Duell, Sloan, and Pearce, 1943), 72.

47. Samuel Glusberg, "Este número," *La vida literatura* 2.14 (September 1929), 8.

48. Waldo Frank, "Carta whitmaniana," trans. Alfonso Reyes, *La vida literaria* 2.14, (September 1929), 1. The full line runs: "Si el pensamiento y el espíritu de Walt Whitman han de mantenerse como factores de nuestra vida americana, fuerza será que encarnen, que se incorporen realmente en el ser de la experiencia americana."

49. Jorge Luis Borges, "El otro Whitman," *La vida literaria* 2.14 (Sept. 1929), 3.

50. Borges, "El otro Whitman," 3: "las complacientes enumeraciones geográficas, históricas y circunstanciales que enfiló Whitman para cumplir con cierta profecía de Emerson, sobre el poeta digno de América."

51. Quoted in Borges, *Obras completas*, 1.263: "Casi todo lo escrito sobre Whitman está falseado por dos interminables errores. Uno es la sumaria identificación de Whitman, hombre de letras, con Whitman, héroe semidivino de Leaves of Grass como don Quijote lo es del Quijote; otro, la insensata adopción del estilo y vocabulario de sus poemas."

52. Whitman, *Poetry and Prose*, 182.

53. See, for instance, Frank's remark in *Primer mensaje* (210) that "[t]he vital work of America consists in a consecration similar to that of Whitman, and its realization in a similar song of harmonious lives and actions" [La tarea vital de América consiste en una consagración similar a la de Whitman, y su realización en un canto similar de vidas y acciones armioniosas].

54. Sánchez, quoted in Benardete, *Waldo Frank in America Hispana*, 111.

55. Borges, *Obras completas*, 1.263: "Imaginemos que una biografía de Ulises… indicara que éste nunca salió de Ítaca. La decepción que nos causaría ese libro, felizmente hipotético, es la que causan todas las biografías de Whitman. Pasar del orbe paradisíaco de sus versos a la insípida crónica de sus días es una transición melancólica. Paradójicamente, esa melancolía inevitable se agrava cuando el biógrafo quiere disimular que hay dos Whitman: el 'amistoso y elocuente salvaje' de *Leaves of Grass* y el pobre literato que lo inventó. Éste jamás estuvo en California o en Platte Canyon; aquél improvisó un apóstrofe en el segundo de esos lugares ('Spirit that Formed This Scene') y ha sido minero en el otro ('Starting from Paumanok,' I). Éste, en 1859, estaba en Nueva York; aquél, el 2 de diciembre de ese año, asistió en Virginia a la ejecución del viejo abolicionista John Brown ('Year of Meteors'). Éste nació en Long Island; aquél también ('Starting from Paumanok') pero asimismo en uno de los estados del Sur ('Longing for Home'). Éste fue casto, reservado y más bien taciturno, aquél efusivo y orgiástico. Multiplicar esas discordias es fácil; más importante es comprender que el mero vagabundo feliz que proponen los versos de *Leaves of Grass* hubiera sido incapaz de escribirlos."

56. Borges's chapter on Whitman in *An Introduction to American Literature* functions as a gloss on this paragraph from "Nota sobre Whitman": "The Walt Whitman of the book is a plural personage: he is the author and he is at the same time each one of his readers, present and future. Thus certain apparent contradicions can be justified: in one passage Whitman is born on Long Island; in another, in the South. 'Leaving Paumanok' begins with a fantastic biography: the poet tells of his experiences as a miner, a job that he never held, and describes the spectacle of herds of buffalo on the prairies, where he had never been" (32).

57. Borges, *Obras Completas*, 1.266: "Walt Whitman, hombre, fue director del Brooklyn Eagle, y leyó sus ideas fundamentales en las páginas de Emerson, de Hegel y de Volney; Walt Whitman, personaje poético, las edujo del contacto de América, ilustrado por experiencias imaginarias en las alcobas de New Orleans y en los campos de batalla de Georgia."

58. On the evasion of Whitman's sexuality in Latin American readings from Martí to Paz, see José Quiroga and Jorge Salessi's "Errata sobre la erótica, or the Elision of Whitman's Body," in *Breaking Bounds: Whitman and American Cultural Studies*, eds. Betsy Erkkila and Jay Grossman (New York: Oxford University Press, 1996), 123–132.

59. Frank, *Primer mensaje*, 198: "¿Qué fecunda semilla de la propia tradición latina implantó ella en el neblinoso, generoso y profético caos nórdico, que había en el alma del joven Whitman?"

60. Frank, *Primer mensaje*, 198: "Quiero imaginarlos juntos, en alguna alcoba secreta del Vieux Carré de Nueva Orleáns."

61. Whitman, *Poetry and Prose*, 438.

62. Whitman, *Poetry and Prose*, 758–759.

63. Borges, *Obras completas*, 1.266.

64. Borges, quoted in Lois Parkinson Zamora and Sylvia Spitta, "Introduction: The Americas, Otherwise," *Comparative Literature* 61 (Summer 2009), 199.

65. Jorge Luis Borges, *Borges en Sur* (Buenos Aires: Emecé Editores, 1999), 240: "el temor candoroso de no ser lo bastante *hardboiled*…es uno de los signos más evidentes (y menos agradables) de las letras norteamericanas de hoy." It is true, as Hernan Díaz has pointed out, that Borges frequently characterized Edgar Allan Poe as an important counterpoint to Whitman in the nineteenth-century US literary tradition, a writer whose belief in "America's continuity with Europe" and "intellectual" formalism provided an important alterative to Whitman's New World naturalism and free verse style (*Borges, between History and Eternity* [New York: Continuum, 2012], 118). Yet in numerous essays Borges expressed his disappointment at the experiential turn in the North American detective novel that derived from Poe.

66. Borges and Zemborain de Torres, *An Introduction to American literature*, 50.

67. Borges, *Obras completas*, 4.85: "Quienes lo acusan de no haber sido asiduamente minero olvidan que si lo hubiera sido tal vez no hubiera sido escritor, o hubiera preferido otros temas, ya que una materia muy familiar suele no ser estimulante."

68. Borges, *Obras completas*, 4.567. The full quote runs: "la sustancia elemental de lo que llamamos el universo es la experiencia"; "más cerca del idealismo que del materialismo."

69. Borges, *Obras completas*, 3.450: "Durante años he repetido que me he criado en Palermo. Se trata, ahora lo sé, de un mero alarde literario; el hecho es que me crié del otro lado de una larga verja de lanzas, en una casa con jardín y con la biblioteca de mi padre y de mis abuelos."

70. Borges, *Obras completas*, 1.478: "Conocer bien el español, recuperar la fe católica, guerrear contra los moros o contra el turco…*ser* Miguel Cervantes."

71. Borges, *Obras completas*, 1.478: "Ser, de alguna manera, Cervantes y llegar al Quijote le pareció menos arduo—por consiguiente, menos interesante—que seguir siendo Pierre Menard y llegar al Quijote a través de las experiencias de Pierre Menard."

72. Carlos Cortínez, "Otra lectura de 'Emerson,'" *Revista Chilena de Literatura* 19 (Apr. 1982), 95.

73. Borges, *Obras completas*, 3.308, 287: "Ese alto caballero americano/ Cierra el volumen de Montaigne y sale/ En busca de otro goce que no vale/ Menos, la tarde que ya exalta el llano"; "De aquel hidalgo de cetrina y seca / Tez y de heroico afán se conjetura/ que, en víspera perpetua de aventura,/ no salió nunca de su biblioteca."

74. Borges, *Obras completas*, 1.305.

75. Ricardo Piglia, *El último lector* (Barcelona: Anagrama, 2005), 189: "'En la carrera de la filosofía gana...aquel que llega último a la meta,'...El último lector responde implícitamente a ese programa."

Chapter 3

1. Lois Parkinson Zamora, *The Usable Past: The Imagination of History in Recent Fiction of the Americas* (New York: Cambridge University Press, 1997), 4, 5.

2. Fredric Jameson refers to Lukács's contribution as the perception of the "profound historicity of the [historical novel] itself" ("Progress versus Utopia; or, Can We Imagine the Future?," *Science Fiction Studies* 9 [July 1982], 150).

3. Gabriel García Márquez, *One Hundred Years of Solitude*, trans. Gregory Rabassa (New York: Harper Perennial Modern Classics, 2006), 415. All subsequent citations in English will be from the Rabassa translation, with slight modifications of quotations where necessary.

4. William Faulkner, *Absalom, Absalom!* (New York: Vintage International, 1986), 24.

5. See, for example, Jessica Hurley's "Ghostwritten: Kinship and History in *Absalom, Absalom!*," *Faulkner Journal* 26 (Fall 2012), 61–79, and Peter Ramos's "Beyond Silence and Realism: Trauma and the Function of Ghosts in *Absalom, Absalom!* and *Beloved*," *Faulkner Journal* 23 (Spring 2008), 47–66.

6. My analysis of Quentin's mode of reconstructing the past runs counter to a strong poststructuralist tradition in Faulkner studies that has described Quentin as a figure of the writer-as-reader. David Krause, for instance, has advanced the Barthesian claim that "for Faulkner, a writer is a kind of reader and a reader is a kind of writer" ("Reading Bon's Letter and Faulkner's *Absalom, Absalom!*" *PMLA* 99 [Mar. 1984], 226).

7. Walter Benn Michaels, *Our America: Nativism, Modernism, and Pluralism* (Durham, N.C.: Duke University Press, 1995), 5.

8. See, for example, Sarah Gleeson-White's "Auditory Exposures: Faulkner, Eisenstein, and Film Sound," *PMLA* 128 (Jan. 2013), 87–100, and Peter Lurie's "Faulkner's Literary Historiography: Color, Photography, and the Accessible Past," *Philological Quarterly* 90 (2011), 229–253.

9. William Faulkner, "A Note on Sherwood Anderson," in *William Faulkner: Essays, Speeches and Public Letters*, ed. James Meriwether (New York: Modern Library, 2004), 8–9.

10. Lois Parkinson Zamora, *Writing the Apocalypse: Historical Vision in Contemporary U.S. and Latin American Fiction* (New York: Cambridge University Press, 1989), 35.

11. García Márquez, *One Hundred Years of Solitude*, 15. In the original Spanish (Madrid: Cátedra, 2005, 101–102), the passage runs: "En el cuartito apartado, cuyas paredes se fueron llenando poco a poco de mapas inverosímiles y gráficos fabulosos, les enseñó a leer y escribir y a sacar cuentas, y les habló de las maravillas del mundo no sólo hasta donde le alcanzaban sus conocimientos, sino forzando a extremos increíbles los límites de su imaginación. Fue así como los niños terminaron por aprender que en el extremo meridional del África había hombres tan inteligentes y pacíficos que su único entrenamiento era sentarse a pensar, y que era posible atravesar a pie el mar Egeo saltando de isla en isla hasta el puerto de Salónica."

12. Deborah Cohn, "'He Was One of Us': The Reception of William Faulkner and the U.S. South by Latin American Authors," *Comparative Literature Studies* 34 (1997), 151. For a

full analysis of the "development of underdevelopment" in *One Hundred Years of Solitude*, see José David Saldívar, *The Dialectics of Our America: Genealogy, Cultural Critique and Literary History* (Durham, N.C.: Duke University Press, 1991).

13. Ángel Rama, *La ciudad letrada* (Montevideo: Arca, 1998), 29.

14. García Márquez, *One Hundred Years of Solitude*, 38.

15. Roberto González Echevarría, *Myth and Archive: A Theory of Latin American Narrative* (New York: Cambridge University Press, 1990), 22. González Echevarría argues that the reference in *One Hundred Years of Solitude* to the *English Encyclopedia* and an earlier mention of *The Thousand and One Nights* are allusions to Borges's "masterbooks" (23).

16. González Echevarría also introduces an important qualification to Rama's theorization of the lettered city by suggesting that "atemporal" myths in twentieth-century Latin American novels often exist alongside and undermine the role of the historical and literary archive. And it is true that in García Márquez's work, as in Faulkner's, myth takes on a mediating role between orality and history, past and present. Yet to compare *One Hundred Years of Solitude* to *Absalom, Absalom!* is to grasp how radically the Latin American archivist differs from the Faulknerian storyteller in making use of the full range of historical, mythical, and folk registers.

17. Toni Morrison, *Song of Solomon* (New York: Vintage International, 2004), 277.

18. Madhu Dubey, *Signs and Cities: Black Literary Postmodernism* (Chicago: University of Chicago Press, 2003), 172.

19. Quoted in " 'The Language Must Not Sweat': A Conversation with Toni Morrison," interview with Thomas LeClair, in *Toni Morrison: Critical Perspectives Past and Present*, ed. Henry Louis Gates, Jr., and Kwame Anthony Appiah (New York: Amistad, 1993), 375.

20. Valerie Smith, "The Quest for and Discovery of Identity in Morrison's *Song of Solomon*," *Southern Review* 23 (July 1985), 731.

21. Susan Willis, "Eruptions of Funk: Historicizing Toni Morrison," in Gates and Appiah, *Toni Morrison: Critical Perspectives*, 325; Wendy Faris, *Ordinary Enchantments: Magical Realism and the Remystification of Narrative* (Nashville: Vanderbilt University Press, 2004), 134.

22. Walter Benn Michaels, *The Shape of the Signifier: 1967 to the End of History* (Princeton, N.J.: Princeton University Press, 2004), 16.

23. Kenneth Warren, *So Black and Blue: Ralph Ellison and the Occasion of Criticism* (Chicago: University of Chicago Press, 2003), 80. In his more recent *What Was African American Literature?* (Cambridge, Mass.: Harvard University Press, 2011), Warren builds on Michaels's claims to argue that Morrison is the central figure in the rise of the "identity novel" in post-civil-rights US literature.

24. Toni Morrison, *Beloved* (New York: Vintage International, 2004), 91–92.

25. John Brenkman, "Politics and Form in Song of Solomon," *Social Text* 39 (Summer 1994), 68.

26. For two important accounts of the relationship between the history of black nationalism and the role of the Seven Days in *Song of Solomon*, see Harry Reed's "Toni Morrison, *Song of Solomon*, and Black Cultural Nationalism," *Centennial Review* 32 (Winter 1988), 50–64, and Ralph Story's "An Excursion into the Black World: The 'Seven' Days in Toni Morrison's Song of Solomon," *Black American Literature Forum* 23 (Spring 1989), 149–158.

27. Amiri Baraka, "The Legacy of Malcolm X and the Coming of Black Nationalism" (166) and "Black Art" (219), in *The LeRoi Jones/Amiri Baraka Reader*, ed. William Harris

(New York: Basic Books, 2000). It is worth noting that in his later "Third World Marxist" phase, Baraka repudiated many of the black nationalist views that he had held from the mid-1960s to the early 1970s. However, Morrison's comments on Baraka from the period when she was composing *Song of Solomon* suggest that she was responding primarily to his 1960s writings. See, for instance, her reference to *Dutchman* in the "Black Studies Center Public Dialogue: Pt. 2" (Portland State University; Morrison, Toni; St. John, Primus; Callahan, John; Callahan, Judy; and Baker, Lloyd, (1975). *Special Collections: Oregon Public Speakers.* 90. http://pdxscholar.library.pdx.edu/orspeakers/90). Accessed 7/13/17.

28. Quoted in Alessandra Vendrame, "Toni Morrison: A Faulknerian Novelist?," *Amerikastudien/American Studies* 42 (Jan. 1997), 680.

29. Zamora, *The Usable Past*, xii.

Chapter 4

1. Ernest Hemingway, *Selected Letters, 1917–1961*, ed. Carlos Baker (New York: Scribner, 1981), 273. Henceforth I will refer to this volume as *SL*.

2. Hemingway did not ultimately resume "Jimmy Breen" even after he returned to the United States in the summer of 1928, instead choosing to finish *A Farewell to Arms*. Hemingway did use the visit—extended when his father unexpectedly committed suicide a few months later—to gather source material for a series of stories about his semiautobiographical character Nick Adams and to travel to Cuba and Key West for the first time.

3. Katherine Anne Porter, *Selected Letters of Katherine Anne Porter: Chronicles of a Modern Woman*, ed. Darlene Unrue (Jackson, Miss.: University Press of Mississippi, 2012), 41.

4. Katherine Anne Porter, *Collected Stories and Other Writings*, ed. Darlene Unrue (New York: Library of America, 2008), 870.

5. Robert Penn Warren, "Katherine Anne Porter: Irony with a Center," in *Critical Essays on Katherine Anne Porter*, ed. Darlene Unrue (New York: G. K. Hall, 1997), 53.

6. Mary McCarthy, *The Groves of Academe* (London: Weidenfeld and Nicolson, 1951), 78.

7. Mark McGurl, *The Program Era: Postwar Fiction and the Rise of Creative Writing* (Cambridge, Mass.: Harvard University Press, 2009), 65.

8. John Dewey, *Art as Experience* (New York: Penguin, 2005), 60, 1.

9. John Dos Passos, *The 42nd Parallel* (Boston: Mariner Books, 2000), xiii.

10. John Dos Passos, *The Big Money* (Boston: Mariner Books, 2000), 192.

11. Ernest Hemingway, "Monologue to the Maestro: A High Seas Dialogue," in *By-line: Ernest Hemingway; Selected Articles and Dispatches of Four Decades*, ed. William White (New York: Scribner, 1967), 215.

12. As *Esquire* editor Arnold Gingrich would later recall, Hemingway's role in the creation of the magazine was paramount: "my newly established rapport with Hemingway began paying off handsomely, and everywhere I went, and everything I did, that late winter and early spring of 1933, I found that the ability to say 'Ernest sent me' had the effect of Open Sesame" (*Nothing but People: The Early Days at Esquire, a Personal History* [New York: Crown, 1971], 88).

13. John Raeburn, *Fame Became of Him: Hemingway as Public Writer* (Bloomington: Indiana University Press, 1984), 46.

14. Ernest Hemingway, *The Sun Also Rises* (New York: Scribner, 2006), 171.

15. Ernest Hemingway, *Death in the Afternoon* (New York: Simon and Shuster, 1996), 2.

16. Hugh Kenner, *A Homemade World: The American Modernist Writers* (New York: Alfred A. Knopf, 1975), 137.

17. Quoted in James Mellow, *Hemingway: A Life without Consequences* (Boston: Houghton Mifflin, 1992), 260.

18. Lionel Trilling, "Hemingway and His Critics," in *Hemingway and His Critics*, ed. Carlos Baker (New York: Hill and Wang, 1961), 62.

19. Michael Soto, *The Modernist Nation: Generation, Renaissance, and Twentieth-Century American Literature* (Tuscaloosa: University of Alabama Press, 2004), 142.

20. "Backstage with Esquire," *Esquire* (Autumn 1933), 7.

21. Edmund Wilson, "The Emergence of Hemingway," in Baker, *Hemingway and His Critics*, 59.

22. Quoted in Mellow, *Hemingway: A Life without Consequences*, 65.

23. See Kevin Maier, "'A Trick Men Learn in Paris: Hemingway, *Esquire* and Mass Tourism," *Hemingway Review* 31 (Summer 2012), 65–83, and David Earle, "Magazine," in *Ernest Hemingway in Context*, ed. Debra Moddelmog and Suzanne del Gizzo (New York: Cambridge University Press, 2013), 86–98.

24. Quoted in Seth Moglen, *Mourning Modernity: Literary Modernism and the Injuries of American Capitalism* (Stanford, Calif.: Stanford University Press, 2007), 193.

25. James Weldon Johnson, introduction, *The Book of American Negro Poetry* (New York: Houghton Mifflin Harcourt, 1983), 7; Langston Hughes, *The Collected Works of Langston Hughes*, vol. 9: *Essays on Art, Race, Politics, and World Affairs*, gen. ed. Arnold Rampersad, vol. ed. Christopher De Santis (Columbia: University of Missouri Press, 2002), 313.

26. Gertrude Stein, *The Autobiography of Alice B. Toklas* (New York: Vintage, 1990), 216.

27. See Stein, *The Autobiography of Alice B. Toklas*. Alice "relates" that Hemingway "was a shadow-boxer, thanks to Sherwood [Anderson], and he heard about bull-fighting from me" (217).

28. The effectiveness of Hemingway's combined textual and corporeal strategy of presenting himself as a writer of experience owed much to the prevalence of biographical literary criticism in the interwar US literary field, an entrenched critical habit of conflating authors, narrators, and protagonists. In the 1920s and 1930s, when the habits of close reading later associated with the New Criticism were still in their infancy, the interpretation of works closely modeled on recent historical events and real-life people (such as *The Sun Also Rises*) almost necessitated some familiarity with the "reality" behind the text. Both Malcolm Cowley's *Exile's Return* and Edmund Wilson's *Axel's Castle* (1931), which studies the influence of French Symbolism on modern writers of the teens and twenties, freely mix literary criticism with analysis of the lives of poets and novelists.

29. John Dewey, *Experience and Nature* (New York: Dover, 1958), 23.

30. Ernest Hemingway, *The Complete Short Stories of Ernest Hemingway: The Finca Vigía Edition* (New York: Scribner, 2003), 276.

31. As Hemingway and Porter got older, their aesthetic creeds increasingly shaded from the pole of experience and adventure toward the pole of memory. Hemingway's posthumous memoir *A Moveable Feast* (1964), for instance, evokes the Paris of the 1920s with evident nostalgia. In 1963, Porter remarked in an interview that "[s]urely, we understand very little of what is happening to us at any given moment. But by remembering, comparing, waiting to know the consequences, we can sometimes see what an event really meant, what it was

trying to teach us" (quoted in Robert Brinkmeyer, *Katherine Anne Porter's Artistic Development: Primitivism, Traditionalism, Totalitarianism* [Baton Rouge: Louisiana State University Press, 1993], 133).

32. See Timo Müller, "The Uses of Authenticity: Hemingway and the Literary Field (1926–1936)," *Journal of Modern Literature* 33 (Fall 2009), 28–42.

33. Mark Cirino and Mark Ott, *Ernest Hemingway and the Geography of Memory* (Kent, Ohio: Kent State University Press, 2010), ix.

34. See, for example, Russ Pottle's "Travel" (367–377) and Emily Wittman's "Travel Writing" (378–387) in Moddelmog and Gizzo, *Ernest Hemingway in Context*.

35. Leonardo Padura, *Adiós, Hemingway* (Barcelona: Tusquets Editores, 2006), 38: "Él sabía que su imaginación había sido escasa y mentirosa, y sólo contar las cosas vistas y aprendidas en la vida le había permitido escribir aquellos libros capaces de rezumar la veracidad que él le exigía a su literatura. Sin la bohemia de París y las corridas de toros no habría escrito *Fiesta*. Sin las heridas de Fossalta, el hospital de Milán y su amor desesperado por Agnes von Kuroswsky, jamás habría imaginado *Adiós a las armas* . . . Sin todos los días invertidos en el Golfo y sin las agujas que pescó y sin las historias de otras agujas tremendas y plateadas que oyó contar a los pescadores de Cojímar nunca hubiera nacido *El Viejo y el mar* . . . Él sí lo sabía: debía hacerse de una vida para hacerse de una literatura, tenía que luchar, matar, pescar, vivir para poder escribir."

36. See Helen Delpar's *The Enormous Vogue of Things Mexican: Cultural Relations between the United States and Mexico, 1920–1935* (Tuscaloosa: University of Alabama Press, 1992), John Britton's *Revolution and Ideology: Images of the Mexican Revolution in the United States* (Lexington, Ky.: University Press of Kentucky, 1995), and Rachel Adams's *Continental Divides: Remapping the Cultures of North America* (Chicago: University of Chicago Press, 2009). Claudio Lomnitz's *The Return of Comrade Ricardo Flores Magón* (Brooklyn: Zone Books, 2014) analyzes the prehistory of the Mexican Revolution in the work of transnational actors such as Turner and the Flores Magón brothers, demonstrating that many of the intellectual and cultural currents that precipitated the Revolution were far more bilateral than previously acknowledged.

37. Lincoln Steffens, "Into Mexico—and Out." *Everybody's Magazine* 34 (May 1916), 533.

38. Katherine Anne Porter, "Mexican Daybook, Notes, Observations, 1920–21," series 2, box 12, folder 14. Katherine Anne Porter Papers, Special Collections, University of Maryland Libraries.

39. Porter, "Mexican Daybook."

40. Mauricio Tenorio-Trillo, *I Speak of the City: Mexico City at the Turn of the Twentieth Century* (Chicago: University of Chicago Press, 2012), 165.

41. Thomas Walsh, *Katherine Anne Porter and Mexico: The Illusion of Eden* (Austin: University of Texas Press, 1992), 122.

42. Sean Latham, *The Art of Scandal: Modernism, Libel Law, and the Roman á Clef* (New York: Oxford University Press, 2009), 7.

43. Edith Walton, "Katherine Anne Porter's Stories and Other Recent Works of Fiction: Flowering Judas and Other Stories." *New York Times*, Oct. 20, 1935, BR6.

44. Quoted in Walsh, *Katherine Anne Porter and Mexico*, 169.

45. John Chamberlain, "Books of the Times," *New York Times*, Oct. 11, 1935, 23.

46. Katherine Anne Porter, "Interview with Henry Lopez," 1965, series 2, box 6, folder 15, Katherine Anne Porter Papers.

47. Darlene Unrue, *Katherine Anne Porter: The Life of an Artist* (Jackson: University Press of Mississippi, 2005), 126.

48. John Gronbeck-Tedesco, "Documenting *The Crime of Cuba*: An Américan Left and the 1933 Cuban Revolution," *American Quarterly* 66 (Sept. 2014), 641.

49. Ernest Hemingway to Maxwell Perkins, Dec. 15, 1936, "Perkins, Maxwell; 1925–1947," Carlos Baker Collection of Ernest Hemingway, Manuscripts Division, Department of Rare Books and Special Collections, Princeton University Library.

50. Ernest Hemingway, *To Have and Have Not* (New York: Scribner, 1996), 3.

51. Ernest Hemingway, *Green Hills of Africa: The Hemingway Library Edition* (New York: Scribner, 2015), 132, 133.

52. Granville Hicks, quoted in Mellow, *Hemingway: A Life without Consequences*, 440.

53. Ernest Hemingway, "Old Newsman Writes: A Letter from Cuba" in White, *By-line*, 181.

54. Katherine Anne Porter, *Letters of Katherine Anne Porter*, ed. Isabel Bayley (New York: Atlantic Monthly Press, 1990), 68.

55. Philip Rahv, "The Cult of Experience in American Writing," in *Image and Idea: Fourteen Essays on Literary Themes* (New York: New Directions, 1949), 9.

56. See Michael Denning's *The Cultural Front: The Laboring of American Culture in the Twentieth Century* (New York: Verso, 1997) and Barbara Foley's *Radical Representations: Politics and Form in U.S. Proletarian Fiction, 1929–1941* (Durham, N.C.: Duke University Press, 1993).

57. Meridel Le Sueur, "I Was Marching," http://xroads.virginia.edu/~ma01/white/anthology/meridel.html, accessed 3/7/15.

58. James Agee and Walker Evans, *Let Us Now Praise Famous Men* (Boston: Mariner Books, 2001), 11, 9.

59. Richard Wright, *Black Boy (American Hunger): A Record of Childhood and Youth* (New York: Harper Perennial, 1993), 375.

60. Cesare Pavese, *American Literature: Essays and Opinions*, trans. Edwin Fussell (New Brunswick, N.J.: Transaction, 2010), 56.

61. Simone De Beauvoir, *America Day by Day*, trans. Carol Cosman (Berkeley: University of Califronia Press, 1999), 57; Italo Calvino, "Hemingway and Ourselves," in *Why Read the Classics?*, trans. Martin McLaughlin (New York: Mariner Books, 2014), 225.

62. Warren, "Katherine Anne Porter: Irony with a Center," 53.

63. McCarthy, *The Groves of Academe*, 220.

64. Quoted in Rahv, "The Cult of Experience in American Writing," 10.

65. On the shifting politics of the New Critics, see Hugh Wilford's *The New York Intellectuals: From Vanguard to Institution* (Manchester: Manchester University Press, 1995).

66. Warren, "Katherine Anne Porter: Irony with a Center," 56.

67. Cleanth Brooks and Robert Penn Warren, *Understanding Fiction* (New York: Appleton-Century-Crofts, 1959), xvii, xix.

68. The writerly opposition to the critical paradigm inaugurated by Warren and Brooks can be seen in Eudora Welty's essay commemorating Porter, "The Eye of the Story." In contrast to Warren and Brooks, Welty foregrounds Porter's pursuit of full immersion and eyewitness testimony, playfully likening Porter's literary practice to that of a meteorologist doggedly seeking out the "eye of the storm." Welty insists that Porter's "stories of Mexico, Germany, Texas all happen there: where love and hate, trust and betrayal happen" and that "[e]xperience itself is stored in no telling how many ways in a

writer's memory." *Modern Critical Views: Katherine Anne Porter*, ed. Harold Bloom (New York: Chelsea House, 1986), 14–15.

69. McGurl, *The Program Era*, 8.

70. Kenneth Burke, *The Philosophy of Literary Form: Studies in Symbolic Action* (Berkeley: University of California Press, 1973), vii.

Chapter 5

1. John Beverley, *Against Literature* (Minneapolis: University of Minnesota Press, 1993), 71.

2. Roberto Fernández Retamar, "Caliban: Notes toward a Discussion of Culture in Our America," (1971), trans. Lynn Garafola, David Arthur McMurray, and Robert Márquez, *Massachusetts Review* (Winter–Spring 1974), 47, 49.

3. A list of the political ventures of writer-intellectuals over the past thirty years includes Mario Vargas Llosa's presidential bid in Peru in 1990, Juan Villoro and Elena Poniatowska's participation in Andrés Lopez Obrador's campaigns in Mexico, Ernesto Laclau and the Carta Abierta group's support of the *kirchnerista* platform in Argentina, and the Marxist-indigenist philosopher Álvaro García Linera's current role as vice president in Bolivia.

4. Roberto Fernández Retamar, "Como yo amé mi Borges," *Hispamérica* 28.83 (Aug. 1999), 45.

5. Fernández Retamar, "Como yo amé mi Borges," 45: "No sólo leí todo lo escrito por él que encontré en la magnífica biblioteca de esa Universidad y otras similares del país, incluyendo materiales en revistas rarísimas, sino que, como su nombre todavía no estaba internacionalizado...pude adquirir en librerías laterales, de publicaciones hispánicas."

6. Ricardo Piglia, *El último lector* (Barcelona: Anagrama, 2005), 107: "La lectura persiste como un resto del pasado, en medio de la experiencia de acción pura, de desposesión y violencia, en la guerrilla, en el monte."

7. Craig Epplin, *Late Book Culture in Argentina* (New York: Bloomsbury, 2014), 3. On the implementation of early twenty-first-century public reading projects in Latin America, see Marcy Schwartz, "Reading on Wheels: Stories of *Convivencia* in the Latin American City." *Latin American Research Review* 51.3 (2016), 181–201.

8. Washington Cucurto, interview with Pedro Pablo Guerrero, "Disparos contra la alta cultura," *El mercurio*, Jan. 16, 2004, 12: "Inversión cero y cambiás la cultura argentina. ¿Quién no va a comprar un libro a un peso y medio en la calle?"

9. Roberto Bolaño, *Entre paréntesis* (Barcelona: Anagrama, 2004), 148, Ricardo Piglia, *Crítica y ficción* (Barcelona: Anagrama, 2001), 89, Juan Villoro, "El 'Quijote', una lectura fronteriza," in *De eso se trata: Ensayos literarios* (Barcelona: Anagrama, 2008), 53.

10. Ricardo Piglia, "Escribir es conversar: Conversación entre Juan Villoro y Ricardo Piglia," in *El lugar de Piglia: Crítica sin ficción* (Barcelona: Candaya, 2008), 210–212: "Bueno me interesa mucho el modo en que Bolaño trabaja la figura del lector. Siempre hay una intriga alrededor de algún texto cuyo sentido no se termina de captar o de comprender, y me parece que también ahí podríamos nosotros pensar en una tradición. Esa tensión entre 'las armas y las letras' o 'cómo salir de la biblioteca' aparece siempre como una especie de problemática, como si la biblioteca estuviera aislada de la vida...Quizá la *beat generation* podría ser uno de los casos, uno de los últimos que yo he visto, en el sentido de la realización

de ese tipo de problemática: salir al camino, la experiencia de Kerouac, la experiencia de Allen Ginsberg; salir, digamos, *on the road*."

11. Idelber Avelar, *The Untimely Present: Postdictatorial Latin American Fiction and the Task of Mourning* (Durham, N.C.: Duke University Press, 1999), 20.

12. Beatriz Sarlo, *Tiempo pasado: Cultural de la memoria y giro subjetivo; una discusión* (Buenos Aires: Siglo Veintiuno Editores, 2005), 166.

13. John Beverley, *Latinamericanism after 9/11* (Durham, N.C.: Duke University Press, 2011), 60–71.

14. Roberto Bolaño, interview with Javier Campos. "Bolaño: son muy pocos los escritores que se la juegan a todo o nada," *El Mostrado.cl*, 3 Aug 2002.

15. Bolaño, "Bolaño: son muy pocos los escritores que se la juegan a todo o nada": "No, yo no tengo entre mis planes viajar a Estados Unidos.… De joven tal vez hubiera sido interesante vivir en Arizona o en California o en Nueva York, que supongo son lugares llenos de energía.… Sinceramente no creo que cuando joven me hubiesen concedido visado para entrar a Estados Unidos. Allí sólo conceden visados a los ricos y a los terroristas. Claro, hubiese podido entrar como espalda mojada, pero es que yo en México ya vivía como espalda mojada, así que en Estados Unidos hubiera sido doblemente espalda mojada. O espalda y pecho mojado, lo que hubiera sido el colmo."

16. Mark Purcell and Joseph Nevins, "Pushing the Boundary: State Restructuring, Regulation Theory, and the Case of U.S.-Mexico Border Enforcement in the 1990s," *Political Geography* 24 (2005), 220.

17. Steffen Mau and Heike Brabandt, *Liberal States and the Freedom of Movement: Selective Borders, Unequal Mobility* (New York: Palgrave Macmillan, 2012), 2.

18. John Tytell, *Naked Angels: Kerouac, Ginsberg, Burroughs, the Lives and Literature of the Beat Generation* (Chicago: Ivan Dee, 1996), 20.

19. William Burroughs, *Naked Lunch* (New York: Grove Press, 2013), 7.

20. William Burroughs, *The Yage Letters* (San Francisco: City Lights, 2006), 22.

21. Bolaño, *Entre paréntesis*, 148: "Viajó por todo el mundo…Y experimentó con todo tipo de drogas…Amaba las armas."

22. Bolaño, *Entre paréntesis*, 148: "Dicen que tuvo todos los vicios del mundo, pero yo creo que fue un santo al que se acercaron todos los viciosos del mundo porque tuvo la delicadeza e imprudencia de no cerrar nunca su puerta."

23. Bolaño, *Entre paréntesis*, 148: "Cuando hablaba de sus lecturas uno tenía la impresión de que lo que hacía era recordar períodos imprecisos de estancias carcelarias."

24. Jorge García-Robles, *Burroughs y Kerouac: Dos forasteros perdidos en México* (Barcelona: Random House Mondadori, 2007), 55: "Burroughs escribe solo en México. Sin desear hacer cultura, sin buscar círculos literarios, mucho menos académicos o intelectuales. Jamás WSB se interesó por la cultura moderna mexicana, nunca cruzó una palabra con alguna lumbrera nacional de la época, jamás asistió a conferencia alguna u obra de teatro. Posiblemente nunca compró un libro suscrito por un mexicano. Cuarenta años después no había oído mentar a Octavio Paz, a Carlos Fuentes, a Juan Rulfo. Si acaso contempló alguna vez los frescos de nuestros egregios muralistas en las paredes del Palacio de Bellas Artes o del Hotel del Prado, sin que le gustaran. Burroughs vivía abstraído de los fuegos artificales de la cultura en México. Sus intereses eran otros."

25. García-Robles, *Burroughs y Kerouac*, 15: "movido por la pasión que me inspira el destino de William S. Burroughs."

26. García-Robles, *Burroughs y Kerouac*, 56: "Ni por enterado de que por esos años Paz publicara *Libertad bajo palabra, El laberinto de la soledad* y *Águila o sol*, de que José Revueltas diera a conocer *Los días terrenales*, de que José Ortiz de Montellano, Xavier Villaurutia y José Clemente Orozco murieran."

27. Jorge Abelardo Ramos, "Feiling, Borges y Komeini," Oct. 7, 1994, www.jorgeabelardoramos.com/articulo.php?id=68, accessed 3/23/2016.

28. These literary-critical efforts culminated in the early 1990s, when two important books of Borges scholarship were published, Beatriz Sarlo's *Borges: A Writer on the Edge* (New York: Verso, 1993) and the US critic Daniel Balderston's *Out of Context: Historical Reference and the Representation of Reality in Borges* (Durham, N.C.: Duke University Press, 1993), which was released in Spanish translation by the Argentine publishing house Beatriz Viterbo in 1996. Sarlo's book centers on Borges's emergence as a "cosmopolitan" writer from the concrete cultural, political, and historical conjuncture of the Argentina of the 1920s and 1930s. Balderston's *Out of Context* demonstrates that the citations, references, and allusions in Borges's stories reveal an author exceptionally attuned to the historical contexts from which and about which he writes. In 1994, Balderston published a translation of *Artificial Respiration*, the first novel by Piglia to appear in English.

29. See, for instance, Piglia's story "Homenaje a Roberto Arlt" (1975), where the narrator-protagonist remarks that "A literary critic is always, in some way, a detective: he pursues over the surface of texts the marks, the traces that allow him to decipher their enigma" [Un crítico literario es siempre, de algún modo, un detective: persigue sobre la superficie del texto las huellas, los rastros que permiten descifrar su enigma], *Nombre Falso* (Barcelona: Anagrama, 2002), 145. As editor of the Serie Negra collection from 1968 to 1976, Piglia also helped to introduce the US hard-boiled detective novel to a Spanish-speaking audience, publishing works by Dashiell Hammett, David Goodis, and Raymond Chandler. Though far more sympathetic to the hard-boiler than Borges, who repeatedly voiced his preference for the British detective story, Piglia similarly located the genre within the US literature of experience: "Because while in the English detective novel everything is resolved through a logical sequence of suppositions, deductions from a sedentary detective, and analytic intelligence…in the North American detective novel there doesn't seem to be any criterion of truth other than experience" [[M]ientras en la narrativa policial clásica todo se resuelve a partir de una secuencia lógica de hipótesis, deducciones con el detective inmóvil, representación pura de la inteligencia analítica…en la novela policial norteamericana no parece haber otro criterio que la criterio de la experiencia], "Cuentos policiales norteamericanos," in *Escritores norteamericanos* (Buenos Aires: Tenemos las máquinas, 2016), 67.

30. Numerous scholars have traced Borges's influence on Piglia. For an important early discussion of Piglia's use of Borgesian citalionalism in *Artificial Respiration*, see José Sazbón's "La reflexión literaria" (*Punto de vista* 4 [1981], 37–44). The best account of the political dimensions of Piglia's reading of Borges is Edgardo Berg's "Ricardo Piglia, lector de Borges," *Iberoamericana (1977–2000)* 22 1 69 (1998), 41–56. For a reading of Piglia's relationship to Borges in the broader context of the Argentine literary tradition, see Jorge Fornet, *El escritor y la tradición: En torno a la poética de Ricardo Piglia* (Buenos Aires: Fondo de Cultura Económica de Argentina, 2007).

31. Beatriz Sarlo, "El crítico literario," in *Siete ensayos sobre Walter Benjamin* (Mexico City: Siglo XXI editores, 2011), 42. For a more panoramic view of Benjamin's reception in

Latin America, see Nicolás Casullo, ed., *Sobre Walter Benjamin: Vanguardias, historia, estética y literatura: una visión latinoamericana* (Buenos Aires: Alianza, 1993).

32. Walter Benjamin, *Selected Writings*, vol. 2, ed. Michael Jennings, trans. Rodney Livingston and Others (Cambridge, Mass.: Belknap Press of Harvard University Press, 1999), 734.

33. Ricardo Piglia, *Respiración artificial* (Buenos Aires: Editorial Sudamericana, 1990), 42: "Ya no hay experiencias...sólo hay ilusiones. Todos nos inventamos historias diversas (que en el fondo son siempre la misma) para imaginar que nos ha pasado algo en la vida."

34. Piglia, *Respiración artificial*, 43–44: "Tarde o temprano, pensaba yo, me voy a convertir en un gran escritor; pero primero, pensaba, debo tener aventuras. Y pensaba que todo lo que me iba pasando, cualquier huevada que fuera, era un modo de ir haciendo ese fondo de experiencias sobre el cual los grandes escritores, suponía yo, construían sus grandes obras. En aquel tiempo, a los 18, 19 años yo pensaba que al llegar a los 35 habría agotado ya todas las experiencias y a la vez iba a tener una obra hecha, una obra tan diversa y de tal calidad que me iba a poder ir cuatro o cinco meses a París a pasarme la gran vida...Mi vida actual, para ponerme a tono con tu última misiva, me parece bastante insensata cuando de golpe, casi sin querer, puedo pensarla. Voy al diario a escribir bosta (para peor bosta sobre literatura) y después vengo acá y me encierro a escribir."

35. Although Piglia often spoke of Ratliff in interviews as a real person, he is in fact a fictional character based on a character from Faulkner's novel *The Hamlet*. In a letter to Jorge Fornet, Piglia claims that Ratliff "is an effect of the attempt to write an autobiography; the character is fictional...but truthful (he could have existed)," (Fornet, *El escritor y la tradición*, 121).

36. Ricardo Piglia, *Prisión perpetua* (Barcelona: Anagrama, 2007), 21: "Era un norteamericano; buscaba hundirse en el fluir de la experiencia para destilar el arte de la ficción."

37. Piglia, *Prisión perpetua*, 18: "No pasaba nada, nunca pasa nada en realidad pero en aquel tiempo me preocupaba. Era muy ingenuo, estaba todo el tiempo buscando aventuras extraordinarias."

38. Piglia, *Prisión perpetua*, 18: "Entonces empecé a robarle la experiencia a la gente conocida, las historias que yo me imaginaba que vivían cuando no estaban conmigo."

39. Piglia, *Prisión perpetua*: "Había una mujer, en Trenton" (52);...Había una mujer en Arizona" (52);...Había un convicto que acababa de salir de la cárcel" (47).

40. Piglia, *Prisión perpetua*, 28: "Viajaban por todo el país y paraban en los hoteles del gueto y le compraban droga a la policía."

41. Piglia, *Prisión perpetua*, 35: "Narrar es fácil...si uno ha vivido lo suficiente para captar el orden de la experiencia."

42. Piglia, *Prisión perpetua*, 54: "[u]n narrador debe ser capaz de crear un héroe cuya experiencia supere la de todos sus lectores."

43. Piglia, *Prisión perpetua*, 19: "Sin él yo no sería escritor; sin él yo no habría escrito los libros que escribí."

44. Piglia, *Prisión perpetua*, 39: "Practicaba la amistad como explotación."

45. Piglia, *Prisión perpetua*, 40: "Se empeñó en que yo aprendiera inglés porque necesitaba al menos un lector en el que probar su novela mientras la escribía. A veces pienso que me hizo leer los libros que hacían falta y me preparó para que yo pudiera comprender con claridad qué era lo que estaba buscando, sin perder, de todos modos, esa ingenuidad que Steve consideraba imprescindible en un lector de ficciones....Me hablaba de la novela

y me leía lo que iba escribiendo y me mostraba las versiones y las variantes y discutía conmigo las alternativas de la trama y yo era una especie de lector privado que estaba ahí, en la mesa del Ambos Mundos sobre la ventana de la calle Rivadavia, esperando la continuación de la historia."

46. Sergio Pitol, *El desfile del amor* (Barcelona: Anagrama, 1984), 11.

47. Luis López Nieves, *Seva: Historia de la primera invasion norteamericana de la Isla de Puerto Rico ocurrida en mayo de 1898* (Bogotá: Grupo Editorial Norma, 2006), 37: "Son pocas las bibliotecas de la peninsula que no he escudriñado anaquel por anaquel, gaveta por gaveta, pulgada por pulgada."

48. Elisabeth Burgos-Debray, introduction to *Me llamo Rigoberta Menchú, y así me nació la conciencia*, by Rigoberta Menchú and Elisabeth Burgos-Debray (México: Siglo Veintiuno Editores, 1985), 18: "una especie de doble suyo, en el instrumento que operaría el paso de lo oral a lo escrito."

49. Roberto Bolaño, *Estrella distante* (Barcelona: Anagrama, 2000), 11: "consultar algunos libros"; "el fantasma cada día más vivo de Pierre Menard"; "la validez de muchos párrafos repetidos."

50. Roberto Bolaño, *Bolaño por sí mismo* (Santiago, Chile: Universidad Diego Portales, 2006), 76: "Yo escribo desde mi experiencia, tanto mi experiencia, digamos, personal, como mi experiencia libresca o cultural, que con el tiempo se han fundido en una sola cosa."

51. Bolaño, *El gaucho insufrible*, 158: "los viajes, el sexo y los libros son caminos que no llevan a ninguna parte, y que sin embargo son caminos por los que hay que internarse y perderse para volverse a encontrar o para encontrar algo, lo que sea, un libro, un gesto, un objeto perdido, para encontrar cualquier cosa, tal vez un método."

52. On Bolaño's repeated use of "cross-cultural comparison" as a structural principle in his works, see David Kurnick's "Comparison, Allegory, and the Address of 'Global' Realism (the Part about Bolaño)," *Boundary 2* 42 (2015), 105–134.

53. Roberto Bolaño, *Los detectives salvajes* (Barcelona: Anagrama, 2005), 178: "La norteamericana me miró a los ojos y asintió. No creo que conociera a Borges demasiado bien. No creo que conociera mi obra en absoluto, aunque a mí me tradujo John Dos Passos. Tampoco creo que conociera mucho a John Dos Passos."

54. Bolaño, *Los detectives salvajes*, 179, 177–178: "viejos putos podridos en sus recuerdos y citas literarias": "Viejo puto mamón de las almorranas de su puta madre, le vi la mala fe desde el principio, en sus ojillos de mono pálido y aburrido, y me dije este cabrón no va a dejar pasar la oportunidad de escupirme, hijo de su chingada madre. Pero yo soy tonta, simpre he sido una tonta y una ingenua y bajé la guardia. Y pasó lo que pasa siempre. Borges. John Dos Passos. Un vómito como al descuido empapando el pelo de Bárbara Patterson. Y el pendejo encima me miró como con pena, como diciendo estos bueyes sólo me han traído a esta gringa de ojos desvaídos para cagarle encima, y Rafael también me miró y ni se inmutó el enano ojete, como si ya estuviera acostrumbrado a que me faltara el respeto cualquier viejo rancio de pedos, cualquier viejo estreñido de la Literatura Mexicana."

55. Bolaño, *Bolaño por sí mismo*, 57: "El viaje, en el imaginario de mi generación, era el viaje de los beatniks."

56. Roberto Bolaño, interview with Ignacio Echevarría, *Introducción a la obra de Roberto Bolaño* [sound recording], Cátedra de las Américas, Barcelona, Nov. 12, 2002, Barcelona: Institut Català de Cooperació Iberoamericana, 2002 (90 min.): "No quiero convertirme en el Jack Kerouac del Tercer Mundo."

57. One of the earliest formal studies of Bolaño's rearticulation of existing discourses on the Latin American dictatorships is Celina Manzoni's "Narrar lo inefable: El juego del doble y los desplazamientos en *Estrella distante*," in *Roberto Bolaño: La escritura como tauromaquia*, ed. Celina Manzoni (Buenos Aires: Ediciones Corregidores, 2002). For an account of Bolaño's rewriting of the *testimonio* genre in *Amulet* and *The Savage Detectives*, see Susana Draper's "Demanding the Impossible...Literature and Political Imagination (*Amuleto*, 1968 in the Nineties)," *Nonsite* 14 (Oct. 2014), www.nonsite.org/article/demanding-the-impossible, accessed 5/16/16.

58. Bolaño, *Entre Paréntesis*, 43: "cantinela de dolor de los exiliados...entonada por latinoamericanos y también por escritores de otras zonas depauperadas o traumatizadas, [que] insiste en la nostalgia, en el regreso al país natal."

59. Bolaño, interview with Echevarría: "Lo que no suscribo de Piglia...es que la literatura, o la novela, o la cosa narrada, es la carcel, que es el reflejo más fiel de la carcel."

60. Roberto Bolaño, *2666* (Barcelona: Anagrama, 2005), 15, 1119: "La primera vez que Jean-Claude Pelletier leyó a Benno von Archimboldi....Poco después [Archimboldi] salió del parque y a la mañana siguiente se marchó a México."

61. Sharae Deckard has read "The Part about the Critics" as an academic satire that initiates the novel's broad critique of the "ascendancy of neoliberal capital" in post-NAFTA Mexico ("Peripheral Realism, Millennial Capitalism, and Roberto Bolaño's *2666*," *Modern Language Quarterly* 73 [Sept. 2012], 355). Although I agree with Deckard that the novel is fundamentally concerned with the imbrication of politics, economics, and aesthetics in late twentieth-century Mexico, her conclusion that the "The Part about the Critics" "self-consciously" raises questions about the "corporatization of humanities scholarship" (372) indicates a misleading tendency to equate Bolaño's literary project with the aims of the Anglo-American academic left. Indeed, while *2666* obsessively thematizes the complicity between cultural and political institutions and state repression in Latin America, there is not even the whiff of an allusion to the contemporary phenomenon of the corporate takeover of academia in the novel. The reason for this, I believe, is as much personal as ideological. Bolaño's own encounter with the Mexican cultural apparatus occurred mainly in the 1970s, when the PRI-ist state had a virtual monopoly over important sectors of the Mexican economy and long before neoliberal measures (including NAFTA) were implemented by Carlos Salinas y Gortari in the 1990s. Thus when Amalfitano, a Bolaño alter ego (same Chilean nationality and year of birth) and a self-described outsider in the backwaters of Mexican academia, refers to the difference between European intellectuals who "work in publishing houses or the press" and Latin American intellecuals who ultimately work for the "State" (116), he is pointing to what he sees as the difference between a market-based and a state-sponsored role for the intellectual. Liz Norton's confession that she doesn't understand what Amalfitano has said does not, as Deckard claims, point to the "depoliticized perspective of [her] arid formalist understanding of comparative literature" (what formalist critic would travel to one of the most dangerous places in the world to track down a writer she is studying!), but rather to her inability to grasp Amalfitano's intricate metaphors about the Mexican state's long history of sustaining and co-opting oppositional intellectuals.

62. Bolaño, *2666*, 985: "No le diré que la experiencia no se obtenga en el trato constante con una biblioteca, pero por encima de la biblioteca prevalece la experiencia."

63. Bolaño, *2666*, 470: "Normalmente no hubiese aceptado el encargo [de ir a Santa Teresa], pues él no era un periodista de crónica policial sino de las páginas de cultura. Hacía reseñas de libros de filosofía."

64. Bolaño, *2666*, 583: "probablemente no les importaba gran cosa lo que ocurría en aquel lejano rincón del país."

65. Marcela Valdes, "Alone among the Ghosts: Roberto Bolano's '2666,'" *Nation* (Dec. 8, 2008), http://www.thenation.com/article/alone-among-ghosts-roberto-bolanos-2666/, accessed Mar. 26, 2016.

66. Bolaño, *Entre paréntesis*, 144: "Porque Easy Rawlings en realidad no es un detective sino un tipo inteligente que de vez en cuando soluciona problemas, busca gente desaparecida, intenta arreglar asuntos de poca monta que inevitablemente se convierten al cabo de pocas páginas en asuntos de vida o muerte, y los problemas se agrandan hasta hacerse insoportables, la máquina de la realidad se pone en funcionamiento y todo lleva a los lectores a pensar que de ésta Easy no saldrá vivo, entre otras cosas porque es negro y pobre y ningún poder político o religioso está detrás de él, un tipo que sólo tiene a su favor un poco de fuerza física, bastante inteligencia, y nada más. Pero Easy siempre sale de los callejones sin salida en que lo pone Mosley."

67. Bolaño, *2666*, 325–326: "Yo lo que digo es que hay que leer libros…Y vosotros que sois tan amables, ahora os estaréis preguntando: ¿qué era lo que leías Barry? Lo leía todo. Pero sobre todo recuerdo un libro que leí en uno de los momentos más desesperados de mi vida y que me devolvió la serenidad. ¿Qué libro es ése?…Pues ése es un libro que se llama *Compendio abreviado de la obra de Voltaire* y les aseguro que es muy útil o al menos para mí fue de gran utilidad."

68. Bolaño, *Entre paréntesis*, 338: "Me conmueven los lectores a secas, los que aún se atreven a leer el *Diccionario filosófico* de Voltaire, que es una de las obras más amenas y modernas que conozco."

69. Bolaño, *2666*, 325: "Lean libros de autores negros. Y de autoras negras. Pero no se queden ahí."

70. Bolaño, *2666*, 359: "Soy americano. Por qué no dije soy afroamericano? Porque estoy en el extranjero?…¿Eso significa que en algún lugar soy americano y en algún lugar soy afroamericano y en algún otro lugar, por pura lógica, soy nadie?" See Brett Levinson's "Case Closed: Madness and Dissociation in *2666*," *Journal of Latin American Cultural Studies* 18 (Dec. 2009), 177–191, for a linguistic analysis of this passage. Although I sympathize with Levinson's attempt to capture the strangeness of Bolaño's rendering of American English into Spanish, I believe that "The Part about Fate" functions more as an engagement with the African American literary and intellectual tradition than as a "parody" of realism and local color.

71. Bolaño, *2666*, 373: "—Oscar—le dijo el jefe de sección—estás allí para cubrir un jodido combate de box.

> —Esto es superior—dijo Fate—, la pelea es una anécdota, lo que te estoy proponiendo es muchas cosas más.
>
> —¿Qué me estás proponiendo?
>
> —Un retrato del mundo industrial en el Tercer Mundo—dijo Fate—, un aide-mémoire de la situación actual de México, una panorámica de la frontera, un relato policial de primera magnitud, joder."

72. Juan Villoro, "Writing in the Midst of Political Upheaval," interview with Carlos Fonseca and Jeffrey Lawrence, www.bombmagazine.org/article/2000006/juan-villoro, accessed 7/18/19.

73. Roberto Bolaño, *Entre paréntesis*, 269: "Todos los novelistas americanos, incluidos los autores de lengua española, en algún momento de sus vidas consiguen vislumbrar dos

libros en el horizonte, que son dos caminos, dos estructuras y, sobre todo, dos argumentos. En ocasiones dos destinos. Uno es *Moby Dick*, de Herman Melville, el otro es *Las aventuras de Huckleberry Finn*, de Mark Twain."

74. Cristina Rivera Garza, "Mis Emilys Dickinsons," www.cristinariveragarza.blogspot .com, posted Aug. 30, 2011, accessed 3/24/16: "Se entiende que el horizonte del que habla Bolaño es el de la narrativa norteamericana en modo, digamos, universal, y que el tiempo al que se refiere es, sin duda, el siglo XIX, que es otro manera de decir el origen de la modernidad. Pero en esa bifurcación tan equidistante, tan bien comportada, tan dada a las comparaciones con aspiraciones a aparecer como naturales o inevitables, se le olvidaba a Bolaño la incómoda, la inclasificable, la con frecuencia alterada tercera vía. Se saltaba, por decirlo así, el tercer libro y, siguiendo a pie juntillas sus palabras, el tercer argumento y, sobre todo, el tercer destino. Se olvidaba de Emily Dickinson. Sí, Emily Dickinson, la poeta que pocas veces salió de casa y cuyos retratos suelen capturarla vestida de negro y con el cabello estrictamente recogido en un moño. La habitante de un cuarto de Amherst, donde leyó todo lo que había y podía leer, por cierto; la inédita. Habrá que recordar que ningún mapa de la literatura norteamericana de ese tiempo estaría completo sin la poeta que consideraba el 'no' la más salvaje de todas las palabras."

75. In the essay "The Uses of the Archive: From the Historical Novel to Documentary Fiction" ("Los usos del archivo: De la novela histórica a la escritura documental," in *Los muertos indóciles: Necroescrituras y desapropiación* [Mexico City: Tusquets Editores México, 2013]), for example, Rivera Garza points to the way certain North American texts such as Rukeyser's *The Book of the Dead* (1938) and Reznikoff's *Testimony* (1934–1979) depart from more conventional forms of the Depression-era documentary genre: "Far from the imperializing gesture of trying to supplant the voice of another with one's own, these poets threw themselves into the task of documenting the struggles and suffering of vast sectors of the US working class, incorporating their voices as they appeared in official documents, oral interviews, and newspaper accounts" (117). Though Rivera Garza cites different kinds of archival material here—oral as well as written, nonfiction as well as fiction—she contrasts this type of "textual curation" to James Agee's and Walker Evans' *Let Us Now Praise Famous Men* (1941), a work written (in Rivera Garza's words) "on the basis of the eight weeks they spent in Alabama" (116).

76. Pola Oloixarac, quoted in Marcela Valente, "Argentina: Women Writers Who Break the Mold," Inter Press Service News Agency, http://www.ipsnews.net/2009/07/argentina-women-writers-who-break-the-mould/, accessed 7/18/17.

77. Of course, many Latin American literary works of the late twentieth century offered a critical perspective on male intellectuals—one thinks of Elena Poniatowska and Carmen Boullosa's fiction in Mexico, and Luisa Valenzuela's and Maria Negroni's work in Argentina. But what distinguishes these *lectora* novels of the first decade of this century, particularly those of Rivera Garza, is that they pursue a genealogical search for precursors akin to the recuperation Piglia undertook with Borges and Roberto Arlt and Bolaño with the *estridentistas* in *The Savage Detectives*.

78. See Claudia Parodi, "Cristina Rivera Garza, ensayista y novelista: el recurso del método," in *Cristina Rivera Garza: Ningún crítico cuenta esto*, ed. Oswaldo Estrada (Mexico City: Eon and University of North Carolina at Chapel Hill with UC Mexicanistas, 2010), 73–84, and Brian Price, "Cristina Rivera Garza en las orillas de la historia," in *Ningún crítico cuenta esto*, 111–133.

79. Cristina Rivera Garza, *Nadie me verá llorar* (Mexico City: Tusquets Editores México, 2014), 71: "cada información lo aproxima un poco más a ella."

80. Rivera Garza, *Nadie me verá llorar*, 79: "En los libros Joaquín se siente a salvo.... El orden de las historias lo orienta en las incógnitas del mundo."

81. Rivera Garza, *Nadie me verá llorar*, 79–80: "Si la ciudad fuera una biblioteca él sería feliz."

82. Rivera Garza, *Nadie me verá llorar*, 81: "el fotógrafo lee todos los libros."

83. Rivera Garza, *Nadie me verá llorar*, 91: "Quiere que Matilda se vuelva dócil y flexible como un bejuco."

84. Rivera Garza, *Nadie me verá llorar*, 248: "Yo sola hallaré la forma de escapar, Joaquín. Nadie me salvará."

85. Rivera Garza, *Nadie me verá llorar*, 205: "Venía...sin meta alguna en la cabeza...y si se había decidido a regresar a Catorce era menos por los afanes de conseguir fortuna y más por el paisaje lunar ante el que alguna vez se había rendido."

86. Rivera Garza, *Nadie me verá llorar*, 199: "pasó por alto todo lo referente a los artistas e intelectuales de la época."

87. Rivera Garza, *Nadie me verá llorar*, 216: "la figura masculina cruza el umbral de la puerta y, desde allí, la mujer ve cómo su cuerpo avanza y se empequeñece en la distancia."

88. Rivera Garza, *Nadie me verá llorar*, "mochila de explorador, una brújula y un par de limones para saciar la sed."

89. Cristina Rivera Garza, *La cresta de Ilión* (Mexico City: Tusquets Editores México, 2014), 17.

90. Cristina Rivera Garza, "La ciudad de los hombres," in *La frontera más distante* (Mexico City: Tusquets Editores México, 2008), 77.

91. Cristina Rivera Garza, *La muerte me da* (Mexico City: Tusquets Editores México, 2007), 30: "[Pensé] en el término asesinatos seriales y me di cuenta de que era la primera vez que lo relacionaba con el cuerpo masculino. Y pensé...que era de suyo interesante que, al menos en español, la palabra víctima siempre fuese feminina."

92. Rivera Garza, *La muerte me da*, 32: "tampoco pude dejar de ver que en la misma superficie del apellido Cortázar se escondían, amenazantes, un *cortar* y un *azar*—palabras que, en ese momento, carecían de toda inocencia."

93. Cristina Rivera Garza, interview with Cheyla Rose Samuelson, "Writing at Escape Velocity: An Interview with Cristina Rivera Garza," *Confluencia: Revista Hispanica de Cultura y Literatura* 23 (Fall 2007), 145.

94. Rivera Garza, *La muerte me da*, 173: "Sin leerla, sin leerla bien, nunca podrás dar con el culpable."

95. Rivera Garza, *La muerte me da*, 188: "Alejandra Pizarnik convirtió el relato ajeno en una especia de refugio."

96. Jorge Luis Borges, *Obras completas* (Buenos Aires: Emecé, 1989), 1.307.

97. Rivera Garza, *La muerte me da*, 202: "En español, lo decía ella misma, no había nadie que le sirviera de modelo. Ni Paz ni Cortázar ni Borges."

98. On Rivera Garza's challenge to the gender codes of the *novela negra* in *La muerte me da*, see Glenn Close's "*Antinovela negra*: Cristina Rivera Garza's *La muerte me da* and the Critical Contemplation of Violence in Contemporary Mexico," *Modern Language Notes* 129 (2014), 394.

99. Mayra Santos-Febres, "La muerte me da o las lectoras de Pizarnik," www .mayrasantosfebres.blogspot.com, posted May 4, 2008, accessed 3/25/16.

100. See Emily Hind's "Lo anterior o el tiempo literario de La muerte me da," in *Ningún crítico cuenta esto*, 313–338 for an analysis of how *La muerte me da* incorporates references to Markson, Charles Bernstein, and Lynn Hadjian.

101. Rivera Garza, *Los muertos indóciles*, 27–28: "una serie de estrategias que…propuso formas de apropiación que, por mucho, dinamitaron nociones más bien conservadoras, si no es que retrógradas, de la autoría y el yo lírico…transformando así al escritor en manipulador de signos o curador del lenguaje contemporáneo."

102. Rivera Garza, *La muerte me da*, 306: "A los lectores les corresponderá…implicarse, si fuera necesario, en ese enigma."

103. Rivera Garza, *Los muertos indóciles*, 83: "una lectura obligada para cualquiera que desee escribir en y con el hoy."

104. Craig Dworkin, "The Fate of Echo," in *Against Expression: An Anthology of Conceptual Writing*, eds. Craig Dworkin and Kenneth Goldsmith (Evanston, Ill.: Northwestern University Press, 2011), xlv.

105. See, for example, Oswaldo Estrada's "Cristina Rivera Garza, en-clave de transgresión," in *Ningún crítico cuenta esto*, 27–46.

Epilogue

1. Sandra Cisneros, "Introduction: A House of My Own," *The House on Mango Street* (New York: Vintage, 2009), xxiv.

2. Ana Menéndez, *Adios, Happy Homeland!* (New York: Black Cat, 2011), 7.

3. Ben Lerner, *Leaving the Atocha Station* (Minneapolis: Coffee House Press, 2011), 68.

4. Valeria Luiselli, *Los ingrávidos* (Mexico City: Sexto Piso, 2011), 24.

5. US Census, "Changing Nation: Percent Hispanic of the U.S. Population: 1980–2050," https://www.census.gov/content/dam/Census/newsroom/facts-for-features/2014/cb14-ff22_graphic.pdf, accessed 7/23/17.

6. Kirsten Silva Gruesz, "Utopia Latina: The Ordinary Seaman in Extraordinary Times," *Modern Fiction Studies* 49 (Spring 2003), 55.

7. Lawrence Buell, *The Dream of the Great American Novel* (Cambridge, Mass.: Belknap Press of Harvard University Press, 2014), 341.

8. Nicolás Kanellos, *Hispanic Immigrant Literature: El sueño del retorno* (Austin: University of Texas Press), 18.

9. Rolando Hinojosa, "A Voice of One's Own," in *The Rolando Hinojosa Reader: Essays Historical and Critical*, ed. José David Saldívar (Houston: Arte Público Press, 1985), 16, 17.

10. Rolando Hinojosa, "Chicano Literature: An American Literature with a Difference," in *The Rolando Hinojosa Reader*, 43.

11. Gloria Anzaldúa, *Borderlands/La Frontera: The New Mestiza* (San Francisco: Aunt Lute Books, 1999), 19.

12. Ilan Stavans, *The Hispanic Condition: Reflections on Culture and Identity in America* (New York: HarperCollins, 1995), 9.

13. The first edition of *The Hispanic Condition* begins with a scene straight out of one of Borges's fantastic fictions, a dream sequence in which Stavans travels to the future and

encounters an aging print engraver who speaks in a fully "Borgesian tone." The engraver then makes a speech about *mestizaje* that Stavans believes he has "read...somewhere before" and that ends with an adaptation of Du Bois's famous quote about the "color line": "the problem of the twenty-first century is the problem of miscegenation" (4–5). This use of Borgesian citationalism to introduce a radical concept—a parallel between white-black relations in the twentieth-century United States and white-brown relations in the twenty-first—echoes the appropriation of Borges among leftist Latin American authors that I discuss in chapter 4.

14. Barbara Epler begins her response to *New Yorker* editor Willing Davidson's question regarding her initial interest in Bolaño with the following anecdote: "Over drinks, my friend Francisco Goldman started chewing my ear off about Roberto Bolaño, and, oddly, just a few days after our date, a pal at another, larger publishing house asked me which new authors I might be stalking, and I mentioned Bolaño, along with a few other writers from abroad" ("This Week in Fiction: The True Bolaño," www.newyorker.com/online/blogs/books/2012/01/this-week-in-fiction-roberto-bolano.html#ixzz2MUVbjgv5, accessed 7/18/17). See Stavans's and Goldman's respective 2007 review essays of Bolaño's work after the US release of *The Savage Detectives*: "Willing Outcast" (*Washington Post*, May 6, 2007); "The Great Bolaño" (*New York Review of Books*, July 19, 2007).

15. Rodrigo Lazo, "Hemispheric American Novels," in *The Cambridge History of the American Novel*, eds. Leonard Cassuto, Claire Eby and Benjamin Reiss (Cambridge: Cambridge University Press, 2011), 1092.

16. Francisco Goldman, *The Divine Husband* (New York: Grove Press, 2004), 3.

17. Francisco Goldman, "Francisco Goldman on Roberto Bolaño's *2666*," wordswithoutborders.org/article/francisco-goldman-on-roberto-bolano-2666, accessed 7/23/17.

18. Francisco Goldman, *Say Her Name* (New York: Grove Press, 2011), 338.

19. Pierre Bourdieu, *The Field of Cultural Production: Essays on Art and Literature*, ed. Randal Johnson, trans. Claud DuVerlie (New York: Columbia University Press, 1993), 64.

20. See Lazo's "The Hemispheric Novel," Glenda Carpio's "Now Check It: Junot Díaz's Wondrous Spanglish," in *Junot Díaz and the Decolonial Imagination* (Durham, NC.: Duke University Press, 2016), 257–290, Rebecca Walkowitz's *Born Translated: The Contemporary Novel in an Age of World Literature* (New York: Columbia University Press, 2015), 37–39, and Sean O'Brien's "Some Assembly Required: Intertextuality, Marginalization, and 'The Brief Wondrous Life of Oscar Wao,'" *Journal of the Midwest Modern Language Association* 45 (2012), 75–94.

21. Junot Díaz, *The Brief Wondrous Life of Oscar Wao* (New York: Riverhead Books, 2008), 90, 225, 244.

22. Monica Hanna, Jennifer Harford Vargas, and José David Saldívar, "Introduction: Junot Díaz and the Decolonial Imagination: From Island to Empire," in *Junot Díaz and the Decolonial Imagination*, 1.

23. Junot Díaz, "Junot Díaz: By the Book," http://www.nytimes.com/2012/09/02/books/review/junot-diaz-by-the-book.html, accessed 7/23/17.

24. Junot Díaz, "Junot Díaz by Edwidge Danticat," http://bombmagazine.org/article/2948/, accessed 7/23/17.

25. Pedro Cabiya, "On the Myopic Self-Righteousness of Firstworlders and Firstworlder Wannabes: Open Letter to Junot Díaz and Edwidge Danticat," http://www.pedrocabiya

.com/2015/06/on-the-myopic-self-righteousness-of-firstworlders-and-firstworlder-wannabes-open-letter-to-junot-diaz-and-edwige-danticat/, accessed 7/23/17.

26. Ana Menéndez, *In Cuba I Was a German Shepherd* (New York: Grove Press, 2001), 205.

27. Ana Menéndez, *Loving Che* (New York: Grove Press, 2003), 10.

28. In a sly aside to those familiar with the Argentine metafictional tradition, Menéndez names Victoria O'Campo as the author of this history of Cuban poetry.

29. David Foster Wallace, "Mr. Cogito," in *Both Flesh and Not: Essays* (New York: Little, Brown, 2012), 121–122.

30. Benjamin Kunkel, "Argentinidad," *n + 1* 11 (Spring 2011), https://nplusonemag.com/issue-11/essays/argentina/, accessed 7/14/17.

31. Ben Lerner, "IFOA Q&A: Ben Lerner on crafting *Leaving the Atocha Station*," http://nationalpost.com/afterword/qa-ben-lerner-on-crafting-leaving-the-atocha-station/wcm/e3d44258-63bc-493d-8fae-05ef816dea1b, accessed 7/23/17.

32. Ulises Gonzáles, "Somos los bárbaros," *Los Bárbaros* 1 (Mar. 2014), 5:

Ya son demasiados años esperándonos.

Nueva York fue tomada hace décadas por los laberintos de Borges. Hoy convive con los detectives que cruzan la ciudad y se duplican con el código escrito en la frente: 2666.

Se ha cerrado el círculo.

En algún momento los departamentos de lenguas de los Estados Unidos albergaron a un pequeño grupo de salvajes llamados Español. Crecieron y sobrevivieron a las multiples corrientes literarias para demostrar lo que muchos hoy ya saben: el mundo hispano ha conquistador el centro, los barbarous hemos tomado el control.

33. Ulises Gonzáles, "El tiempo de los bárbaros," *Los Bárbaros* 3 (Feb. 2015), 5: "Su lengua es la de hombres de provincia que después de haber sido comidos por los piojos, leyendo a Reyes, a Paz y a Borges, llegaron aquí para entender mejor a Salinger, a Whitman, a Faulkner y también a Foster Wallace. Los bárbaros no pueden mirar el atardecer sobre el Hudson ni el bote que cruza la bahía de Manhattan al amanecer sin que en algún lugar de su memoria se les aparezca una imagen que requiere las palabras de Martí, de Onetti, de Arguedas; los versos de Pizarnik, de Vallejo y de Lorca, la inteligencia de Parra."

34. Luiselli, *Los ingrávidos*, 24: "tras el éxito de Bolaño en el mercado gringo...habría un siguiente boom lationamericano"; "algo que podamos publicar."

35. Luiselli, *Los ingrávidos*, 43: "Así es como funciona el éxito literario, por lo menos a una escala."

36. Luiselli, *Los ingrávidos*, 72: "El departamento de Letras Hispánicas de la Universidad de Austin, abrió un 'Archivo Owen'; aparecieron los artículos que Owen había escrito para *El Tiempo* de Bogotá en los años treinta y cuarenta, que un professor reunió y publicó en un tomo de Porrúa, en la ciudad de México, y que enseguida tradujo y publicó la Harvard University Press."

37. Luiselli, *Los ingrávidos*, 87: "Owen se convertiría, sin duda, en un nuevo Bolaño."

38. Sarah Pollack, "After Bolaño: Rethinking the Politics of Latin American Literature in Translation," *PMLA* 128 (May 2013), 661.

39. Luiselli, *Los ingrávidos*, 29: "Había pasado la noche...hojeando una antología aburridísima de poetas mexicanos amigos de Octavio Paz traducidos al inglés.... [H]ay tal vez por ahí un ergo, pero no sé bien dónde colocarlo."

40. Luiselli, *Los ingrávidos*, 24: "¿Ya oíste, Minni? Tenemos el honor de trabajar con la única latinoamericana que no fue amiga de Bolaño."

41. See Héctor Hoyos, *Beyond Bolaño: The Global Latin American Novel* (New York: Columbia University Press, 2015).

42. See Francisco Carrillo Martín, *Excepción Bolaño: Crisis política y reescritura de la derrota* (San Juan, P.R.: Instituto de Cultura Puertorriqueña, 2014); Oswaldo Zavala, *La modernidad insufrible: Roberto Bolaño en los límites de la literatura latinoamericana contemporánea* (Chapel Hill: North Carolina Studies in the Romance Languages and Literatures, UNC Department of Romance Languages, 2016).

43. Mara Pastor, "El otro día nos volvimos a ignorar," in *Candada por error* (San Juan, P.R.: Atarraya Cartonera, 2009), 5.

44. Mara Pastor, "Conozco a Manuel," in *Candada por error*, 15.

45. Luis Othoniel Rosa, "Luis Othoniel reseña a Mara Pastor (Puerto Rico), https://elroommate.com/2011/02/14/othoniel-resena-a-mara-pastor/, accessed 7/23/12/: "no la literatura como referencia a una tradición intelectual, sino la literatura como una actividad, como una forma de vivir, que condiciona la situación económica, doméstica, emocional y geográfica."

46. Mara Pastor, "La trompeta del arcángel," in *Poemas para fomentar el turismo* (Mexico City: Cartábon de nube, 2012), 22: "Yo he aterrizado tantas veces/y nunca pensé en traficar conmigo/ una crisis mundial."

47. Mara Pastor, "Los estudiantes," in *Poemas para fomentar el turismo*, 69:
del que nos paramos con contestaciones
leídas a espaldas de maestros de creación literaria
y con poemas de Parra en la Biblioteca Lázaro
en donde hicieron un huerto los estudiantes en huelga

48. Pastor, "Los estudiantes," 70:
Y mientras tanto ocupar.
Y mientras tanto ocupar.
La juventud se quitó las alas
con una suavidad insospechada.

49. Nicole Cecilia Delgado, in *Poemas para fomentar el turismo*, 11: "una politización inminente de su discurso"; "naciente agudeza crítica que le permite observar y compartir la realidad social que la rodea."

50. Luis Othoniel Rosa, "Luis Othoniel Rosa y lo que se abre a partir de *Otra vez me alejo*," http://www.pagina12.com.ar/diario/suplementos/espectaculos/4-26671-2012-10-08.html, accessed 7/23/17: "'no estoy contando mi vida, no es que mi literatura nace de mí, sino que yo nazco de mi literatura'"; "Escribir, para mí, es un yo planeando su modo vivir."

51. Luis Othoniel Rosa, http://evaristocultural.com.ar/2013/01/14/el-otro-yo-entrevista-a-luis-othoniel-rosa/, accessed 7/23/17: "es un movimiento o un corrimiento interesante, porque antes la academia estadounidense era el campus, era la torre de marfil total, literalmente campus, con paredes y todo. Y de momento, el académico que antes estaba protegido en su burbuja, está ahora de nuevo en la calle, tenemos que entender o aprender de nuevo cuál es nuestro lugar en la sociedad."

{ INDEX }